Economic Adjustment and Reform

Economic Adjustment and Reform in Eastern Europe and the Soviet Union

Essays in Honor of Franklyn D. Holzman

Edited by *Josef C. Brada, Ed A. Hewett, and Thomas A. Wolf*
Duke Press Policy Studies

Duke University Press   Durham and London   1988

Contents

IV. PARTICIPATION IN THE LARGER WORLD ECONOMY

Acknowledgments

Most of the chapters in this *Festschrift* to Franklyn D. Holzman are substantially revised versions of papers originally presented at a conference on "The Soviet Union and Eastern Europe in the World Economy" hosted by The Kennan Institute for Advanced Russian Studies of The Wilson Center in Washington, D.C., in October 1984. The editors are grateful for financial support of the conference from The Kennan Institute, the Stanley Foundation, the U.S. Department of State, The Ford Foundation, and the National Endowment for the Humanities, and for support from the Joint Committee on Eastern Europe of the American Council of Learned Societies and the Social Science Research Council.

Abbreviations

BIS	Bank for International Settlements
CDP	Central Development Program
CGE	Computable General Equilibrium
CMEA	Council for Mutual Economic Assistance
CPE	Centrally Planned Economy
CPSU	Communist Party of the Soviet Union
EC	Enterprise Council
ECWA	Economic Contract Work Association
EEC	European Economic Community
EFF	Extended Fund Facility
FTO	Foreign Trade Organization
ftp	foreign trade price
FYP	Five-Year Plan
GATT	General Agreement on Tariffs and Trade
GDP	Gross Domestic Product
GDR	German Democratic Republic
GNP	Gross National Product
GSP	Generalized System of Preferences
HSWP	Hungarian Socialist Workers' Party
IBRD	International Bank for Reconstruction and Development
ICP	International Comparisons Project
IDA	International Development Association
IEO	International Economic Organization
IFC	International Finance Corporation
IIB	International Investment Bank
IMF	International Monetary Fund
ITO	International Trade Organization

KISZ	Communist Youth Organization (Hungary)
KWF	Financial Indicator of Export Efficiency (Poland)
KWN	Last-Phase Export Efficiency Coefficient (Poland)
LDC	Less Developed Country
LIBOR	London Interbank Offered Rate
MESZOV	County-level Cooperative Association
MFA	Multifiber Agreement
MFN	Most Favored Nation Tariff Status
MFT	Ministry of Foreign Trade
mmt	million metric tons
MPE	Modified Planned Economy
MTE	Market-type Economy
NEM	New Economic Mechanism
NIC	Newly Industrialized Country
NMP	Net Material Product
NTB	Nontariff Barrier
OECD	Organization for Economic Cooperation and Development
PFAZ	State Vocational Activation Fund (Poland)
PPP	Purchasing Power Parity
QR	Quantitative Restriction
SDR	Special Drawing Right
SEI	Socialist Economic Integration
TR	Transferable Ruble
UNCTAD	United Nations Conference on Trade and Development
VVB	Association of National Enterprises (GDR)
VVER	Pressurized Water Reactor (USSR)
wmp	world market price
WOG	Large Economic Organization (Poland)

Foreword

Joseph S. Berliner

The foundations of American scholarship on the Soviet economy were laid in the decade following the Second World War. The central methodological question at the time was whether an economy without markets, without consumer sovereignty, and with a price system that made no provision for rent, interest, or profit could be understood at all with the analytic equipment of non-Marxian economic theory, which at the time meant neoclassical microeconomics and Keynesian macroeconomics. A number of seminal works soon appeared that demonstrated the power of modern economic theory — imaginatively adapted to the special conditions of a centrally planned socialist economy — to guide the measurement of Soviet economic performance and to produce illuminating normative and positive propositions about that performance. Among the earliest and most influential of these works was Franklyn D. Holzman's *Soviet Taxation: The Fiscal and Monetary Problems of a Planned Economy* (1955).

A rich scholarly career is like a river fed by a variety of streams. One such stream was Holzman's wartime experience. Most contributors to the early development of modern economic analysis of the Soviet economy had served in the armed forces or in government during the war. None had moved closer to the subject of their future careers than Holzman, who served for a time at the U.S. Air Force base in Poltava, maintaining the B-17 bombers at the Soviet end of the American shuttle-bombing raids over Germany and occupied Europe. That assignment gave him not only a working knowledge of the Russian language, but also firsthand experience with Soviet life and its institutions that was rare among the young scholars of the postwar years.

The second stream was his first postwar job, in the Office of International Finance of the U.S. Treasury Department. That experience established his interest and provided his initial analytic training in the two fields in which he eventually made his major contributions—monetary and international economics. When he later enrolled in graduate study, he had hands-on experience in applied economics that was the envy of his graduate student colleagues (like me), for whom economics was something that happened in books and journals. Before he wrote his Ph.D. dissertation he had published several major journal articles on international trade and on inflation theory; none, however, dealt with the Soviet economy, which he had just begun to study.

Graduate study in economics at Harvard was the third stream. In the ordinary course of things his career probably would have moved into standard international and monetary economics, but then an extraordinary event occurred which set the direction of many graduate students' careers at the time. Research institutes in Soviet studies were established at Harvard and Columbia, and fellowships became available for training and dissertation support in this new field. If not for that development, "he might not have been a Roosian," as W. S. Gilbert might have said.

Before the establishment of research institutes, study of the USSR was sometimes a lonely occupation, with few people to talk to about one's esoteric pursuits. The research institute provided a community of scholarship, and with it the heady sense that one was engaged with others in a pioneering venture—the scholarly exploration of the new terrain of Soviet society. Holzman was offered a fellowship at the new Russian Research Center at Harvard, and for the rest of his graduate career was a student of one of Harvard's great teachers and scholars, Alexander Gerschenkron. It was under his direction that Holzman wrote the dissertation that culminated in the book *Soviet Taxation*.

There is a fourth stream, perhaps merely a streamlet, but one that must be reported if the reader is to have a full appreciation of Holzman's career. In 1964 his expertise on Soviet finance led to an invitation from the U.S. Arms Control and Disarmament Agency to undertake a study to determine whether the budgetary and financial data published by the Soviet government could be used to verify arms control agreements with the USSR. Having a deep and long-standing commitment to the cause of peace, he accepted the invitation with enthusiasm. One outcome of the research was his book *Financial Checks on Soviet Defense Expenditures*.

The project, however, introduced him to the arcane art of estimating Soviet defense expenditures, and that became a lifelong commitment. The CIA, which is the primary source of American governmental estimates of Soviet defense expenditures, has no more knowledgeable and dogged reader of its publications, critic of some of its work, and supporter of other aspects of the agency's work. His chief criticism has been of the CIA's estimates of Soviet defense expenditures in U.S. dollar prices and the use of those estimates for assessing the military balance. It is on this topic, more than on any other, that Holzman has brought his expertise to the public forum, serving as a one-man truth squad in rebutting ill-founded alarmist assessments of the military balance derived from dollar-based estimates of Soviet military spending.

These several streams merged to produce the scholarly career of Franklyn Holzman, the fruits of which are recorded in the list of his selected publications. Much of his early work was theoretical—on discrimination in international trade, on the foreign trade multiplier, and on inflation theory. It was on the basis of the latter work that he was commissioned by the American Economic Association and the Royal Economic Society to coauthor the survey of the state of inflation theory at that time. Beyond his contributions to pure theory, however, it was the use of theory to illuminate the nature of empirical economic relationships that is the major source of his influence on the development in the fields of comparative economics generally and Soviet economics in particular. He was, for example, the first to identify overfull employment planning rather than credit policy as the cause of Soviet inflationary pressures, a contribution that flowed directly from his work on general inflation theory. On the basis of that insight, he also pointed out that various management practices like hoarding and the safety factor are more properly viewed as consequences of the shortages generated by overfull employment planning, rather than of the practice of central planning itself.

The most celebrated and illuminating instance of the close interplay between theory and data goes back a long way. Early in his career there appeared two influential papers in a major journal claiming to prove that the USSR exploited the East European countries by the use of extensive price discrimination in Soviet trade with them. The papers made a strong case, and only someone with a thorough knowledge of the underlying economic relationships would have been initially skeptical of the inferences drawn from the available data. Drawing on customs union theory, Holzman published an important paper demonstrating that the model that had been used to prove that the USSR exploited Eastern Europe could also be used to prove the improbable result that each member of the Soviet Bloc exploited all the others, including the USSR. To demonstrate empirically that this was so, however, required the trade data of at least one other East European nation, which unfortunately were not available to U.S. scholars in the late fifties. Everyone who knew Franklyn Holzman at the time will remember the excitement when the Bulgarians unexpectedly published a set of foreign trade data that he somehow discovered; and, just as he had predicted, the model that showed the Soviets to be exploiting Bulgaria when Soviet data were used also showed the Bulgarians to be exploiting the USSR when Bulgarian data were used.

Every graduate student in comparative economics now knows, or should know, that famous case, and should avoid committing the original analytic sin. The issue continues to reemerge, however, currently in the form of the thesis that the USSR, rather than exploiting the East European countries, subsidizes them in return for various political benefits. While all the returns on the current controversy are not yet in, Holzman has returned to the fray, again applying the customs union model to question the interpretation of the data.

There is another instructive example in this piece of history that is perhaps more important than the lessons that data in the absence of theory can tell some strange stories. Western students of the Soviet Union are, by and large, hostile to the government and political system of that country. It is difficult to maintain the canons of objective scholarship under those circumstances, although in my opinion the field as a whole does a remarkably good job. Nevertheless, findings that show the Soviet Union in an unfavorable light are probably less critically evaluated than findings that show them in a favorable light. It takes an unusual dedication to objectivity in this field of scholarship to say, in effect

—unfavorable or favorable light, the important thing is that the conclusion be supported by the evidence. The most valuable lesson that Franklyn Holzman has taught his colleagues and students is that, regardless of one's political position, the deepest obligation is to describe the situation accurately.

Academics teach in various ways. Many teach their own students in classrooms and in seminars, as Holzman has done for thirty-five years, first at the University of Washington and later at Tufts. Some also teach by their writings, to many more students, in other teachers' classrooms, and to their colleagues whose understanding is broadened by their works. And a few teach also by seeking out and encouraging promising younger scholars whose works they have read and whose careers they have helped to advance. All three classes of Franklyn Holzman's students are presented in this *Festschrift* as an expression of their esteem.

Selected Publications of Franklyn D. Holzman

BOOKS

Soviet Taxation: The Fiscal and Monetary Problems of a Planned Economy, Cambridge, Mass.: Harvard University Press, 1955.

Readings on the Soviet Economy (Editor and Contributor), Chicago: Rand McNally, 1962.

Foreign Trade Under Central Planning, Cambridge, Mass.: Harvard University Press, 1974.

Financial Checks on Soviet Defense Expenditures, Lexington, Mass.: Lexington Books, 1975.

International Trade Under Communism: Politics and Economics, New York: Basic Books, 1976.

Economics of Soviet Bloc Trade and Finance, Boulder, Colo., and London: Westview Press, 1987.

MONOGRAPHIC STUDIES

"The Financial System of Outer Mongolia," in *Mongolian People's Republic*, vol. 3, Human Relations Area Files, New Haven, Conn.: Yale University Press, 1956.

The Soviet Economy: Past, Present, and Future, Foreign Policy Association, Headline Series, September–October 1982.

SELECTED ARTICLES

"Discrimination in International Trade," *American Economic Review*, vol. 39, no. 6 (December 1949), pp. 1234–44.

"Income Determination in Open Inflation," *Review of Economics and Statistics*, vol. 32, no. 2 (May 1950), pp. 150–58.

"Dollar Capital Flows in the South African Balance of Payments," *South African Journal of Economics*, vol. 8, no. 3 (September 1950), pp. 285–95.

"Commodity and Income Taxation in the Soviet Union," *Journal of Political Economy*, vol. 58, no. 5 (October 1950), pp. 421–33.

"The Soviet Budget, 1928–1952," *National Tax Journal*, vol. 6, no. 3 (September 1953), pp. 226–49.

"The Burden of Soviet Taxation," *American Economic Review*, vol. 43, no. 4 (September 1953), pp. 548–71.

"The Profit-Output Relationship of a Soviet Firm: Comment," *Canadian Journal of Economics and Political Science*, vol. 19, no. 4 (November 1953), pp. 523–31.

"Soviet Economic Growth," *World Politics*, vol. 7 (October 1954), pp. 133–56.

"Unemployment in Planned and Capitalist Economies," *Quarterly Journal of Economics*, vol. 69, no. 3 (August 1955), pp. 452–60.

"Financing Soviet Economic Development," *Capital Formation and Economic Growth,* NBER Study, Princeton, N.J.: Princeton University Press, 1955, pp. 229–73. Also "Reply," Ibid., pp. 282–90. Reprinted in Morris Bornstein and Daniel Fusfeld, eds. *The Soviet Economy*, Homewood, Ill.: Irwin, 1962, pp. 145–62; and Richard Byrd and Oliver Oldman, eds., *Readings in the Tax Policy of Developing Nations*, Baltimore: Johns Hopkins University Press, 1964, pp. 71–91.

"Equity of the Livestock Tax of Outer Mongolia," *American, Slavic, and East European Review*, vol. 15, no. 4 (December 1956), pp. 506–11.

"The Tax System of Outer Mongolia, 1911–1955: A Brief History," *Journal of Asian Studies* (formerly *Far Eastern Quarterly*), vol. 16, no. 2 (February 1957), pp. 221–36.

"The Budget Expenditures of Outer Mongolia," *Public Finance, Finance Publique*, vol. 12 (1957), pp. 35–48.

"Taxes and Standard of Living in the USSR: Postwar Developments," *National Tax Journal*, vol. 10, no. 2 (June 1957), pp. 138–47.

"The Adjusted Factor Cost Method of Valuing National Income: Comment," *Soviet Studies*, vol. 8, no. 1 (July 1957), pp. 32–36.

"An Estimate of the Tax Element of Soviet Bonds," *American Economic Review*, vol. 47, no. 3 (June 1957), pp. 390–96. Also "Reply," ibid. (September 1958).

"The Soviet Ural-Kuznetsk Combine: A Study in Investment Criteria and Industrialization Policies," *Quarterly Journal of Economics*, vol. 71, no. 3 (August 1957), pp. 368–405.

"The Foreign Trade and Balanced Budget Multipliers" (with Arnold Zellner), *American Economic Review*, vol. 48, no. 1 (March 1958), pp. 73–91.

"Consumer Sovereignty and the Rate of Economic Growth," *Economia Internazionale*, vol. 11, no. 2 (May 1958), pp. 193–210.

"The Soviet Income Tax: A Comparative Study," *National Tax Journal*, vol. 11, no. 2 (June 1958), pp. 99–113.

"Forty Million Missing Persons: The Soviet Labor Shortage," *Mercurio* (October 1958), pp. 25–29.

"Investment Criteria and the Rate of Growth" (in Spanish), *El Trimestre Economica* (25th anniversary issue), vol. 25 (December 1958), pp. 664–73.

"Creeping Inflation," *Review of Economics and Statistics*, vol. 41, no. 3 (August 1959), pp. 24–29.

"Some Financial Aspects of Soviet Foreign Trade," *Comparisons of the United States and Soviet Economies*, vol. 2, Joint Economic Committee, Congress of the United States, Washington, D.C.: U.S. Government Printing Office, 1959, pp. 427–43.

"Inflation: Cost-push and Demand-pull," *American Economic Review*, vol. 50, no. 1 (March 1960), pp. 20–42. Also "Correction and Re-Statement" (September 1960), pp. 723–24.

"Soviet Inflationary Pressures, 1928–1957: Causes and Cures," *Quarterly Journal of Economics*, vol. 74, no. 2 (May 1960), pp. 167–88.

"Effectiveness of Soviet Monetary Policy: Comment," in Gregory Grossman, ed. *Value and Plan*, Berkeley: University of California Press, 1960, pp. 125–31.

"The Strategy of Economic Development in Communist China: Comment," *American Economic Review*, vol. 51, no. 2 (May 1961), pp. 518–21.

"Soviet Foreign Trade Pricing and the Question of Discrimination," *Review of Economics and Statistics*, vol. 44, no. 2 (May 1962), pp. 134–47.

"Soviet Bloc Mutual Discrimination: Comment," *Review of Economics and Statistics*, vol. 44, no. 4 (November 1962), pp. 496–99.

"Foreign Trade," in Abram Bergson and Simon Kuznets, eds. *Economic Trends in the Soviet Union*, Cambridge, Mass.: Harvard University Press, 1963, pp. 283–332.

"American Problems and Policies Regarding Unemployment and Economic Growth," in I. Puhan and S. Gross, eds. *Selected Problems of Social Sciences and Humanities*, Skopje, Yugoslavia, 1963, pp. 41–53. Also published in Serbo-Croatian in *Stopanski Pregled (Economic Review of Macedonia)*, no. 5 (1962), pp. 45–59.

"Survey of Inflation Theory" (with M. Bronfenbrenner), *American Economic Review*, vol. 53, no. 4 (September 1963), pp. 593–661. Reprinted in *Surveys of Economic Theory*, vol. 1, London and New York: Macmillan and St. Martin's Press for the American Economic Association and the Royal Economic Society, 1965, pp. 46–107. Reprinted in Bobbs-Merrill Reprint Series.

"Escalation and Its Use to Mitigate the Inequities of Inflation," in *Inflation, Growth, and Employment*, for the Commission on Money and Credit, Prentice-Hall, Englewood Cliffs, N.J.: 1964, pp. 177–230.

"More on Soviet Bloc Trade Discrimination," *Soviet Studies*, vol. 17, no. 1 (July 1965), pp. 44–65.

"Foreign Trade Behavior of Centrally Planned Economies," in Henny Rosovsky, ed. *Industrialization in Two Systems: Essays in Honor of Alexander Gerschenkron*, New York: John Wiley and Sons, 1966, pp. 237–63. Reprinted in Morris Bornstein, ed. *Comparative Economic Systems: Models and Cases*, Homewood, Ill.: Richard D. Irwin, 1969.

"The Operation of Some Traditional Adjustment Mechanisms in the Foreign Trade of Centrally Planned Economies," *Economies et Societes: Economie Planifiee*, Cahiers de L'I.S.E.A. (February 1968), vol. 2, no. 2, pp. 407-44.

"Soviet Central Planning and Its Impact on Foreign Trade Behavior and Adjustment Mechanisms," in Alan Brown and Egon Neuberger, eds. *International Trade and Central Planning*, pp. 280-305, Berkeley: University of California Press, 1968.

"Economic Organization of Communism: Public Finance," in *International Encyclopedia of the Social Sciences*, vol. 3, New York, 1968, pp. 146-51.

"The Ruble Exchange Rate and Soviet Foreign Trade Pricing Policies, 1929-1961," *American Economic Review*, vol. 58, no. 4 (September 1968), pp. 803-25.

"Comparison of Different Forms of Trade Barriers," *Review of Economics and Statistics*, vol. 51, no. 2 (May 1969), pp. 159-65.

"Import Bottlenecks and the Foreign Trade Multiplier," *Economic Inquiry* (formerly *Western Economic Journal*), vol. 7, no. 2 (June 1969), pp. 101-8.

"Soviet Trade and Aid," in J. C. Hurwitz, ed. *Soviet-American Rivalry in the Middle East*, (Proceedings of the American Academy of Political Science (March 1969), pp. 104-20. Republished in 1969 by Frederick A. Praeger.

"Economic Planning," *Encyclopedia Americana*, New York, 1969, pp. 598-600.

"Some Notes on Overfull Employment Planning, Short-run Balance, and the Soviet Economic Reforms," *Soviet Studies*, vol. 22, no. 2 (October 1970), pp. 255-61.

"On the Technique of Comparing Trade Barriers of Products Imported by Capitalist and Communist Nations," *European Economic Review*, vol. 2, no. 1 (Fall 1970), pp. 3-22.

"The Real Cost of Foreign Economic Aid," *Journal of Development Studies*, vol. 7, no. 3 (April 1971), pp. 245-56.

"East-West Trade and Investment Policy Issues," in *United States International Economic Policy in an Interdependent World*, vol. 2, Papers submitted to the Commission on International Trade and Investment Policy, Washington, D.C.: U.S. Government Printing Office, July 1971, pp. 363–96.

"La Theorie du commerce exterieur des economies centralement planifiees," *Revue de L'Est* (July 1972), pp. 5–36.

"Foreign Trade in the Balance of Payments and GNP Accounts of Centrally Planned Economies," *Occasional Paper*, University Center for International Studies, University of Pittsburgh, 1973, 27 pp.

"East-West Trade and Investment Policy Issues: Past and Future," in Joint Economic Committee, Congress of the United States, *Soviet Economic Prospects for the Seventies*, Washington, D.C.: U.S. Government Printing Office, 1973, pp. 660–89.

"Future East-West Economic Issues," in C. Fred Bergsten and John Mathieson, eds. *The Future of the World Economic Order*, Washington, D.C.: Brookings Institution, 1973, pp. 265–92.

"Foreign Trade Accounting Methodology in Centrally Planned and Capitalist Economies," *Journal of International Economics*, vol. 3, no. 1 (February 1973), pp. 59–66.

"Trade and Growth: A Sino-Soviet Comparison," in F. D. Holzman, *Foreign Trade Under Central Planning*, Cambridge, Mass.: Harvard University Press, 1974, pp. 86–89.

"The Economics and Politics of East-West Relations," with R. Legvold, *International Organization*, vol. 30, no. 1 (Winter 1975), pp. 275–322. Republished in: C. Fred Bergsten and Lawrence B. Krause, eds. *World Politics and International Economics*, Washington, D.C.: Brookings Institution, 1975. Reprinted in E. P. Hoffman and F. J. Fleron, eds. *The Conduct of Soviet Foreign Policy*, New York: Aldine, 1980.

"The Soviet Economy: Internal and International Issues" (with Joseph Berliner) in William Griffith, ed. *The Soviet Empire: Expansion and Detente*, for the Rockefeller Commission on Critical Choices for Americans, Lexington, Mass.: D. C. Health, 1976, pp. 85–144.

"Trade, Technology, and Leverage: The Limits of Pressure" (with Richard Portes), *Foreign Policy* (Fall 1978), pp. 80–90. Reprinted in Gary Bertsch and John McIntyre, eds. *National Security and Technology Transfer: The Strategic Dimensions of East-West Trade*, Boulder, Colo.: Westview Press, 1983, pp. 77–84.

Economic Relations Between East and West: Problems and Prospects, Washington, D.C.: Brookings Institution, 1978, 35 pp. (Tripartite report by fifteen experts from the United States, Germany, and Japan.)

"CMEA's Hard Currency Deficits and Ruble Convertibility," in Nita Watts, ed. *Economic Relations Between East and West*, International Economic Association Volume, New York: St. Martin's Press, 1978, pp. 144–63.

"Notes on Ruble Convertibility: Discussion," in C. T. Saunders, ed. *Money and Finance in East and West*, New York: St. Martin's Press, 1978.

"Some Systemic Factors Contributing to the Convertible Currency Shortages of Centrally Planned Economies," *American Economic Review*, vol. 69, no. 2 (May 1979), pp. 76–80.

"Some Theories of the Hard Currency Shortages of Centrally Planned Economies," in *Soviet Economy in a Time of Change*, vol. 2, Joint Economic Committee, Congress of the United States, Washington, D.C.: U.S. Government Printing Office, 1979, pp. 297–316.

"Communist Challenges to the Liberal Economic Order," in Ryan Amacher, Gottfried Haberler, and Thomas Willett, eds. *Challenges to the Liberal Economic Order*, Washington, D.C.: American Enterprise Institute, 1979, pp. 346–53.

"Are the Soviets Really Outspending the U.S. on Defense?" *International Security*, vol. 5, no. 1 (Spring 1980), pp. 86–104. Reprinted in part in *Bulletin of the Atomic Scientists* (June 1980), and in *Challenge*, vol. 23, no. 4 (September/October 1980).

"The CMEA Financial System and Integration: Comment," in Paul Marer and J. Michael Montias, eds. *East European Integration and East-West Trade*, Bloomington: Indiana University Press, 1980, pp. 139–42.

"Internal and External Balance under Central Planning: Comment," in Egon Neuberger and Laura Tyson, eds. *The Impact of International Economic Disturbances on the Soviet Union and Eastern Europe*, New York: Pergamon Press, 1980, pp. 113–18.

"Creditworthiness and Balance of Payments Adjustment Mechanisms of Centrally Planned Economies," in Steven Rosefielde, ed. *Economic Welfare and the Economics of Soviet Socialism*, Cambridge: Cambridge University Press, 1981, pp. 163–84. Also published in Hungarian in the Proceedings of the Joint U.S.-Hungarian Conference, edited by I. Dobozi and M. Simai, Budapest, 1979, pp. 113–43.

"The Second Economy in CMEA: A Terminological Note," *The ACES Bulletin*, vol. 23, no. 1 (Spring 1981), pp. 111–15.

"Does the Recent United States Anti-Dumping Regulation for Centrally Planned Economies Bridge the Systemic Gap?" in D. Wallace, G. Spina, et al., eds. *Interface Two*, Washington, D.C.: 1981, pp. 514–22 and 5 unpaginated charts and tables.

"The Performance of the Soviet Economy: Past and Future," in *Future Trends in the World Economy*, Washington, D.C.: Evans Economics, 1981, 80 pp.

"Soviet Military Spending: Assessing the Numbers Game," *International Security*, vol. 6, no. 1 (Spring 1982), pp. 78–101.

"Dumping by Centrally Planned Economies: The Polish Golf Cart Case," in Padma Desai, ed. *Marxism, Central Planning, and the Soviet Economy: Economic Essays in Honor of Alexander Erlich*, Cambridge, Mass.: MIT Press, 1983, pp. 133–48.

"Administration Misrepresentations of Soviet Military Spending," in Ronald Dellums, ed. *Defense Sense: The Search for a Rational Defense Policy*, Cambridge, Mass.: Ballinger, 1983, pp. 96–105.

"Systemic Bases of the Unconventional International Trade Practices of Centrally Planned Economies," *Columbia Journal of World Business*, vol. 18, no. 4 (Winter 1983), pp. 3–8. Reprinted in Thomas Wolf, ed. *International Economic Perspectives: Current Research on East-West Trade*, vol. 10, no. 4, U.S. Information Agency, 1985.

"A Comparative View of Foreign Trade Behavior: Market vs. Non-Market Systems," in Morris Bornstein, ed. *Comparative Economic Systems: Models and Cases* (5th ed.), Homewood, Ill.: Richard D. Irwin, 1985, pp. 367–86.

"The Effects of Aggregation on the Difference between Laspeyres and Paasche Indices" (with Gilbert DeBartolo), *Journal of Comparative Economics*, vol. 9, no. 1, (March 1985), pp. 71–79.

"Comecon: A Trade Destroying Customs Union?" *Journal of Comparative Economics*, vol. 9, no. 4 (December 1985), pp. 410–23.

"Can Military Expenditure Figures Provide any Useful Information?" *Russia*, vol. 11 (1985), pp. 26–34.

"The Significance of Soviet Subsidies to Eastern Europe" *Comparative Economic Studies*, vol. 28, no. 1 (Spring 1986), pp. 54–65.

"Further Thoughts on the Significance of Soviet Subsidies to Eastern Europe," *Comparative Economic Studies*, vol. 28, no. 3 (Fall 1986), pp. 59–64.

PART I

Overview

CHAPTER I

Economic Stabilization, Structural Adjustment, and Economic Reform

Josef C. Brada
Ed A. Hewett
Thomas A. Wolf

In the 1960s Western analysts studying Eastern Europe and the Soviet Union, along with many of their Eastern colleagues, were preoccupied with the prospects for success of the unfolding economic reforms. In general, macroeconomic issues were relegated to the background and given far less attention than the myriad microeconomic issues highlighted by the reform debates. To be sure, macroeconomic policy issues were not totally neglected in the centrally planned economies (CPEs). The debate over industrialization policy in the Soviet Union in the 1920s and the literature on economic cycles in Eastern Europe had focused on macroeconomic issues, and Franklyn Holzman's own analysis of the tendency toward overfull employment planning in CPEs had drawn attention to the macroeconomic implications of planners' behavior in planned economies.[1]

Nonetheless, the 1960s were the years of reform, and the literature on Eastern Europe reflected that. If there had been a slogan designed to capture the spirit of writing on CPEs in the 1960s and early 1970s, it would have been ". . . get the prices right, then all else will fall into place." Rational prices and incentives would force a major reallocation of resources, shifting the structure of these economies toward an increasingly efficient configuration, one more closely oriented to the satisfaction of both domestic and foreign buyers. Economic reform, and the discussion of it, focused on structural adjustment in the form of resource movements between industries and within each industry, on shifts in resources toward the production of commodities in demand on world markets as well as on increased efficiency of production. The implicit assumption seemed to be either that price generated micro-balances would yield macro-balance, or that macroeconomic balance would somehow come out of a macro-policy skillfully designed to accommodate, rather than interfere with, the structural adjustment.

By the beginning of the 1970s most of the reform packages introduced in the Soviet Union and Eastern Europe had been de facto, if not de jure, reversed. Hungary was the only exception, having begun late with one of the most comprehensive packages; but even there the reversal had begun by 1972. By the beginning of the 1970s it was clear that reforms and the needed structural changes that prompted them would be extraordinarily difficult to implement in the light of the formidable economic and political barriers that stood in their way (Bornstein 1977; and Brus 1979).

Then came a combination of events, whose consequences have not yet fully run their course, that would form a watershed for Eastern Europe. In 1972 Presidents Nixon and Brezhnev reached a series of agreements and understandings that set off a short, but rapid and far-reaching, relaxation of tensions. The result was an explosion in trade and capital flows, involving mainly Eastern Europe, that continued through the remainder of the decade.

The 1973–74 oil price shock magnified the structural imbalances in Soviet trade with the smaller East European countries while at the same time its consequences encouraged the latter to postpone or ignore the need for drastic changes in macroeconomic and structural policies. Within the Council for Mutual Economic Assistance (CMEA), Soviet willingness to run large trade surpluses vis-à-vis Eastern Europe and the slow adjustment of energy prices to world market levels forestalled the need for austerity and encouraged slow or even perverse changes in industrial structure. At the same time, the willingness of western banks to provide loans to Eastern Europe permitted these countries to continue to take advantage of the newly created opportunities to import technology and capital from the West without the need to reallocate exports to, or restructure the pattern of production with regard to the needs of, the world market. Only as leaders in Eastern Europe gradually began to realize the unavoidability of macroeconomic adjustment and the increasingly compelling need for structural change in the latter years of the 1970s did the focus of Western studies of these countries shift from reform to macroeconomic and structural policies.

Although the issue of economic reform has never been eclipsed by the issues of macroeconomic stabilization and structural change, East European policymakers and economists, as well as Western economists who study those systems, found themselves increasingly devoting attention to the very difficult issue of how to reduce the balance-of-payments deficits and, once having done so, how to restore vigor to economies that had become stagnant and structurally ossified from the lengthy application of deflationary policies (see Balassa 1986, for a view of the effects of deflationary policies on international competitiveness). Economic reforms, while they might reduce deficits in the long run, might increase them in the short run. East European leaders, searching for low-risk policies with relatively short lags, naturally gravitate away from reforms toward more traditional demand-suppression instruments inherent in the material balances system. Similarly, reflation combined with structural change might be seen as requiring strong central guidance in order to avoid a repetition of the investment booms of the 1970s.

On the other hand, economic reforms cannot be discarded as a consideration, either by policymakers, or by the analysts who seek to follow events in these countries. Eastern Europe's balance-of-payments problems have a strong structural component, and economic reforms are a promising avenue for addressing that source of the difficulty. If the remainder of the balance-of-payments problems are attributable to excess demand for goods as a whole, then excess demand for investment goods is a likely cause, and here too an economic reform may provide a promising long-run remedy.

Economic reform, structural adjustment, macroeconomic stabilization, and participation in the larger world economy are in fact interconnected aspects of the same issue: the long-term economic viability of centrally planned economies in the rapidly changing economic environment of the modern world. Any economic strategy that focuses on only one or two of these aspects at the expense of the others is likely to fail; yet even those strategies that build on all these pillars may well fail

TABLE 1.1. CMEA Country Trade Balances with Market Economies (Customs Basis),[1] 1971–84 (in billions of U.S. dollars)

	1971–75 (Cumulative)	1976–80 (Cumulative)	1980	1981
Bulgaria	−0.4	1.6	1.0	0.7
Czechoslovakia	−0.5	−2.2	0.1	0.3
German Democratic				
Republic	−3.6	−7.4	−1.7	—
Hungary	−2.6	−4.2	−0.7	−0.8
Poland	−3.3	−12.1	−1.0	—
Romania	−0.4	−4.0	−1.9	0.2
Eastern Europe	−10.8	−28.3	−4.3	0.4
USSR	−2.4	6.4	3.4	−0.7

SOURCES: UN, ECE *Economic Survey of Europe in 1984–85*, pp. 204–5.
    [1]F.o.b., except for Hungarian imports, which are c.i.f.

unless political leaders can muster exceptional skill, garner international support, and enjoy good luck.

The contributions to this volume reflect the recent research on these issues by various specialists on the economies of the Soviet Union and Eastern Europe. Because these issues are so interrelated, most of these papers discuss two or more facets of the problem. Yet each author does emphasize either the macroeconomic stabilization aspect, structural adjustment, participation in the larger world economy, or the economic reform aspect, and this has led to the placement of essays in the four sections.

MACROECONOMIC STABILIZATION

In market economies, the usual symptoms of excess demand pressures are open inflation and a deterioration of the balance of payments. They are less reliable indicators of the extent of excess demand in centrally planned economies because both of these symptoms can easily be suppressed through administrative intervention (Wolf 1985a). Growing inflationary pressures in a planned economy may be difficult for the outsider to detect, especially in the early stages. Most domestic prices are administratively fixed or closely regulated, and these pressures may only be manifested in a buildup in excessive household liquidity ("forced savings"), "forced substitution", and lowered labor pro-

1982	1983	1984	
0.7	0.3	0.5	
0.4	0.8	1.0	
1.5	1.3	1.0	
−0.3	−0.1	0.1	
1.5	1.4	1.5	
1.4	2.3	3.0	
5.2	6.1	7.1	
4.3	6.2	6.7	

ductivity, each of which is very difficult to quantify. Because foreign trade and payments are under administrative control, there need not be a direct spillover of domestic inflationary pressures into the balance of payments (Allen 1982).

Such suppression of the usual symptoms of excess demand, however, cannot continue indefinitely. Indeed, in the late 1970s and early 1980s most East European countries experienced a degree of open inflation not seen since the early postwar period. At the same time virtually all countries in the region incurred convertible currency trade deficits, as well as ruble deficits with the Soviet Union, and accumulated external debt in unprecedented amounts (see table 1.1). Poland was only the most spectacular case of macroeconomic disequilibrium in the region.

Large trade deficits over a period of several years do not automatically indicate the existence of fundamental macroeconomic disequilibrium. In Poland, for example, large convertible currency trade deficits lasting several years were actually planned by the authorities in the early 1970s. By importing massive amounts of machinery, equipment, and technology from the West in those years, the Poles hoped to modernize their industry and ultimately to pay off the increased debts through growing exports of industrial output to the West (Foreign Trade Research Institute 1972, 1973). Had the authorities been able to limit import growth to a moderate level, to develop effective export incentives, to accompany this policy with control over domestic demand, and had world markets not been jolted by the oil price shock of 1973–74 and the ensuing recession of 1974–75, the Polish strategy conceivably might have worked and the debacle of the late 1970s through the early 1980s might have been avoided.

The past fifteen years offer analysts a fertile field for studying emerging macroeconomic disequilibria in the USSR and Eastern Europe and for evaluating the types of policies followed to adjust to the imbalances. The severity of these problems varied across the countries of the region; so too did the nature and timing of the adjustment policies aimed at eliminating the imbalances. The contribution to this volume by Tyson, Robinson, and Woods (chapter 3) focuses on these differences between Hungary and Yugoslavia in the early 1980s. Aside from the question of why these differences existed, the study of macroeconomic stabilization in these economies raises important and difficult issues regarding methodology and measurement. Many of these issues are addressed in the following two sections.

Sources of Macroeconomic Imbalances

One issue of continuing interest involves the causes of economic imbalances in Eastern Europe and the Soviet Union. Part of the problem is distinguishing between the sources and symptoms of disequilibrium. Even if the sources can be clearly identified, a further problem involves sorting out the relative contribution of the different sources.

Many economists in Eastern Europe stress the role of investment fluctuations as a disequilibrating force. It is not disputed that investment growth rates tend to fluctuate quite dramatically in planned economies. But it is less clear that these fluctuations have a well-defined cyclical character; and the source of these fluctuations is much more controversial. A debate continues over whether responsibility for such fluctuations should be assigned primarily to the planning and higher levels of the economic hierarchy or, instead, to the enterprises themselves. From an earlier emphasis on planners' errors and their tendency to formulate overly ambitious plans for the investment sector (Holzman's [1953] notion of overfull employment planning was a way of conceptualizing this problem), much of the discussion of investment cycles has evolved to a point where the blame is placed on enterprises that purposely understate their total investment requirement when "hooking on" to the plan. The result is a surge in the demand for investment goods that spills over into the foreign trade sector. The resulting balance-of-payments deficit forces planners to clamp down on total investment, bringing about an improvement in the trade balance. The gradual improvement in the external balance creates an environment conducive to a reemergence of excess demand for investment goods, and the cycle begins again.

This type of explanation is particularly persuasive to economists from those countries with modified systems, such as Hungary or even Poland at certain times over the past fifteen years (see Hewett 1981; and Wolf 1985a). If enterprises' excess demand is the culprit here, it would be the result of policy mistakes, such as too lax a credit policy, and of subtle systemic features of the planned economies, such as implicit output maximization rather than profit maximization as the goal of enterprises, an inefficient price system, and the "soft budget constraint," by which the authorities accommodate the credit and subsidy demands of enterprises, thereby weakening financial discipline (on the soft budget constraint see Kornai 1980a, 1980b). It is very difficult to disentangle these factors; yet this must be done if useful recommendations for reform of both policies and institutions are to be possible. It is an open question whether an analytical distinction between system and policy, often used by comparativists, is really very useful in this case.

If investment fluctuations are an important determinant of changing levels of macroeconomic imbalance in planned economies, we would expect increases in the growth rate of investment to be positively correlated with some measure of excess household liquidity, as real resources are diverted from consumption to investment, and negatively correlated with the overall trade balance. It is difficult to identify such empirical regularities, however, because it is no simple task to measure excess demand pressures for consumer goods in planned economies, and in any event other factors will also be affecting macroeconomic balance in these countries.

Despite these difficulties in measurement, it is perhaps significant that in four of the five countries for which the relevant data appear in official statistics (Bulgaria, Czechoslovakia, Hungary, and Poland), those years in the period 1970 to 1984 in which the proportion of domestic expenditure going to investment was highest—that is, when the "accumulation fund" as a percentage of "net material product distributed" was greatest—tended to correspond to those years in which the overall trade deficit in relation to net material product (NMP) was greatest.[2] By the same token in virtually all these countries the years of relatively low investment in relation to aggregate expenditure, namely the early 1980s, are correlated very strongly with those years in which the trade deficit relative to NMP was minimized or trade surpluses were generated. Year-to-year changes in the two ratios are less clearly correlated, however, so that this evidence of the preeminent role of investment spending in determining the external deficit is relatively crude. Clearly, much more work needs to be done in analyzing and empirically identifying the role of investment in economic fluctuations in planned economies.

Fluctuations in investment, measured either by changes in the aforementioned share of investment in domestic expenditure or changes in the real growth rate of investment spending, were most pronounced among the CMEA countries in Bulgaria, Hungary, and Poland. It is perhaps not coincidental that the latter two countries were in the forefront of economic reform in the early and mid-1970s. Indeed, some observers have seen partial decentralization of decisionmaking regarding investment, wages, and other economic activity as having aggravated the problem of macroeconomic balance in planned economies. (On wage regulation, see Adam 1980; and Marrese 1981.) The papers in this volume by Tyson et al. on Hungary and Yugoslavia (chapter 3), and by Plowiec on Poland (chapter 13) raise this issue and thereby join the two issues of macroeconomic stability and reform.

Although the domestic authorities' own economic policies must ultimately be held responsible for the perpetuation and in some cases worsening of internal and external macroeconomic imbalances, many of the problems of Eastern Europe in the 1970s and early 1980s were clearly influenced by exogenous factors. All the East European countries except Poland were adversely affected by the oil price shock of 1973–74. Those countries relatively poorly endowed with energy resources were particularly hard hit: Czechoslovakia, the GDR, and Hungary. The resulting terms of trade deterioration meant a one-shot loss in real income for these countries, and policymakers faced the choice of permitting the convertible currency trade balance to deteriorate pari passu with the decline in terms of trade, or to enforce cutbacks in the rate of growth of domestic spending to correspond to the real income loss. This shock emanating from the convertible currency area was followed by a change in 1975 toward greater flexibility in the intra-CMEA foreign trade price system, which also set in motion the continuing deterioration of East

European terms of trade vis-à-vis the Soviet Union documented in the paper by Marrese and Vaňous (chapter 7).

The oil price shock of the period 1973–74 was followed in the West by the recession of 1974–75, and this, together with stepped-up protectionist pressures in the industrialized countries, limited the growth potential for East European exports. At the same time, and continuing up to the present, the newly industrialized countries (NICs) and other developing countries have become an increasingly significant competitive force to be reckoned with on world markets for manufactured goods (Poznański 1986). Although changes in partner country commercial policies and increasing competitive pressures on export markets are not intrinsically macroeconomic issues, these external shocks of a structural nature have materially affected the ability of the East European countries to eliminate their external deficits, and have forced most of them to rely mainly on cuts in imports to achieve the convertible currency trade surpluses needed to service the large debt accumulated in the 1970s.

Although it is true that the recycling of petro-dollars and the Western stagflation of the mid- and late 1970s led to an unprecedented availability of credit to the Soviet Union and Eastern Europe in this period, the responsibility for growing external indebtedness must ultimately rest with the policymakers of these countries. The same must be said with respect to the management of these countries' external debt following the second oil price shock of 1979, that led to renewed inflationary pressures in the convertible currency area accompanied by a decline in the real rate of interest in international financial markets. The CMEA countries were not compelled to continue to run external deficits financed by what was temporarily very cheap credit, and not all of them did so. By the late 1970s Bulgaria was running trade surpluses, on a customs basis, with the nonsocialist world, as was the Soviet Union. Czechoslovakia was able to achieve balanced trade by 1980 and a substantial surplus as early as 1981. At the other extreme, Hungary did not bring its nonsocialist trade into balance until 1984.[3] As these countries' debts grew, and debt service obligations developed swiftly, the need to reduce aggregate spending in order to generate trade surpluses with which to service the debt became even more urgent. This brings us to the subject of macroeconomic adjustment more generally.

Policies for Macroeconomic Adjustment

The foregoing discussion suggests that most of the CMEA countries were buffeted in the 1970s both by external economic shocks, such as the two oil price explosions and rising protectionist pressures, as well as by economic disturbances, such as investment booms and harvest failures, that originated in the domestic economy. Some of the domestic disturbances, and in particular the fluctuations in investment, were the result of complex and as yet inadequately understood interactions between the authorities themselves and lower-level decisionmaking units. A case can be made for the view that policy response to such disturbances in most planned economies is likely to take place in two analytically distinguishable steps.

Stage One. In the first stage, which may run from several months to a few years, authorities adhere to the basic investment goods priority that has characterized economic development in most planned economies since the establishment of the Soviet-type system. Whether in response to a supply- or demand-side disturbance, the authorities may not oppose and in fact may even encourage the diversion of resources from consumption to investment. In the event of a supply-side disturbance, this diversion of resources helps to buffer the investment sector; there is no reason, however, to suppose that the rate of investment would actually be stepped up in the face of such a disturbance. At the same time, the rigidity of the producer and consumer price system, combined with the planners' interest in fixed prices for planning purposes and their commitment to stable prices at the retail level for sociopolitical reasons, will generate little if any upward movement in administratively set prices in response to the emerging inflationary pressures.

The investment goods priority combined with price stability means that short- and medium-run adjustment will involve primarily quantity rather than price changes, and that these quantity responses will appear in growing excess demand pressures in the consumption sector as the growth in output of consumer goods fails to keep up with rising household incomes, as well as in a deterioration in the balance of trade. The latter may occur if the country initially has plentiful international reserves or easy access to foreign credit and if the diversion of resources into investment eats into exportable surpluses and, together with emerging shortages of consumer goods, leads the authorities to step up imports (see Wolf 1985a). As noted earlier, there is some rough evidence of a positive correlation between the share of investment in domestic spending and trade deficits for several of the CMEA countries in the 1970s.

Another potential symptom of short- and medium-run disequilibrium in planned economies—"forced saving" among households—is more difficult to measure. Indeed, the measurement of excess demand in the market for consumption goods, which, roughly speaking, is the corollary to forced saving, has been a hotly debated issue among Western experts on the planned economies over the past decade. In a stationary economy it might seem at first glance that an increase in the share of domestic expenditure devoted to investment would, given fixed prices and inflexible wages, necessarily lead to excess demand for consumer goods. This is not an inevitable outcome, however, because the increased spending on investment goods could be just offset by increased imports of these products. (The increase in investment would just be offset by an increase in the difference between NMP distributed and NMP produced, a development reflected by an increase in the external deficit.)

The measurement problem becomes much more complicated in a dynamic context. Disequilibrium, either excess demand or excess supply, may already exist in consumption, and income will be changing from one period to the next. If the marginal propensity to save out of income is greater than the average propensity to save, a less than proportionate change of actual consumption with changes in income need not imply an increase in excess demand for consumer goods. And because the possibility of disequilibrium must be allowed for, standard approaches for estimating this propensity in market economies cannot be used for the planned economies (Portes and Winter 1980). Moreover, because administratively set relative prices are unlikely to reflect accurately the relative scarcities in the economy, many individual consumer markets will be in disequilibrium regardless of the macroeconomic situation. This will cause aggregate consumption to be below desired levels, and it will not be clear whether the resulting excessive buildup in household liquidity, even if it could be measured, is due to micro- or macro-disequilibria, or both. Consequently we cannot draw direct inferences about the state of the market for consumption goods, and hence about excessive household liquidity, on the basis of movements from period to period in the share of spending or output devoted to investment.

Emerging widespread shortages of consumer goods and a deteriorating trade balance are not the only possible indicators of short- and medium-run disequilibrium. The growing burden of price subsidies may lead the authorities to authorize some increase in retail prices. The Hungarian authorities adopted this course as early as 1975–76 in response to the emerging disequilibrium in that country. Another possible symptom of imbalance, particularly in CPEs that have undergone significant decentralizing reforms, may be a reversal of the reform process as the authorities attempt to regain macroeconomic control. This was evident in the recentralizing efforts in Poland as described in the contribution by Plowiec to this volume (chapter 13) and in Hungary in the mid-1970s (see Hewett 1981; and Tyson et al. in chapter 3).

Stage Two. In the second stage, which in effect more closely resembles what is usually considered as adjustment, planners attempt to bring the external deficit under control and to restore some degree of balance to the market for consumption goods. Resources are diverted away from investment and imports and into consumption (or at least the former *share* of consumption in aggregate spending would be restored) and diverted into exports. This adjustment stage may arrive slowly because of the inertia that characterizes economic management in planned economies and because of the relatively heavy reliance on quantity rather than price adjustments. Its advent may also be significantly delayed if external credit conditions are particularly favorable.

Some facets of the macroeconomic experience of the USSR and the East European countries over the past fifteen years are summarized in table 1.2. Official data are reported on: annual average growth rates, for certain subperiods, of net material product (NMP); aggregate spending, or NMP distributed; and the consumption fund and the accumulation or investment fund. Also reported are the unweighted average annual investment/NMP ratios and the overall trade surplus (NMP produced minus NMP distributed), as a percentage of NMP.[4] The subperiods are 1971–73; 1974–75, the years immediately following the first oil price shock; 1976–80; and 1981–84. Given the data problems inherent in many of these countries' statistics, the data should be taken as being at best only broadly indicative of changes in these macroeconomic variables.

A common feature for these countries is that in those periods in which investment growth outpaced the growth of consumption, aggregate spending tended to grow faster than output, or NMP. When investment growth slowed relative to that of consumption, aggregate spending increased at a lower rate than output. This general pattern is consistent with both the stage one and two behavior described earlier.

In the 1971 to 1973 period, domestic absorption or spending in Bulgaria grew on average at about the same rate as NMP, with investment growth a little higher than that of consumption. In that period the trade deficit averaged about 4 percent of NMP. Immediately following the first oil price shock—concurrently with the Western recession of 1974–75 and the revamping of the intra-CMEA foreign trade price system—the growth rate of investment spending actually increased dramatically in Bulgaria, as did the growth rate for overall domestic absorption.[5] The overall trade deficit equaled 9.5 percent of NMP. The ratio of investment to NMP distributed peaked in 1975, and real investment actually declined in 1976. Since 1976 investment growth on average has been negligible although positive; the rate of growth of spending has been kept well under the growth rate of NMP, and the NMP-normalized trade deficits have been considerably reduced. Although large imbalances were permitted to develop in Bulgaria in 1974–75, in historical and regional perspective the Bulgarians appear to have moved fairly rapidly from stage one to stage two of the adjustment process, and this may have permitted that country to avoid the draconian investment cuts and negligible consumption growth experienced by most other East European countries in the early 1980s.

Macroeconomic developments in Czechoslovakia in the 1971 to 1973 period were similar to those in Bulgaria. Although Czechoslovakia also stepped up investment growth in 1974–75 despite the external shocks, these increases as well as the deterioration in the external balance were less dramatic than for Bulgaria. Like their Bulgarian counterparts, Czechoslovak authorities reined in investment spending quickly, so that by 1977 real investment declined and the overall trade balance was restored. Also, as in Bulgaria, the growth rate of real consumption was roughly halved between 1974–75 and 1976–80. Unlike Bulgaria, the rate of growth of real consumption was further cut in the early 1980s; consumption declined by 1.1 percent in 1982, and investment growth was negative.

We can have less confidence in the figures reported for the GDR in table 1.2 because the implicit overall trade surpluses for that country in the 1970s simply do not match with the sizable deficits that show up in its foreign trade statistics. It is likely, nevertheless, that the general

TABLE 1.2. Aggregate Output and Expenditure Indicators for Five CMEA
Countries, 1971–84

			Average annual growth rates (in percent)		
Country	Period	(1) NMP	(2) NMP distributed	(3) Consumption fund	(4) Accumulation fund
Bulgaria	1971–73	7.6	6.7	6.8	7.5
	1974–75	8.2	11.4	7.4	21.4
	1976–80	6.1	2.8	4.0	−3.2
	1981–84	4.2	3.4	3.8	2.1
Czechoslovakia	1971–73	5.5	6.0	5.9	6.3
	1974–75	6.0	6.3	4.6	11.7
	1976–80	3.7	2.3	2.6	1.5
	1981–84	1.3	−0.7	1.7	−9.3
German Democratic Republic	1971–73	5.2	5.0	5.6	3.4
	1974–75	5.7	4.4	5.1	2.2
	1976–80	4.1	3.6	3.8	3.0
	1981–84	4.3	0.3	2.2	−6.8
Hungary	1971–73	6.4	3.0	4.1	−0.5
	1974–75	6.0	9.5	5.8	22.3
	1976–80	2.8	1.7	3.0	−2.8
	1981–84	2.1	−0.9	1.4	−12.1
Poland	1971–73	9.8	12.2	8.3	21.2
	1974–75	9.7	10.7	9.2	13.5
	1976–80	1.2	−0.2	4.5	−11.8
	1981–84	−1.9	−3.0	−1.7	−7.9
Romania	1971–73	11.4	N.A.	N.A.	N.A.
	1974–75	11.1	N.A.	N.A.	N.A.
	1976–80	7.3	6.9	7.1	6.6
	1981–84	4.1	−1.0	1.4	−6.5
Soviet Union	1971–73	6.1	5.7	5.6	5.0
	1974–75	4.9	4.1	5.1	−0.5
	1976–80	4.3	3.8	4.7	2.3
	1981–84	3.6	3.2	2.8	3.2

SOURCES: column 1, ECE (1985); columns 2–4, ECE (1985) for 1971–80, and Vaňous (1985) for
1981–84; columns 5–6, Vienna Institute for Comparative Economics (1984) and Vaňous (1985).

trends suggested in the table are a reliable reflection of what actually
did transpire. The basic picture conveyed is one of moderately growing
investment and expenditure more generally, with only minor changes in
the proportions of spending devoted to consumption and investment. It
is well known that the GDR, together with Czechoslovakia and Hungary,

(5) Accumulation fund NMP distributed	(6) Trade balance[1] NMP
.270	(.040)
.315	(.095)
.256	(.006)
.250	(.020)
.230	(.027)
.255	(.050)
.244	.008
.187	.087
.230	.017
.225	.030
.220	.038
.187	.130
.213	(.100)
.235	(.090)
.238	(.058)
.147	.035
.297	(.010)
.350	(.060)
.296	(.034)
.215	.007
N.A.	N.A.
N.A.	N.A.
N.A.	N.A.
.282	.143
.283	.013
.275	.010
.262	.014
.260	.020

[1]Includes "losses" and in some cases other minor items.

has been particularly hard hit by terms of trade losses since the mid-1970s. GDR policymakers avoided an investment boom in 1974–75, but they did attempt to maintain both consumption and investment spending growth at almost preshock levels well into the late 1970s. Given the external terms of trade deterioration, they had to pay for this with trade deficits, not registered in table 1.2, financed with foreign credit. Indeed, real investment in the GDR did not fall in a significant way until 1978. By the early 1980s, balance-of-payments pressures necessitated large cutbacks in real investment and continued to slow the growth in consumer spending.

In Hungary domestic investment actually shot out of control in the aftermath of the first oil price shock and, despite the terms of trade deterioration that the country had begun to experience, domestic aggregate spending was permitted to significantly outpace the rate of growth of output. Although real investment declined slightly in 1976, another boom took place in 1977–78 and the pattern of absolute declines in real fixed investment, which continued through 1985, did not begin until 1979. Through 1978 aggregate spending continued to grow excessively relative to output, and as a result Hungary incurred sizable trade deficits for the rest of the decade. Only through sustained and significant cutbacks in real investment since 1979, together with significant reductions in the growth of consumption in the 1980s, was Hungary finally able to generate an overall trade surplus by 1982. By delaying the second stage of adjustment so much longer than the preceding three countries, Hungary was having to pay a larger price in terms of absolute reductions in investment and negligible growth in consumption in the early 1980s. A more detailed analysis of the Hungarian situation in the 1970s may be found in Hewett (1981), and the more recent period is reviewed by Tyson et al. in chapter 3 of this volume.

The figures in table 1.2 illustrate fairly clearly the somewhat unusual case of Poland. Already in 1971–73, having embarked on the "new development strategy" under Gierek, investment in Poland was growing at about 20 percent a year in real terms, and the growth of NMP distributed was outpacing what was itself a very high growth rate for NMP. This policy, or at least its manifestation, changed very little in the ensuing two years. Between 1970 and 1975 the ratio of investment to NMP distributed had increased from 27 to 35 percent and the NMP normalized trade surplus of 3 percent in 1970 had deteriorated to a normalized deficit of 7 percent by 1975. Although investment growth was slowed materially in 1976 and turned negative in 1977, consumption continued to grow through 1980. Inasmuch as Poland did not face a material deterioration in its terms of trade through the mid-1970s, the main disturbance faced by the Polish authorities was mainly of their own making. The period 1971–76 in one respect was a kind of caricature of the investment cycle in planned economies. The magnitude of the disturbance, and the seriousness of the internal and external imbalances that developed in the first stage of adjustment to it, led to the virtual collapse of the economy when the long-delayed second stage of adjustment was finally set in motion.

The second stage of adjustment in all these economies was undertaken largely by means of conventional measures of central planners —administrative intervention. Even in countries such as Hungary and Poland, which had initiated relatively bold reforms in certain spheres of the economy in the early 1970s and again in Hungary in 1980, adjustment was carried out largely by administrative interventions designed to reduce investment and imports. (See the papers on Hungary and Poland respectively by Tyson et al. and Plowiec.) Exports were also frequently pushed in total disregard of considerations of profitability. Traditional macroeconomic stabilization instruments utilized in market economies, such as currency devaluations, are generally of limited use in the more centrally planned economies (Wolf 1985b). However, as discussed in the contribution by Wolf (chapter 2), recent and prospective reform measures in Hungary imply at least the potential effectiveness of the exchange rate as a stabilization instrument in that country. As demonstrated by Wolf, the effectiveness of exchange policy is critically dependent on the monetary policy stance adopted by the authorities, and on the degree to which they can abstain from traditional patterns of pervasive intervention in the microeconomic affairs of enterprises. (Also see chapter 13 by Plowiec on Poland, and the comments thereon by Fallenbuchl and Kemme in chapters 14 and 15.) Other policy instruments designed to affect aggregate demand may also someday prove useful in modified planned economies (MPEs) such as Hungary and Poland, although as discussed in the essay by Tardos (chapter 9), their effectiveness will depend on further institutional reforms and integration of the commodity, money, and factor markets in these economies.

The second stage of adjustment, entered into by most East European economies in the late 1970s or early 1980s, also involved novel approaches toward resolving the external debt problem. As discussed in the papers by Marer (chapter 8) and Tyson et al. (chapter 3), three of these countries, Poland, Romania, and Yugoslavia, entered into rescheduling of their external debt with foreign bankers and governments. Both Romania and Yugoslavia utilized their membership in the International Monetary Fund (IMF) and the World Bank (the International Bank for

Reconstruction and Development, IBRD) to assist their adjustment process. Hungary was able to join these institutions in 1982 at a critical juncture in its own external debt crisis. Poland applied for membership before martial law was imposed, and by becoming a member in 1986 it acquired potential access to the credit facilities and the technical assistance of the IMF and the IBRD. Marer's contribution to this volume discusses the pros and cons of East European membership in the international economic organizations, and also highlights some of the differences in Fund and Bank relationships with these countries.

The foregoing conceptualization of macroeconomic adjustment as consisting essentially of two steps is of course an oversimplification of reality. It is also not meant to apply to all planned economies under all circumstances. Nevertheless, the broad patterns of adjustment suggested by this conceptualization are apparent in the cases of Bulgaria, Czechoslovakia, Hungary, and Poland. Only in the GDR and the USSR, among those countries for which we have data, is there a lack of empirical evidence for these patterns. Indeed, if the figures in table 1.2 can be believed, policymakers in the GDR appear to have avoided the type of diversion of resources from consumption into investment in response to the shocks of 1973–75 and in subsequent years that are suggested by the two-stage hypothesis. This may have eased somewhat the burden of adjustment in later years, but it was not enough to avoid a severe deterioration of the GDR's external balance and a threatening liquidity crisis in the early 1980s due to continued terms of trade deterioration unaccompanied by a sufficient slowdown in the growth of real domestic spending. As indicated in table 1.2, the growth of investment was somewhat effectively reined in throughout this period in the Soviet Union as well, and this, together with a spectacular improvement in terms of trade, enabled the USSR to avoid the balance-of-payments problems of Eastern Europe.

What is perhaps most striking for several of these countries is not the evidence of stage one type of adjustment in the mid-1970s in the form of increased investment/NMP-distributed ratios and trade deficits, but rather the actual acceleration of real investment growth rates in Bulgaria, Czechoslovakia, Hungary, and Poland precisely at the time that the external environment, both outside and inside the CMEA, was deteriorating. Those countries that were able to put the brakes on excess demand pressures relatively quickly, such as Bulgaria and Czechoslovakia, appear to have been able to restore some measure of internal and external balance more easily by the late 1970s.

A uniform characteristic of all these countries was the dramatic slowing of NMP growth rates between the early 1970s and early 1980s, and the even more dramatic slowdown in domestic spending. Clearly these slowdowns are attributable to structural and systemic factors, as well as to various imbalances caused by the macroeconomic problems of the past fifteen years. It may be significant that the countries with the greatest apparent macroeconomic stability in the 1970s, the GDR and the USSR, have shown the smallest declines in NMP growth of the seven countries in table 1.2, as well as the second and third highest average growth rates for NMP distributed in the early 1980s, after Bulgaria. Only a much more in-depth analysis, however, could attempt to derive definitive conclusions with respect to the impact of short-term macroeconomic policymaking on economic growth in the planned economies.

STRUCTURAL ADJUSTMENT AND INTRA-CMEA RELATIONS

The 1970s and early 1980s were a period during which the Soviet Union and the socialist countries of Eastern Europe experienced pressures for structural change of an intensity perhaps matched only during the Stalinist industrialization drive of the 1930s in the Soviet Union and during the early postwar years in Eastern Europe. At the same time the obstacles to structural change were especially severe, particularly toward the end of the 1970s and during the early 1980s.

Pressures for Structural Change

Marxist regimes are, by virtue of their ideology, committed to rapid economic development and, in particular, to a development based on structural changes favoring industry in general and, within industry, those sectors where factor productivity is highest or growing rapidly, or that have the potential for improving productivity in other sectors. The ideological basis for this commitment is the need to build communism through the achievement of high levels of productivity, largely through investment in ever newer and more productive technologies.

Since the socialist countries lag behind the industrialized capitalist countries in the development and application of such technologies, much of the perceived pressure for technological progress and the structural changes it implies is exogenous. The socialist countries must seek to close the gap between the technical and structural sophistication of their economies and those of the developed capitalist countries for a number of reasons. First, the eventual overtaking of capitalist countries clearly cannot be achieved without it; both the leadership and the populace are likely to view the building of communism and the competition with capitalism in terms of the relative modernity of the two systems' industrial structures and the technological sophistication of the goods that these structures can produce. Moreover, the outcome of the competition between capitalism and socialism in the third world depends in large part on the relative economic attractiveness of the two systems. The relative ability of the two systems to facilitate structural change is likely to be a primary determinant of system appeal, particularly among the more prosperous developing countries where industries competitive on a global scale are evolving. While the overtaking of advanced capitalist countries is, of course, a long-term objective, it does serve to color the thinking of socialist leaders both about the economic progress that they have achieved in the recent past and about the structural changes that they as follower countries will have to undertake in the near future. It is worth bearing in mind that such changes will have to be brought about through conscious decisions on the leadership's part and not through the impersonal working of the market that leads to structural changes in market economies that are also at the follower level of economic development.

From the vantage point of the mid-1970s, decisionmakers in CPES could observe important structural changes taking place in the industrialized West. While these structural changes involved some shifts of emphasis from one industry to another, it was the creation and rapid growth of subsectors of certain industries that appeared to impart the greatest stimulus to structural change. In engineering, for example, new branches such as power engineering, computers, and instrumentation were particularly dynamic. Between 1960 and 1975 the share of these new sectors in engineering output had grown from 41.7 to 50.3 percent in the United States, from 29.1 to 48.1 percent in Japan and from 18.5 to 27.3 percent in the Federal Republic of Germany (Kurenkov 1979). Similar changes took place in the chemical industry where new branches such as organic chemicals, synthetic materials, and pharmaceuticals had increased their share of the industry's output from 51.6 to 67.2 percent in the United States and from 35.9 to 59.9 percent in Japan. Not only could East European policymakers discern these changes in the structure of Western industries, but they could also extrapolate them into the second half of the 1970s and into the 1980s. Indeed, the growing importance of computers could be expected to create ever greater changes in process technologies and automation as well as in information processing. Similarly, biogenetics and other advances in the chemical industry offered possibilities for the restructuring of other industries.

A second source of pressure for restructuring came from security considerations. First, many of the new technologies, such as computers and microelectronics, had direct application to the production of new weapons, as did the technology for the production of new synthetic materials, numerically controlled machine tools, and biogenetics. On a broader scale, if the East European countries were to become dependent on the West for the products of these new technologies, they would become increasingly vulnerable to economic warfare from the West. In this connection, the Reagan administration's efforts to hold up shipments of gas-pipeline compressors to the Soviet Union was a useful reminder of the need to maintain technological independence.

The need for structural change was also amply evident from the evolution of the trade of the Soviet Union and of Eastern Europe, both with the rest of the world and with each other. In the increasingly competitive conditions that characterized the world market after the oil price shock, East European exports of manufactures to the West were unable to hold their ground against competitors from newly industrializing and developed market countries. This could be attributed in part to the slow adjustment of industrial structures within the socialist countries.

Within the CMEA, pressures for structural change also increased as a result of the oil price increase. The opportunity cost of Soviet deliveries of oil and other raw materials to Eastern Europe increased not only because these exports could have been redirected to the world market where prices were higher, but also because the Soviet Union could have imported better manufactured goods from the West than were available within CMEA. The magnitude of these opportunity costs was large, as Marrese and Vaňous indicate in their contribution to this volume (chapter 7). Even if one were to accept their widely debated conclusion that the Soviet Union bears these costs as a form of payment for Eastern Europe's loyalty and support, there is no reason to believe that Soviet leaders would not prefer to obtain a better deal in their trade with Eastern Europe. (For alternative explanations of Soviet subsidies to Eastern Europe, see Brada 1985, forthcoming; and Holzman 1986.) Thus the Soviets have both placed limits on their energy exports to CMEA and pressured the East Europeans for better manufactured goods. As Lavigne's essay (chapter 5) shows, this has led to changes in the way in which intra-CMEA integration is to be pursued and the manner in which structural changes are to be coordinated among the CMEA countries.

The oil price increase also created a more general need for industrial restructuring in Eastern Europe that would reflect the new terms of trade implied by higher energy and raw material prices. Among such changes would be increases in domestic energy production and cutbacks in energy-intensive sectors in order to reduce dependence on external sources of energy. By contrast, as Lavigne's essay (chapter 5) suggests, in the Soviet Union the problem was to expand energy intensive industries and to speed the development of oil and natural gas production and distribution networks.

Conditions for Implementing Structural Change

The successful implementation of structural changes to improve export performance and promote more rapid economic growth depends on a number of internal and exogenous factors. Among the most important of these is the availability of resources to direct toward priority sectors. In the early 1970s, the supply of capital would appear to have been ample, both because increasing shares of domestic output were being devoted to investment and because of foreign capital inflows. In the latter part of the 1970s and early 1980s, exactly the reverse was the case in Eastern Europe. The implementation of deflationary policies and the effort to reduce external debt sharply reduced the volume of investment. This must have made it difficult for planners to consider possibilities for the rapid expansion of new industries while at the same time sharply cutting investments in traditional sectors. Beyond the general cutback in investment, newly emerging industries must have been particularly hard hit by the severe restrictions on imports from the West, in part due to the fact that much of the equipment and technology for advanced sectors could be obtained only in the West. Thus those countries, such as Hungary, whose structural policies were particularly dependent upon imports of machinery and purchases of Western licenses and know-how, faced serious obstacles in attempting to restructure their economies (Brada 1984).[6] An equally serious, but less visible, dependence on Western sources is in the area of components and assemblies. In general, new sectors are developed from the top down. Thus the final assembly stage is developed first, with many components imported from the West. While it is hoped that domestic subcontractors or backward integration by the assembler will eventually reduce the reliance on outside sources for components, such hopes have been no better realized in Eastern Europe than they have been in many developing countries. Consequently, a good deal of productive capacity in new sectors has gone underutilized in the 1970s and 1980s because of a shortage of imported components. (On the Polish experience, see Kemme and Crane 1984.)

There is, of course, a degree of simultaneity between the slowdown in structural change due to the effects of deflationary policies and the performance of the foreign trade sector. While poor foreign trade performance necessitated the deflationary policies, the cumulative effect of slower structural change due to these policies must be poorer export performance in the future. Thus East European policymakers face the dilemma that short-run policy measures to establish payments equilibrium may exacerbate future payments' problems. Thus there is a dependence of Eastern Europe: on the West for creating the economic conditions under which East-West trade flows can grow; on the Soviet Union for serving as a satisfactory market for East European manufactures; and on both the United States and the Soviet Union for providing the political atmosphere within which East-West economic exchanges can flourish.

One way of resolving this dilemma would be to attempt to rely on economic reform to facilitate the movement of productive resources from low productivity, uncompetitive sectors to those where productivity and competitiveness on export markets is high. As the essay by Brada (chapter 4) suggests, central planning, as currently practiced in Eastern Europe and the Soviet Union, does not ensure that capital and labor are directed to sectors at the command of planners. The allocation of resources is rather the outcome of a bargaining process between the center and strong sectoral and regional interests. It is thus not clear whether a decentralizing reform would facilitate structural change or whether, instead, it would eliminate the center as a source of countervailing power on behalf of nascent industries in their competition against established sectors for scarce resources. What is certain is that under any decentralizing reform the battle for exceptions would be fought just as intensively on the investment front as it would be to obtain exemptions for individual enterprises from market pressures. On the other hand, centralizing reforms have their own drawbacks. They stifle the ability of the system to introduce new technology into use; they attenuate the ties between foreign markets and domestic producers; and they eliminate competition. Such reforms do, nevertheless, make planners feel that they are able to exercise some control over the allocation of resources in such a way as to affect social welfare. Thus, in the end, the question of systemic change to promote growth and better export performance revolves around the question raised by Tardos (chapter 9) regarding the ability of central authorities to promote social welfare and harmony while simultaneously serving as the custodians of society's productive resources.

At this point it is unclear whether system change is being viewed as the means of escape from the East European dilemma. An alternative approach, the strengthening of CMEA integration, may hold more appeal for both the Soviet Union and Eastern Europe. One reason for the appeal of this course is that it is much safer than reform. As Lavigne points out (chapter 5), CMEA integration is based increasingly on elements of a plan, or possibly of supernational dirigisme based on the predominant role played by the Soviet economy as a supplier of natural resources, as an insatiable market for manufactures and as a generator of implicit subsidies to Eastern Europe. Whether such a concertization, to use Lavigne's term, of economic policies can produce positive results for CMEA members is an open question. The CMEA as an institution has few defenders in the West, and scarcely more in the member countries (Holzman 1976, chapter 3; Holzman 1985). It is difficult to deny that it has caused a good deal of trade diversion and that its mechanisms have, in the past, been unable to avoid duplication in capacity and to promote intra-industry trade on a scope comparable to that found in market economies or optimal from the point of view of its member countries. On the positive side, it is worth noting that CMEA specialization is progressing and that, as Brada concludes (chapter 4), those countries that have made structural changes that reflect CMEA market needs appear to have achieved some success in export performance. As Lavigne argues, it is difficult to predict the outcome of current integration efforts. Nevertheless, the type of subsidies ascribed to Soviet-East European trade by Marrese and Vañous would be more likely to continue to strengthen CMEA integration than to support reform experiments in Eastern Europe.

Prospects for the Future

Eastern Europe's leaders face severe pressures to implement structural changes in the face of serious systemic and exogenous obstacles and in light of the perceived need to maintain relatively restrictive investment policies. The possibilities for breaking the vicious cycle of slow growth, low investment, and little structural change appear limited, and many of the key variables, such as East-West relations, the success of reforms, and CMEA integration, are beyond the control of any individual country. Much will depend on the ability of the Soviet economy to break out of the trend of increasingly slower economic growth. Nevertheless, care should be taken to avoid excessive pessimism. East European and Soviet leaders clearly view structural change as a key issue, one that they have successfully dealt with in the past, albeit under different circumstances. Moreover, deflationary policies must eventually bear fruit, not only by restoring internal and external balance and creditworthiness, but also by forcing upon these countries a negative form of structural policy, one where industries decay and shrink at differing rates. Thus the type of resource reallocation impossible to implement with growing investments in the short run may prove easier to implement in the long run with stagnant or declining investment levels, and Eastern Europe may recover from its current difficulties with a stronger industrial structure than it had at the beginning of the 1970s. While the analysis of structural change over the past fifteen years is critical for understanding what may occur as reflation begins in the region, both policymakers and students of the planned economies must recognize that only change is permanent.

PARTICIPATION IN THE LARGER WORLD ECONOMY

For the CMEA countries, particularly for Eastern Europe, the issue of structural change is inextricably intertwined with the issue of participation in the larger world economy outside of CMEA. Western economies offer a range of goods and a supply of capital resources unparalleled within CMEA. Every CMEA country must decide how it will use the foreign sector, and in particular economic relations with the West, in its strategy for structural transformation. A successful effort to tap the

West's rich goods and capital markets, skillfully interwoven with a domestic program for structural change, holds the potential for performance gains that otherwise would be unattainable. An unsuccessful effort could place a country in a situation such as that faced by Poland over the past decade.

The decision in any CMEA country concerning a strategy for economic relations with the West is a complicated one involving many variables, only some of which are under the control of that country. The most obvious and important distinction here is between the USSR and Eastern Europe. For the USSR, political considerations weigh heavily in its decisions on economic relations, not only because of its position as a superpower, but also because of the strong economic position it enjoys as a result of its rich resources. The USSR is the only CMEA member that can afford the luxury of relatively modest participation in international product and capital markets, and therefore that can afford to subordinate economic to political considerations in its decisions on participation in the world economy.

Eastern Europe, on the other hand, must specialize and trade in order to prosper. Limited domestic markets and skewed, generally poor, resources, leave these countries with few other options. The critical issue is the mix between relations with the East and those with the West. To some extent the degree of effort the East European countries put into developing their relationship with the West is influenced by the state of Soviet relations with the West. Thus, whatever the economic calculations the East Europeans might make concerning the best approach to economic relations with the West, the political considerations of their relationship with the USSR may add a constraining element.

In recent years, as the Soviet-East European relationship has matured, and as Soviet economic difficulties have grown more serious, Eastern Europe's maneuverability in its relations with the West has increased. The result has been the beginning of a gradual process of increasing East European participation in the larger world economy. Hungary, Poland, and Romania are members of the IMF and the World Bank and along with Czechoslovakia, are also contracting parties to the General Agreement on Tariffs and Trade (GATT). Several East European countries, particularly Hungary, operate in Western capital markets with a growing sophistication.

There are two important implications of Eastern Europe's increased participation in international economic organizations, both discussed in detail by Paul Marer (chapter 8). First, the fact of active membership means that these countries have pledged to make an honest effort to play by the rules of the game in the most important institutions shaping the postwar international economy. Secondly, membership in the IMF implies a willingness on the part of governments and parties in Eastern Europe to share with international economic organizations the determination of economic policy, a fundamental change from what Eastern Europe would accept, or the Soviet Union would tolerate, even fifteen years ago. Inevitably this gives to international economic organizations some influence not only over economic policy, but over the basic course of economic reforms, a point discussed by Tyson et al. (chapter 3), which we consider below.

The increasing complexity of the East European economic relationship with the West has the added consequence of drawing the USSR and the West, particularly the United States, into a joint, albeit implicit, responsibility for resolving some of Eastern Europe's economic difficulties. For example, Poland's membership in the IMF represents an internationalization of the Polish economic/political dilemma, and the implication is at the very least a tacit division of responsibilities among the USSR, the West, and Polish leaders regarding the resolution of Poland's problems.

In fact, we seem to be in the early stages of a normalization of East-West relations in which they begin to lose some of the particular characteristics that distinguish them from other economic relations in the world economy. The pace of changes in this direction will, in part but not solely, be determined by U.S.-Soviet relations. In addition, the systemic changes occurring in Eastern Europe will also play an important role in setting the institutional foundation indispensable to much deeper changes.

These changes, and the resulting expansion in opportunities for expanded East-West economic relations, could prove to be an important consideration in Eastern Europe's ability to address effectively the economic problems common to the region. But East-West relations do not constitute the most critical variables. Those lie in the economic systems themselves, particularly in the capabilities of these systems to actually institutionalize pressures for structural change. A system that is undergoing successful reforms will be able to identify and use opportunities available in East-West economic relations far more effectively than a system that bases its strategy primarily on an opening to the West. Thus, the most important issue, on which all others turn, is the nature of economic reform.

ECONOMIC REFORM

Much of the postwar Western research on the Soviet and East European economies has focused on the interrelated issues of economic reforms, structural adjustment, and links between the domestic economy in each of these countries and the world economy. The impetus for reform typically originates in persistent structural rigidities that lead to long-term inefficiencies and inertia in technological change. In the East European economies these create persistent balance-of-payments pressures, the joint consequence of difficulties in producing and selling manufactured goods competitive on world markets, and a persistent high demand for imports, both tendencies analyzed by Franklyn Holzman (see Holzman 1974a, 1979). The effects are similar in the Soviet Union, but the consequences are different. The Soviet Union's rich resources have enabled it to avoid serious balance-of-payments pressures in spite of a persistent weakness in manufactured exports for hard currency (Hewett 1983). In sum, one case for economic reform is the structural adjustments that will result, and their consequences: increased efficiency, more rapid innovation in both product and process technology, dramatic improvements in the quality, cost, and mix of goods and services available for domestic and potential foreign customers.

The case against economic reform rests on the potential economic and social disruption from bankruptcies, unemployment, and inflation that may result from rapid structural change; the potential for macroeconomic destabilization; and the potential loss of control over important social processes. The first two considerations are most important from the economic point of view. Economists have convincing arguments to show that, once it has been implemented, a systemic reform will improve performance. But economic theory is virtually of no help in charting the way through the transition from the old to the new system. It is understandable that politicians interested in retaining their power and the sovereignty, however limited, of their country have heretofore judged the uncertain costs of reform sufficiently large to justify advancing very slowly and turning back at early signs of trouble.

A quarter of a century of experience with reforms—with multiple waves in various countries, most notably Hungary and Yugoslavia —provide a rich data set for understanding the process and its implications for the economy. A number of essays in this volume address aspects of this topic from different perspectives. In addition, there are issues relating to structural change, in particular those linked to foreign economic relations, that are only partially separable from economic reform per se, and receive separate attention in several essays.

The Process of Reform

The history of economic reforms in Eastern Europe since the late 1950s is generally a discouraging one, both for those following the reforms, and for those devising them—the spectators and the players. The lessons are somewhat different for those two groups, but the conclusions regarding the feasibility of reform are the same.

For the players, those who actually took part in debates surrounding the reforms, and who may have played some role in their implementation, the simple lesson is that it is very much harder to do than anyone would have guessed beforehand. The Hungarian experience is quite instructive in this regard, and Marton Tardos (chapter 9) indicates the difficulties involved.

Some of the problems, noted by Marer in his comments on Tardos's essay, stem from the fact that the traditional centrally planned economy constitutes a set of institutions, habits, and expectations deeply embedded in social institutions, as well as in the psyche of the population. Multiple lines of formal authority and long-term relationships reinforce each other in an intricate hierarchy. Ministries are linked to enterprises as parent to child, not just through obligatory plans but also through the authority to appoint management, the ability to help management out of tight spots, and the implicit willingness to support management when they seek special treatment to compensate for inefficiencies (see Kornai 1986). A similar, although not always consistent, symbiotic relationship exists between each enterprise and local party and government officials.

The Hungarian reforms of 1968 sought to change these relationships, but only by changing one of their most visible aspects: obligatory plans. The symbiotic relationships remained essentially intact, the old habits and ways of thinking essentially unchanged. For that reason alone the reform has fallen far short of its claims. Since 1968 enterprises continue to find that their most promising path to decent profits is through negotiation with their superiors, and not through an all-out effort to satisfy the needs of customers. The effect has been to continue, in no insignificant way, the old prereform pattern of individual deals linking each enterprise with superior authorities in a complex set of differentiated subsidies, taxes, and mutual obligations. The plan is gone, but the other strands of the umbilical cord linking the enterprise to the center remain and may have become even stronger to compensate for the loss of the obligatory plan as an instrument for central control of enterprises.

This persistence in keeping the important components of the old system under the cover of reform is the essentially unanticipated outcome of a cautious approach to changing a number of institutions simultaneously. Furthermore, the urge to maintain, or even strengthen, central control is a natural consequence of deeper flaws in the design of reforms that ultimately touch on the essence of socialism as it has been defined in Eastern Europe and the Soviet Union. As Tardos so convincingly shows in his contribution, the lack of close links between product, factor, and money markets in Hungary produces pressures in which the state must continue to act as a surrogate for those missing institutions. That leads to the perpetuation of individual deals; indeed, it justifies them. Any serious effort to change this situation would have to involve the introduction of capital markets and the resolution of some very difficult dilemmas regarding the existence of individual property rights under socialism. Tardos explores the options, but it is clear that the required decisions will be difficult for political authorities.

The various links between the Party and local government officials and enterprises present their own set of problems, for the most part yet to be addressed in Eastern Europe. As Ellen Comisso notes in her comments on Tardos's essay, there are ways one could construct incentives that would interest the party in economic reforms and in enterprise autonomy. But the use of such incentives has not yet been attempted in Hungary and may not be for some time to come.

For the spectators following economic reforms in Eastern Europe the lessons of Hungary are important, but as yet they are not adequately reflected in the academic literature. First, reform decrees should be treated as no more than reformers' hypotheses concerning what might happen. These decrees need to be tested through implementation so that the actual behavior of the actors can breathe life, or death, into them. Second, much that determines the fate of a reform may not be evident contemporaneously, but will only be revealed some time later. What Hewett (1981) called the battle for exceptions, when enterprises ask that they be made a special case during implementation of the reform, occurs as soon as reforms are implemented, but quietly, in the various offices of central government and party agencies. It is only some years later that it becomes evident how that battle went. Finally, it is clear that reforms, following Brus (1979), come in waves, and that the reform process is long, subject to setbacks, and with no guarantee of forward movement. How many waves there will be, and how successful they will be in weakening the opposition, are issues in the politics of reform. Unfortunately, neither political scientists nor economists have been drawn to this very important topic, but that may be changing (Gustafson 1981; and Colton 1984). The lessons of the Hungarian experience are useful, if judiciously applied, to analyzing the prospects for reform in other centrally planned economies. Irrespective of the differences between Hungary and the USSR, there are still many useful clues in Hungary's experience about the pitfalls awaiting those seeking to reform the Soviet economy. All of the symbiotic links between enterprises and party and government officials exist in the USSR, where they are probably stronger than they ever were in Hungary. The problems of creating integrated factor, product, and financial markets are no less daunting in the USSR than in Hungary. The institutions, habits, and expectations of the traditional centrally planned economy are surely more deeply rooted in the Soviet Union, where socialism in its present form has existed for over half a century, than they are in Hungary where socialism has had a shorter tenure.

Hewett's article in this volume (chapter 12) explores the prospects for reform in the USSR, following the working assumption that fifteen years from now its economic system could well be essentially the same as it is today and as it has been for more than half a century. He explores the impediments to reform, the pressures favoring reform, and concludes that it is not implausible to predict that no significant systemic change will take place in the USSR during this century.

Hungary's experience is probably more relevant for other East European countries seeking to introduce similar reforms. Plowiec's essay outlines the efforts to introduce reforms in Poland in the aftermath of Solidarity and prior to the adoption of the "second stage" of economic reform in 1986–88. The Hungarian experience and the recent Polish situation, as analyzed by Fallenbuchl and Kemme in chapters 14 and

15, both suggest that reform in Poland and other countries will be a very long process indeed.

Economic Reforms and Economic Performance

With the accession of Romania, Hungary, and, most recently, Poland to the IMF and the World Bank, the distinction between spectator and player in the reform process has begun to blur somewhat. As the IMF and World Bank lend money to these countries and become involved in negotiating conditions associated with the loans, they simultaneously become the most well-informed spectators in the West as well as marginally important players. They cannot dictate policy, but they can recommend or argue for policy, with real money behind their arguments. Both the Marer and Tyson et al. chapters discuss this important set of developments.

As a result of the increased role of these international organizations in influencing the path of reforms, the relationship between economic reforms and economic performance becomes even more important than it was heretofore. This is an area in which very little research has been done, and while this volume has no articles that directly address the issue, several important points do emerge. Among the many performance indicators that are watched carefully by East European leaders and Western analysts alike, two stand out: the growth rate of GNP and the balance of trade. The first indicator is traditional for all industrial economies and, with all its imperfections, it is a shorthand measure of the growth of social welfare. The second indicator is particularly useful as a rough summary indicator of numerous variables: product quality and productive efficiency, both linked to technological progress, and the macro policies implemented by the government.

Economic reforms, in theory, will have a beneficial effect on both of these indicators. They work mainly through structural changes in which firms producing efficiently and using modern technologies can grow in importance, probably for the most part through modernization of older enterprises. The result is increased factor productivity, that in turn accelerates economic growth. The growth in production of higher quality products, combined with increased efficiency, improves export performance and may allow for rational import substitution, both of which bring about an improvement in the balance of trade. All of this depends, of course, on the ability of the government to pursue policies that support the effects of the reform.

The interesting question is whether a quarter-century of experience with economic reforms in Eastern Europe supports the implied hypotheses linking reforms to economic performance in Eastern Europe. At first glance, the answer would not seem to be very encouraging; but further thought suggests that in fact the experience with reforms to date is too inconclusive to offer much information on this issue.

The two countries with the most extensive reform experience are Yugoslavia and Hungary. Except for the contribution by Tyson et al., the Yugoslav experience is not addressed in this volume. It is clear, however, from previous research (Tyson and Eichler, 1980; and Burkett 1986) that macroeconomic performance in this economy is characterized by serious shortcomings. A major problem with Yugoslavia is its unique set of quasi-independent republics which create political impediments to full implementation of reforms and rational economic policies. Thus Yugoslavia is usually not used as even a casual source of information on how economic reforms affect economic performance in a centrally planned economy.

Hungary might seem to be a more promising source of information. Hungary's growth performance over the last fifteen years has been no more than average for Eastern Europe (table 1.2) and its balance-of-payments record is worse than that of many East European countries (table 1.1). From this one might conclude that the Hungarian reforms, whatever their effects, had no measurable positive impact on growth or on the balance of payments. Indeed, Tardos indicates that Hungarian authorities seem inclined to draw just such a conclusion. The question that deserves much more attention, however, is whether the Hungarian reforms were indeed reforms as they are usually discussed by economists. If—as we believe and Tardos has indicated—the Hungarian system did not change anywhere near as much as the decrees suggested, then the economic performance data from the post-1968 period are not useful information for how reforms in general will affect economic performance. And if that is the case, then we in fact do not yet have a test of what effects radical reforms will have on economic performance.

A second important caveat relates to economic policy, and in particular macroeconomic policy. Economic reforms involve a transition by the government to a system in which aggregate demand is managed primarily by indirect instruments rather than directly through the material balance system. The importance of aggregate demand policy in a partially reformed CPE is stressed both in Tardos's contribution and in that of Wolf—reform of institutions and the price system, without an accompanying prudent macroeconomic policy, cannot be expected to yield positive results. Indeed, if governments mismanage this part of the transition, allowing aggregate demand to get out of hand, then the balance of payments can deteriorate quickly and create pressures to reassert central control through traditional techniques. The problem here is not the economic reforms themselves, but a failure on the part of authorities, probably through inexperience, to respect the accompanying policy requirements.

FUTURE RESEARCH

We hope that this volume settles some issues in the reader's mind, and raises many others. We are at the beginning of a new and different period in which the Soviet Union and Eastern Europe appear to be trying to accelerate the process of integrating themselves into the world economy, a process symbolized by the membership now of three European CMEA members in the IMF and World Bank. Many issues will be raised as this process unfolds, issues that are best addressed from a solid foundation of knowledge about how these systems operate and how they are changing.

Much remains to be done to build that foundation. There is still much to be learned about Eastern Europe's response to the oil price shocks and to changing credit conditions. The reform cycles of the 1960s to the 1970s deserve much more attention than they have received. New reform cycles are underway or are likely to begin soon in several East European countries. The process of generational and systemic change finally seems to have commenced, but a long and very uncertain road lies ahead.

To fully understand this unfolding process will require the insight of several social sciences, most notably political science and economics. There is no clearer message from the experience of the East European countries over the last several decades than that the problems they face and the solutions they attempt can neither be understood nor evaluated using the tools of economics alone. The issue is both political and economic, and those who wish fully to comprehend it shall have to somehow develop analytical approaches as broad as the problem.

PART II

Macroeconomic Stabilization

CHAPTER 2

Devaluation in Modified Planned Economies: A Preliminary Model for Hungary

Thomas A. Wolf

I. INTRODUCTION

Changes in the official exchange rate are usually presumed to have little or no impact on the trade balance in classical centrally planned economies (CPES). As foreign trade decisionmaking is decentralized, however, and links are established between domestic and foreign currency prices, the exchange rate may play a role in attaining both internal and external balance. Among the members of the Council for Mutual Economic Assistance (CMEA), modification of the foreign trade system and of the broader economic mechanism has been most far-reaching in Hungary. In the Hungarian context, the convertible currency exchange rate now plays a potentially much more important role in economic stabilization than does its counterpart in the classical CPE.[1] Nevertheless, the impact of a currency devaluation in Hungary may still differ in some important respects from its effect in market economies of comparable size and income level.

One approach to evaluating the impact of a devaluation in Hungary would be to estimate econometrically the convertible currency trade balance response to various changes in the Hungarian exchange rate over the past decade. Unfortunately, however, such an approach would encounter a number of problems. First, the exchange rate system itself has been modified within the past several years, since the separate commercial and noncommercial rates were finally unified in 1981. Second, and probably more significantly, the Hungarian price system has recently undergone major changes and is subject to continuing modification. The price system of the 1970s based on prime cost was largely converted, insofar as tradables were concerned, into a so-called "competitive" system in 1980. Since 1980, this system in turn has undergone further important modifications. Third, policies regarding export subsidization, as well as trade and exchange controls, have been modified over the past decade. Finally, the structure of trade restrictions faced by Hungary on convertible currency markets has changed in recent years, although the changes would be extremely difficult to quantify. Taken together, these institutional and policy changes would make it very difficult to estimate empirically the marginal impact of a devaluation on the trade balance. Even if this impact could be reliably estimated for the period, say, 1974–84, recent and prospective changes in and extension of the competitive price system would limit the relevance of such estimates for the period ahead.

This essay develops a preliminary model for analyzing the short- and medium-run effects of devaluation in a modified planned economy (MPE), using some of the main institutional features of the present Hungarian economic mechanism as the basis for the model. (See Wolf 1985a, for a discussion of the main features of the MPE.) It is often argued that the Hungarian authorities have pursued an active exchange rate policy in the past mainly to help attain a certain target for the domestic rate of inflation, rather than to attempt to influence significantly the convertible currency trade balance. While this may be an accurate characterization of Hungarian exchange policy in the past, it does not preclude the possibility of the exchange rate being actively used to pursue other goals as well in the future. The emphasis of this essay, therefore, is on the trade balance impact of a devaluation and not on its effect on the domestic price level per se. The study attempts to clarify the main determinants of the effectiveness of the convertible currency exchange rate in improving the convertible currency balance of trade. It should be recognized that although the specific features of this analysis are meant to apply to Hungary, the basic features of the model itself are sufficiently general so as to make it potentially applicable to other emergent modified CPES as well.

By no means should this essay be considered a definitive or comprehensive analysis of the role of the exchange rate in economic stabilization in Hungary. Aside from making a number of simplifying assumptions regarding the Hungarian economy, the model developed and discussed here also does not give an explicit account of several factors that certainly must bear on the impact of exchange rate changes. For instance, to facilitate construction of the model, Hungary is assumed to be a price taker on nonruble markets, even with respect to its exports (for relaxation of this assumption, see Wolf in press). For simplicity, just one convertible currency exchange rate is assumed; therefore the issue of the real effective exchange rate is ignored here. Other limitations include the omission of intermediate goods trade in the formal analysis (again, see Wolf in press) and the abstraction from differences between producer and consumer price structures and systems. Finally, an area that needs a great deal more research is the response by consumers in a modified planned economy to devaluation-induced excess demand pressures in fixed price markets. Moreover, it would be useful to attempt to incorporate the possibility of initial excess demand, at the macro level or micro level or both, more explicitly into the formal model. Some of these limitations could be overcome in future analytical work, although in certain cases, such as the relationship between consumer and producer prices, more information would be needed first.

Section 2 of the essay briefly outlines the fundamental characteristics of the Hungarian price and exchange rate systems. In section 3 a simple model is described and used to highlight the basic responses to devaluation that might be expected in an MPE such as Hungary. The model is employed in section 4 to discuss the possible impact that certain characteristic features of the Hungarian economy may be expected to have on the effectiveness of exchange rate changes. The model is also used to analyze the impact that further economic reforms and policy changes might have on the effectiveness of the exchange rate in improving the trade balance. The formal model, and some numerical calculations, are developed and interpreted in detail in the Appendices.

2. THE HUNGARIAN PRICE AND EXCHANGE RATE SYSTEMS

The basic features of the Hungarian price and exchange rate systems relevant to our problem may be summarized using the terminology and notation of Wolf (1985b). In equation (1) the *transaction* price of the ith tradable (P_i'') is defined as the product of (1) the convertible currency price of this good (P_i^*); (2) the convertible currency exchange rate (e), defined here as the forint price of convertible currency; and (3) a parameter (t_i) equal to 1.0 plus the explicit ad valorem trade tax (subsidy) rate on that commodity:

$$P_i'' = P_i^* e t_i. \tag{1}$$

This transaction price may or may not be equal to the price at which this product is traded on domestic markets (P_i). Price reform over the past fifteen years, however, has meant that an increasing number of Hungarian tradables have domestic prices that are directly or indirectly linked to changes in world market prices and in the exchange rate.

In 1985 several methods for setting prices coexisted in Hungary; about 80 percent of industry was subject to the competitive system, by which domestic producer prices were linked directly or indirectly to transaction prices. In that year, essentially all manufacturing output (about 35 percent of industry) was to be sold on the basis of one or more of the three rules of the competitive system (see Marer 1986c; and Wolf 1985b). Enterprises accounting for 35–40 percent of manufacturing were expected to qualify for the most liberal application of the competitive rules in 1985. Subject to a display that they were successful exporters and a demonstration of responsible behavior with respect to utilization of domestic market power, these enterprises would only be constrained, in domestic price setting, by the actual or hypothetical import transaction prices of the products marketed. In effect, this means that the domestic sales price for the ith product (P_i) could be no greater than the transaction price paid (received) for imports (exports) of that product or, if not traded, no greater than the hypothetical import transaction price.

Domestic producer prices of basic nonagricultural materials and energy, which accounted for about 45 percent of industry, were also keyed to transaction prices of these products determined for convertible currency trade. If these intermediates were imported from the convertible currency area, their effective domestic price was to be the transaction price. If produced domestically or imported from other CMEA countries, the authorities charged the users a variable "producers' differential turnover tax" equal to the difference between the convertible currency transaction price and the domestic cost or forint equivalent of the CMEA import price respectively. In order to be certain that changes in world market prices for such products were more than transitory, the authorities might wait three to five months after significant world market price changes occurred before adjusting the producers' differential turnover tax.

In the remaining 20 percent of industry, most domestic trade was subject to producer prices that might bear little relationship to their transaction prices. Only about one-third of producer prices in agriculture were free. Procurement prices for the remaining agricultural products were set annually.

Producer price flexibility in most nontradable branches was considerably less than in tradables. Only about one-quarter of the value of output in construction and transportation-communication was subject to free pricing. Some of the producer prices on tradables and nontradables that were not free, however, were still permitted to fluctuate within narrow limits or are subject to a price ceiling. For the economy as a whole, including foreign trade, about 70 percent of all producer prices were said to be free or administratively tied directly to convertible currency transaction prices.

Trade with the nonruble area was carried out mainly in convertible currencies, and enterprise export revenue and import expenditures in forints were calculated at transaction prices. Ruble area trade, however, was transacted at transferable ruble prices, which reflected only indirectly, and by no means consistently, world market prices in convertible currency. Because the structure of intra-CMEA prices tended to be inconsistent with the world market price structure, forint price discrepancies on individual products that were faced by enterprises trading with the CMEA could not be eliminated simply by pegging the forint/transferable ruble exchange rate at some correct level. To eliminate or at least reduce these discrepancies and the resulting impact they might have on enterprise profitability, the authorities followed a "price equalization" policy in ruble trade. For ruble area trade in basic intermediates this policy involved, as noted above, a system of variable producers' differential turnover taxes. There was price equalization for other products as well, but it was not necessarily carried out on a strict commodity-specific basis. The system of so-called "modernization grants" to enterprises in effect involved a form of price equalization, but these grants appeared to be related to the specific investment projects or to the overall profitability level of enterprises engaged in ruble trade.

A number of questions remain regarding the forint pricing of ruble area trade. Changes in domestic prices for intermediates imported from the ruble area might lag behind changes in convertible currency transaction prices for these products. Was the lag, of possibly three to five months, long enough to induce enterprises, responding to changes in relative prices, to shift sources of supply? Were there constraints in doing so, at least insofar as CMEA suppliers were concerned? Exactly how were domestic prices set for finished products imported from CMEA? What if many of these products had no close substitutes in the convertible currency area? Would changes in convertible currency transaction prices caused by changes in the convertible currency exchange rate affect ruble area transaction prices in the same way and at the same speed as changes induced by movements in world market prices? Exactly how did the tax-subsidy system work in ruble trade; did it effectively eliminate all enterprise incentive to reallocate trade in response to changes in relative prices?

Until now only producer price changes have been considered. At the retail level, approximately one-half of the trade in state and cooperative shops, two-thirds of services, and all of handicraft and other small-scale market types of goods and services had "free" prices (i.e., without officially set limits) in 1983. Between 90–95 percent of producer prices in light industry and the food industry were free. Without knowing, however, the precise extent to which products and services with free or partially flexible retail prices are produced with free or competitive system priced inputs at the various stages of production—as well as the various price elasticities of supply and demand and the extent to which a devaluation could be expected to reduce aggregate real domestic expenditure—only a rough guess can be made concerning the probable "pass-through" of an exchange rate change to the consumer price index. Some Hungarian economists have estimated the elasticity of the domestic producers' price level with respect to an exchange rate change to be about 0.60–0.65. These estimates appear to be based, however, on the implicit assumptions that: (1) the economy is a price taker with respect to imports; (2) the relative price elasticity of export demand is

TABLE 2.1. Estimated Weights for the Five Composite Goods in
Hungarian Gross Output, 1983 (in percentages)

1. Competitive nonruble tradable	43
2. Fixed price nonruble tradable	16
3. Ruble area tradable	7
Total tradables	66
4. Flexible priced nontradable	18
5. Fixed priced nontradable	16
	100

SOURCE: See appendix 2.2.

Note: Tradables accounted for roughly 57 percent and nontradables 43 percent of Hungarian GDP in 1983.

infinite; and (3) that monetary policy would fully accommodate the price level effect of devaluation.[2]

Any stylized analysis of the balance of trade impact of a devaluation must proceed in terms of "composite" goods. The notion of a composite good is dependent on the assumption that relative price changes among the individual products making up the composite will not occur or at most will be negligible, at least in response to whatever disturbances are permitted in the stylized model. In the case of Hungary, the foregoing description of the price system suggests that it would be inadequate simply to divide the economy into the familiar dichotomy of a composite tradable, the price of which is fixed by the world market price and the exchange rate, and a flexibly priced composite nontradable.

The model developed in appendix 2.1 and described in the next section represents an attempt to respond to the evident complexity of the Hungarian trade and price system, while at the same time to retain enough simplicity to make the model mathematically tractable and describable in a literary exposition. Its forebearers are the classic one asset (money), tradable-nontradable market economy models of Dornbusch (1973) and Krueger (1974), and the relatively briefly sketched modified CPE model of Wolf (1978), the latter containing simply a flexibly priced tradable and a composite fixed price tradable-nontradable.

3. A Simple Framework for
Devaluation Analysis

The discussion of the structure of Hungarian prices in the preceding section suggests that the most apt stylized model of the Hungarian economy would include both fixed and flexibly priced tradables and nontradables. Adding to these products a composite good representing trade with the ruble area would give us five composite goods. The estimated weights for these goods in Hungarian gross output in 1983 are presented in table 2.1.

The competitive nonruble tradable includes those tradables that are either traded with the nonruble area (excluding energy exports that for simplicity are assumed to be entirely reexports), or produced and sold domestically at prices that, at the initiative of either the enterprises or the authorities, move proportionately with convertible currency transaction prices. (For simplicity throughout this essay, the distinction between nonruble and convertible currency trade is ignored.) In other words, the price of the nonruble tradable is assumed to vary in direct proportion to the convertible currency exchange rate.[3] Virtually all products making up this composite product are included in the competitive price system. It is estimated, using 1983 data, that about 43 percent of the gross value of output would fall into this category at the producer level. (See appendix 2.2 for the methodology used in these calculations.)

A second composite would include all those domestically produced tradables that are sold at home at fixed prices. These would be mainly agricultural commodities with fixed procurement prices and various industrial raw materials and semimanufactures. About 16 percent of Hungarian gross output would fall into this category in 1983.

Exports to the ruble area, which accounted for about 7 percent of gross output (18 percent of gross domestic product, henceforth GDP) in 1983,[4] make up the third composite, the ruble area tradable. Despite the questions raised in the previous section about our understanding of how these goods are valued in forints, it will be assumed here for simplicity that their domestic prices are modified, with little or no delay, in line with changes in convertible currency transaction prices for similar goods. Consequently, an increase in the convertible currency exchange rate is assumed to have no effect on the price of the ruble area good relative to that of the competitive tradable.

These two goods are nevertheless differentiated, not so much because the two groups may be mutually quite heterogenous (especially in respect of manufactures), but because there is assumed to be negligible or zero substitution between these goods in the short run for institutional reasons. Hungary's ruble trade is still planned and carried out on the basis of bilateral trade agreements and cleared by what still amounts to a bilateral clearing mechanism.[5] Therefore, even to the extent that forint relative price changes involving the ruble area good do occur vis-à-vis the fixed price tradable and nontradable, the pressure on enterprises to fulfill, but not significantly to over-fulfill on the export side, their ruble area trade plans may serve to minimize their supply response to these relative price changes. For this reason it will be assumed that short-run, say, within one year, relative price supply and demand elasticities involving the ruble area are zero.

The fourth composite would include all nontradables that have prices determined freely by the market. This category amounted to about 18 percent of gross output in 1983. The fifth composite would include all nontradables with fixed prices. This composite accounted for about 16 percent of gross output in 1983. Observe that no more than 50 percent of prices, (i.e., of the competitive and ruble area tradables) will in principle move proportionately with the exchange rate; another 18 percent have flexible prices, but, as explained below, these may not move in proportion to the exchange rate. About one-third of the prices are assumed to be fixed in the short run.

While ideally we would like to specify our model in terms of these five composite goods, such a procedure is not mathematically tractable. Solution of the model for the balance of trade impact of a devaluation involves, inter alia, the use of elasticities of substitution among the different composite goods. When the number of substitutes is increased beyond two goods, these elasticities become endogenous to the model and the simplicity and usefulness of the model are severely limited. For the purpose of model building, therefore, we have reduced the number of goods to three, involving two substitutes, the competitive tradable (T good) and a nontradable (N good), and the ruble area tradable, the R good. No provision is therefore made for a fixed price tradable. Regarding the combination of fixed and flexibly priced nontradables, however, price control is introduced by means of permitting the degree of uniform price control on the nontradable composite to vary (i.e., from an N good price that is determined solely by the market to one that is held fixed by the authorities). The full model of devaluation and its formal solution is discussed in detail in appendix 2.1.

Beginning from an assumed initial position of full stock-flow equilibrium that includes full employment and balanced trade, the basic short-run impact of devaluation of the forint vis-à-vis the convertible currency can be summarized as follows. The economy is assumed to be a price taker in nonruble trade; therefore the increase in the convertible currency exchange rate will lead to an automatic proportionate increase in the transaction prices for all goods actually traded with the nonruble area. Higher prices for these traded products will increase the relative profitability and supply of nonruble exports and diminish the demand for nonruble imports. This will lead to domestic excess demand for all remaining competitive tradables produced at home and will put upward pressure on their prices. Because by assumption these tradables can be traded with the nonruble area at the new, higher transaction prices, there will be nothing to stop their prices from also moving proportionately to the exchange rate.[6]

The effective transaction price for all goods traded with the ruble area will also be fairly rapidly increased by the authorities in proportion to the exchange rate modification. In other words, the price of the composite T and R goods will rise essentially in proportion to the convertible currency exchange rate. The increase in nominal prices for these two composite goods will likewise raise proportionately the relative prices of these goods vis-à-vis the N composite good. This change in relative prices will encourage producers to reallocate resources into production of the T good (recall that the R good is not considered a substitute in the short run), away from the N good. At the same time, consumers of the T good, faced with its higher relative price, will begin to shift their purchases toward the N good. While this is happening, the higher prices for the T and R goods will put upward pressure on the overall domestic price level. If the aggregate real demand elasticity with respect to a change in the price level is negative (because of the decline in real money balances, the real wage, or both) the higher price level will induce a general reduction in real expenditure.

Reallocation of output away from the N good and the shift in demand toward it will create excess demand in this market. If there are no price controls on this good, excess demand will cause its price to rise. The increase in the price of the N good has several effects. It contributes to the rise in the overall price level, and thus reinforces the general decline in real aggregate demand and therefore, given the assumption of initial equilibrium, the decline in real expenditure. A higher nominal and therefore now higher relative price for the N good will tend to diminish the excess demand for this product by reducing somewhat the incentive for producers to reallocate production toward the T good, and by diminishing the interest of consumers in shifting expenditure toward it.

If the authorities fix or limit the increase of the price of the N good, excess demand pressures for the good will not be fully alleviated and potential consumers will be accumulating excessive money balances. Those consumers who remain frustrated in obtaining the N good face a choice which is complex and relatively difficult for formal economic analysis. They can simply accumulate unwanted money balances, hoping that the controlled product will become more available in the not-too-distant future. They can reduce their effort at work or attempt to work fewer hours—this will in general lead to a fall in output, including the production of the N good. They can attempt to acquire this good on the black market, at higher prices than prevail in the state-controlled outlets. In addition, entrepreneurs may be able to respond to these higher prices with additional output produced outside the socialized sector or by enterprise work associations using the capital stock of this sector. Finally, consumers can engage in forced substitution of the T good for this fixed price good. In this event they end up consuming more of the T good than they prefer at prevailing relative prices, but on the margin they may well prefer greater consumption of this good to increased holdings of money.[7] To the extent that forced substitution, reduced labor effort, and diversion of resources to "second economy" production of the N good occur, emergent excess supplies of the T good will of course be reduced.

These are the general responses to a devaluation in this stylized three composite-good modified planned economy. In sum, the nonruble trade balance will improve to the extent that the devaluation induces excess supply of the competitive tradable. Expressed differently, the improvement in the nonruble trade balance will be equal to the reduction in aggregate demand caused by the increase in the price level, plus the amount of any excess demand for the N good that is not accommodated through forced substitution.[8]

Whether the devaluation will indeed lead to an improvement in the trade balance, and by how much, is not evident from the above verbal discussion. These questions can only be answered with the aid of the analytical model developed in appendix 2.1. Equations (A19)–(A20) in that appendix are expressions (at different levels of generality) for the income-normalized improvement in the trade balance starting from balanced trade. Rather than replicate here those equations and their fairly technical interpretation, however, we will attempt a literary summary of those results.

The income-normalized improvement in the nonruble trade balance (i.e., the change in the balance of trade divided by GDP, both expressed in forints) is shown in appendix 2.1 to be a function of: (1) the percentage change in the convertible currency exchange rate; (2) the elasticity of real aggregate expenditure with respect to the price level (which in turn is a function, inter alia, of the tightness of monetary policy); (3) the different weights of the three composite goods in national output (expenditure); (4) the elasticities of demand for and supply of the T good with respect to a change in its relative price (hereinafter, for simplicity, referred to as substitution elasticities); (5) the elasticity of real expenditure on each good with respect to a change in aggregate real expenditure; and (6) coefficients indicating the extent to which the devaluation-induced increase in the price of the N good is limited by the authorities and the degree to which the resulting excess demand for the N good is accommodated by forced substitution. The attempt explicitly to incorporate labor supply and black market responses to disequilibrium is left for future work.

The interaction of the above determinants can be classified into expenditure-*reducing* and expenditure-*switching* effects, although the two effects are in fact interrelated. The necessary and sufficient conditions for the improvement of the nonruble trade balance are either (1) some limitation by the authorities of the devaluation-induced increase in the price of the nontradable and some degree of substitution between this good and the competitive tradable, together with less than total accommodation of the resultant excess demand by forced substitution; or, lacking this, (2) both a negative elasticity of real aggregate expenditure with respect to the price level *and* some degree of substitution between the nontradable and the competitive tradable. It is important to realize that in the event that the elasticity of real aggregate expenditure is negative (i.e., monetary policy does not fully accommodate the price level effects of the devaluation), the price of the N good will rise by only a fraction of the percentage increase in the price of the T good. This will ensure that all domestic prices will *not* rise proportionately, as is sometimes alleged in studies of the effectiveness of devaluation in

Hungary. Indeed, under these conditions table 2.1 suggests that at most only about one-half of all prices would rise proportionately with the exchange rate.

Changes in virtually any of the aforementioned elasticities, sectoral weights, and other parameters will affect both the expenditure-reducing and expenditure-switching facets of the response to devaluation. From a formal, technical standpoint the net effect of changes in one or more parameters on the trade balance impact of devaluation may be ambiguous. Changes in some of the parameters and their likely *net* effects are discussed in the next section.

4. DETERMINANTS OF THE SIZE OF THE TRADE BALANCE IMPACT OF A DEVALUATION

Some of the specific determinants of the trade balance impact of a devaluation mentioned in the last section can be fairly easily quantified, or at least approximated. These include the sectoral weights of the various composite goods and the velocity of money, the latter entering into the calculation of the elasticity of real aggregate demand with respect to the price level. Most of the other determinants, however, may not be subject to empirically based quantification. Because we lack empirical estimates, for example, of various substitution elasticities between different composite goods and forced substitution coefficients, the discussion that follows will be largely in qualitative rather than quantitative terms. It examines several characteristic features of the Hungarian economy and their possible impact on the effectiveness of the convertible currency exchange rate as a stabilization instrument. Some of these features are amenable to change through further extension of the economic reforms that have taken place in Hungary since 1968.

The Price Structure and Price Reform

One significant characteristic of the Hungarian economy is the coexistence of several domestic price systems. Roughly one-third of the economy is still subject to more or less fixed prices, while an additional 7 percent of gross output, in the form of trade with the ruble area, is characterized by forint pricing that presumably has little or no impact on resource allocation; indeed, we have assumed for simplicity that the composite R good constitutes a kind of ruble core of transactions that is impervious, at least in the short run, to changes in relative prices. The existence of fixed price composite goods makes the analysis of devaluation much more complicated than it would be in a stylized market economy with the familiar dichotomy of flexibly priced tradable and nontradable goods. The answer to whether devaluation has a greater or smaller impact in an economy with one-third of its products subject to fixed prices is, "it depends."

Clearly, the potential scope for substitution effects between the N and T goods is greater, ceteris paribus, in the event that the authorities control the price of the former. We cannot be certain, however, that the excess demand for the N good that results from price control may not be effectively eliminated either partially or totally by forced substitution of the T good for this product. Price controls on the nontradable will also tend to reduce the expenditure reducing impact of devaluation. We should not therefore automatically assume that the existence of important groups of fixed or controlled priced goods in the Hungarian economy will necessarily enhance the impact of devaluation. (The simpler stylized MPE model of Wolf (1978) did indeed leave this impression.) Moreover, the maintenance of fixed prices on a considerable range of output in Hungary is motivated by many of the same socioeconomic goals—such as relative price stability, equitable income distribution, and enterprise stability—that influence various features of the economic mechanism and economic policies, which in turn may reduce the sensitivity of enterprises to changes in relative prices. For this reason, it might be reasonable to suppose that the extension of flexible pricing in the MPE, which would presumably be accompanied by other reforms, would tend to enhance the values of the substitution elasticities.

In sum, further price liberalization would probably reduce the relative price effect of devaluation, but at the same time it would enhance the expenditure-reducing effect and, to the extent it was to be accompanied by increased elasticities of substitution, on balance would be likely to increase the balance of trade impact of devaluation.

Other Obstacles to Efficient Resource Allocation

Although the Hungarian economy relies on price signals as a guide to resource allocation to a far greater extent than the classical CPE, it is still subject to many of the rigidities inherited from the earlier stage of central planning. Specifically, despite the increased stress now being placed on enterprise profitability, enterprise managers still are probably not motivated, or in any event in most cases not permitted, to maximize profits as they might in a market economy. Genuinely profitable enterprises may find their profits heavily taxed by the budget in order to finance the subsidization of other firms' losses. Profile restrictions still limit the ability of enterprises to shift or expand into new lines of activity. In addition, factor reallocation among enterprises and among industries is cumbersome and inefficient, particularly in respect of capital. Moreover, a policy of soft budget constraints for enterprises reinforces the other deterrents to rapid resource reallocation, at least on the part of enterprises faced with a decline in profits as a result of the relative price effects of the devaluation. Consequently, the expectation shared by a number of Hungarian economists is that the short-run substitution effect of a devaluation is likely to be quite small, if not negligible, on the supply side. The same would apply to the demand side as well, insofar as enterprise demand for capital equipment and intermediate products is concerned.[9]

Reforms aimed at raising the profit incentive of enterprise managers, easing profile restrictions and improving factor mobility, along with policies that encourage greater enterprise financial discipline, should enhance the short-run substitutability of the different composite goods on the supply side. Differentiation and manipulation of equations (A16)–(A20) in appendix 2.1 indicate that policy changes and modifications of the economic mechanism that raise relative price elasticities have, strictly speaking, an ambiguous impact on the effectiveness of the exchange rate as a policy instrument. As a practical matter, however, the impact is likely to be positive, as intuition would suggest. This is particularly so if the initial substitution elasticities between the N and T goods are relatively low, which is likely to be the case and indeed provides one of the main impetuses for reform in the first place.

Initial Aggregate Excess Demand

Until now we have been assuming that there is no initial excess demand in the economy at either the aggregate level or in any of the individual composite good markets. This assumption facilitates the technical analysis in appendix 2.1, and it also means that at the macro level we could necessarily expect a decline in aggregate real expenditure following devaluation as long as the monetary authorities do not fully accommodate the price level effects of the change in the exchange rate.

If the economy initially is characterized by excess demand for goods as a whole, there must exist quantitative restrictions on trade. This excess demand will also be equal to the excess of the economic agents' net flow supplies of money less their notional flow demand for money balances. In other words, at the current level of income, their holdings of real balances are in excess of what they desire were they to be unconstrained in consumption. If the currency is now devalued, the resultant increase in the price level will reduce the value of aggregate real balances, but unless the devaluation is large enough, it will not eliminate these surplus balances.

In a situation of initial excess demand, the elasticity of aggregate expenditure with respect to the price level must necessarily be smaller than in the event of initial macro-level equilibrium. If the authorities do not further restrict the availability of goods on the domestic market —through a tightening of trade controls—and if the increase in the price level following devaluation is not great enough to eliminate the excess demand, there is no reason to suppose that real expenditure will fall. Indeed, if the existing quantitative restrictions are lifted or at least eased, it may increase. In general, then, the expenditure-reducing effect of the devaluation will be diminished in the case of initial excess demand (see appendix 2.1 for more detail).

In this connection it may also be instructive to examine briefly the consequences for the impact of a devaluation of an absolute increase in the (negative) value of the elasticity of real aggregate expenditure with respect to the exchange rate. This may come about because of a tightening of monetary policy, elimination of a currency overhang, an exogenous increase in the demand for money, or an increase in the speed at which money holders attempt to remove any disparity between the amount of money held and the amount demanded. Manipulation of the expressions in the Appendix would show that the impact of such changes on the magnitude of the trade balance effect of devaluation is also formally ambiguous. Of course the expenditure reducing impact of a given price level increase following devaluation would be enhanced, and this dampening effect on aggregate demand would cause the price of the N good to rise less than otherwise. This would promote a greater degree of substitution between the N and T goods, but the diminished increase in the price of the N good would cause the actual net increase in the overall price level, and thus the fall in aggregate demand, to be smaller than before. It can be shown, however, that if the sum of the two substitution elasticities is more than negligible, exogenous and/or policy changes causing an increase in the absolute value of the elasticity of real aggregate expenditure will enhance the effectiveness of the exchange rate in improving the balance of trade.

Initial Excess Demand for the Competitive Tradable

Another possibility is that while initial aggregate excess demand pressures may have been eliminated—through a combination of a tighter credit policy, a shift in output proportions from investment to consumption goods, and increases in administered prices—initial disequilibrium may persist at the micro level. For example, we may imagine excess demand for the T good at the prevailing domestic (= transaction) price, this excess demand being exactly offset by excess supply in some other sector. Observe that unalleviated excess demand for the T good can only be enforced through direct controls on trade. In addition, note that the N good cannot be in excess supply, if it has a flexible price. Furthermore, in terms of our model, the ruble tradable also cannot be in excess supply due to an incorrect relative price. Consequently, excess demand for the T good as the result of a wrong relative price would only be consistent, in the event that aggregate excess demand is zero, with an administered relative price for the nontradable that is set above its market clearing level.

Frustrated consumer demand with respect to the T good will mean excessive money holding by consumers. This will just offset the above-plan enterprise inventories of the good or goods in excess supply. If consumers have not completely eliminated this excess liquidity through forced substitution and other responses, and excessive enterprise inventory accumulation has been effectively financed by the credit authorities or the government budget, money holders as a group will end up with excessive liquidity. The result, as discussed in the preceding section, will be a lower real aggregate expenditure elasticity and a reduced expenditure-*reducing* impact from devaluation.

Devaluation will normally, of course, cause the nominal and relative price of the T good to rise. In the nontradable sector, characterized by excess supply, the relative price change will lead to reduced output and increased demand for this product, thereby diminishing the excess supply. In the T sector, the higher relative price of this good will stimulate output and reduce demand. Because there was initially excess demand in this sector, however, the increase in output of the T good will also mean a rise in real expenditure on this product. Under these circumstances, therefore, the expenditure-*switching* effect of devaluation may also be minimal. Devaluation under these circumstances might permit, however, the reduction and possible elimination of the trade restrictions on the T good.

The Ruble Core

As noted earlier, about 7 percent of the gross value of Hungarian output in 1983 was exported to CMEA countries on the basis of TR clearings. These exports account for 46 percent of total nonenergy exports; the percentage is similar on the import side. There is, of course, some short-run substitution between these products and other goods, especially insofar as consumer goods demand is concerned. And given the importance of energy, raw materials, and intermediate products in Hungary's ruble imports, this sector is not really totally insulated from developments elsewhere in the Hungarian economy.

Hungarian economists emphasize, however, the lack of substitutability of ruble and nonruble tradables in the short run, and it was argued in section 3 that the institutional mechanisms and policies under which this ruble trade is carried out suggest very low or negligible short-run substitutability. Furthermore, while consumers may view some ruble tradables as substitutes for other products, exports of these goods will in effect have no domestically quoted consumer prices (hence there is no basis for a substitution effect) and imports of consumer goods comprise only about 10 percent of total Hungarian imports from the ruble area. Moreover, to the extent that ruble area trade flows are indeed modified in the short run to accommodate developments in other markets, these changes very likely occur primarily through various forms of administrative intervention and not in response to changes in domestic relative prices. For purposes of a stylized analysis, therefore, it seems reasonable to assume zero short-run substitutability of R goods for other products in response to changes in relative prices.

Intuition suggests that insulating 7 percent of total output (11 percent of combined tradable output) from relative price effects must have some effect on the nonruble trade balance impact of a devaluation. To the extent that the allocation of resources to ruble area exports has had a more than proportionate effect on the output of nonruble tradables, as compared to the output of nontradables, the market clearing relative price for nontradables in Hungary would be less than otherwise.[10] It is not possible, however, to demonstrate analytically that the existence of a "ruble core" will unambiguously either raise or lower the elasticities between the N and T goods.

Although the R good is assumed to be nonsubstitutable in the short run with other composite products, a devaluation vis-à-vis the convertible currency will still in general lead to excess supply domestically of this good. This is because if there is any reduction in real expenditure following devaluation, it may affect demand for the ruble tradable as well. Either enterprises will reduce imports of the R good, thereby running a trade surplus with CMEA partners, or they will accumulate unwanted inventories. (Forced substitution is assumed not to occur, given the zero substitutability assumption.) Whatever the precise response, this effect is implicitly taken into account in the equations in appendix 2.1. This induced excess supply effect in the ruble sector is similar to the analytical finding of Nivollet (1983) that a devaluation vis-à-vis the nonruble area, which in effect would constitute a real relative appreciation of the forint against the transferable ruble, could cause an MPE's ruble trade balance to improve, if the country's trade elasticities were low enough in trade with the CMEA (i.e., if the Marshall-Lerner condition were not satisfied). To the extent that a devaluation does lead to excess supply of the R good that is not exportable to the nonruble area, its impact on the nonruble trade balance is correspondingly diminished.

5. CONCLUSIONS

This essay has developed an analytical model of a small modified planned economy, such as Hungary, with three composite goods: a tradable priced according to the rules of the so-called competitive system; a good traded only with the ruble area; and a nontradable. Our analysis has yielded the following main conclusions with respect to the short- and medium-run trade balance effect of a devaluation in such an economy. First, contrary to the impression of many observers, not all domestic prices in Hungary will move proportionately with the exchange rate in the short run following devaluation. Indeed, in the model used here, which admittedly does not give an explicit account of the impact of increased prices for imported intermediates on the costs and thus possibly indirectly on the prices of various products outside the competitive sector, at most about one-half of all domestic prices in Hungary would move more or less proportionately with the exchange rate.

The model also demonstrates another basic fact of price formation in Hungary that is often overlooked in analyses of exchange rate policy in that country. Specifically, the extent to which the prices of flexibly priced products outside the competitive sector (i.e., nontradables) will rise following devaluation is critically determined by the state of initial aggregate demand and the extent to which the monetary authorities accommodate devaluation-induced price rises by increasing the nominal supply of money. The greater the initial excess aggregate demand, and the more accommodating the monetary policy, the smaller will be the expenditure-reducing impact of devaluation; the greater the short-run increase in nontradable prices, and the smaller the scope for substitution effects leading to expanded exports and reduced imports.

The model shows that if the economy is initially in equilibrium in all markets, the necessary and sufficient condition for improvement in the nonruble trade balance following devaluation—in the event that the price of the nontradable is controlled—is that there be some degree of substitution in supply or demand or both between the nontradable and the competitive tradable, and that forced substitution of the latter for the nontradable, which now will be in excess demand, does not totally eliminate this excess demand. Should the price of the nontradable be uncontrolled, the necessary and sufficient condition for trade balance improvement then becomes the combination of a less than fully accommodative monetary policy *and* some degree of substitution in supply or demand or both between the flexibly priced nontradable and the competitive tradable.

Although satisfaction of the above conditions ensures a trade balance improvement following devaluation, there are several characteristics of the Hungarian economy that suggest that the magnitude of the trade balance impact of a devaluation may at the present time be smaller than in an otherwise comparable stylized small market economy. For instance, many economists are of the opinion that short-run substitution elasticities in Hungary, particularly on the supply side, are relatively low. This judgment stems from the belief that, despite almost twenty years of economic reform, the profit incentives of enterprises may still be weak, labor, and particularly capital mobility between individual enterprises and between sectors, is low in the short run, and the authorities have not as yet systematically subjected Hungarian enterprises to sufficient financial discipline. Active use of the so-called "indirect tax rebate" policy on exports, however, suggests that the price responsiveness of exporting enterprises may not be as low as is sometimes alleged.

A second factor that would limit the effectiveness of devaluation, but one about which there is less consensus, is the possibility of continued excess liquidity in the economy as a whole. As noted earlier, if there were initial excessive liquidity in the economy, the expenditure-reducing impact of a devaluation would be lessened. Although there is disagreement about the presence of excess demand for goods at the macro level, continuing quantitative controls on a portion of competitive nonruble tradables do suggest that excess demand pressures persist at least within this sector. To the extent that such excess demand does exist, devaluation will have both a smaller expenditure-switching and reducing impact than the initial equilibrium result would suggest. Devaluation could at least be seen, however, as a means to reduce or even possibly to eliminate this excess demand, thereby permitting the further reduction or abolition of present trade controls.

Part of the potential balance of trade impact of a devaluation in Hungary may come from the control over many nontradable prices and the resultant excess demand pressure on this market induced by the devaluation. If this excess demand persists it will be offset, in theory, by excess supply of the competitive tradable, which, in turn, constitutes part of the nonruble trade surplus. It is unlikely, however, that persistent excess demand for the nontradable will not at least partially be accommodated by some combination of reduced labor supply, second economy activities, and forced substitution of the nonruble tradable in consumption. To the extent that this forced substitution occurs, the surplus of the competitive tradable for net export will be reduced.

A final factor affecting the convertible currency exchange rate as a stabilization instrument is the share of gross output exported under ruble clearing arrangements. In our stylized model, this trade is characterized as a ruble core of products which is not substitutable with other composite products in the short run. The ruble composite thus constitutes a core of tradables that are largely unaffected by devaluation. Unfortunately, no analytical result could be derived that unambiguously indicated the impact that the existence of this ruble core would have on the elasticities of substitution between the competitive tradable and the nontradable. The diversion of output toward the ruble core does tend to diminish the expenditure-reducing effect of devaluation on the nonruble trade balance, however, as the possible decline in expenditure on the ruble composite leads to a trade surplus in ruble trade or excess inventory accumulation of this good rather than to increased net exports to the nonruble area.

Having noted some of the factors that might diminish the effectiveness of a devaluation in Hungary, it will be instructive to review briefly the impact that recent and future reforms of the Hungarian economic mechanism might have on the role of the exchange rate as a stabilization instrument. As with each of the reforms discussed in the paper, an extension of free or competitive pricing to additional products would have, in terms of a formal model, an ambiguous effect on the trade balance impact of devaluation. As discussed in section 4, however, a positive effect from further freeing of prices could probably be expected on balance.

Many of the ongoing reform efforts in Hungary are aimed at increasing the price sensitivity of enterprise managers and improving the mobility of factors of production. To the extent these reforms are successful, the relative price substitution elasticities between the different goods should increase, particularly on the supply side. As long as the initial substitution elasticities are relatively low, and this would appear to be the case in Hungary, an increase in these elasticities will unambiguously enhance the trade balance impact of a devaluation.

Improvements in the mechanism by which credit is extended, along with policies that eliminate excess liquidity, would in effect increase the (absolute) value of the elasticity of real aggregate expenditure with respect to the price level. While an increase in this elasticity formally has an ambiguous effect on the trade balance effect of devaluation, for plausible values of the model's parameters it will indeed increase the effectiveness of exchange rate policy, as intuition suggests.

As discussed in sections 1–3, the model developed in this essay still has a number of limitations insofar as its applicability to the actual Hungarian economy is concerned. I would submit, however, that it is still useful as a preliminary framework for examining the main channels by which an exchange rate change might affect economic activity in an MPE such as Hungary. Contrary to the impression held by many, the present price and exchange rate system in Hungary would appear to offer potential for both the substitution and expenditure-reducing effects of a devaluation. At the same time, such as in the case of nonruble tradables that have fixed prices domestically and for which devaluation would generate additional excess demand pressures, devaluation could present the authorities with difficult policy choices. Thus several factors, characteristic although not unique to Hungary, probably diminish the effectiveness of the exchange rate at the present time. Successful implementation of the most recent as well as prospective modifications of the Hungarian economic mechanism, however, would probably enhance the role of the exchange rate as a policy instrument.

APPENDIX 2.1: A PRELIMINARY MODEL OF DEVALUATION
IN A MODIFIED PLANNED ECONOMY

1. The Model

Consider a fully employed modified planned economy (MPE) with three composite goods: a nonruble area tradable subject to a price system similar to the most liberal form of the competitive pricing rules in Hungary (T); a nontradable product (N); and a product traded with the ruble area (R), which is neither a substitute for nor a complement to the other composite goods in the short run, and the domestic price of which is administratively manipulated so as to vary directly with the price of the T good. Domestic output of the R good is fixed in the short run, while output of the T good (N good) is a positive (negative) function of the domestic price of the T good relative to that of the N good $(q = P_T/P_N)$:[11]

$$S_T = S_T(q), \qquad (A1)$$
$$S_N = S_N(q), \qquad (A2)$$
$$S_R = \bar{S}_R. \qquad (A3)$$

Here S_T, S_N, and S_R refer to output of the nonruble tradable, the nontradable and the ruble tradable respectively.

Domestic demand for the nonruble tradable (nontradable) is negatively (positively) related to the relative domestic currency price of the two products, and domestic demand for all three products is a positive function of the level of real aggregate expenditure (a):

$$E_T = E_T(q,a), \qquad (A4)$$
$$E_N = E_N(q,a), \qquad (A5)$$
$$E_R = E_R(a), \qquad (A6)$$

where E_T, E_N and E_R denote domestic demand for the T, N, and R goods respectively.

The domestic price of the nonruble tradable is linked to its foreign currency price by the familiar international commodity arbitrage equation, except that in this case the relationship is assured through the pricing rules rather than necessarily by international commodity arbitrage per se:

$$P_T = P_T^* e, \tag{A7}$$

where P_T and P_T^* are the domestic and foreign currency prices of the T good, respectively, and e is the exchange rate, defined as the domestic currency price of foreign exchange. The foreign currency price is invariant with respect to a change in the exchange rate; that is, the MPE is a small country in its trade with the nonruble area. The exchange rate is set by the authorities.

The price of the nontradable (P_N) is either fixed by the authorities or is determined freely by the market as the price that equates domestic demand and supply of the nontradable:

$$S_N = E_N. \tag{A8}$$

The price of the ruble tradable (P_R) is fixed by the authorities in relation to the price of the nonruble tradable:

$$P_R = \eta P_T, \tag{A9}$$

where η is a constant.

The nonruble balance of trade (B_T) is defined as the *effective* excess supply of the T good. By effective excess supply of the T good is meant the difference between domestic output and the notional domestic demand for the nonruble tradable, less the proportion of any not otherwise alleviated notional excess demand for the nontradable that gives rise to "forced substitution" by domestic consumers of the nonruble tradable for the nontradable:[12]

$$B_T = P_T(S_T - E_T) - P_N(E_N - S_N)\delta \tag{A10}$$

where δ denotes this proportion (i.e., the parameter of forced substitution). Actually this coefficient may vary, say, with the degree of excess demand for the nontradable.

Real aggregate expenditure is equal to the difference between real income (y), which is at its full employment level, and real hoarding (h):

$$a = y - h. \tag{A11}$$

Real hoarding equals, in flow equilibrium, real desired hoarding (h*):

$$h = h^*. \tag{A12}$$

Real desired hoarding in turn is a positive function of the difference between the desired level of real money balances (M^*P^{-1}) and the stock of real money balances held at the beginning of the period (MP^{-1}):

$$h^* = \lambda[y^\gamma P^{\phi-1} - MP^{-1}], \tag{A13}$$

where P is the price level, γ and ϕ are the elasticities of money demand with respect to real income and the price level respectively ($M^*P^{-1} = y^\gamma P^{\phi-1}$), and λ is a coefficient indicating the speed of adjustment of real desired hoarding to any imbalance between the desired and actual real money stocks.

The price index is constructed in terms of expenditure weights:

$$P = P_T^{\alpha_T} P_N^{\alpha_N} P_R^{\alpha_R}, \tag{A14}$$

where α_T, α_N, and α_R are the weights for the nonruble tradable, nontradable, and ruble tradable respectively.

Equations (A1) through (A14) contain 14 endogenous variables. The production possibilities of the economy are considered to be fixed and the economy is assumed to remain at full employment output. Policy instruments are the exchange rate and the nominal money supply, although the latter will also be jointly determined by economic agents according to the hoarding equations (A12)–(A13). Except for section 4, the following discussion will assume that the economy begins in full stock-flow equilibrium; that is, h^* in equation (A13) is equal to zero.

2. The Price and Trade Balance Effects of a Devaluation

In the event that the N good has a flexible price, there is nothing to keep that market from moving to a new equilibrium after the responses to a devaluation have run their course. Consequently, the induced change in domestic supply of this nontradable must be equal to the induced change in domestic demand. The latter effect has two components: an expenditure and a substitution effect. Totally differentiating both sides of equation (A8) with respect to the convertible currency exchange rate, assuming zero initial excess demand in all markets, and making use of the relationship between the elasticities of substitution of the T and N goods, respectively $[\epsilon_T = (-\alpha_N \epsilon_N)/\alpha_T]$, and simplifying, yields:

$$\epsilon_T^N = 1 - \frac{\epsilon_a^N \epsilon_e^a}{\dfrac{\alpha^T}{\alpha_N}(\epsilon_T^d - \epsilon_T^s)}, \tag{A15}$$

where ϵ_T^N is the elasticity of the price of the nontradable with respect to a change in the domestic currency price of the nonruble tradable; ϵ_a^N is the elasticity of real expenditure on the nontradable with respect to a change in aggregate real domestic expenditure; α_T and α_N are the weights for the T and N goods (in *both* expenditure and output, under the above assumptions); and ϵ_T^d and ϵ_T^s are the elasticities of demand for and supply of the nonruble tradable respectively, with respect to a change in its relative price (q).

The elasticity of aggregate real domestic expenditure with respect to a change in the exchange rate (ϵ_e^a) on the right-hand side of equation (A15) is endogenous to the model and is derived by totally differentiating (A11) with respect to the exchange rate and making various substitutions. This elasticity is in turn a function, inter alia, of ϵ_T^N:

$$\epsilon_e^a = \lambda \epsilon_e^P V^{-1}(\epsilon_p^m - \phi), \tag{A16}$$

where λ and ϕ are defined as before, V is the income velocity of money; ϵ_p^m is the policy-determined effective elasticity of the nominal supply of money (independent of hoarding) with respect to a change in the price level; and ϵ_e^P is the elasticity of the domestic price level with respect to a change in the exchange rate, where:

$$\epsilon_e^P = (\alpha_T + \alpha_N \beta \epsilon_T^N + \alpha_R), \tag{A17}$$

and β is the proportion of the free market increase in the price of the nontradable permitted by the authorities.

Solving (A15)–(A17) simultaneously for ϵ_T^N yields:

$$\epsilon_T^N = \frac{\dfrac{\alpha_T(\epsilon_T^d - \epsilon_T^s) - \epsilon_a^N \lambda(\epsilon_p^m - \phi)(\alpha_T + \alpha_R)}{\alpha_N \qquad V}}{\dfrac{\alpha_T(\epsilon_T^d - \epsilon_T^s) + \epsilon_a^N \lambda(\epsilon_p^m - \phi)\alpha_N.}{\alpha_N \qquad V}} \tag{A18}$$

If equation (A10) is totally differentiated with respect to the exchange rate, multiplied by de/Y and simplified, it may be written as equation (A19). This equation is an expression for the income-normalized improvement in the nonruble trade balance:

$$dB_T/Y = \hat{e}[\alpha_T(1 - \beta \epsilon_T^N)(\epsilon_T^s - \epsilon_T^d)(1 - \delta) - \epsilon_e^a(\alpha_T \epsilon_a^T + \delta \alpha_N \epsilon_a^N)], \tag{A19}$$

where $\hat{e}$ is the percentage change in the exchange rate; β is defined above; ϵ_a^T is the elasticity of real expenditure on the nonruble tradable with respect to a change in aggregate real domestic expenditure; and the other parameters are as defined earlier.

The first term within brackets on the right-hand side of equation (A19) is the *expenditure-switching* effect of a devaluation. From (A18) it can be shown that the partial derivative $\partial \epsilon_T^N / \partial (\epsilon_p^m - \phi)$ is positive, which means that the tighter monetary policy is at the time of devaluation, the smaller the increase will be in the market-determined price of the nontradable good (that is, the smaller will be ϵ_T^N), and consequently the larger ceteris paribus will be the expenditure-switching effect of the devaluation.

If the authorities do not permit the price of the nontradable to rise to its market-clearing level after devaluation, β will be less than unity and this will permit an even larger relative price effect of the devaluation and hence, ceteris paribus, a larger expenditure-switching impact. To the extent the resulting unalleviated excess demand for the nontradable leads to forced substitution of the nonruble tradable for the nontradable in domestic consumption ($\delta > 0$), however, the effective expenditure-switching effect will be reduced as will the positive trade balance impact of the devaluation. Which effect will dominate, in this case in which the price of the nontradable is controlled, can be shown to be formally ambiguous, lacking a more specific assumption about the relationship between β and δ. In general, if the price of the nontradable is market-determined, $\beta = 1.00$ and $\delta = 0$, and (A19) may be written in a simpler form as:

$$dB_T/Y = \hat{e}[\alpha_T(1 - \epsilon_T^N)(\epsilon_T^s - \epsilon_T^d) - \epsilon_e^a \alpha_T \epsilon_a^T]. \tag{A20}$$

The second right-hand side term within brackets in expressions (A19)–(A20) is the direct *expenditure-reducing* effect of the devaluation. Although the strength of the expenditure-reducing effect on the trade balance is formally ambiguous with respect to a change in the tightness of monetary policy, it can be shown, as intuition would suggest, that for plausible values of the parameters in equations (A16)–(A18), the positive expenditure-reducing effect of a devaluation on the nonruble trade balance will be greater, the less accommodative is monetary policy to the price-level effects of the devaluation (i.e., the lower is ϵ_p^m).

From equations (A19)–(A20) it can be seen that the necessary and sufficient conditions for the improvement of the nonruble trade balance are either: (1) some limitation by the authorities of the devaluation-induced increase in the price of the nontradable ($\beta < 1.00$) and some degree of substitution between this good and the competitive tradable

($[\epsilon_T^s - \epsilon_T^d] > 0$), together with less than total accommodation of the resultant excess demand by forced substitution ($\delta < 1.00$); *or*, lacking this, (2) both a monetary policy that does not fully accommodate the price level effects of the devaluation ($\epsilon_P^m < \phi$; therefore $\epsilon_e^a < 0$) and at least some degree of substitution between the N and T goods ($[\epsilon_T^s - \epsilon_T^d] > 0$).

Observe that if the aggregate demand elasticity were negative and the price of the nontradable were flexible, but both substitution elasticities were zero, the trade balance would not be responsive to devaluation. In this case, the devaluation-induced increase in the relative price of the T good would cause no excess demand in the N sector. There would, in the meantime, be a price level and therefore an aggregate demand response to the increased price of the T good, and demand for the N good would decrease as well. This would create a situation of excess supply of the N good. Because the price of the nontradable is flexible and full employment is assumed, P_N would decline until the excess supply were eliminated. This means that P_N must fall by enough exactly to offset the rise in the overall price level caused by the increase in P_T. On balance, therefore, aggregate demand would remain unchanged and there would be no expenditure-reducing effect as well as no substitution effect. (This result can be seen by setting ($\epsilon_T^d - \epsilon_T^s$) in (A18) equal to zero. The resulting expression for ϵ_T^N, equal to $-(\alpha_T + \alpha_R)/\alpha_N$, can then be substituted into (A17), yielding a zero price level effect and a zero expenditure-reducing effect in (A16) and (A20).)

3. The Impact of Increased Elasticities of Substitution

Totally differentiating equation (A19) with respect to the combined relative price elasticities of supply and demand of the nonruble nontradable ($\epsilon_T^s - \epsilon_T^d$), shows that the effect on the trade balance impact of devaluation of an increase in these elasticities is formally ambiguous. This is because an increase in elasticities will: (1) increase the substitution effects between the T and N goods, on both the supply and demand side, for a given change in the relative price; (2) increase the price level effect of devaluation and hence its expenditure-reducing effect, by virtue of causing a greater increase in the price of the nontradable; (3) but, by the same token, the larger increase in the price of this good will reduce the rise in the relative price of the T good, which is the very basis for the substitution effect noted under (1).

Despite the formal ambiguity of the partial derivative $\partial[dB_T/Y]/$

$\partial[\epsilon_T^s - \epsilon_T^d]$, however, it can be shown that the lower the *initial* substitution elasticities are, relative to the degree of tightness of monetary policy, the more likely an increase in these elasticities will enhance the trade balance effect of a devaluation.

4. The Impact of Initial Aggregate Excess Demand

If there is initial aggregate domestic excess demand for goods, this implies excess liquidity in the domestic economy, or $h^* < 0$ in equation (A13). Under these conditions, ϵ_e^a will no longer be defined by the simple expression of equation (A16). Instead, we now have:

$$\epsilon_e^a = \lambda PV^{-1}[\epsilon_e^p[(\phi-1)y^\gamma P^\phi M^{-1} + (1-\epsilon_p^m)] \qquad (A21)$$
$$+ \hat{e}^{-1}(y^\gamma P^\phi M^{-1} - 1)],$$

which, if we assume for simplicity that the demand for money is unit elastic with respect to the price level and monetary policy is perfectly nonaccommodative ($\phi = 1.00$ and $\epsilon_p^m = 0$), can be reduced to:

$$\epsilon_e^a = -\lambda PV^{-1}e^{-1}[\hat{P} + (M^*/M - 1)], \qquad (A22)$$

where $\hat{P}$ is the rate of domestic inflation induced by the change in the exchange rate. For the devaluation actually to lead to a reduction in real aggregate expenditure ($\epsilon_e^a < 0$), the expression in brackets on the right-hand side of (A22) must be positive. This will occur only if the rate of induced inflation is greater than the size of the initial liquidity overhang as a percentage of the money stock. Otherwise, aggregate demand may fall, but not actual expenditure.

APPENDIX 2.2: CALCULATION OF COMPOSITE
GOOD SHARES FOR HUNGARY – 1983

In the accompanying table all sectors are divided into tradables and nontradables. For each sector or group of sectors is listed: in column (1) gross value of output, calculated from official Hungarian statistics; (2) f.o.b. value of exports, based on figures provided by the Hungarian authorities; (3) f.o.b. value of exports to the nonruble area; (4) f.o.b. value of exports to the ruble area; (5) gross output available for domestic consumption $(=(1)-(2))$; (6) percentage of output subject to free prices; (7) value of output available for consumption subject to free prices at the producer level $(=(5)\times(6))$, where for simplicity it is assumed that the percentages in column (6) are applicable to "output available for consumption" as well as to "output"; and (8) value of output available for consumption subject to fixed or limited flexibility prices at the producer level $(=(5)-(7))$. All recorded energy exports (see bottom of table) are assumed, for simplicity, to be reexports.

Using the individual sectoral gross output values in column (1), the individual free price percentages for mining, metallurgy, construction materials, and chemicals are used to calculate a weighted free price percentage for these sectors as a group. This percentage (67 percent) is then implicitly applied to miscellaneous industry as well.

The individual composite good shares are calculated by dividing the following gross output totals for each good by the aggregate gross output of 2,273.2 billion forints (based on official Hungarian statistics). (1) Competitive nonruble tradable: assumed composed of nonruble exports (excluding energy) of 183.9 billion forints and free priced tradables consumed domestically of 798.5 billion forints; (2) Fixed price nonruble tradable: equal to fixed price tradables (366.2 billion forints); (3) Ruble area tradable: equal to ruble exports (excluding energy) of 158.8 billion forints; (4) Flexible priced nontradable: equal to 414.3 billion forints; (5) Fixed price nontradable: equal to 351.5 billion forints.

APPENDIX TABLE 2.1. (Output and Exports in Billions of Forints)

Sector	(1) Gross value of output	(2) Total exports (f.o.b.)	(3) Non-ruble exports	(4) Ruble exports
TRADABLES				
Mining	66.9			
Metallurgy	105.0			
Construction materials	36.9	107.3[a]	68.9[a]	38.4[a]
Chemicals	221.5			
Miscellaneous	16.1			
Engineering	278.0	96.4	27.0	69.4
Industrial consumer goods	156.9	53.0	26.2	26.8
Food processing	221.5	57.0	39.0	18.0
Agriculture and forestry	404.6	29.0	22.8	6.2
Subtotal	1,507.4	342.7	183.9	158.8
NONTRADABLES				
Construction	162.1	—		
Transportation, commun.	124.8	—		
Other material sectors	173.6	—		
Electric energy	50.7	—		
Nonmaterial sectors	254.6	—		
Subtotal	765.8			
Total	2,273.2			
Energy exports			30.2	1.2
Total exports			214.1	160.0

a. Includes mining, metallurgy, construction materials, chemicals, and miscellaneous.

(5) Output available for domestic consumption $((1)-(2))$	(6) Proportion of free prices	(7) Output available at free prices $((5)\times(6))$	(8) Output not available at free prices $((5)-(7))$
	0.20		
	0.99		
339.1[a]	0.87	227.2[a]	111.9[a]
	0.63		
	0.67		
181.6	1.00	181.6	—
103.9	0.94	97.7	6.2
164.5	0.93	153.0	11.5
375.6	0.37	139.0	236.6
1,164.7		798.5	366.2
162.1	0.25	40.5	121.6
124.8	0.23	28.7	96.1
173.6	1.00	173.6	—
50.7	0.07	3.5	47.2
254.6	0.66	168.0	86.6
765.8		414.3	351.5

CHAPTER 3

Conditionality and Adjustment in Hungary and Yugoslavia

Laura Tyson
Sherman Robinson
Leyla Woods

This essay examines the influence of the International Monetary Fund (IMF) on the adjustment efforts of Yugoslavia and Hungary during the 1980 to 1984 period. Both countries received IMF and World Bank loans during this period and both benefited from the implicit seal of approval associated with such loans in their negotiations with private lenders. In both countries access to IMF lending depended on the design of adjustment programs incorporating explicit conditions of performance or conditionality that had to be met if lending was to continue. Such conditionality is always a part of IMF lending and raises a number of questions that we pursue in this essay. First, what were the basic objectives of the adjustment programs and did the forms of conditionality hammered out in IMF negotiations with the authorities of each country support or impede these objectives? Second, did the forms of conditionality chosen reflect the unique economic systems of Hungary and Yugoslavia, or were they typical of conditionality programs designed for market economies? Finally, did the involvement of the IMF actually make any difference to what happened? In particular, what were the effects of IMF involvement on the policies chosen, on the speed of adjustment, and on actual economic performance?

Precise answers to these questions are elusive for two reasons. First, a veil of secrecy traditionally surrounds IMF agreements with individual countries. Without privileged access, it is nearly impossible to ascertain all of the details of such agreements. Some information leaks into the public domain mainly through the commercial banks and through the press, but it is always incomplete and sometimes inaccurate. Consequently, the discussion in this essay rests on fragmentary information. Not all of the conditions of IMF agreements with Yugoslavia and Hungary are known and, even when a particular type of condition is known, quantitative targets or constraints associated with its enforcement are generally not. The paucity of information is particularly pronounced in the case of Hungary because the Hungarian authorities have not made public any of the details of their negotiations with the IMF. In contrast, heated public debates over conditionality among public figures in Yugoslavia provide a rich source of information. In the Hungarian case, therefore, the discussion rests on a number of assumptions, including the assumption that the overall terms of conditionality were qualitatively similar to those of the Yugoslav case.

The difficulty of doing counterfactual history poses a second methodological problem in the search for precise answers to the questions that motivate this essay. It is impossible to assess accurately the effects of IMF involvement in policy choices and economic outcomes without knowing what would have happened in the absence of such involvement. Since we cannot replay history, the basic methodological approach in this essay must be one of informed speculation. In particular, we will try to assess the effects of IMF involvement by comparing what actually happened, to what the economic systems and recent economic histories of Hungary and Yugoslavia suggest would have happened in the absence of such involvement.

The remainder of the essay proceeds as follows. In section 1 we examine the basic objectives and features of standard IMF adjustment programs. The main types of conditionality usually contained in such programs are described, and their underlying assumptions about how the economy works are identified. Section 2 focuses on some of the unique features of the Yugoslav and Hungarian economies that make them different from the economies for which the assumptions and features of standard IMF programs have been fashioned. Sections 3 and 4 address the major questions of the essay. In section 3 the role of the IMF in mobilizing finance to support adjustment during the 1980 to 1984 period is assessed, and some of the basic forms of conditionality adopted in the IMF programs are identified and discussed. Several types of conditionality are examined, including conditions relating to basic macroeconomic targets and to critical prices, the interest rate, the exchange rate, and the wage rate. Finally, in section 4, economic performance under the IMF program is evaluated; and the differences and similarities between the experiences of the two countries are described.

1. ADJUSTMENT PROGRAMS AND CONDITIONALITY

The IMF is essentially interested in short-term adjustment. Its primary function is to grant short-term loans to help countries finance balance-of-payments deficits that are either temporary or intended to be temporary because of the adoption of adjustment policies. The IMF can help finance a country's adjustment efforts in two ways: (1) directly by short-term loans and (2) indirectly by providing a seal of approval that shores up the country's creditworthiness and restores its ability to draw on private capital markets. In recent years, because of the growing importance of the IMF's seal of approval in mobilizing private capital, the IMF's own lending, while often quantitatively small, has been qualitatively important in putting together the necessary private finance to support an adjustment program.[1]

The herd instinct exhibited by the private banking community has enhanced the IMF's leadership role by increasing its leverage. In several countries, including Hungary and Yugoslavia, private banks collectively lent to the point where adjustment was undesirably postponed and then sought to reduce their exposure in ways that compounded liquidity problems. At that point, the IMF's involvement in the formation and financial support of an adjustment program became critical to a country's ability to maintain reasonable access to private credit.

The starting point for the IMF's advice in the development of an adjustment program is an estimate of how large an improvement in a country's current account deficit is required and over what time period. This estimate depends, in turn, on an assessment of the available foreign capital inflow and its sustainability. The IMF does not have complete discretion in choosing how dramatic or rapid a country's adjustment program should be, but is constrained by conditions in international capital markets. Of course, the issue of leverage is important; and the IMF's involvement may assist a country in raising money from private sources.

Once the IMF has established a current account target, it considers next the issue of internal balance—what is the level of demand that can be sustained without generating pressure for accelerating inflation?[2] Total domestic demand for both domestically produced and imported goods or absorption is given by the sum of consumption, investment, and government expenditure: $D = C + I + G$. Total supply to the domestic market is the sum of gross domestic product (GDP) and the difference between imports and exports, $S = GDP + M - E$. Ex post, demand equals supply, $D = S$, and we have, solving for GDP, the traditional identity: $GDP = C + I + G + E - M$. If the trade account must be improved, and output cannot be increased, total absorption must fall.

It is important to emphasize that this relationship is true for all economies regardless of differences in economic system. If capital market conditions necessitate an improvement in the trade account, there must be some combination of an increase in real output, or a fall in domestic absorption. In this important sense, austerity in domestic demand cannot be blamed on the IMF. The IMF can affect both the severity of austerity (mainly through its influence on the pace at which the trade account improves) and the policies used to realize austerity with politically charged distributional implications, but it is not responsible for austerity per se.

A standard IMF adjustment program aims primarily at the introduction of policies to cut domestic demand by controlling the flow of nominal income to the major domestic spending groups: households, government, and enterprises. Such programs usually involve controls on wages to lower real household income and consumption, controls on aggregate credit to lower investment expenditure, and increases in taxes and reductions in government expenditure, both to reduce government demand directly and to reduce government pressure on credit and money markets. In addition to controls on demand, controls on the rate of growth of credit are traditionally a central part of the package designed to control inflation.

These expenditure-reducing policies are also usually accompanied by expenditure-switching policies designed to encourage exports and discourage imports. A devaluation raises the domestic prices of both exports and imports, encouraging demanders to substitute domestically produced goods for imports and suppliers to divert goods from the domestic market to the export market. Substantial devaluation is, thus, usually an important part of an IMF policy package.

All that has been said to this point about the IMF's analysis is consistent with either Keynesian or monetarist views on how the economy operates. Both schools imply that an improvement in the current account requires expenditure-switching policies to improve a country's international competitiveness and stabilization policies to reduce domestic demand consistent with the required fall in absorption. Moreover, in theory, neither approach requires that these policies reduce GDP except when initial output exceeds long-run capacity. If an adjustment program results in a fall in either or both the level and rate of growth of domestic output, this will hinder the stabilization program since it results in less supply as well as less demand. In practice it seems to be true that a severe contraction in both supply and demand leads to a larger decrease in demand than in supply; and so it is possible to establish balance at a lower level of GDP.[3]

There are several reasons why one might expect to find that an IMF stabilzation program leads to a contraction in GDP. One is simply that the actual set of policies adopted results in overkill; domestic demand may be inadvertently cut more than is required to match reduced absorption. A second reason is that economies are much less flexible in practice than either the Keynesian or monetarist model suggests so that the shift of resources toward tradable sectors implied by expenditure switching leads to short-run supply difficulties and declines in aggregate output. A third reason is that the only way a country can meet a current account target in the time allowed may be to cut imports of intermediate and capital goods for which there are no immediately available domestic substitutes. Output falls for lack of crucial inputs. Finally, demand-management policies often fall disproportionately on investment, leading to lower growth of capital and capacity over a period of time.

The second and third arguments, which might be termed "structuralist," imply that excessively ambitious and rapid adjustment progams can result in significant waste of resources because of limited substitution possibilities in the short run in demand and production. Unfortunately, of course, constraints in international capital markets may leave both the IMF and the country it is advising with little choice but to accept such a program and the loss of output it implies. However, it is important to understand that, in the short run, output losses, due to excessive adjustment policies in an environment where there are serious rigidities, may far exceed any efficient gains from better resource allocation. There is a real trade-off which is especially important for developing countries and is often neglected in theory.

Concern over the output effects of demand-management policies and an underlying belief in the efficiency of markets have led the IMF to include supply-side policies in most standard adjustment programs. The basic objectives of such policies are to improve price signals, achieve correct pricing, and to encourage greater reliance on prices in resource allocation. Supply-side policies frequently recommended include the liberalization of trade and payments regimes and the freeing of certain critical product and input prices, including the prices of food and basic services, the interest rate, and the exchange rate. An implicit assumption of such policies is that economic actors respond to price signals in the manner and to the extent that they do in abstract models of the market mechanism. As we shall see, this assumption does not conform very well with important aspects of Yugoslav and Hungarian economic reality, just as it does not conform very well with the reality of economic systems in many developing countries despite their ostensibly greater reliance on market mechanisms.

Together, the IMF's recommendations for both demand-management and supply-side polices are negotiated between the IMF and the country seeking access to IMF lending; and the policies agreed upon are embodied in a set of conditions specified in a letter of intent. These conditions include both performance criteria that, if violated, involve suspension of further disbursements by the IMF until a new agreement is reached, and policy understandings that do not carry any explicit sanctions for nonfulfillment. Discussions of IMF conditionality usually do not distinguish between these two types of conditions, and the remainder of this essay follows this convention.[4]

2. BASIC FEATURES OF THE ECONOMIC SYSTEMS OF HUNGARY AND YUGOSLAVIA

In order to answer questions about the effects or the appropriateness of IMF conditionally in Hungary and Yugoslavia, it is necessary to understand the basic features of the economic systems of these two countries. Unfortunately, this is no small task since both systems have many unique features that distinguish them both from one another and from the systems of other developing countries with which the IMF is traditionally involved. Moreover, there are no standard theoretical models that capture these features very well. Both the traditional market-type economy (MTE) model that is the usual starting point for analyses of developing countries and the centrally planned economy (CPE) model and its recent shortage-economy variant overlook important aspects of economic reality in Yugoslavia and Hungary.[5] In the following discussion, we present a thumbnail description of these economies during the 1980 to 1984 period, emphasizing only those features that are most relevant to the questions at hand.[6]

Economic reforms in Hungary and Yugoslavia have had, as their basic goal, the replacement of the central planning system by a price-guided market system based on socialist ownership. While traditional quantitative planning has been eliminated, however, it has been replaced by a system that is hard to characterize as a market-socialist system for several reasons. First, enterprises remain subject to vertical control exercised by both state and party organizations in a variety of ways, some formal, some informal, some permanent, and some temporary. Sometimes vertical control affects the price signals influencing an input or output decision—for example, through either economy-wide taxes or subsidies or enterprise-specific ones. Such methods of vertical control working through prices will be called indirect methods in this discussion. Price controls and detailed regulations on price formation are important examples of such methods. Other methods of vertical control set more direct restrictions on input and output choices—for example, through quantitative limitations on input availability, detailed conditions on input use, or detailed specifications of output composition. Such methods of vertical control will be called direct or administrative methods in this discussion.

Overall, economic reforms have weakened administrative controls over enterprise output choices; but such controls have retained a strong grip on input choices, especially those involving the use of capital, foreign exchange, and, in the case of Hungary, labor. Even in product markets administrative restrictions sometimes play a substantial role, especially when the products involved are important to fulfilling trade contracts with members of the Council for Mutual Economic Assistance (CMEA).[7] Even the relative absence of administrative measures does not imply the absence of significant vertical influence on product market conditions in the short run through indirect policies affecting prices, such as taxes, subsidies, and pricing regulations, and in the longer run through administrative controls on input use.

Even more fundamentally, product markets, as well as input choices, are influenced by the profound effects of vertical control on enterprise objectives. In theory the decisions of Hungarian and Yugoslav enterprises are to be guided by considerations of profitability; and various reforms have linked both managerial and worker rewards to profitability performance. In theory, too, this motivational structure is designed to make enterprises responsive to changing price and cost indicators in their output and input choices. Practice has diverged from theory, however, for two important and related reasons. First, considerations of equity or fairness in income distribution have led to a variety of indirect and administrative policies undermining the link between profitability and rewards. Second, enterprises have operated with the expectation that, because they are socially owned and because vertical authorities are ultimately responsible for their welfare and performance, such authorities will bail them out of financial difficulties. The result of this expectation is the so-called soft budget constraint that significantly reduces enterprise sensitivity to considerations of price, cost, and profitability compared to what it would be in a hypothetical market economy.

Even though Yugoslavia and Hungary share the feature of soft budget constraints with their East European neighbors, it is an oversimplification to characterize them as shortage economies in which enterprises struggle to produce as much as possible with little regard to costs or salability of output. Evidence drawn from enterprise surveys and interviews indicates that enterprise managers and workers are informed and concerned about costs and prices and that, with the imposition of domestic austerity measures after 1980, they have become increasingly concerned about excess capacity and falling domestic sales.[8] The real issue is one of the degree of sensitivity of enterprise decisions to such market information—not the existence of such sensitivity. What seems certain is that such sensitivity is weaker than it would be in market economies based on private ownership, profit maximization, and hard budget constraints. As a result, supply-side policies to get the prices right are likely to be considerably less effective in the Hungarian and Yugoslav systems than in such market systems.

As far as input allocation is concerned, supply-side policies designed to correct the prices of critical inputs, such as capital and foreign exchange, may be undermined both by the softness of budget constraints and by the fact that, for reasons of policy, administrative measures are the preferred and predominant method of control. For example, in both Hungary and Yugoslavia, administrative controls over the allocation and use of capital and foreign exchange are used, not only because the prices of the inputs may not be market clearing, but also because they give state and party authorities control over the distribution of critical resources among competing enterprise, sectoral, and regional claimants.

Administrative measures to influence the distribution of capital and foreign exchange at the microeconomic level are also important tools for the realization of macroeconomic targets. Administrative policies to control the distribution and use of foreign exchange are critical to efforts to control the balance of payments, and administrative policies to control the level and distribution of enterprise funds and the level and allocation of bank and state credit are critical to efforts to control aggregate investment spending. Obviously, such methods do not guarantee that macro targets will be realized, as evidenced by balance-of-payments difficulties and recurrent investment cycles in both countries.[9] But when macroeconomic objectives become paramount, often in response to an unsustainable balance-of-payments situation, such methods prove effective and are traditionally relied upon in lieu of the monetary, fiscal, and exchange rate policies usually associated with demand management in MTES. The use of such methods allows the authorities to achieve tighter control over the distribution of macroeconomic cutbacks both among categories of spending and among groups of spenders than is normally possible with the indirect macro controls of the MTES.

So far the discussion has emphasized the basic similarities between the Yugoslav and Hungarian systems, but the issue of macroeconomic control brings up important differences between them. Even the most casual glance at evidence from the 1970s indicates that macroeconomic control has been considerably weaker in Yugoslavia than in Hungary. There are several reasons for this. First and of the utmost importance, reforms in Yugoslavia gradually eliminated the ability of state and party authorities to control nominal incomes in socialist industry. Repeated and varied approaches to income policies have failed in the realization of macro targets for nominal income growth. The inability to control nominal incomes has meant an inability to control real incomes as well. The behavior of real wages has been the result of the uncontrolled interaction of nominal income growth and inflation and, given the history of inflationary expectations, cost-based pricing regulations, and the strong links between domestic price increases and devaluations, inflation has been both uncontrollable and unpredictable in the short run. In contrast to the situation in Yugoslavia, the authorities in Hungary have retained strong control over nominal incomes; and this has been a critical ingredient in their ability to control the inflation rate.

The decentralization of economic policymaking is a second important characteristic of the Yugoslav system that sharply distinguishes it from the Hungarian one and is responsible for Yugoslavia's weak macroeconomic control. Authority for making and implementing policy and the indirect and administrative tools for the realization of policy objectives rest mainly with powerful, competing regional authorities in Yugoslavia. National policy formation requires a consensus among these authorities and policy execution relies on the implementation of policy measures by them. During times of economic difficulty, underlying unresolved questions about the distribution of economic costs among different regions impede the process of policy formulation and weaken the degree of policy implementaion. On a more fundamental level, distributional conflicts among powerful regional interests make if difficult to maintain effective administrative controls over the use of capital and foreign exchange resources. Yet, in the absence of macroeconomic tools at the national level, macro stability depends on the implementation of such controls at the regional level.

Overall, underlying differences in the degree of political unity explain differences in economic policy formulation and implementation in Hungary and Yugoslavia. As the discussion at the beginning of this section suggests, there are important structural similarities between these two economies; but politics affect both the objectives of policy and the ability to use the existing structure to realize these objectives. While the economic objectives of the two countries have been similar, the ability to formulate and implement policy has not. Decentralization and regional conflict have significantly weakened this ability in Yugoslavia while continued centralization and party unity have strengthened it in Hungary.

TABLE 3.1. IMF Loans to Yugoslavia and Hungary, 1980–84

HUNGARY	
November 1982	$78.5 million in compensatory finance
	$517.8 million one-year standby agreement
January 1984	$436 million one-year standby agreement
YUGOSLAVIA	
June 1980	$441 million two-year standby agreement
January 1981	$1,960 million three-year standby agreement
	(replaces June 1980 agreement)
April 1984	$379 million one-year standby agreement

3. COMPARISON OF IMF CONDITIONALITY
IN HUNGARY AND YUGOSLAVIA

The Influence of the IMF on Adjustment Lending

Given this picture of the basic features of IMF adjustment programs and of the Hungarian and Yugoslav systems, we now examine the influence of the IMF on adjustment programs in both countries during the 1980 to 1984 period. Table 3.1 provides the basic information about the timing and extent of IMF finance in these programs. Relative to the total of medium- and long-term loans from private convertible currency sources, IMF lending was an important source of finance in both countries. For example, the 1984 IMF loan amounted to about 38 percent of the value of medium- and long-term funds raised by Hungary from private capital market sources in 1984. In Yugoslavia capital inflow from IMF lending in 1984 amounted to about 45 percent of the value of long-term capital inflow from the commercial banks in that year.[10]

In Yugoslavia the IMF played a critical role in organizing the 1983 emergency lending package which was the equivalent of a rescheduling agreement. The package amounted to about $6.5 billion in loans financed by approximately 500 western commercial banks, fifteen Western governments, the IMF, the Bank for International Settlements (BIS), and the World Bank. It was understood by all participants that the package was to underwrite the 1983 adjustment program whose targets and policy measures were laid out in the third year of the IMF standby agreement. Without the IMF's seal of approval, it is unlikely that the aid package would have been supported by Yugoslavia's major creditor banks, which were reportedly reluctant to extend new lending even with this approval.[11] Similarly, it is clear that, without continued IMF involvement in Yugoslavia in 1984, creditor banks would have been unwilling to reschedule debt or to extend new credits to the extent they did.

In Hungary IMF involvement was also critical to the flow of lending from other sources during the 1982 to 1984 period. Hungary applied for IMF membership at the end of 1981 at a time of great financial difficulty. During the first quarter of 1982, there was a sharp outflow of short-term funds from Hungary, and its convertible currency reserves fell sharply. During this period, Hungary had great difficulty raising any new finance from private sources. After it became clear that Hungary's application to the IMF would be accepted, the lending situation began to ease.

In April 1982 Hungary received a $210 million bridging loan from a group of thirteen central banks (not including the U.S. Federal Reserve Bank) arranged by the BIS with strong support from the Bank of England. The BIS granted a further six-month credit of $300 million in September (after refusing an urgent request in July) on the understanding that Hungary would become eligible to draw on IMF facilities before the end of the period. In August a syndicate of fifteen Western banks, led by Manufacturers Hanover, granted Hungary a three-year loan of $260 million at 1.25 points over the London interbank offered rate (LIBOR).[12] This loan was hailed as the first commercial bank credit to any East European country since the imposition of martial law in Poland.

The seal of approval given by the IMF to Hungarian adjustment efforts was critical to Hungary's ability to raise funds from Western sources. Given the general nervousness of the international private banking community about the situation in Eastern Europe and their strong herd instinct, Hungary would not have been able to arrange any significant loans on its own during this period. The participation of the IMF provided a mechanism for the private banks to distinguish among the various East European countries and to make a reasonable assessment of creditworthiness. Hungary's participation in policy dialogue with the IMF and its adoption of IMF-approved adjustment policies reassured the banks and demonstrated the IMF's leverage.

Overall, it seems clear that, at the very least, IMF involvement in the adjustment efforts of Hungary and Yugoslavia did have one beneficial effect on both countries—it bought them more time for adjustment by promoting additional lending. This allowed both countries to avoid the sharp contractions in output that would have resulted from tighter capital market constraints. In other words, contrary to an often-voiced opinion, the severity of domestic austerity in both countries was probably reduced rather than increased by IMF involvement.

The Influence of the IMF on Adjustment Policies and Objectives

In this section we identify the basic conditions of IMF standby agreements with Yugoslavia and Hungary and evaluate their objectives and their effectiveness or appropriateness relative to these objectives. We also discuss whether other types of conditions might have been more suitable to achieve these objectives given the special features of the Yugoslav and Hungarian systems. As we indicated in the introduction, we know much more about conditionality in Yugoslavia than in Hungary. What we do know supports our assumption that the general structure of the standby agreements was similar in both countries, and we will rely on this assumption in the following discussion.

As is traditional in IMF agreements with other countries, the IMF agreements with Yugoslavia set out a number of conditions relating to demand management. The basic objective of these conditions was to reduce domestic absorption to achieve targets of improved external performance. At various points during the 1980 to 1984 period, these targets included increases in foreign exchange reserves, limits on new foreign borrowing, and improvements in the current account. Similar targets were undoubtedly set in the IMF agreements with Hungary.

In the Yugoslav case demand-management conditions specifying quantitative limits on the growth of net domestic assets (domestic credit creation) of the banking system, central bank credit to the federal government, and public sector revenues and expenditures were designed to restrain the growth of domestic demand.[13] Presumably, similar monetary and fiscal conditions were also set for Hungary. In addition, in Hungary a quantitative target for real wage growth was set, whereas in Yugoslavia the authorities agreed to restrain nominal income growth although no quantitative limit was set. This difference in treatment may reflect IMF recognition that the Yugoslav authoritites exercised significantly weaker control over incomes than did the Hungarian authorities. Or it may reflect an IMF assessment that real income declines in Yugoslavia as a result of accelerating inflation were likely to be sufficiently large to cut domestic consumption as much as the Fund thought necessary. In neither country did the IMF agreement specify a limit on the allowable rate of inflation and, indeed, as the later discussion of exhange rate conditionality and price liberalization indicates, the IMF clearly accorded lower priority to controlling the inflation rate than to other policy objectives. In this respect, its policy preferences proved at odds with the policy preferences of both the Hungarian and the Yugoslav authorities.

Several observations can be made about the appropriateness of the demand-management conditions identified here. First, given the softness of enterprise budget constraints, there are no single predictable links between credit conditions and enterprise behavior. This point is obvious once hard or soft budget constraints in the accounting sense are distinguished from hard or soft budget constraints in the behavioral or expectational sense. In the expectational sense, enterprise budget constraints are soft when enterprises do not expect that their short-run survival or their long-run growth depends on operating within their current budget constraints in the accounting sense (Kornai 1980a). In an environment of soft budget constraints in the expectational sense, a hardening of enterprise budget constraints in the accounting sense is not likely to affect enterprise behavior to the same extent and in the same manner as would be the case in a standard market environment where current financial performance affects enterprise survival and growth.

Effective ceilings on net domestic credit extended by the banking system to both enterprises and the government certainly harden enterprise budgets in the accounting sense. If credits to finance enterprise activity contract, and if the government is unable to offset this contraction by an increase in enterprise subsidies because of binding limits on government bank borrowing, then enterprises will certainly face a reduction in credit available to finance their fixed and working capital needs. Faced with such a reduction, enterprises can respond in several ways, and their choices will be influenced by the softness of their budget constraints in the expectational sense. In an environment of hard budget constraints characteristic of market economies, firms have four options: first, to the extent that they have excess liquidity, they can economize on their holdings of cash to substitute for an unexpected shortfall in credit, resulting in an increase in the velocity of money at the aggregate level; second, they can scale back on their working capital needs by cutting inventories, reducing money wages, and/or laying off workers and cutting back on current production levels; third, they can increase their prices to try to cover higher borrowing costs associated with rising interest rates as credit contracts; and fourth, they can scale down investment spending, resulting in a diversion of output from investment to either consumption or net exports at the aggregate level.[14] Assuming that other demand-management conditions of the IMF's adjustment program rule out persistent excess demand in domestic consumer goods' markets, this fourth response will generate the desired macro outcome of an improvement in the external balance by switching resources from domestic to foreign use.

As Taylor's (1983) work on the effects of IMF stabilization programs in developing countries suggests, even in market economies with hard budget constraints, the fourth response—which is the one consistent with the ultimate objective of Fund adjustment programs—is not the only or even the most important response observed in practice. Enterprise liquidity does fall and velocity does increase offsetting to some extent the contractionary effects of credit restrictions on domestic demand. Production and employment levels fall and prices rise, and enterprises react to a squeeze on working capital finance, resulting in stagflationary conditions at the macroeconomic level. Thus the required diversion of output to net exports is more costly to domestic absorption because it takes place in an environment of falling aggregate output.

When enterprise budget constraints are soft in the expectational sense, enterprise production and investment plans are likely to be less sensitive to a reduction in credit availability than they are in a market economy with hard budget constraints, at least in the short run. The Yugoslav experience with repeated cycles of credit contraction in the 1960s and 1970s reveals a typical reaction pattern (Tyson 1977a). Despite a cutback in available credit, firms initially attempt to maintain current levels of production and employment and current investment plans. To obtain the finance required for their needs, they simultaneously cut back on their liquidity, driving it down to levels that are insufficient to cover regular payments due to suppliers, banks, government, and occasionally even to workers, and they attempt to replace bank credit with trade credit by postponing payment on outstanding obligations. The result of such behavior is a dramatic explosion in the stock of inter-enterprise trade credit, reflecting an equally dramatic increase in the stock of overdue, unpaid bills and accompanied by growing illiquidity in the enterprise sector. Such an explosion clearly accompanied the Fund's stabilization programs during the 1981 to 84 period as the figures in table 3.2 indicate.

In addition to running down their liquidity to unsustainably low levels and to defaulting on outstanding obligations, Yugoslav firms confronting a reduction in bank credit also tend to raise their prices in an ill-fated effort to increase their revenues. This response is similar to that documented by Taylor for firms in other developing countries. Yugoslav firms also tend to understate the credit requirements of their investment plans in an attempt to get the loan approval necessary to initiate or continue such plans. All of these responses are consistent with the existence of soft budget constraints in the expectational sense. Indeed, the tendency to underestimate financing requirements for investment projects is a standard explanation for recurrent investment cycles in most socialist economies, including Yugoslavia and Hungary.

Eventually, of course, if enterprise budget constraints have truly hardened in the accounting sense, Yugoslav firms have no recourse but to adjust their actual production and spending levels. But by the time they begin to react, the economy confronts a major financial crisis that threatens a large fraction of socialist enterprises with outright bankruptcy. Bankruptcy, however, is a politically and ideologically dangerous option, one which the authorities are anxious to avoid. Moreover, there is no guarantee that the firms that find themselves in the most precarious position are necessarily the weakest ones from a long-run efficiency point of view. A firm may find itself near bankruptcy because it is the unwilling creditor of a large number of weaker firms. As the threat of default and bankruptcy grows, so does the pressure on the authorities to ease credit policy, in effect to monetize the debt created by the inter-enterprise credit transactions. As long as the authorities are constrained by the IMF's conditions they will not be able to yield to this pressure, and in this sense the difficulty of the budget constraints in the accounting sense will of necessity begin to influence enterprise production and spending behavior in ways that support the necessary diversion of resources to net exports.

As the preceding discussion suggests, limits on domestic credit creation do not harden enterprise budget constraints in the expectational sense in Yugoslavia, at least in the short run. Hence, there are no single predictable links in the short run between such limits and enterprise pricing, production, or spending patterns. If the object of IMF policy is

TABLE 3.2. Macroeconomic Indicators for Hungary and Yugoslavia, 1975–84 (average annual rates of growth in percent)

	1975–79	1979–80	1980–81	1981–82
HUNGARY				
Gross domestic product	4.1	0.1	2.9	2.8
Consumption	3.4	0.6	2.9	1.2
Fixed investment	4.3	−5.8	−4.3	−1.6
Domestic absorption	3.0	−0.6	1.4	−0.1
Producer prices	3.1	15.3	6.3	4.7
Consumer prices	5.6	9.1	4.6	6.9
Real wages	1.3	−1.7	1.1	−0.7
YUGOSLAVIA				
Gross domestic product	6.9	2.6	1.1	0.5
Consumption	5.8	0.6	−1.4	0.4
Fixed investment	8.6	−5.9	−9.8	−6.2
Domestic absorption	7.0	−1.0	−1.3	−0.3
Producer prices	9.3	27.3	45.0	25.0
Retail prices	14.3	30.4	46.0	30.0
Real wages	3.2	−7.5	−5.7	−4.2
Money supply	29.5	23.0	26.6	26.6
Interenterprise trade credit	NA	NA	36.7	51.3

SOURCES: Growth rates of national account aggregates are based on World Bank data. Estimates of price and wage growth are based on data contained in official country sources. Estimates of

to cut investment spending, such limits are neither sufficient in the short run nor are they necessary since the Yugoslav authorities have a variety of administrative means to control such spending. Such means are more likely to be effective than credit limits in tightening control over aggregate investment spending in the short run. They are also preferred by the Yugoslav authorities because they permit greater control over the microeconomic incidence of investment cutbacks.

Although the preceding discussion has focused on Yugoslavia, it has relevance to Hungary as well. Recent empirical evidence by Kornai and Matits (1983) indicates that budget constraints in Hungary remain soft in the expectational sense. Neither firm survival nor growth depend on financial solvency and responsibility in the short run. Because of greater administrative control over firm behavior in Hungary—particularly on the wage and pricing side—and the continued large share of enterprise

1982–83	1983–84
0.7	2.6
0.5	1.2
−3.4	−4.4
−1.7	0.2
5.6	3.9
7.3	8.3
−3.2	−2.6
−1.3	2.1
−0.3	−0.7
−9.0	−10.0
−2.1	1.2
32.0	57.0
39.0	57.0
−11.0	−5.7
20.1	43.1
250.0	59.1

growth in money supply and interenterprise trade credit for Yugoslavia are based on data contained in the National Bank of Yugoslavia (June 1984 and 1985).

finance provided by government subsidies, liquidity crises in response to reductions in bank credit have not yet been observed in Hungary; but it would be reasonable to predict that such cycles would develop as administrative control over firm price, wages, and spending continues to weaken.[15] And investment cycles have certainly persisted in Hungary, despite several rounds of economic reform (Tyson 1983). Thus, in Hungary as in Yugoslavia, it seems reasonable to conclude that there are no simple links between credit cutbacks and enterprise behavior in the short run. In Hungary, too, it is obvious that if the object of policy is to cut enterprise investment spending, the authorities tend to rely on administrative measures to do so. A cutback in bank credit and state subsidies is better understood as the passive reflection of a decision to reduce investment spending by administrative means, rather than as the active instrument used to realize such a reduction.

Confronted with the existence of soft budget constraints in the expectational sense and with the existence of administrative methods for achieving control over enterprise investment spending, how might the IMF have amended its traditional demand-management conditions to be more appropriate to the Yugoslav and Hungarian economic systems? Rather than rely on aggregate credit limitations whose effects were very difficult to predict, a more promising approach would have involved working with the Yugoslav and Hungarian authorities to set explicit limits on investment, and lending technical assistance to guide the microeconomic incidence of investment cutbacks to reduce their long-run efficiency costs. Such an approach, if combined with traditional limits on bank credit to the government and demand-management conditions limiting consumption, would have had a more predictable effect on the level and composition of domestic absorption than traditional overall credit limitations.

The traditional use of monetary-credit limits for demand-management objectives in IMF agreements is premised on a model that assumes certain simple, predictable links between monetary growth on the one hand and prices and balance-of-payments deficits on the other.[16] As the preceding discussion indicates, several systemic factors in both Hungary and Yugoslavia—including soft budget constraints in the expectational sense, distinctions between hard and soft enterprise funds, inter-enterprise trade credit, resulting variations in velocity, and regulations on domestic price formation—weaken these links and make predictions about the price or balance-of-payments effects of a given credit limit misleading. As is suggested by the Yugoslav case, a given dose of nominal credit contraction often results in a harsher than anticipated dose of real credit contraction, resulting in illiquidity, threatened bankruptcy, and overkill in the contraction of domestic demand.

A final observation about the appropriateness of the IMF's demand-management conditions concerns their underlying distributional objectives. In both Yugoslavia and Hungary the IMF negotiated conditions to influence the incidence of austerity among consumption, investment, and government spending in what it perceived to be desirable ways. In the Yugoslav case demand-management conditions included limits on the growth of public sector revenues and expenditures and limits on central bank credit to the Federal government. Limits of this type are traditional in IMF agreements with developing countries, most often because there are close links between deficit financing, money creation, and inflation in such countries. In the Yugoslav context of balanced or surplus budgets for most levels of government and a relatively small federal deficit, these links are unimportant and another explanation for IMF policy must be sought. The most plausible explanation, consistent with both the IMF's general concern over longer-term, supply-side issues and its preference for private market actors, is its desire to redirect resources away from nonproductive government activities to productive investment activities.

A similar explanation applies to the limitations on real wage growth in the IMF standby agreement with Hungary. In the 1979 to 1982 period, prior to the negotiation of this agreement, the Hungarian authorities had reduced domestic demand by sharp cuts in investment spending while consumption (both private and collective) had continued to increase, albeit at reduced rates. This pattern of demand restriction reflected Hungary's long-term commitment to protect consumption gains even during a time of macroeconomic stress, but was at odds with the IMF's traditional preference to cut back both consumption and government spending to reduce the crowding out of investment due to overall austerity.

In addition to demand-management conditions, the IMF agreements with Yugoslavia in 1983 and 1984 contained explicit exchange rate conditions. These conditions took the form of targets for the required real devaluation of the dinar to be realized by a specified date. The basic objective of such targets was to promote expenditure switching by improving the incentives for exports, enhancing the competitiveness of exports on Western markets, and reducing the incentives for imports. The rationale behind such targets was the IMF view that Yugoslavia's poor export performance during the 1976 to 1983 period was mainly the result of an incentive bias against exports due to an increasingly overvalued exchange rate.

It is impossible from available information to determine whether the IMF agreements with Hungary included explicit exchange rate conditions. Apparently, IMF negotiators did press Hungary to devalue the forint to improve export incentives, but the Hungarians resisted the adoption of a specific devaluation target as an explicit condition. A more active exchange rate policy may have been a policy understanding between the IMF and the Hungarians.[17] This would certainly be consistent with the pattern of forint depreciation in 1983 and 1984. (See the next section for an analysis of exchange rate changes in Hungary during the 1980 to 1984 period.)

Clearly, IMF pressure on exchange rate policy was much greater in Yugoslavia than in Hungary both because the inflation differential between Yugoslavia and its Western trading partners was much greater than that between Hungary and its Western trading partners, and because the available evidence suggested that the degree of overvaluation of the dinar was substantial.[18] In addition, the IMF was in a more powerful bargaining position vis-à-vis Yugoslavia than vis-à-vis Hungary for a variety of reasons. The macroeconomic situation in Yugoslavia seemed much more precarious, and the Yugoslav authorities appeared much less able to maintain macro control. The Yugoslav leadership was divided and decentralized while the Hungarian leadership presented a united front in discussions with the IMF.[19] Finally, during 1981–82, the Yugoslavs failed to fulfill policy understandings on exchange rate policy, leading the IMF to substitute explicit conditions with sanctions for such understandings in the 1983–84 agreements.

Although exchange rate policy is a traditional ingredient of IMF policy advice, there are several reasons to question its effectiveness in the Yugoslav and Hungarian settings. During the 1980 to 1984 period, the pricing practices and regulations in force within both economies established a tight link between the exchange rate and the domestic prices of both tradable and nontradable goods. In Yugoslavia increases in the costs of imported inputs and increases in the dinar prices of exports translated into direct upward pressure on domestic prices. The result was predictable given Yugoslavia's past experience with the inflationary consequences of devaluation and the experiences of many other semi-industrial countries as well.[20] Fear of the inflationary consequences of devaluation was the major reason for heated Yugoslav opposition to the imposition of exchange rate conditions by the IMF.

On its side the IMF appeared willing to accept what it believed to be the short-term costs of an acceleration of inflation for the benefits of improved export incentives and competitiveness resulting from devaluation. The IMF was also relatively sanguine about the inflationary consequences of devaluation because these consequences were viewed as necessary to produce declines in real incomes and domestic absorption in the Yugoslav setting. The IMF was surprised by the strength of the inflationary pressure accompanying the 1983–84 devaluations, especially in light of the sharp reductions in the real money supply occurring at the same time.[21] Clearly, the simple macro models linking money, demand, and prices on which standard IMF policy is based proved to be misleading predictors of price changes in Yugoslavia at least in the short to medium run.

A fear of the inflationary consequences of devaluation also motivated Hungarian opposition to exchange rate conditions. In Hungary, the prevailing pricing regulations meant that a devaluation would automatically increase the domestic prices of both tradables and nontradables. Perhaps the transparent nature of the links between devaluation and the domestic price level in the Hungarian pricing system was one reason why the IMF did not push harder for explicit exchange rate conditionality.

Of course, the fact that devaluation was likely to have an inflationary impact in both Hungary and Yugoslavia does not mean that it could not play a role in the adjustment process in both countries. As long as any initial excess demand in both countries was eliminated by the inflationary effects of devaluation and complementary expenditure-reducing policies, and as long as the price level effects of devaluation were not fully accommodated by the monetary authorities—a reaction limited by effective credit restrictions—then the domestic prices of tradables could be expected to increase relative to the domestic prices of nontradables. Although domestic price controls would complicate the extent and timing of the relative price changes resulting from a devaluation, such changes could be expected to occur. Indeed, to the extent that the price authorities continued to keep the prices of certain important nontradables below market-clearing levels, devaluation would definitely lead to the anticipated change in relative prices in favor of tradables.[22]

If the effects of devaluation on the price level and on the relative prices of tradables and nontradables in both Yugoslavia and Hungary were predictable, its effects on the trade balance (the ultimate target of exchange rate policy) were not. Imports in both countries were subject to a variety of formal and informal rationing schemes and were mainly limited to raw material and other productive inputs for which there were no easily available domestic or CMEA substitutes. Even if a devaluation eliminated the excess demand pressure for imports—thereby eliminating the need for quantity rationing—overall imports could not be expected to fall. And the preference of the authorities to regulate both the composition of imports and their distribution among enterprises could be expected to undermine most of the efficiency gains normally associated with devaluation and a move away from quantity rationing.

Given the inflationary effects of devaluation and the likely absence of its effects on aggregate imports in these economies, a more appropriate policy approach to improving the trade balance might have focused on direct measures to stimulate exports. Given soft budget constraints in the expectational sense—something that the authorities could not have eliminated in the short run even if they had been willing to do so—both Yugoslav and Hungarian firms could be expected to be quite insensitive to the relative price effects of devaluation at least compared to enterprises in systems with harder budget constraints. In addition, especially in Hungary, lack of experience in Western markets meant that there were serious structural impediments to exports in such markets that a devaluation would not address. Given the costs and uncertainties associated with breaking into these markets, enterprises could be expected to continue to prefer selling their goods on domestic or bloc markets, even when devaluation made sales on Western markets nominally more attractive.

In this setting, the price signals of a devaluation could not be expected to support the kind of export boom required to break the foreign exchange shortage strangling growth in these economies. Additional policies to promote exports directly were required. Yet such policies were not included in the conditions of IMF agreements with Yugoslavia, and available evidence also suggests that they were not included in IMF agreements with Hungary. This finding is in line with the traditional IMF bias against explicit export subsidies or other policies that result in dual exchange rate or multiple exchange rate systems. While understandable from a longer-term perspective, this bias is questionable in a short-run situation of severe foreign exchange shortage. Even more remarkable from this perspective is the fact that, in its 1984 agreement with Yugoslavia, the IMF actually called for cuts in public spending to be concentrated on export subsidies.

Finally, in the Hungarian case the IMF supported a reduction in a variety of subsidies in accordance with the general reform objective of bringing Hungarian prices more closely into line with world prices. As part of this reform process, export subsidy rates on dollar trade fell in a variety of critical export sectors between 1981 and 1983.[23] The net effect of the decline in export subsidies, accompanied by stricter controls on imports that made domestic sales conditions more attractive, was a decline in incentives to export.[24] This occurred at the very time that the IMF was pressing for a devaluation to improve these incentives.

In both countries the IMF seemed to lack a sense of policy priority. Its support of measures to reduce government interference in the economy and to rationalize the price structure actually conflicted with what should have been accorded top policy priority, namely, a rapid and dramatic improvement in export earnings in the short run. This is not to deny that such measures might improve the efficiency of resource use in the long run or that a policy of differential subsidies and administrative export targets that expanded exports in the short run might not result in significant efficiency losses in the long run. The real issue is one of tradeoffs or priorities. In the short-run foreign exchange crises in which Yugoslavia and Hungary found themselves, the supply-side effects of easing the foreign exchange constraint by additional exports undoubtedly exceeded the supply-side effects of efficiency gains from a more rational incentive structure, especially given enterprise insensitivity to relative price signals resulting from soft budget constraints in the expectational sense.

Conflicts between short-run and long-run policy priorities are also evident in the imposition of IMF conditions to correct price distortions in Yugoslavia and Hungary. Both the Hungarian and Yugoslav authorities were outspoken in their concern about inflation and its economic and political consequences in their negotiations with the IMF. Yet the IMF pushed for a variety of policy measures to relax price controls and to adjust sensitive consumer and producer prices that were heavily subsidized. In the Yugoslav case the IMF actually imposed conditions relating to the termination of a general price freeze in 1984 and to the upward adjustment of critical energy and transportation prices. Similar conditions may have been set in earlier agreements during the 1981 to 1984 period. In the Hungarian case we do not know if explicit conditions regarding prices were set, but we do know that the IMF expressed a preference to achieve the target reduction in real wages by a reduction in consumer price subsidies.

Although the correction of domestic price distortions is a desirable objective in the long run, the short-run costs of such a policy direction must be considered relative to other objectives. In Yugoslavia, where accelerating inflation in 1983–84 was producing unexpectedly large declines in real incomes, undermining public confidence in the divided leadership, and aggravating social and political tensions, policies to control overall prices and the relative prices of critical inputs might have been a useful short-term adjunct to other demand-management measures to quell inflationary expectations. In these circumstances Yugoslav leaders viewed the struggle against inflation as the primary objective of policy and correctly viewed the IMF's conditions on devaluation and the relaxation of price controls as running counter to this objective. In Hungary the leadership was committed to a gradual process of price rationalization, but fear of inflation limited the pace of the process. Ironically, however, the price pressures generated by the reduction in subsidies made the Hungarians more opposed to devaluation since the room for politically acceptable inflation was used up by price increases resulting from price rationalization. Thus, the IMF might have been more successful in its negotiations with the Hungarians to push for larger devaluations had it been more willing to support a slowdown in the pace of price liberalization in the short run.

In addition to the demand-management, exchange rate, and price-liberalization conditions already noted, the 1984 IMF agreement with Yugoslavia contained an especially controversial condition relating to interest rates. The condition set a schedule for large increases in nominal rates with the objective of realizing positive real interest rates within a specified period of time. Although there was some sentiment in support of such a policy within Yugoslavia, there was also vigorous opposition. Many Yugoslav officials argued that such a policy would further aggravate inflationary pressure. Others raised concern about the excessive burden that positive real interest rates would impose on enterprises that depended heavily on credit for both working and fixed capital. According to these critics, if enterprises were to lose the substantial subsidies they were receiving in the form of credits at negative real interest rates, their already precarious financial situation would be seriously aggravated.

It is hard to understand why the IMF attached so much importance to interest rate policy in its 1984 standby with Yugoslavia. On the macro side sharp reductions in real credit availability and a plethora of administrative restrictions had produced sharp reductions in aggregate investment spending and Yugoslavia had met most, if not all, of its demand-management conditions. Although the IMF might have preferred that the incidence of these reductions be guided by price signals for efficiency reasons, it must have been clear that nonprice considerations would continue to have a dominant influence on investment allocation even if interest rates rose to positive levels. Positive real interest rates were necessary but hardly sufficient to the realization of greater efficiency in the Yugoslav institutional setting. Moreover, in the short run, because a large percentage of Yugoslav enterprises would not be able to operate profitably at such levels, the predictable results would be further softening of enterprise budget constraints and further growth in interenterprise trade credit. The alternative was widespread bankruptcy with severe losses in output and employment—an alternative that was not politically feasible.

The most plausible explanation of IMF pressure for real interest rates was concern over the possible effects of negative real interest rates on saving and capital flight. The dramatic deterioration in the errors and omissions term in the Yugoslav balance-of-payments accounts in 1983 suggested that such concern might be warranted.[25] According to anecdotal information, both enterprises and Yugoslav migrant workers were leaving a substantial fraction of their foreign exchange earnings abroad. If such earnings could be attracted to Yugoslavia by positive real interest rates, the tasks of rebuilding foreign exchange reserves and improving the current account would be made easier. Such reasoning depended, of course, on the underlying assumption that interest rate considerations were important to decisions about earnings repatriation. Although this may have been the case, there was no empirical evidence to support it. Furthermore, in the Yugoslav context, fears of further devaluation and of additional, unpredictable restrictions on the use of repatriated foreign exchange by both consumers and producers were probably at least as important as interest rate considerations in repatriation decisions.[26]

Overall, in light of the bitter controversy surrounding the interest rate conditions and the fact that they aggravated already serious inflationary pressure and widespread liquidity problems, the IMF's decision to impose them seems questionable. Since the real crisis was one of foreign exchange shortage, more direct policies to stimulate greater foreign exchange earnings through export subsidies would seem to have been preferable to an interest rate policy to encourage greater repatriation of such earnings, especially when the effects of the interest rate policy were very uncertain. The export subsidy approach also had the attraction of political support while the interest rate policy did not. This made the odds for the effective implementation of the subsidy approach much greater in the decentralized Yugoslav system.

4. THE INFLUENCE OF THE IMF FUND ON ECONOMIC PERFORMANCE IN HUNGARY AND YUGOSLAVIA DURING THE 1980 to 1984 PERIOD

Both Hungary and Yugoslavia were forced to accept reductions in domestic absorption levels during the period 1980–84 in order to improve their external balances in conformity with tighter external capital market conditions. Austerity in domestic demand would have been required even in the absence of IMF involvement; indeed, in Hungary austerity began in 1979—three years before its first agreement with the IMF. As noted earlier, IMF involvement actually brought in more external financing than would have been available otherwise and thus allowed for a slower pace of downward adjustment in domestic absorption in both countries during the 1980 to 1984 period.

The data in table 3.2 indicate that investment spending bore the disproportionate share of the cutback in domestic absorption in both Hungary and Yugoslavia. In both countries investment rates fell each year and in 1984 were sharply below preausterity levels. In Yugoslavia aggregate personal consumption also fell between 1980 and 1984, while in Hungary it rose over the same period; it both countries consumption's share in total domestic demand increased.

In neither country was the decision to concentrate cuts in domestic demand on investment the result of IMF conditionality. Indeed, as noted earlier, the IMF traditionally exhibits a preference to moderate the crowding out of investment in austerity programs. In both Hungary and Yugoslavia, as in the other countries of Eastern Europe that underwent austerity during this period, this decision was the result of several domestic considerations. First, as a matter of policy, political leaders chose to protect consumption levels from deep sustained reductions to avoid the overt and covert political dissatisfaction that such reductions were likely to entail. Since private consumption was the largest single component of domestic demand, this choice necessitated a very heavy burden on investment.

A second reason for the disproportionate impact of austerity on investment was the effort by state authorities to minimize short-term output losses associated with import cuts. In order to maintain the flow of imports of raw materials and other inputs required for immediate production, imports of capital goods required for investment projects and future productive capabilities were squeezed disproportionately hard. This was a rational policy response from a short-term perspective but was questionable from a longer-term point of view.

Finally, as noted earlier, both the Yugoslav and Hungarian authorities had a variety of administrative means at their disposal to control the level of investment and, during past periods of macroeconomic stabilization, they had relied on such means as the primary method of curtailing domestic demand. Thus, their behavior during the 1980 to 1984 period was consistent with their past behavior and does not suggest any aberration due to IMF pressure.

In both countries the interest rates on investment finance increased during the 1980 to 1984 period, in Hungary as a result of an internal policy decision and in Yugoslavia as a result of IMF pressure. In Hungary higher interest rates were used mainly as one of several measures to reduce enterprise discretionary funds and not as a price signal to allocate funds among competing users.[27] In Yugoslavia, despite IMF pressure, interest rates in real terms remained negative through the middle of 1984, and administrative rationing of credit by banks and state authorities remained the dominant method of investment control. By the last quarter of 1984 real interest rates had risen approximately to zero as the Yugoslav authorities struggled to meet the condition of the 1984 IMF agreement.[28] Throughout the entire period, given the softness of enterprise budget constraints, the regionalization of capital markets, and the continued desire of regional and national authorities to direct investment to priority objectives, administrative rationing was both desired and necessary to realize effective control over investment.[29]

Compared to Yugoslavia, Hungary had much tighter control over the course of nominal incomes in the socialized sector. Nominal income growth in this sector was a target of economic policy in Hungary and detailed administrative controls over enterprise income and wage distribution were used to pursue it. In Yugoslavia the authorities were not able to control nominal incomes in much of the socialized sector, despite repeated and varied efforts, although they were able to restrict nominal income growth in government and quasi-government organizations. The inability to target the course of nominal incomes or to control the rate of inflation meant that, even in the socialized sector, the behavior of

TABLE 3.3. Convertible Currency Merchandise Trade of Hungary and Yugoslavia, 1978–84 (billions of U.S. dollars)

	1978	1979	1980	1981
HUNGARY				
Merchandise exports	3.18	4.06	4.86	4.88
Merchandise imports	3.96	4.23	4.59	4.43
Trade balance	−0.78	−0.17	0.27	0.45
Current account balance	−1.24	−0.82	−0.37	−0.73
YUGOSLAVIA				
Merchandise exports	3.97	4.77	5.65	5.72
Merchandise imports	−8.37	11.34	11.32	10.60
Trade balance	−4.40	−6.57	−5.80	−4.88
Current account balance	−1.27	−3.30	−2.20	−1.82

SOURCES: World Bank and IMF data sources and official country statistics.

*The Yugoslav statistics are distorted by the use of unrealistic statistical exchange rates that are used to convert trade denominated in other convertible currencies to dollar values. In periods,

real incomes was not a meaningful policy target as it was in Hungary. In Hungary the decline in real socialized sector wages in 1982, 1983, and 1984 conforms with the performance criteria calling for a 2–4 percent decline in real wages in the 1982 IMF agreement and does suggest that IMF pressure may have been an important influence. In Yugoslavia, by contrast, IMF involvement exercised only an indirect influence on real wages through the cumulative effects of other conditions on the inflation rate.

As far as the pattern of external adjustment is concerned, in both Hungary and Yugoslavia a decline in convertible currency imports was an important component of the improvement in the convertible currency trade balance realized during the 1980 to 1984 period. In 1984 convertible currency imports in nominal terms were only 81 percent of their 1980 value in Hungary and 69 percent in Yugoslavia. In both countries a portion of this decline is attributable to the appreciation of the dollar which caused the nominal dollar value of other convertible currency imports to decline. Nevertheless, available evidence on the behavior of import prices suggests that convertible currency imports declined in real terms in both countries as well. For example, a recent study by Robinson (1986) indicates that convertible currency imports in real terms declined at an average annual rate of 2.2 percent a year in Hungary between 1981 and 1984.[30] Official Yugoslav statistics indicate that aggregate imports declined in real terms at an average

1982	1983	1984
4.88	4.86	4.97
4.11	3.97	3.73
0.77	0.88	1.24
−0.06	0.32	0.33
5.85	6.27	6.59
9.64	8.07	7.76
−3.79	−1.80	−1.17
−1.42	0.30	0.87

such as that of 1981–1984, when actual European exchange rates were declining relative to the dollar, the use of statistical exchange rates that diverged from actual market rates tended to inflate the dollar value of Yugoslav trade.

annual rate of 8.8 percent a year between 1980 and 1984, and this decline was concentrated in convertible currency imports (table 3.3).[31]

As in past periods of macroeconomic stabilization in both countries and similarly to the recurrent slowdown phases in investment cycles in other East European countries, administrative quantitative controls on convertible currency imports were relied upon to realize improvement in the trade balance. Thus, it seems likely that this pattern of adjustment would have emerged, as it did throughout Eastern Europe, even in the absence of IMF involvement.

The IMF influence may have been an important determinant of export performance in Yugoslavia. Under strong IMF pressure, the real effective exchange rate in Yugoslavia fell sharply by about 45 percent between 1981 and the end of 1983 (table 3.4). After growing by only about 1.7 percent per year between 1980 and 1982, Yugoslavia's nominal exports to convertible currency markets grew by about 6.1 percent per year between 1982 and 1984, and some of this growth may be attributable to the improved incentives stemming from dinar devaluation.[32] Estimates of the behavior of the real quantity of convertible currency exports reported by Bajt (1985) confirm the view that the exchange rate depreciation may have provided a stimulus to exports. According to Bajt's calculations, real convertible currency exports increased at an average annual rate of nearly 11 percent in 1983 and 1984 after falling at an average annual rate of 7.6 percent in 1981 and 1982. Earlier

TABLE 3.4. Real Effective Exchange Rates: Hungary and Yugoslavia*
(1979 = 100)

	1979	1980	1981	1982	1983	1984
Forints per dollar**	100	88.6	79.0	77.7	82.4	84.3
Dinars per dollar***	100	106.4	113.5	132.3	165.0	170.1

*Local currency cost of $1.00.

**Based on the real effective exchange rate for the forint calculated by Balassa. His calculations are derived by weighting Hungary's trade with its major partner countries among the developed market economies (using export and import weights) and by adjusting nominal values for differences in the rate of inflation of wholesale prices in Hungary and in these partner countries.

***Based on the real effective exchange rate for the dinar calculated by the National Bank of Yugoslavia. Calculations are derived by weighting the exchange rate of the dinar against convertible currencies using their weights in total current account receipts and payments. The nominal values are adjusted by differences in the rates of inflation of wholesale (producer) prices in Yugoslavia and in its convertible currency trading partners.

work on the adverse effects on exports of the increasing dinar overvaluation during the 1976 to 1980 period is also consistent with this interpretation.[33]

The introduction in Yugoslavia of new export subsidy measures and the strengthening of existing ones, as well as the linking of import rights to export earnings at the enterprise level, also enhanced incentives to export during the 1980 to 1984 period. Consequently, it is difficult to assess the effects of exchange rate policy alone. Given the magnitude of the real devaluation that occurred—the real effective value of the dinar fell by about 60 percent between 1980 and 1984—the growth in export earnings seems relatively weak and suggests that the price elasticities of export supply and export demand were relatively small, at least in the short to medium run. At the present time there is no careful empirical work to support this supposition. Relatively low price sensitivity on the supply side, however, is consistent with the behavioral implications of soft budget constraints.

In Hungary the forint appreciated in real terms by about 22 percent between 1979 and 1982. This trend was reversed in 1983 and 1984 when the forint depreciated in value by about 8.5 percent. IMF pressure may have been behind the exchange rate adjustments in 1983 and 1984. Despite these adjustments, however, the forint had still appreciated in real effective terms by some 16 percent between 1979 and 1984. In addition to the net disincentive effects of these exchange rate trends, the competitive pricing rules in effect after 1980 tended to discourage convertible currency exports.[34] As noted earlier, the reduction in a variety of subsidies in line with reform objectives apparently also had a similar discouraging effect by reducing the forint price of exports relative to the forint price of domestic sales (Kis, Robinson, and Tyson 1985). Given this constellation of policies and their effects on export incentives, it is not surprising that Hungary's convertible currency exports stagnated in nominal terms and that it lost market share in the developed market economies.[35] Recent estimates indicate, however, that in real terms convertible currency exports may have increased at an annual rate of about 6–6.5 percent between 1980 and 1984.[36] Interviews and other anecdotal evidence suggest that this export growth was largely the result of a vigorous party campaign waged at the enterprise level to mobilize exports and an accompanying import control program that linked enterprise access to foreign exchange to its export performance.[37] In other words, mainly administrative measures rather than IMF price policies were relied on by the Hungarian authorities to stimulate exports during the period.

A final stiking difference between austerity in Hungary and austerity in Yugoslavia lies in the behavior of the inflation rate. In Hungary the inflation rate for producer prices during the 1980 to 1984 period was comparable to that realized in the 1975 to 1980 period. The acceleration in the inflation rate for retail prices registered in 1979 and again in 1983 and 1984 was, in large part, the consequence of a reduction in subsidies called for by reform and did not indicate a serious intensification of inflationary pressure.

In Yugoslavia, in contrast, the inflation rates for both producer and retail prices between 1980 and 1984 were sharply higher than in 1975–79, and they accelerated toward the end of the period. Sharp and sustained contractions in real credit availability and domestic demand were accompanied by high and accelerating rates of inflation. Although paradoxical when viewed from the traditional monetarist models on which IMF advice rests, this result is consistent with a variety of empirical studies of the inflation process in Yugoslavia that show a weak link between demand conditions and prices and a strong cost-push pattern of inflation (see, for example, Tyson 1977b; Tyson and Neuberger 1979; and Mencinger 1974). If these studies, based on past Yugoslav behavior, are a guide to what happened in the 1980 to 1984 period, then it seems clear that the real devaluation policy specified as part of IMF conditionality aggravated inflationary pressure as most Yugoslav critics feared it would. The real interest rate policy imposed in 1984 may also have had a similar effect by increasing the nominal costs of enterprise capital, thereby exerting upward pressure on producer prices. Finally, IMF pressure to terminate an overall price freeze and to raise the prices of certain basic services also contributed to an upward jump in the inflation rate in 1984. Overall, it seems very likely that, as a result of some of the conditions adopted in the IMF agreements with Yugoslavia, the inflation rate during the 1980 to 1984 period was higher than it would have been otherwise. If the IMF had accorded a higher priority to reducing inflation and, if it had dropped its traditional excess demand interpretation of inflationary pressure, it might have been able to develop alternative conditions that achieved the same degree of success in reducing domestic demand and improving external performance at a lower inflationary cost.

5. CONCLUSIONS

Our review of IMF conditionality in Yugoslavia and Hungary during the 1980 to 1984 period provides partial answers to the questions we posed at the beginning of the paper. First, the basic objectives of IMF conditionality in both countries were a reduction in domestic demand and an improvement in external performance. Most of the conditions actually imposed tended to support these objectives although sometimes the pursuit of other objectives, particularly the reduction of price distortions, actually made the realization of the primary objectives more difficult in the short run.

Second, there was nothing unique about most of the forms of IMF conditionality in either Hungary or Yugoslavia. The conditions chosen seemed to rest on the assumption that the traditional demand-management explanations of and cures for balance-of-payments deficits drawn from the experiences of market economies applied to both Hungary and Yugoslavia despite their unique institutional settings.

Third, our analysis indicates that IMF conditionality did affect what actually happened in both countries to some extent. Both countries benefited from the additional finance made available as a result of IMF approval of their austerity plans. In Hungary, IMF pressure for a reduction in real wages probably played a role in the reduction that actually occurred in 1983 and 1984, and IMF pressure for an exchange rate adjustment may have played a role in the 1983–84 depreciation of the forint. In Yugoslavia, IMF conditionality was behind the introduction of real exchange rate and real interest rate policies and the relaxation of price controls. As a consequence of these policies, the inflation rate in Yugoslavia was probably higher than it otherwise would have been and export performance may have been stronger. Overall, as might be expected given the relative negotiating strength of both countries vis-à-vis the IMF, our findings indicate that IMF influence on what actually happened was much stronger in Yugoslavia than in Hungary.

Finally, in both countries the major results of austerity—a disproportionate share of the cutback in domestic demand on investment, stagnation, or cutbacks in convertible currency imports, and an expansion of convertible currency exports—were the result of domestic policy choices taken in response to external capital market constraints and were not fundamentally affected by IMF involvement. Moreover, the authorities in both countries continued to rely on traditional administrative means to realize these results. Investment was restricted by direct controls over the use of enterprise funds and quantitative credit rationing in accordance with national or regional priorities. Imports were subject to a variety of formal and informal quantitative rationing methods, and exports were encouraged by external pressure on enterprises to realize enterprise-specific export targets and to link export earnings to their own import needs.

In the absence of reforms to harden enterprise-budget constraints and create significant foreign exchange and capital markets, administrative measures of this type perforce remained more effective at realizing macroeconomic targets than IMF policy conditions aimed at eliminating price distortions. In addition, such measures allowed the state and party authorities to continue to guide the distribution of resources rather than to cede their authority to the dictates of market forces as standard IMF prescriptions would have them do.

PART III

Structural Adjustment and Intra-CMEA Economic Relations

CHAPTER 4

Industrial Policy in Eastern Europe

Josef C. Brada

INTRODUCTION

This study examines the formulation and implementation of industrial policy in six East European countries, Bulgaria, Czechoslovakia, the German Democratic Republic, Hungary, Poland, and Romania. Industrial policy is taken to mean something more specific and at the same time broader than structural policy. The latter may be viewed as planners' choices about the relative growth rates of various sectors of industry. While industrial policy also implies choices about the rate of expansion or contraction of various economic activities, it attempts to provide a rationale for making such choices by evaluating the ability of individual sectors to promote specific objectives. Among these objectives are domestic growth, export competitiveness, energy and raw materials utilization, and the performance of downstream or consuming sectors. Industrial policy also differs from planners' expressions of preferences about structural change because industrial policy involves the creation of new, often extra-plan, mechanisms for promoting the development of priority sectors, for allocating resources to them, and for linking them to international markets.

Pressure on the East European countries to formulate and implement effective industrial policies intensified sharply in the 1970s and continued unabated in the 1980s. The slowdown in economic growth brought about by the exhaustion of the extensive factors of growth and the general unwillingness to implement meaningful economic reforms during this time left industrial policy as one of the few attractive alternatives for attaining sustained growth. On the international front, a number of factors induced East European policymakers to focus on industrial policy. Not the least of these international developments was the continuing success of the Japanese economy—attributed by many observers to that country's implementation of a comprehensive industrial policy. Secondly there was a desire to take advantage of the scientific-technical revolution and to close the technological gap between the East and the West. This was particularly important for the export industries in these countries, since these industries were facing increased competition on Western markets from the newly industrializing countries and on the CMEA market from the exports of Western Europe, the United States, and Japan. The increase in energy and raw material prices created a need to promote new, less energy- and material-intensive industries while dealing with the contraction or reinvigoration of those that were rendered uncompetitive on world markets or uneconomic due to their excessive consumption of imported inputs.

In the early 1970s international forces tended to facilitate the implementation of industrial policy. The easing of tensions between East and West facilitated the flow of equipment and technology from the latter to the former while the buildup of deposits in Western banks provided the wherewithal to finance such imports. In the latter part of the decade and in the early 1980s the situation was reversed. Credits to Eastern Europe dried up and, as the East European countries sought to reduce their debts, imports of technology and equipment were sharply reduced. At the same time the need to run balance-of-payments surpluses reduced the availability of domestically produced investment goods, further complicating the implementation of industrial policy by reducing the volume of resources that could be devoted to its implementation, thus forcing ever more difficult choices on planners.

It is not surprising that within this complex environment the policies adopted by the six countries studied in this chapter—varied as they are in terms of level of development, quality of decisionmaking, economic system, and national aspirations—should differ in terms of sectors selected for promotion, of means adopted for allocating resources to these sectors, and in the ultimate success of their efforts.

The next section sets out the bases of industrial policy and develops an analytical framework within which the industrial policies of East European economies can be compared and evaluated. The policies themselves are set out in the following section. Next, I examine and analyze the available evidence on structural change in the sample countries. The chapter then closes with some conclusions on industrial policy in Eastern Europe.

To this tour d'horizon I must add a caveat. Although the plan of attack is comparative, there are inherent limitations. Some of these limitations stem from intercountry differences in the quality of published economic discourse on the subject and also differences in the conceptualization of the questions surrounding industrial policy. Similarly, the quantitative analysis of industrial policy is hampered by differences in the amount of data available regarding the industrial structure of each country. Despite these limitations, a comparative overview of industrial policy in all the East European countries is critical to the understanding of the changing industrial structure in Eastern Europe and of the evolving trade relations within CMEA as well as between CMEA and the rest of the world.

AN ECONOMIC BASIS FOR INDUSTRIAL POLICY

The objective of industrial policy is to improve economic performance by favoring, either directly or indirectly, certain sectors of the economy. The sectors thus favored are expected to grow more rapidly or decline more slowly than they would without aid. The improvement in economic performance, whether judged by aggregate growth, export growth or import substitution, productivity, or employment, thus results from the fact that the favored sectors are larger than they otherwise would be.

Varieties of Industrial Policy

The promotion of favored sectors of the economy can be achieved in a number of ways. The broadest conception of industrial policy is one that is economy-wide and that seeks to improve the functioning of the economic mechanism. In market economies such policies would eliminate market imperfections by dismantling trade barriers, improving the working of the capital market, promoting labor mobility, and fostering competition to the advantage of dynamic sectors whose growth could be promoted by the more efficient operation of markets. In planned economies, economic reform plays an analogous role. To the extent that shortcomings in the system of economic management impede the transfer of resources to potentially dynamic sectors or fail to stimulate the rapid adoption of new products and technologies, the system may be viewed as a barrier to the growth of the most promising sectors of the economy. Reforms, whether centralizing or decentralizing, that improve the system's functioning in these areas are thus also a form of industrial policy.

A more specific form of support for favored sectors is one that promotes activities that are thought to especially favor them. Among such policies are support for independent research and development activities or increased state activity in the field of research. Since new sectors are often viewed as technology based, the presumption is that a greater volume of research and development activity will be particularly favorable to their growth. Efforts to increase the volume of investment are another means of promoting emerging sectors by making the needed inputs more readily available. Forming pools of venture capital that are earmarked for priority sectors supplements such efforts by directing a larger share of total investment to emerging sectors. Governments also can rely on a wide variety of policies in the area of human resources: training programs for workers, efforts to increase labor mobility, and wide-ranging educational programs. Finally, the creation of infrastructure thought favorable to the emergence of priority sectors also falls into this category of industrial policy.

More focused industrial policies are those that seek to assist specific industries or sectors of industries directly. Such policies may involve fiscal assistance, trade policy assistance, better access to inputs, and the creation of infrastructure by the government. Efforts to promote mergers, to limit competition among firms in the sector, and to provide for controlled access to foreign technology are all used to promote sectoral growth. In the countries discussed in this essay, the need to achieve economies of scale may imply that policies aimed at the promotion of a sector effectively imply the support of an individual enterprise, since it may either completely dominate its domestic competitors or have none. Such emphasis on firm-specific sources of comparative advantage has found theoretical support in the work of Krugman (1980).

The Need for Industrial Policies in Centrally Planned Economies

The argument for the use of industrial policy in market economies rests largely on the existence of market imperfections that create differences between private and social costs and benefits. Among the more germane ones are economies of scale, whether at the firm or sectoral, assembly or component production level. Other nonconvexities in production include learning by doing and firm-specific advantages resulting from size, past research, and experience. There are also imperfections in labor markets such as the under-provision of general human capital by firms to workers, or the destruction of firm-specific human capital in declining sectors. Similarly, proponents of industrial policy point to imperfections in capital markets that may favor established firms over nascent ones.

There may also be imperfections in output markets. One of these is that the social benefits (or spillovers) from the output of one sector are not reflected in the price that consumers of the sector's product pay. Computers, for example, are a product believed to be important to the efficiency of other industries and to the ability of entire economies to remain competitive and contemporary on a global basis. Second, there may be possibilities for creating market imperfections by gaining a monopolistic or oligopolistic market position, possibly through the strategic anticipation of the workings of the international product life cycle.

The industrial policy of the planned economy can be understood in two ways. First, since economic activity is planned, the state has a de facto industrial policy that operates at all levels from that of the economy down to the level of the industry and indeed the enterprise. In such a conception of industrial policy, which equates industrial policy with structural policy, nonconvexities that cause market imperfections in market economies may also exist, but they do not cause any difficulties under socialism. Consequently there should be no need to introduce industrial policy measures beyond the economic plan itself. Such a view rests on the belief that planners are sufficiently aware of convexities and can construct a plan that takes them into account. It also assumes that there is nothing in the nature of the economic mechanism that hampers the implementation of the plan—or that whatever elements do hamper the implementation of the plan do not hamper disproportionately those activities related to structural change and innovation. If these conditions are met, then the structural aspects of plans would represent the entirety of industrial policy in a planned economy.

Evidence abounds that these assumptions are not valid. Enterprises are unwilling to make use of new technology; difficulties in the vertical coordination of production preclude the creation of economies of scale and specialization; vested labor, regional and industrial ministry interests hamper the movement of factors of production from one industry to another. All these are well-known phenomena in planned economies, and, even if one were to grant planners sufficient information to formulate an optimal structural policy, it is evident that there are important forces at work impeding the implementation of the structure determining aspects of the plan.

There is also indirect evidence of these barriers. That is, there exists in many planned economies an industrial policy that supplements the plan and the mechanisms that are employed to promote plan implementation. Among the measures used to aid in the implementation of industrial policy outside the normal mechanisms are organizational changes, priority access to labor, capital and imported inputs, and subsidization of production and research (Brada and Montias 1984, 1985). Thus it is important to recognize that industrial policy in Eastern Europe operates both at the level of the plan and at the level of semiautonomous policies and allocation mechanisms that operate outside the plan and the existing economic mechanism.

Components of Industrial Policy

A useful way of viewing industrial policy in a comparative setting is to divide it into the four following elements:

Selecting Industries for Expansion or Shrinkage. As discussed in the previous section, there are some economic bases for industrial policy in the planned economy; to these it is necessary to add political ones. Moreover, the economic reasons for choosing sectors for promotion are somewhat subjective, so that the optimism of policymakers is given greater leeway than in other areas of economic policy. Thus an effective industrial policy is one that makes realistic assessments of the possibilities of achieving economies of scale, advantages in imperfect product markets and firm-specific competitive strengths. Similarly governments must be willing to apply similar criteria to sectors that no longer appear to be competitive and are in need of either support or elimination.

Selecting Markets. In selecting the industries that are to receive government support, the characteristics of the production process are of course important. The government must seek out industries where productivity and productivity growth are high, and where economies of scale will create the potential to preempt rivals from other nations. However, the demand-side characteristics of these industries are just as important. That is, the income elasticity of new products ought to be high, as should the price elasticity of market share of established products. Industries aimed at the leading edge of the product life cycle in advanced economies will benefit from longer lives than industries geared to older products, since, as advanced-country markets become saturated, the markets for these products in less developed countries begin to expand.

In the case of Japan, for example, the postwar decision to promote capital-intensive industries was as much influenced by their appealing supply-side characteristics as by the realization that—at the time decisions on industrial policy were made—the United States was the only large market open to Japanese exports. The Japanese predilection toward high productivity growth sectors was reinforced by the need to serve a large, sophisticated market with high income elasticity of demand for goods produced under conditions of increasing returns to scale, or by industries characterized by relatively uncompetitive price policies.

Allocating Resources. Even if the government is able to identify winners and losers, it faces the problem of reallocating resources from the latter to the former. Existing industries have a vested interest in remaining in existence and both management and labor are likely to exert strong pressure to turn industrial policy into a policy of protecting declining industries. Similarly, representatives of industries viewing themselves as potential winners are likely to pressure government decisionmakers to make allocations favorable to them. Since established sectors are likely to have greater political leverage than nascent or nonexistent ones, the possibilities for developing new industries would appear to be limited. Moreover, given the political demands of many labor and management advocates from different sectors, the government may be forced to disseminate the access to additional capital and labor among too many industries, thus precluding the possibilities of capturing economies of scale.

Generating Production and Exports. To the extent that the government is able to direct resources toward favored sectors the possibility of a successful industrial policy exists. The achievement of success will depend on effective production, so that economies of scale and potential productivity gains are realized. This requires appropriate management skills as well as the ability to create the necessary technology or to master technology imported from abroad. Once produced, goods must be marketed effectively in the target countries.

A Survey of Individual National Policies

Bulgaria

Of the CMEA countries, Bulgaria has been the most consistent in the choice of sectors selected for preferential treatment and has maintained the clearest relationship between the demands of its target markets and the choice of priority sectors. At the same time, Bulgaria's industrial policy more nearly resembles a structural policy; for much of the period under review there appears to be no extraordinary changes in economic system, organization, and incentives to favor priority sectors' access to resources. In part this may be due to Bulgaria's relatively low level of development that facilitated the expansion of priority industries through the central allocation of new resources rather than through the reallocation of existing ones.

Although Bulgaria's priority sectors, metallurgy, machine building, electronics, and chemicals do not appear to differ much from the traditional concept of a socialist development strategy, Bulgaria has succeeded in developing narrower specializations in several of these sectors that have enabled it to achieve economies of scale, firm-specific advantages, and the ability to apply new technologies with a higher payoff in terms of trade performance than achieved by other socialist countries.

The least successful example of Bulgarian industrial policy has been metallurgy. With Soviet assistance two large steelmaking complexes were constructed; the Lenin works in Pernik, and in the 1960s the Kremikovitsi works outside Sofia. The latter complex was constructed in the expectation of the development of local ore deposits which failed to materialize, forcing the complex to rely on imports of both enriched ores and coking coal from the Soviet Union. Due to high transportation costs for these inputs within Bulgaria, the complex has not been profitable and as a consequence appears not to have operated at full capacity in the 1970s (Lampe 1986, pp. 167–68). Like steel firms in many other countries, Kremikovitsi has received government support for its operations and has been permitted to pay above-norm wages in order to retain its work force. During the 1970s the government injected fresh funds into the complex in order to increase its capacity for working the steel produced into pipes, rods, and other finished products (Jackson 1981, p. 610). At the same time a new steel complex is being constructed near Burgas on the Black Sea coast. While the new mill's location should make it less costly to operate with imported inputs, metallurgy cannot be regarded as a successful example of industrial policy on the basis of dynamism or contribution to export competitiveness.

Machinery has been a much more dynamic and successful example of the promotion of sectors for both structure-determining and export purposes. Indeed, Bulgaria ranks only behind Czechoslovakia and the GDR in the share of machinery in total exports. During the 1970s machinery's share in exports increased from 30 to 50 percent and by 1985 had reached 56 percent. Given Bulgaria's relatively high export to NMP ratio, this suggests that a large part of Bulgarian machinery production is intended for export markets. The centerpiece of this export-oriented machinery sector is Balkancar that, with 45,000 employees, accounts for 20 percent of Bulgarian industrial output, making it the largest industrial enterprise in Bulgaria (Lampe 1986, p. 176). Balkancar is most famous for its forklift trucks, of which it is the world's largest producer, but it also produces a wide range of other material handling equipment. About three-fourths of Balkancar's production is exported, mainly to the Soviet Union and to the other CMEA countries. Given the scale of production and Balkancar's experience and reputation, it seems reasonable to attribute its success not only to economies of scale, but also to firm-specific advantages of name recognition and learning by doing. Some of Balkancar's competitive position must also be attributed to Bulgaria's efforts to prevent the development of competitors within CMEA by appealing to CMEA specialization principles and by lobbying against import-competing investments in forklift truck production within CMEA. Lampe (1986 p. 176) reports that the Bulgarians persuaded the Soviet Union not to carry out a plan to construct a large plant for the manufacture of forklift trucks in the USSR. Bulgaria also appears to have been successful in developing the production of metalworking machinery, trucks, buses, ships, and agricultural machinery, often either on the basis of CMEA specialization agreements or of bilateral agreements with the Soviet Union. The latter have been particularly important for the expansion of the production and export of components for Soviet enterprises, as in the production of automobiles and computers in the Soviet Union. As a result, in 1981, 37 percent of Bulgarian machinery exports were covered by CMEA specialization agreements, while the Soviet Union imported about three-fourths of these.

Another successful area of emphasis has been in electronics, especially in computers. The latter are viewed as important for structure-determining reasons, being viewed as significant for the development of other high technology activities such as the manufacture of robots as well as for the management of industrial operations and agro-industrial complexes. Like machinery, electronics have also been a dynamic component of exports, largely to CMEA, with the Soviet Union the main buyer. Bulgaria accounts for about 40 percent of the CMEA's output of microcomputers, and Bulgarian diskettes and personal computers appear to be relatively well received in other CMEA markets.

In the late 1960s and early 1970s Bulgaria, like many other CMEA countries, also gave priority to the chemical industry largely due to its structure-determining characteristics. Until the mid-1970s both production and exports grew rapidly. However, in the face of worldwide overcapacity in the petrochemical industry and the limitation on the supply of Soviet oil that represented the feedstock for the Bulgarian chemical industry, this sector has languished since the mid-1970s (Jackson 1986a).

While the organization of Bulgarian industry and reforms of the planning system have generally followed East European trends—including the formation of associations and the declining emphasis on physical indicators—there is little evidence in Bulgarian writings that such measures had any specific elements intended to facilitate the promotion of priority sectors. The reform measures announced in 1986, on the other hand, do have the specific intention of promoting the effective and speedy application of scientific breakthroughs to industry. The reform measures create three superministries—one of which deals with the economy and thus controls all industry—hopefully eliminating some of the autarchic tendencies of individual industrial ministries. Such a superministry should be able to shift resources from one sector to another to promote the growth of priority sectors, especially in view of the simultaneous downgrading of the state planning committee. Another Bulgarian institutional innovation for promoting technological progress is support for small or out-of-plan enterprises. Through the Bulgarian Industrial Association units of enterprises can obtain funds and resources to support proposals for productive activities outside the plan. The objective is to introduce an element of flexibility into the allocation of resources, particularly to promote the adoption of advanced technology and to promote hard-currency exports.

Czechoslovakia

In Czechoslovakia a declining growth rate, the exhaustion of labor reserves, and deteriorating international competitiveness made the development of an industrial policy of critical importance, particularly because there was no possibility of an economy-wide reform after 1968.[1] Moreover, unlike Bulgaria, Czechoslovakia was an industrialized economy and therefore industrial policy had to be more focused than the more general industrialization drive in Bulgaria.

An explicit industrial policy was first formulated for the fifth five-year plan (FYP), 1970–75. The objectives of this policy were to "concentrate scientific-technical forces on a limited number of objectives where [Czechoslovakia] seeks and has the prerequisites for reaching leading technical and economic levels or achieving important noneconomic objectives" (Vavroušek 1986). Policy objectives were organized into eighteen state programs for technological progress that were then broken down into some sixty programs of most important structural changes. The actual implementation of the program at the level of associations and enterprises was embodied in hundreds of tasks or assignments. Coordination of each program was assigned to a general director who was to be responsible for both the conception and execution of activities needed to carry out the program. In 1973 these directorships were abolished and the programs fell under the aegis of newly formed departments of the Federal Ministry (later State Committee) for Technology and Investment, a change in organization that opened the programs to parochial interference by branch ministries (Vavroušek 1986, pp. 848–49).

The conception of industrial policy in Czechoslovakia suffered from two faults. First, the criteria for determining which sectors were to be promoted were never clearly articulated, and thus the choice of the state programs in 1970 was an intuitive one made on the "basis of practical experience" (Vavroušek 1986, p. 848).[2] Despite this rather ad hoc choice of priority sectors, the list of state programs for technological progress remained largely unaltered for over fifteen years. A second problem was that these programs were developed outside the normal process of drawing up the five-year plans. Thus, although approved at the time of the passage of the FYP into law, the development programs were never considered during the discussion of the plan, nor were they an organic part of it (Bačková 1986). This led to excessive investments during the implementation of the fifth FYP as well as a general scramble for resources on the part of enterprises. In subsequent FYPs the coordination of investment outlays was improved, but little else was done to bring program tasks into the ambit of the plan. Moreover, enterprises participating in these programs—28 percent of all Czechoslovak enterprises in 1976–80 and 39 percent in 1981–85— had special allocations for hard currency imports, priority access to labor (Altmann 1982), as well as special allocations of investment resources.

Among the sectors included in the state programs were electronics and electrical engineering, computers and cybernetics, chemicals, nuclear technology, metallurgy, and machine building to name only some of the more traditional favorites of Czechoslovak planners. Somewhat more surprising choices were programs to make better use of forest resources, to improve materials handling, to achieve self-sufficiency in animal feeds, and to improve food supplies. Clearly not all programs were accorded the same importance and consequently the same level of resources, and by the time of the 1981–85 FYP a number of the state programs had only a few ongoing tasks, while others served merely as umbrella designations for uncoordinated research and development efforts at the enterprise or association level.

Despite the lack of clear-cut criteria for selecting priority sectors, the disfunctional recentralization of the Czechoslovak economic system, and the excessively broad themes of the state programs, there are a number of positive features in Czechoslovak industrial policy that bear mention. The first of these is a consistency in terms of programs promoted and in terms of the target market. Although the number of tasks at the level of the most important structural changes has been reduced over the years, it appears that key programs in nuclear energy, machine building, and electronics have continued to receive support for a significant period of time. A second area of consistency is the choice of the target market that has clearly been CMEA and the Soviet Union in particular. Like Bulgaria, Czechoslovakia has assiduously cultivated the Soviet market, seeking to obtain a secure market for its products through Soviet-Czechoslovak bilateral agreements on product specialization, cooperation in research and development, and on trade as well as through similar multilateral agreements with all CMEA members (Blaha 1986; Terek 1985; and Skolkova 1986).

The program that best fits the popularly conceived objectives of industrial policy—and one that in many ways may be both the largest and most successful of the Czechoslovak development programs—is the nuclear energy program (Kucera 1984). Czechoslovakia undertook to develop the capacity to construct nuclear power reactors of the Soviet VVER–440 (Pressurized Water Reactor) design and subsequently its larger version the VVER–1000. The program was based on traditional Czechoslovak skills in metallurgy and heavy engineering. At first the program concentrated on components such as pressure vessels, tubing, and turbines, but has been considerably broadened over time, so that Czechoslovakia is the major co-constructor, along with the Soviet Union, of nuclear power plants within CMEA. In view of the growing demand for nuclear power in the region, and the improbability of serious competition from suppliers outside CMEA, Czechoslovakia has achieved a significant monopoly position in an important and growing market.

German Democratic Republic

As in the case of Czechoslovakia, slow economic growth, the exhaustion of labor reserves exacerbated by the loss of workers to the West, and declining export competitiveness led to the formulation of a comprehensive industrial policy. Although reforms had begun in 1963, the pace of economic reform accelerated sharply in 1967 as part of the effort to implement an industrial policy based on the fullest use of science and technology. The strategy of the GDR's industrial policy was expressed by the slogan "uberholen ohne einzuholen," which may be translated as, "to surpass without equaling," indicative of a desire not merely to catch up technologically with advanced Western countries but rather to surpass them through bold technological breakthroughs.

This policy was to be implemented by means of systemic changes, by organizational restructuring of industrial units, and by providing favorable access to resources for enterprises engaged in priority activities, the structure determining tasks. The most significant organizational change involved the formation of industrial associations, called VVBS (associations of national enterprises) in the GDR, that took over many of the functions of the industrial ministries. Subordinate to the VVBS were the Kombinate, or combines, formed from large enterprises and their subcontractors, and enterprises. The VVB organized the productive activities of its subordinate units, imposed targets on them and could transfer investment and wage funds from one unit to another. It also financed and organized research and development activities (Granick 1975, pp. 138–44). There is little evidence that such a concentration of industrial production reflected an industrial policy geared toward capturing economies of scale in production. Rather, given the science-based nature of the GDR's policy, such concentration was viewed as valuable because it led to economies of scale in research and development. On the other hand, the organization of the combines was viewed as assisting a science-based industrial policy by coordinating relations between suppliers and consumers of industrial components (Bentley 1984, chapter 6).

The formation of the VVBS was accompanied by systemic changes, although these were, somewhat paradoxically, less important for priority than for nonpriority sectors. Profitability replaced output as the main indicator of enterprise performance and the tautness of plans was reduced so that VVBS could shift resources in order to increase profitability. A centrally determined and VVB-specific proportion of profits was retained to finance investment. VVBS also assumed responsibility for setting prices. Structure determining tasks, and the units charged with executing them, remained under central control. In contrast to the general use of financial levers to guide enterprise performance, structure determining tasks were centrally planned in physical terms that then served as targets for producing units. Thus units engaged in structure determining tasks had less leeway to make adjustments that would increase profitability and thus their investment funds. On the other hand, central direction in physical terms may have been viewed as a useful way of breaking enterprise resistance to the introduction of new technologies and products (Bentley 1984, chapter 7).

However much units in priority sectors may have suffered from their inability to adjust in order to earn higher profits, they benefited from priority access to resources. In terms of bank credits, enterprises engaged in structure determining tasks were not subject to bank-imposed penalties for low profitability and also had preferential access to credits. The number of workers that priority enterprises could employ was determined only by the state planning commission and by the appropriate vvb, whereas labor allocations to nonpriority enterprises were subject to regional economic councils. Moreover, local authorities assisted priority firms in attracting their allotment of workers by financing workers' housing. Finally, within the supply system, enterprises engaged in structure determining tasks had priority for the supply of inputs over other enterprises, except those providing raw materials and inputs needed for the normal functioning of the economy.

This experiment with an ambitious science-based industrial policy implemented by centralized directive, but within a relatively decentralized environment, was short-lived. This may partly have reflected the transfer of leadership from Ulbricht to Honecker. In any case, amidst complaints of excessive levels of investment and shortages of raw materials, all production, rather than only that of priority products, was centralized and subject to physical planning. In 1972 structure determining was dropped as an appellation for priority sectors and replaced by the less urgent adjective, important. With the increased centralization, vvbs lost many of their former powers and during the course of the decade were disbanded with their functions taken over by the branch ministries or by the combines. Similarly, the use of financial levers declined to be replaced by the volume of production, value added, and material intensity as the primary enterprise indicators (Csaba 1983, pp. 36–37). The process of forming the combines was completed in the early 1980s, and the state undertook a series of measures to exploit the new organizational form. The Kombinaten were given broad responsibilities for research and development. The hope was both to make research and development more relevant to industrial needs and to speed its diffusion. The fact that in most combines the director was also the director of the leading enterprise ensured that the Kombinat's technological decisions were made by someone with practical experience.[3] The combines were also given the right to engage in foreign trade transactions, under the supervision of the Ministry of Foreign Trade, and the responsibility within the kombinat for overseeing export performance fell on the deputy director. All Kombinaten were expected to export, and export performance influenced their investment and bonus funds. Despite this wholesale organizational and systemic overhaul, a number of elements of the original industrial policy remain. These include slack planning, emphasis on the application of science and technology, and a belief that large economic units are best suited to the discovery and application of new technologies.

Unfortunately, while the means for implementing industrial policy in the GDR have been amply documented, the objectives of this policy, in terms of sectors to be promoted and markets to be served, can only be conjectured. Between 1967 and 1971 the structure determining tasks were a secret and in the mid-1970s the GDR ceased publishing a sectoral breakdown of industrial investment. Nevertheless, one can infer the GDR's structural priorities both from the statements of the leadership and by examining rates of growth of output of various sectors of industry on the assumption that priority sectors did grow more rapidly than others. During 1967–70, the period of attempted leapfrogging of world technological levels, fast-growing sectors included chemicals, especially petrochemicals and pharmaceuticals; machine building, especially machine tools, chemical plants, and agricultural machinery; and electronics and instruments including data processing machines, fine mechanical optical apparatus, and process control equipment. In the 1970s lignite and brown coal production clearly became priority sectors, despite their incongruence with the high-tech profile of industrial policy. In chemicals the stress on petrochemicals abated but pharmaceuticals continued to be emphasized. In engineering the emphasis on machine tools and complete plants and refineries appears to have been supplemented by cars, railroad rolling stock, and ships. The emphasis on electronics continues, as this sector is viewed as critical not only for the country's export performance but also for the general level of competitiveness that can be achieved by other sectors of the economy through the application of computers, robots, and other electronic devices (Machowski 1985, pp. 49–51). Whether all of these have been or still are the objects of industrial policy is unclear, and thus it is difficult to assess whether industrial policy has had a favorable effect on the economy. On the positive side, the performance of the economy in the 1980s compares favorably with that of the other countries in our sample. Nevertheless, there are expressions of dissatisfaction in the GDR over the inability to narrow the range of engineering products and to effectively link science and industry, two objectives of any science-based industrial policy.

Hungary

Hungary has pursued industrial policies both under the traditional system of central planning and during the period of the New Economic Mechanism (NEM).[4] Thus the Hungarian experience is a particularly instructive one in that it offers some insight into the possible role of economic reform as a general industrial policy aimed at a more rational use of resources and an increase in factor mobility.

As early as the 1950s Hungary chose to promote large-scale production of diesel engines, motor vehicles, machine tools, telecommunications equipment, and machinery for the food industry. The impetus for these programs came from the existence of a large market for such products in the Soviet Union and what the Hungarian authorities perceived as the existence of firm-specific advantages and the potential for capturing economies of scale. These efforts proved, to a large extent, to be unsuccessful (Schweitzer 1980). Because policies were imposed from above, anticipated firm-specific advantages were not carried forward to the new products. Moreover, the high degree of vertical integration of Hungarian enterprises forced the enterprises to produce most of the required components. Thus potential economies of scale at the assembly stage were offset by diseconomies encountered in the production of components.

With the introduction of NEM came new instruments for the promotion of priority sectors. Capital was provided by central development programs (CDPS) and by means of credits, taxes, and subsidies that were set at the level of the firm (A. Balassa 1975). Six CDPS were planned for 1971–75. They included the expansion of the natural gas network; the development of the aluminum, petrochemical, and motor vehicle industries; the promotion of computer manufacture and utilization; and the use of lightweight structures in construction. Some sectors, such as gas, computers, and petrochemicals, were to provide externalities for other sectors of the economy; vehicles, aluminum, petrochemicals, and computers were to be exported to CMEA markets; and computer production was expected to replace imports from the West. Neither the vagueness of these criteria nor the domestic and CMEA orientation of the program survived the impact of the oil price shock.

At the October 1977 meeting of the Central Committee of the Hungarian Socialist Workers' Party a new approach to industrial policy was put forward (Nemeth 1977). This stressed energy production and utilization, engineering, light industry, and agriculture as priority sectors. Within each industry production was to be narrowed in order to focus on modern high quality products that could compete on both Western and CMEA markets. A special fund of 45 billion forints was established to finance investments that would increase exports to the West.

Despite these changes, Hungarian industrial policy has continued to be the object of a lively debate within Hungary. The emphasis on economies of scale as a criterion has been criticized because the vertical integration of Hungarian firms and the practical impossibility of an effective intra-CMEA supply of components prohibit the achievement of such economies (Roman 1978). The emphasis on CMEA as a reference market has also been the subject of some controversy, in that it is viewed as an undemanding market that does not force Hungarian producers to meet world standards. While it is true that the CMEA market absorbs many low quality goods that are at the mature stage of their product life cycle, it clearly would not reject modern high quality goods. The problem then would seem to be one caused by the domestic system rather than by the characteristics of the CMEA market. Finally NEM itself has been regarded as a barrier to industrial policy in that investment continues to be more centralized de facto than the blueprint of the NEM suggests.

Poland[5]

Poland's effort to formulate a coherent industrial policy based on specialization dates from 1968 when Gierek proposed that foreign trade become the determining factor in Polish economic progress, which to date had been disappointing. Certain branches of industry were to become leading sectors whose above-average growth would pull the remainder of the economy to a higher growth path. These branches were to be selected for their ability to earn foreign exchange effectively and to penetrate world markets. Although all enterprises would be expected to seek to export, it was proposed that within each priority branch one or more enterprises would be singled out for the production of exports. Priority sectors and firms were to benefit from earmarked investment outlays and from special access to bank credits and foreign exchange.

The selection of sectors to be so favored sparked a debate between minimalists, maximalists, and compromisers. Minimalists argued for the promotion of industries where economies of scale and firm-specific advantages already existed, as in shipbuilding, railroad cars, construction equipment, and textiles from natural fibers. Maximalists, on the other hand, wanted to promote structure-determining sectors, such as electronics, nuclear technology, chemicals, and synthetic fibers. The compromisers proposed criteria that looked to foreign market conditions, the growth or size of world demand, as criteria for selecting industries to promote.

The proposed policy was never implemented. In part this was due to the eagerness of all firms and sectors to become a priority sector and thus to benefit from the advantages offered to the favored firms. Excess production was to be favored, which of course meant that, in fact, none could be favored. In any case, the Polish government had by then adopted a macroeconomic strategy that obviated the need to make choices among sectors. All Polish industry could be favored by means of imports of Western technology and equipment. However, this dispersion of resources failed to produce any economies of scale, firm-specific advantages, or spillovers to other sectors.

As in several other countries in our sample, there are serious weaknesses in the implementation of industrial policies in Poland. In part the weaknesses stem from similar causes, among them the unwillingness or inability of central authorities to deny resources to entrenched ministry and enterprise interests, the lack of adequate incentives to promote efficiency and innovation, and general macroeconomic disequilibrium. In contrast to the lack of strong incentives for participating in industrial policy apparent in Czechoslovak experience, Poland appears to have had excessive incentives for enterprise participation and a faulty or ineffective means of screening out those enterprises unlikely to be successful. There was also less consistency in industrial policy: Polish criteria for choosing priority sectors were unsettled and changed over time. The most striking difference between the industrial policies of the countries examined so far and Polish industrial policies, however, was that these countries' choice of sectors appeared to have been made with reference to the needs of the CMEA market while, at least in the 1970s, Polish industrial policy was being framed with a view toward developing the capacity to export to Western markets. Despite these differences, Poland's choices of industries to develop overlaps those of the other CMEA countries' list in a number of categories including cars, machinery, and electronics.

Romania

Industrial policy in Romania has been strongly influenced by environmental and foreign policy factors. Like Bulgaria, Romania began socialist development as a relatively agrarian economy, and thus industrial policy was more a structural one based on the rapid expansion of industry through large infusions of capital and of labor released from agriculture. At the same time the industrial sectors that grew most rapidly partially reflected Romania's natural resource endowments. Unlike Bulgaria, Romania neither sought to create special niches to exploit within the branches of industry associated with traditional socialist industrialization, nor selected priority sectors with a view toward the needs of the CMEA market. Rather, similarly to Poland, domestic needs, possibilities for exporting to developing countries and the developed market economies, as well as the possibilities for importing machinery and technology from the West predominated in decisions regarding priority sectors. The sectors demonstrating most rapid growth since the 1960s have been electrical power generation, metallurgy, machine building, chemicals, and clothing and textiles.

The development of the metallurgical sector in Romania has played a pivotal role in Romania's developmental and foreign policies. It was the Romanian-Soviet dispute over the expansion of steelmaking capacity in Romania that focused attention on Romania's conflicts with CMEA and helped to turn Romanian trade toward the West. Despite a dependence on imports of ore and coking coal, Romania has continued to push for the expansion of steelmaking, to the point where domestic demand, in the aggregate if not in terms of individual steel products, is more than met by the output of the Romanian steel industry. In recent years efforts have been made not only to continue the expansion of steel production so that Romania's steel production should exceed, on a per capita basis, that of all other CMEA countries save Czechoslovakia, but also to improve the product mix of the industry (Jackson 1977, pp. 914–15). The latter goal appears to be motivated by the desire to reduce imports of specialty steels, steel plate, and steel forms.

Like the development of the steel industry, the development of the machine building sector in Romania was based on a strategy of import substitution. At first Romanian machinery production was characterized by long production runs of fairly simple machines geared primarily to the needs of the domestic market. In the 1970s a trend could be discerned toward the production of more sophisticated machinery, including cars, aircraft, computer peripherals, tractors, and electronic equipment. In these sectors, promoted in large part on the basis of their structure-determining characteristics, an interesting form of support was the extensive use of foreign technology and equipment. Indeed to some extent Romanian efforts to industrialize by using Western technology and credits parallel those of Poland. There are, however, important differences between the role of the West in each country's industrial policy. In the case of Romania, there was a rather creative approach to the use of joint ventures and industrial cooperation with Western firms to facilitate technology transfer and the export of industrial products to the West, although, in contrast to Poland, the actual amount of Western capital imported was a small proportion of total machinery investment. Despite its rapid development, the Romanian machine building industry continues to suffer from an inability to specialize production and focus efforts on a narrower and more internationally competitive product line. In large part this may result from Romania's failure to select an appropriate target market. With trade split between CMEA and the West, Romania cannot serve either market effectively. The country's large size and voracious appetite for investment goods has permitted the domestic market to drive industrial policy. A World Bank survey (Tsantis and Pepper 1979) observed that "[u]ntil a few years ago, it would have been difficult to identify industrial projects developed primarily for the export market." Even products in which Romania has some relatively focused export advantage, such as oil-field equipment, tractors, and chemical plants, were developed at first to meet domestic needs and only began to be exported when domestic production, perhaps fortuitously, outpaced demand.

Because Romania's oil fields had been extensively developed before the Second World War, Romania had the requisite skill to expand the chemical industry. At first the petrochemical sector was expanded on the basis of domestic production. However, oil production could not keep up with both the needs of the expanding chemical sector and the energy needs of the rest of the economy. Consequently during the 1970s, and particularly after 1975, Romania began to import large quantities of oil, not from the Soviet Union but rather from developing countries. Romania thus was wagering that, even by paying world market prices for feedstock for its petrochemical sector, a profit could be earned by exporting the products of the petrochemical sector in the West. Unfortunately, the excess refining and chemical capacity in the West kept the price of such products from rising as rapidly as did the price of crude oil (Jackson 1986b, pp. 500–502). Thus in Romania's one export-oriented sector both declining domestic sources of advantage and developments abroad have conspired to sharply reduce gains to the economy.

In view of Romania's abundance of labor, it would seem rational to develop some labor-intensive sectors in order to move workers from agriculture to industry and thus to expand that proportion of the labor force that is disciplined to factory labor and the use of industrial equipment. While they do not fit the Romanian leadership's view of modernity as do the sectors discussed above, the textile and clothing sectors do provide opportunities for creating numerous low skill and low capital intensity jobs. Because of this, these two sectors have experienced rapid growth, both when compared to more prestigious sectors and to the rest of light industry (Tsantis and Pepper 1979). The exports of these goods to developed countries also have expanded rapidly despite occasional difficulties over allegations of dumping.

There is little evidence of extra-plan mechanisms for allocating resources to priority sectors. The Romanian planning system is rather simple and oriented toward physical indicators. Planners appear able to direct funds to meet their investment objectives and there is sufficient labor to man new plants. Consequently the type of extra-plan mechanisms evident in Czechoslovakia and Hungary do not appear to be needed in Romania. Romania has nevertheless promoted its priority sectors in two ways. First, it has sought to create favorable opportunities for export. In the West this has taken the form of efforts to improve access to developed and developing country markets by means of an aggressive diplomacy. Romanian pressure for most favored nation (MFN) status from the United States, a flexible attitude toward negotiations with the European Community, and an effort to present Romania as a nonaligned developing country are more notable examples of such a policy. Romania has also priced its products aggressively and, as a result, both steel and textile products have been subjected to restrictions by the United States and the European Community. Within CMEA Romania has attempted to build an export position based on specialization, but, given Romania's maverick economic and foreign policies and the decisive importance of Soviet cooperation for the success of such specialization, it is not surprising that little has been achieved. The other form of support for priority sectors has come from the importation of technology and capital from the West, often through industrial cooperation and joint ventures with Western firms. However, given the overall size of Romania's industry and the small scope of cooperative ventures with Western firms, the impact of such measures on the performance of Romanian industry must be small.

A COMPARISON OF EAST EUROPEAN INDUSTRIAL POLICIES

The foregoing survey of industrial policies in Eastern Europe reveals many similarities as well as some important differences between countries. The specificity and completeness of criteria for selecting sectors to be promoted are not impressive in any of the countries studied. Nevertheless, in all countries the same major sectors, engineering, chemicals, and electronics have been targeted for special attention. One reason why such similar choices were made by the East European countries is their overriding need to keep up economically and technologically with the developed market economies. Since there exists a considerable technological gap between Eastern Europe and the developed market economies, the pattern of structural change needed in the East is evident from the recent experience of the West. Thus the choice of priority sectors in Eastern Europe must revolve much more around which specific aspects of recent structural changes in the West are to be promoted through industrial policy and which ones are best left to others. In this sense the choice of sector is considerably easier than it is in developed market economies, because the broad outlines of what needs to be done already exist and both the technical feasibility and market acceptance of new lines of endeavor have been demonstrated.

The similarities in the effects of industrial policy on the pattern of industrial employment and production are shown in tables 4.1 through 4.6. In order to show the effect of industrial policy on the reallocation of resources tables 4.1 through 4.3 show the rates of growth of employment by sector. Tables 4.4 through 4.6 present similar data for sector outputs. The periods chosen for examination are 1968–73, a period before the oil crisis, 1973–78, when some adjustment to new conditions should have begun to make itself felt, and 1978–81, the most recent period for which data are available. Several general conclusions can be drawn from these tables. First, in terms of both employment and output, priority sectors discussed above have experienced above-average

TABLE 4.1. Rate of Growth of Employment in CMEA Countries, 1968–1973 (percentage per year)

ISIC	Industry	Bulgaria	Czecho-slovakia	GDR	Hungary
210	Coalmining	−2.7	−0.9	0.7	−4.0
220	Petroleum and gas	−20.0	0.8	NA	3.4
311	Food products	−2.6	1.0	2.6	3.1
313	Beverages	5.8	−1.2	2.6	2.7
314	Tobacco	−1.0	0.0	2.6	0.0
321	Textiles	4.0	0.5	−1.1	−0.8
322	Wearing apparel	2.1	1.0	2.0	2.6
323	Leather and leather products	5.3	0.8	2.0	1.3
324	Footwear	3.3	0.8	2.0	0.0
331	Wood products	1.0	−0.9	2.0	−9.0
332	Furniture and fixtures	6.4	0.3	2.0	1.9
341	Paper and paper products	4.8	1.9	2.0	2.5
342	Printing, publishing	2.2	0.7	2.0	2.0
351	Industrial chemicals	4.6	3.4	0.5	3.2
352	Other chemical products	3.1	0.7	0.5	3.2
353	Petroleum refineries	NA	0.0	0.5	3.1
354	Petroleum, coal products	16.2	0.0	0.5	NA
355	Rubber products	17.0	−5.5	0.5	1.3
356	Plastic products nec.	7.4	NA	0.5	1.3
361	Pottery, china	−1.1	−1.9	NA	4.8
362	Glass and glass products	2.8	2.1	NA	2.9
369	Nonmetal products nec.	3.0	0.0	0.9	−1.2
371	Iron and steel	2.4	0.2	0.7	0.7
372	Nonferrous metals	2.4	1.6	0.7	3.1
381	Metal products	7.2	3.3	1.3	0.5
382	Machinery nec.	6.4	−0.8	1.3	−1.2
383	Electrical machinery	4.3	1.1	4.1	3.3
384	Transportation equipment	1.3	−1.3	NA	−2.6
385	Professional goods	NA	3.2	4.1	2.3
390	Other industries	1.9	11.2	NA	−0.7

rates of employment and output growth, suggesting that, at the level of aggregation employed here, resources were directed toward and effectively utilized by priority sectors. Somewhat surprising is the ability to reduce employment in nonessential sectors in the 1968 to 1978 period, not only in labor-short countries such as Czechoslovakia, the GDR, and Hungary, but also in Bulgaria and Romania. Less encouraging is the inability to reduce the production of nonpriority products in 1968–78. Only in 1978–81 is there any evidence of declines in the

Poland	Romania	USSR
1.0	NA	−2.8
−4.4	NA	0.5
4.3	3.6	0.5
2.0	3.6	1.3
0.0	3.6	1.1
2.5	7.9	0.3
6.7	8.4	1.7
7.2	5.1	0.3
5.3	5.1	1.1
5.3	2.0	−0.7
5.6	2.0	2.2
2.9	2.6	0.9
2.9	0.9	NA
1.4	6.7	2.9
5.6	6.7	1.4
7.3	NA	1.4
1.9	NA	1.4
4.1	6.7	2.7
10.0	6.7	8.0
2.4	NA	2.0
3.9	8.5	1.5
1.7	8.5	1.9
2.5	3.1	0.8
2.4	2.2	NA
4.3	8.5	3.0
3.8	8.5	3.0
6.2	8.5	3.0
2.9	8.5	3.0
5.6	8.5	3.0
8.7	NA	−0.3

production of energy- and material-intensive products in countries other than Poland and Romania where the economic crisis rather than industrial policy was at work.

To provide some systematization of the information in tables 4.1–4.6, tables 4.7–4.9 report the cosine of the angle between the vectors of growth rates of sectoral outputs for all pairs of East European countries and the Soviet Union. Table 4.7 reveals values for the cosine of the angle between the vectors close to 1 for most East European countries

TABLE 4.2. Rate of Growth of Employment in CMEA Countries, 1973–1978 (percentage per year)

ISIC	Industry	Bulgaria	Czecho-slovakia	GDR	Hungary
210	Coalmining	−0.6	0.4	1.4	−1.9
220	Petroleum and gas	13.3	−20.0	NA	−6.1
311	Food products	2.1	1.7	2.5	1.2
313	Beverages	1.8	0.0	2.5	1.6
314	Tobacco	−4.3	0.0	2.5	0.0
321	Textiles	0.7	−0.4	−1.4	−3.3
322	Wearing apparel	0.8	−1.6	−0.4	−2.9
323	Leather and leather products	−4.1	0.0	−0.4	−4.1
324	Footwear	2.4	0.0	−0.4	−3.5
331	Wood products	−2.0	−0.3	−0.4	−1.1
332	Furniture and fixtures	−0.2	1.3	−0.4	−1.2
341	Paper and paper products	2.3	1.3	−0.4	−1.2
342	Printing, publishing	3.5	2.0	−0.4	−1.0
351	Industrial chemicals	8.0	0.7	0.4	0.5
352	Other chemical products	4.4	−4.6	0.4	0.7
353	Petroleum refineries	NA	1.8	0.4	0.0
354	Petroleum, coal products	−8.7	8.0	0.4	NA
355	Rubber products	−1.4	1.5	0.4	−1.7
356	Plastic products nec.	1.9	NA	0.4	−5.7
361	Pottery, china	6.6	0.0	NA	1.4
362	Glass and glass products	3.3	0.6	NA	2.5
369	Nonmetal products nec.	2.2	1.0	0.9	−2.7
371	Iron and steel	2.3	−2.2	1.1	−1.0
372	Nonferrous metals	2.3	−5.4	1.1	0.0
381	Metal products	−0.3	6.1	1.5	−4.9
382	Machinery nec.	3.3	2.4	1.5	−2.0
383	Electrical machinery	4.5	1.8	0.3	2.2
384	Transportation equipment	7.5	4.5	NA	−0.2
385	Professional goods	NA	−26.5	0.3	1.4
390	Other industries	1.1	1.0	NA	−10.6

and the Soviet Union. The closer the value of the cosine is to one, the more similar are the patterns of growth. Bulgaria and Hungary experienced structural change that was the least similar to the Soviet pattern of growth, suggesting an industrial policy aimed at developing sectors relatively neglected in the target market. Also of interest are the high values for Polish-Czechoslovak and Polish-GDR cosines, suggesting Poland's efforts to achieve a more advanced pattern of production. The cosines for Romania reveal a similar tendency.

Poland	Romania	USSR
1.9	NA	0.6
0.0	NA	1.3
1.2	−0.6	1.5
−3.8	−0.6	2.1
−2.1	−0.6	2.1
−0.9	−0.2	0.8
1.7	−4.0	1.0
0.9	−5.1	0.7
−0.9	−5.1	0.9
0.2	−2.2	−0.5
1.1	−2.2	1.0
−1.4	−0.6	1.4
−0.4	−6.3	NA
−0.6	6.1	1.4
−1.9	6.1	1.7
2.9	NA	1.7
0.0	NA	1.7
0.8	6.1	2.7
7.3	6.1	2.2
2.9	NA	2.9
1.8	−1.6	1.9
−1.3	10.2	1.4
1.9	3.7	0.6
3.5	6.7	NA
1.2	6.7	2.3
3.3	6.7	2.3
5.1	6.7	2.3
0.9	6.7	2.3
0.7	6.7	2.3
7.1	NA	5.1

The effects of the oil crisis on industrial policy are evident in table 4.8. The Soviet-East European cosines fall appreciably, reflecting both efforts to expand energy production in Eastern Europe and the effort to shift production of energy-intensive products from Eastern Europe to the Soviet Union. The pattern of sectoral growth among the countries of Eastern Europe, on the other hand, reveals a greater homogeneity —reflecting similarities in the sectors chosen for promotion at this time. The period 1978–81 covered by table 4.9 is dominated by the

TABLE 4.3. Rate of Growth of Employment in CMEA Countries, 1978–1981
(percentage per year)

ISIC	Industry	Bulgaria	Czecho-slovakia	GDR	Hungary
210	Coalmining	3.8	1.0	1.6	−0.4
220	Petroleum and gas	7.4	13.3	NA	2.3
311	Food products	−0.7	0.4	0.5	−1.0
313	Beverages	0.0	0.0	0.5	0.0
314	Tobacco	−2.2	0.0	0.5	0.0
321	Textiles	0.1	−0.1	−0.7	−2.3
322	Wearing apparel	1.8	−1.2	−0.3	−0.4
323	Leather and leather products	2.0	0.0	−0.3	−0.0
324	Footwear	0.9	−0.5	−0.3	−0.9
331	Wood products	3.7	0.5	−0.3	−1.9
332	Furniture and fixtures	−2.1	−1.1	−0.3	−1.1
341	Paper and paper products	2.5	1.4	−0.3	−2.2
342	Printing, publishing	0.6	0.0	−0.3	−1.7
351	Industrial chemicals	3.3	1.1	−0.1	−0.8
352	Other chemical products	−1.4	1.4	−0.1	−2.5
353	Petroleum refineries	NA	0.0	−0.1	−5.1
354	Petroleum, coal products	2.7	0.0	−0.1	NA
355	Rubber products	−0.8	−1.3	−0.1	0.0
356	Plastic products nec.	7.1	NA	−0.1	2.7
361	Pottery, china	2.2	−3.5	NA	0.0
362	Glass and glass products	0.4	0.9	NA	0.0
369	Nonmetal products nec.	3.5	1.1	−0.3	−1.7
371	Iron and steel	1.5	0.2	1.5	−1.8
372	Nonferrous metals	1.5	−1.2	1.5	−5.1
381	Metal products	−1.9	0.0	0.4	−2.3
382	Machinery nec.	−5.4	1.0	0.4	−0.8
383	Electrical machinery	7.9	0.9	0.6	−2.2
384	Transportation equipment	8.7	0.4	NA	−2.2
385	Professional goods	NA	−3.9	0.6	−1.7
390	Other industries	1.1	0.8	NA	−4.6

consequences of the economic crisis in Poland and Romania that forced
the curtailment of production in a number of sectors; thus giving these
countries negative cosines with the other CMEA countries whose industrial output continued to grow. For the rest of the CMEA, cosines with
the Soviet Union increased, suggesting that the tendency of all countries to promote similar sectors through their industrial policies—evident
in the period 1968–73—is returning.

Excessive reliance on data aggregated to the levels employed in the

Poland	Romania	USSR
0.7	NA	0.8
0.0	NA	1.5
1.2	−1.2	0.2
0.6	−1.2	0.3
0.0	−1.2	0.0
−1.3	3.1	−0.3
1.2	0.0	0.5
−1.4	2.9	0.0
0.3	2.9	0.5
0.6	0.2	−0.3
−2.9	0.2	−0.3
−0.6	0.0	0.8
−0.7	3.9	NA
−1.1	−2.9	1.6
−3.0	−2.9	1.1
2.2	NA	1.1
0.0	NA	1.1
1.3	−2.9	3.2
2.8	−2.9	1.6
2.2	NA	0.1
−0.5	3.2	−0.2
−1.7	−2.2	0.1
−1.1	5.5	0.3
−5.0	1.2	NA
0.0	2.1	0.3
−0.4	2.1	0.6
0.1	2.1	0.6
−1.0	2.1	0.6
−2.5	2.1	0.6
20.9	NA	0.7

foregoing analysis can lead to the erroneous conclusion that all East European countries are following identical industrial policies and thus are competing with each other, either for a finite CMEA market or, by means of import substitution, for their domestic market. To some extent this is the case, as many of the authors of East European literature on CMEA integration complain. At the same time it must be recognized that a parallel development of the same sectors need not be competitive if it stimulates intra-industry trade. The Czechoslovak nuclear energy

TABLE 4.4. Rate of Growth of Output in CMEA Countries, 1968–1973 (percentage per year)

ISIC	Industry	Bulgaria	Czecho-slovakia	GDR	Hungary
210	Coalmining	0.0	2.6	0.8	−2.7
220	Petroleum and gas	NA	0.0	NA	2.7
311	Food products	NA	4.1	NA	4.2
313	Beverages	NA	5.3	NA	4.2
314	Tobacco	NA	3.4	NA	4.2
321	Textiles	7.6	5.9	4.2	−0.2
322	Wearing apparel	4.9	5.2	5.4	3.3
323	Leather and leather products	8.4	6.4	6.0	4.2
324	Footwear	8.2	5.1	6.0	2.5
331	Wood products	5.1	6.3	6.6	−0.5
332	Furniture and fixtures	13.6	7.5	6.6	8.3
341	Paper and paper products	8.0	5.3	4.2	4.1
342	Printing, publishing	5.4	5.6	NA	NA
351	Industrial chemicals	6.8	10.1	7.3	NA
352	Other chemical products	10.4	8.6	7.3	8.7
353	Petroleum refineries	NA	9.4	8.6	13.1
354	Petroleum, coal products	NA	4.0	8.6	NA
355	Rubber products	21.0	7.0	6.8	6.2
356	Plastic products nec.	NA	NA	9.2	6.2
361	Pottery, china	4.9	4.8	7.0	7.3
362	Glass and glass products	7.6	8.0	7.0	5.6
369	Nonmetal products nec.	7.2	5.6	6.0	−1.8
371	Iron and steel	10.8	5.0	6.9	3.7
372	Nonferrous metals	NA	5.3	6.9	8.1
381	Metal products	8.4	7.6	5.7	0.7
382	Machinery nec.	16.3	7.6	5.9	0.2
383	Electrical machinery	10.4	9.5	9.6	8.5
384	Transportation equipment	11.9	7.2	NA	8.8
385	Professional goods	NA	8.2	NA	8.3
390	Other industries	8.6	11.2	NA	8.5

program, Hungarian bus production, and Bulgarian forklift trucks are examples of such a policy, with each country specializing in one sector of the engineering industry. With such a strategy, all CMEA countries could choose machinery, chemicals, and electronics as priority sectors, as they have done. With sufficiently narrow specializations within each of the sectors, intra-sector trade in components and final products could be based on providing a national advantage. The Bulgarian strategy of providing components to Soviet enterprises is one example of such a

Poland	Romania	USSR
4.6	7.2	3.2
6.8	2.2	6.7
6.4	6.3	5.6
8.2	6.3	3.3
1.1	6.3	7.0
6.9	11.9	4.9
9.9	13.6	6.6
7.3	8.3	3.6
5.6	8.3	3.1
5.2	7.8	5.1
9.6	7.8	8.5
5.7	8.0	7.5
6.3	3.5	NA
10.3	15.6	10.8
12.0	9.2	9.1
13.3	5.7	7.8
2.3	2.5	3.0
9.3	NA	7.9
13.3	NA	13.1
8.5	15.8	9.1
9.8	15.8	9.8
7.7	10.3	7.6
5.8	10.0	5.4
12.4	NA	5.4
12.0	13.3	10.4
12.6	14.9	10.4
12.6	18.0	10.4
10.8	14.9	10.4
17.8	NA	8.3
10.9	NA	NA

strategy. Czechoslovakia has signed long-term specialization agreements with the Soviet Union in a number of industries. In chemicals, the Soviet Union exports energy-intensive and bulk chemicals to Czechoslovakia in return for pharmaceuticals and fine chemicals (Skolkova 1986). In the engineering sector the two countries have agreements for bilateral specialization in, and exchanges of, engines, tractors, and agricultural machinery (Terek 1985).

To coordinate intra-industry specialization among the East European

TABLE 4.5. Rate of Growth of Output in CMEA Countries, 1973–1978 (percentage per year)

ISIC	Industry	Bulgaria	Czecho-slovakia	GDR	Hungary
210	Coalmining	1.4	1.6	1.4	−2.5
220	Petroleum and gas	NA	1.8	NA	2.4
311	Food products	NA	4.1	NA	$\left.\begin{array}{c}4.7\\4.7\\4.7\end{array}\right.$
313	Beverages	NA	3.3	NA	
314	Tobacco	NA	4.3	NA	
321	Textiles	6.8	4.7	5.4	1.6
322	Wearing apparel	6.1	5.0	4.1	−1.0
323	Leather and leather products	0.0	4.7	$\left.\begin{array}{c}6.2\\6.2\end{array}\right.$	1.2
324	Footwear	6.5	5.0		1.5
331	Wood products	3.7	7.8	$\left.\begin{array}{c}6.6\\6.6\end{array}\right.$	4.0
332	Furniture and fixtures	9.6	9.5		4.7
341	Paper and paper products	8.5	6.5	5.9	4.4
342	Printing, publishing	10.5	5.8	NA	4.4
351	Industrial chemicals	14.0	7.8	$\left.\begin{array}{c}7.4\\7.4\end{array}\right.$	NA
352	Other chemical products	13.5	7.9		6.9
353	Petroleum refineries	NA	6.5	$\left.\begin{array}{c}6.4\\6.4\end{array}\right.$	8.1
354	Petroleum, coal products	NA	0.6		NA
355	Rubber products	5.6	7.9	6.7	5.9
356	Plastic products nec.	NA	NA	11.2	5.9
361	Pottery, china	9.4	3.3	$\left.\begin{array}{c}7.8\\7.8\end{array}\right.$	8.0
362	Glass and glass products	9.3	6.9		6.4
369	Nonmetal products nec.	9.9	5.9	5.9	0.2
371	Iron and steel	9.5	4.5	$\left.\begin{array}{c}5.5\\5.5\end{array}\right.$	3.0
372	Nonferrous metals	NA	5.4		4.4
381	Metal products	7.2	7.5	6.9	1.3
382	Machinery nec.	14.3	8.9	6.9	−0.4
383	Electrical machinery	11.8	11.2	9.6	10.6
384	Transportation equipment	15.7	7.3	NA	12.0
385	Professional goods	NA	9.6	NA	10.3
390	Other industries	7.0	4.8	NA	7.4

countries requires a degree of supernational planning and coordination that CMEA does not have. As a result, most CMEA countries have taken the Soviet market as the reference market for their industrial policies. The pivotal role of the Soviet Union in promoting this tendency for intra-sector specialization is shown in tables 4.10 and 4.11. Table 4.10 clearly shows that the Soviet market absorbs the bulk of products produced within CMEA under specialization agreements (Machovski 1985; and Clement 1985). Moreover, to the extent that countries' priority

Poland	Romania	USSR
4.8	6.6	1.4
−9.5	0.4	7.0
5.5	8.1	3.6
7.1	8.1	8.2
4.9	8.1	6.6
7.2	11.7	3.9
7.1	12.5	6.2
6.0	9.6	3.6
7.0	9.6	5.7
5.7	8.6	1.8
13.8	8.6	6.8
4.6	9.2	4.0
10.3	3.9	NA
6.5	13.6	8.9
9.3	11.5	6.7
10.2	6.5	NA
−0.7	14.7	NA
8.2	NA	6.8
18.9	NA	10.0
14.5	10.6	8.5
12.5	10.6	11.4
1.6	14.3	4.1
6.0	12.4	4.4
8.8	NA	4.4
9.6	13.2	10.8
13.1	16.5	10.8
15.0	17.3	10.8
10.0	16.5	10.8
12.1	NA	10.8
14.2	NA	NA

sectors are reflected in the specialization positions they obtain within CMEA, those countries whose industrial policies are oriented toward the Soviet markets account for higher shares of CMEA exports of these products. Thus Bulgaria, for example, accounts for 16 percent of CMEA exports of specialized products while Poland, a much larger country, accounts for only 11 percent. That such specialization occurs at the level of intra-industry rather than inter-industry trade is illustrated by table 4.11, which shows the growing role of specialization in the chemical industry.

TABLE 4.6. Rate of Growth of Output in CMEA Countries, 1978–1981 (percentage per year)

ISIC	Industry	Bulgaria	Czecho-slovakia	GDR	Hungary
210	Coalmining	2.5	−1.0	3.9	0.0
220	Petroleum and gas	NA	0.3	NA	−1.7
311	Food products	NA	1.2	NA	⎰1.4
313	Beverages	NA	1.5	NA	⎱1.4
314	Tobacco	NA	1.3	NA	1.4
321	Textiles	2.6	2.3	1.9	0.3
322	Wearing apparel	2.6	2.2	0.9	2.6
323	Leather and leather products	4.6	1.7	⎰2.7	−1.9
324	Footwear	5.1	1.4	⎱2.7	0.0
331	Wood products	3.9	2.3	⎰0.3	−3.9
332	Furniture and fixtures	5.0	2.2	⎱0.3	0.0
341	Paper and paper products	4.5	1.7	2.2	1.9
342	Printing, publishing	2.8	1.9	NA	NA
351	Industrial chemicals	5.4	1.8	⎰2.1	NA
352	Other chemical products	8.8	3.8	⎱2.1	3.8
353	Petroleum refineries	NA	−0.5	⎰2.5	−0.2
354	Petroleum, coal products	NA	0.0	⎱2.5	NA
355	Rubber products	5.4	2.5	1.8	⎰2.4
356	Plastic products nec.	NA	NA	1.5	⎱2.4
361	Pottery, china	5.2	2.9	⎰3.3	1.8
362	Glass and glass products	1.3	1.1	⎱3.3	2.1
369	Nonmetal products nec.	2.8	1.7	−0.3	−1.0
371	Iron and steel	8.1	1.4	⎰3.8	−1.2
372	Nonferrous metals	NA	0.3	⎱3.8	2.1
381	Metal products	−1.7	2.1	2.6	−4.8
382	Machinery nec.	5.9	2.9	4.0	0.7
383	Electrical machinery	6.7	3.8	6.1	2.0
384	Transportation equipment	−1.2	12.7	NA	1.0
385	Professional goods	NA	3.1	NA	3.3
390	Other industries	3.5	1.7	NA	0.3

*1978–1980.

Only Poland and Romania have not chosen the CMEA market—and the Soviet market in particular—to guide their choice of priority sectors to the same extent as have the other CMEA countries. In the case of Poland the reference market was the world market and, particularly reflecting the predominance of the developed market economies in world trade, the developed West. In the case of Romania the domestic market —and to a lesser extent the developed West—appeared to be the mar-

Poland	Romania	USSR
−6.9	8.2*	−0.7
−1.7	−4.6*	2.1
−3.7	5.8	0.3
−6.1	5.8	2.7
−13.2	5.8	6.1
−4.8	5.1	1.5
−0.9	4.7	3.4
−2.6	4.0	0.6
−3.0	4.0	2.2
−4.2	3.1	0.0
−1.9	3.1	4.5
−3.5	2.2	3.6
−4.7	1.0	3.6
−3.6	3.2	4.0
−4.3	4.9	2.4
−6.3	1.5*	NA
−4.0	−5.4*	NA
−4.0	NA	1.6
−3.7	NA	6.3
1.4	6.3	3.4
−1.8	6.3	2.9
−6.7	1.3	0.9
−6.5	1.9	0.6
−1.4	NA	0.6
−5.1	8.0*	3.8
−3.2	12.0*	3.8
−3.9	NA	3.8
−5.1	NA	3.8
−3.1	NA	3.8
4.2	NA	NA

kets whose needs guided industrial policy. It is noteworthy that such choices of reference markets implied a reduction in reliance on CMEA and a willingness to expand relations with the West, both for increased imports of technology and equipment and as a market for exports. The efforts of both countries in this regard proved unsuccessful, although whether the failure was due to shortcomings in industrial policy or to lamentably poor macroeconomic policies is unclear. What is certain is

TABLE 4.7. Cosines of Sectoral Output Growth, 1968–73

	Czechoslovakia	GDR	Hungary	Poland	Romania	USSR
Bulgaria	.676	.743	.688	.660	.550	.654
Czechoslovakia		.954	.805	.959	.916	.955
GDR			.856	.934	.887	.933
Hungary				.797	.687	.774
Poland					.909	.966
Romania						.906

that to date no socialist country has successfully implemented industrial policies geared toward Western markets.

In the means used to promote the growth of priority sectors, there are both similarities and differences among the East European countries. While changes in the system of economic management as a means of stimulating the performance of priority sectors has been attempted in virtually all countries, there appears to be little agreement on which changes are likely to be more beneficial. While the GDR and Czechoslovakia have moved toward greater central control over resource allocation, Hungary has decentralized, yet no clear-cut advantage appears to adhere to either approach. Much greater agreement seems to exist on the benefits of reorganizing industrial enterprises into larger units, or associations, which can cut across industry lines and can combine production with research and development and foreign trade activities. Most obviously in the case of the GDR, but in the other countries as well, enterprise amalgamation has been seen as an important means of increasing export competitiveness through accelerated technical progress.

The allocation of resources to priority sectors is relatively commonplace in all countries. Perhaps the greatest difference is to be found in the importation of Western technology and equipment for priority sec-

TABLE 4.8. Cosines of Sectoral Output Growth, 1973–78

	Czechoslovakia	GDR	Hungary	Poland	Romania	USSR
Bulgaria	.894	.931	.843	.823	.912	.151
Czechoslovakia		.952	.811	.908	.936	.394
GDR			.857	.910	.956	.291
Hungary				.778	.812	.130
Poland					.871	.376
Romania						.313

TABLE 4.9. Cosines of Sectoral Output Growth, 1978–81

	Czechoslovakia	GDR	Hungary	Poland	Romania	USSR
Bulgaria	.404	−.341	.238	−.668	−.506	.582
Czechoslovakia		.157	.319	−.553	−.523	.754
GDR			.307	.141	.291	.141
Hungary				−.127	−.117	.418
Poland					.552	−.633
Romania						−.567

tors. This has been a key element of industrial policies in Poland and Romania, and is used to an appreciable extent in Bulgaria, Hungary, and the German Democratic Republic. In Czechoslovakia it has played a minor role. Among the more developed countries there is greater evidence of extra-plan mechanisms for allocating capital and labor to priority sectors, mechanisms that appear to be dispensable in the less industrialized economies. Given the complaints in the literature of many countries about the diversion to other uses of resources obtained by means of these priority allocations, it is evident that such extra-plan means of allocating resources may not be very effective in stimulating the output of the products intended.

Finally, the promotion of exports has been carried out largely within the framework of CMEA specialization and in particular within bilateral specialization agreements with the Soviet Union. Romania and Poland have been less effective in this respect than have the other socialist countries, primarily because they chose not to view the Soviet Union as a reference market. To what extent economists wish to view the other CMEA countries as being successful in their trade promotion efforts

TABLE 4.10. Intra-CMEA Trade in Specialized Products in 1981

	Share of specialized exports destined for USSR (%)	Share of total CMEA specialized exports (%)
Bulgaria	76.7	16
Czechoslovakia	61.8	17
GDR	78.9	26
Hungary	69.0	12
Poland	75.5	11
Romania	44.6	5

SOURCE: Heinrich Machowski, "Die Productions-spezialisierung im RGW am Beispiel der DDR." In Heinrich Machowski (ed.) *Harmonisierung der Wirtschaftspolitik in Osteuropa* (Berlin, 1985).

TABLE 4.11. Intra-CMEA Trade in Specialized Chemical Products as a
Percentage of Total Intra-CMEA Chemical Trade, by Country in Percentages

Country	1975	1982
Bulgaria	24.1	35.0
Czechoslovakia	25.5	47.2
GDR	4.6	22.9
Hungary	19.4	68.7
Poland	8.8	80.3
Romania	0.0	51.1

SOURCE: Wilhelm Jampel, "L'industrie chimique à l'Est." *Le Courier des Pays de l'Est*, no. 302, January 1986.

depends in large part on the individual's assessment of CMEA integration. Clearly there have been difficulties in the conceptualization and implementation of socialist economic integration. At the same time intra-industry trade, particularly in those sectors where industrial policy is at work, has increased within CMEA.[6] Perhaps the clearest conclusion here is that the Soviet Union plays just as important a role in the success of the industrial policies of the East European countries as it does in overall CMEA trade.

CHAPTER 5

The Evolution of CMEA Institutions and Policies and the Need for Structural Adjustment

Marie Lavigne

The June 1984 summit that brought together the party leaders of the CMEA member countries was generally viewed in the West as a nonevent. The previous summit had taken place in 1969 and led to the adoption in 1971 of the Comprehensive Program "for deepening and improving economic cooperation, and developing socialist economic integration."[1] The 1984 summit was not expected to launch a similar project. However, as it had been advocated as early as 1981 in a speech by Brezhnev at the Twenty-sixth Congress of the Communist Party of the Soviet Union, (henceforth CPSU), and since many controversial issues do exist in the socialist commonwealth, many expectations were raised. One of them was related to price setting, which appeared as a major source of conflict between the USSR and the East European countries. Although some Western observers heralded a change in the CMEA price formula, no definite alteration was announced.

A closer investigation of the declaration "on the main directions of further development and deepening of economic, scientific, and technological cooperation of member countries of the CMEA," related to the development of socialist economic integration (SEI) in the 1980s, clarifies the present prospects. The most interesting passage of the declaration is an extraordinarily blunt statement—quite unusual in CMEA documents where a particular country is never singled out, apart from special circumstances, as was the case for Poland in 1981–82:

For creating the economic conditions allowing the Soviet Union to maintain and continue its supplies of raw materials and energy so as to satisfy their import needs on a level defined through plan coordination and long-term agreements, the interested CMEA countries, in the framework of a coordinated economic policy, will gradually and consistently develop the structure of their production and export, and implement the required measures in the field of investment, reconstruction, and rationalization of their own industry, so as to supply the Soviet Union with the goods it needs, namely food products, industrial consumer goods, some types of construction materials, machinery and equipment of high quality and meeting the world technological level. The mutually agreed decisions on these questions will be carried out taking into account the objective economic conditions of the USSR and the other CMEA countries, as well as the structures of production and mutual trade of these countries. This will ensure a mutually advantageous compensation of production costs and open opportunities for a further deepening of a stable, long-term production specialization in the framework of the socialist community. (Translated by the author from *Ekonomicheskaia Gazeta*, no. 26, June 1984)

At first reading this passage suggests that socialist economic integration (SEI) is now basically a bilateral relation between the Soviet Union as supplier of energy and raw materials and the other countries as suppliers of food and manufactured goods. To meet Soviet requirements, the CMEA countries have to adjust, through a far-reaching, long-term restructuring of their own economies, the final outcome being an all-embracing specialization within the CMEA. However, before reaching this conclusion, several issues must be addressed.

First, what happened to the Comprehensive Program? It was a specific combination of "market" and "plan" integration in a multilateral framework and was supposed to reach its aims in the latter half of the 1980s. Is that program totally obsolete? If so, what new concepts have been introduced? If not, what still remains? Second, since the beginning of the world energy crisis, Western analyses of CMEA have almost exclusively focused on the Soviet-East European relationship, particularly on energy and on the terms of trade changes occurring after 1975. This has led them to regard CMEA institutions, concerted plans, and target programs, set up in the same period as more or less empty boxes. Is that a justified assumption? If not, then in what areas outside pricing do CMEA institutions have a tangible effect on trade and resource distribution? Does the recent CMEA summit imply fundamental changes in this respect? This leads to the last question: what are the structural adjustments required from the six smaller CMEA countries? How do they fit into the adjustments already realized in these countries in the past years? (van Brabant 1984a, p. 128). The issue is associated with the transition from extensive to intensive growth, in other words, with the need for a faster growth of factor productivity. This aim has been formulated in the official documents of all the East European countries from the beginning of the 1970s.[2] Only a decade later was it clearly linked with the formal mechanism of SEI. We have now, on the one hand, specific requirements addressed to the six by the USSR and embodied in the mechanism of CMEA institutions. On the other hand, each country has its own concept on how to adapt the long-term strategy to its own economic conditions and aims. The outcome remains open because the feasibility of any of those national concepts may be questioned.

THE CONCEPT OF SOCIALIST INTEGRATION: FROM THE COMPREHENSIVE PROGRAM TO THE 1984 SUMMIT

The Comprehensive Program of 1971 defined SEI in a pragmatic way, through the aims and methods of the international socialist division of labor. It viewed integration as a long-term process, to be achieved through a balance of market and production or plan mechanisms. The use of monetary-market mechanisms implied the following according to the program: a limited liberalization of mutual trade through the increase in the share of goods exchanged without fixed quotas specified in value or in quantities; a further improvement in the price-setting system; introduction of a limited convertibility of domestic currencies, that is, among themselves and with the transferable ruble, but not with the capitalist currencies. Production integration meant coordination in planning through a complicated system with different time spans. Long-term programs, up to twenty years in duration, coordination of five-year planning, and joint planning for specific products were to be combined in order to ensure a growing cooperation and specialization in production.

When he first suggested a CMEA summit in February 1981, at the twenty-sixth Congress of the CPSU, Leonid Brezhnev launched some new ideas that greatly influenced subsequent theoretical developments and announced the approach to be defined at the 1984 summit (Csaba 1984a). He stressed three basic forms of SEI that were to supplement the traditional means of plan coordination: the concertation (soglaso-vanie) of economic policies; the convergence (sblizhenie) of the structures of national economic mechanisms; and finally the future development of direct interfirm and interassociation links, including the creation of joint firms (Brezhnev 1982, pp. 9–10). Similar formulations have appeared regularly since then.[3] The declaration of the summit meeting incorporated these concepts, along with an unbalanced updating of the 1971 Comprehensive Program, the market component of which was almost entirely put aside.

The New Concepts

The concertation of economic policy is defined in the declaration as " . . . the elaboration, on a collective level, of the main ways to solve large economic problems, bearing a mutual interest and having a significant meaning for the determination, by *each* brother country, of the orientations of economic growth and long-term cooperation; the *joint* definition of direct interaction in the fields of science, technology, material production, and investment" (*Ekonomicheskaia Gazeta,* June 1984, p. 4, my italics).

Clearly, economic policy in the summit document refers to growth strategy, along the lines of what Western economists would label an industrial policy. The components of this strategy include those of the concept of intensive growth as defined in Soviet and East European textbooks: rationalization of factor utilization, higher technical level, and quality of production. To these components the text adds "the development of the export potential, mainly in the manufactured goods sections of the economy," and "a more rational location of productive forces." The first term might be supporting an export-led growth strategy in general. It might also point to the specific requirement that the USSR receive more high-quality manufactured goods from its partners. The mention of the regional allocation of productive forces apparently refers to a scheme advocated by the USSR as early as the late 1970s, according to which energy and raw materials-intensive activities were to be developed on the territory of the USSR, while the smaller CMEA countries would concentrate on less material-intensive production.

The concertation thus implies that the CMEA would interfere with the industrial policy of individual countries. In this context there is some obscurity in the division between fields of mutual cooperation, where all member countries should take part in the concertation, and "other fields of social and economic development," where only interested countries should decide to harmonize their interests to the extent to which they should find it necessary. The concept of interested countries is a basic one in the CMEA statute, and has up to now prevented the organization from exerting supernational powers. It means that all decisions within the CMEA must be made unanimously, but that unanimity is restricted to interested countries. This principle has repeatedly allowed some countries, such as Romania, not to take part in joint measures or specialization patterns of which they disapproved. On the other hand, this principle helped to implement some actions—for instance, the creation of international economic organizations and the realization of large joint investments—by a fraction of the member countries, leaving aside the members not interested. Thus the real significance of concertation depends upon the exact limits of those areas or branches which require a "joint definition of ways of direct interaction" according the wording of the declaration.

Let us now turn to Brezhnev's second formulation, the convergence (sblizhenie) of the structures of the economic mechanism. One should probably not attach too much importance to the ambiguity of this formulation. Was Brezhnev alluding to the convergence of the national systems of planning and management? Or was he insisting upon the convergence of the macroeconomic proportions of the national economies through a more intricate specialization? No clarification is given in the declaration that simply reproduces the expression.

However, it seems that the first line of a convergence between the national economic systems has to be rejected, even if it was on Brezhnev's mind and a part of Soviet intentions. During his short time in office Andropov pointed to the advantage of utilizing some of the experiences of the brother countries, without an alignment on the basis of a dominant model. The national systems of economic management are now substantially different, and the reforms implemented in Hungary, in Poland, and even in Bulgaria diverge from the classical Soviet model. In this context, one may quote a source published in Moscow, but edited as a joint publication of the academies of sciences of six CMEA countries (Romania did not take part): *Problems of Balancing the Socialist Economy.* The last chapter of this book deals with foreign relations and suggests that there are basically two types of mechanisms appropriate to achieving or restoring balance in this field. The first one would rely upon those elements of the economic mechanism that would help to promote exports through the price system, credit conditions, as well as through the planning and organization of foreign trade. The second one would be a directive type of planning based upon the distribution of tasks and resources among ministries and enterprises; this is clearly the Soviet model although it is not specified (Mikul'skii 1984, p. 286). No preference is expressed in favor of either of these models; it is simply suggested that the first one may be more effective in the long run and the second in the short run.

If we interpret the convergence of the structures as a strategy of specialization in the field of foreign trade and production, we are certainly closer to the spirit of the declaration. This may be a dominant Soviet view as opposed to the wishes of the partner countries, although similar views have been expressed in Czechoslovak (Maly 1984) and GDR (Mittag 1985) economic literature and official statements. Again, one may cite the conclusions of a multilateral conference in April 1983 sponsored by the International Institute for Economic Problems of the World Socialist System, one of the two CMEA institutes (International Institute for Economic Problems of the World Socialist System 1984). The text stresses that, although a definite convergence in macroeconomic structures occurred among the European CMEA countries, the outcome cannot be considered as satisfactory. In almost all countries the share of investment in national income is too high compared to the share of consumption—the same can be said about the share of producers goods, "group A," within industrial production; and all countries have a high resource-intensity of production. In addition, the conference report complains that many countries maintain parallel production lines and manufacture the same goods. Czechoslovakia manufactures 70 percent of the world assortment of machinery; in Hungary, Poland, and the GDR it is about 60 percent. As a result, their production suffers from high costs, low quality standards, excessive energy and raw materials intensity, and limited export potential.

Of course the present state of things stems from an industrial policy that has been developed as a result of Soviet influence and control going back to the 1950s. The report does not mention this point, which is rarely alluded to in East European literature but is obvious enough.[4] Thus the CMEA countries have to take collective action in order to reverse the negative results of the previous policy. This action is a part of the concertation defined above. It implies adjustments through intra-branch specialization at the microeconomic level which will be discussed later on, together with the mechanisms of SEI.

The third and last development suggested in Brezhnev's definition was the achievement of direct links between economic units. This appears in the declaration only as "an important orientation," in a rather restrained formulation. For instance, the creation of joint firms is not declared as desirable; it is only said that favorable conditions should be created for such actions. One may perhaps consider as a favorable condition the adoption in the USSR of a very little-publicized bill on the operation on the Soviet territory of joint firms with socialist partners; but the bill was not implemented in any way.[5] A Hungarian author, Csaba (1984a, p.33), quite firmly states: "there is absolutely no sign of a tendency of a gradually growing basis for micro-integrational forms in CMEA, as some analysts suggest."

The concept of SEI emerging from the June 1984 summit appears to be a compromise between Soviet views and the concepts of the smaller six, particularly as far as the division is concerned between the strategic fields of mutual cooperation and the other fields left to national initiative. The very uncertainty about where the dividing line goes may allow for some margin of maneuver.

The Withering of Market Integration

The main fact is that the market component of SEI has almost completely disappeared. It emerges only at the very end of the 1984 declaration: "the organic combination of cooperation in the field of planning and active use of monetary-market categories remains actual." Immediately following is a short statement according to which the price system is going to be improved and the transferable ruble to be strengthened.

This emphasis upon production or plan integration, as opposed to market integration, is in line with the Soviet views, but perhaps also with those of a majority of the East European countries, except Hungary (Csaba 1984b; Pecsi 1981; and Nyers 1983). This does not necessarily conflict with the general assumption that Eastern Europe is resisting the Soviet conception of integration (Marer, 1984). The smaller East European countries object to the present mechanisms of integration, especially to the involvement in joint investments, because of the strain

TABLE 5.1. Mechanisms of Socialist Economic Integration (1973–90)

Factors influencing SEI	Instruments	Forms
Structural: –dependence of Eastern Europe on energy and raw material supplies from the USSR –lack of self-sufficiency in agriculture –relative technological lag compared to the West External: –the oil shocks –Western recession –Western sanctions	Five-year "concerted plan for multilateral integration measures" 1976–80 1981–85 1986–90 "Long-term target programs for cooperation" 1978/79–90 "Long-term bilateral cooperation programs" between the USSR and the CMEA countries 1979/80–90 + Special long-term program Poland and USSR 1984–90	Joint investments (especially, if not exclusively, in five-year concerted plan no. 1 and long-term target program no. 1) Cooperation and specialization in production

it puts on their resources. But this does not mean that they should favor market integration because any development in this direction—through a larger mutual trade in goods not specified by quotas and a more active role of prices or of monetary instruments—would require an appropriate development in the reform of the domestic economies. In addition, the more the system of CMEA institutions has in fact moved away from a market-type operation, the less significant are market categories. The price issue is a case in point. Here again one may quote a Hungarian author: "in the system of trade within the CMEA relying on bilateral interstate agreements . . . the fact that a given product is exported or not does not depend on the price that may be attained, nor on the profitability of the given export deal . . . but on the particular logic of the given system of bilateral relations" (Köves 1983, p. 129).

The Mechanism for Developing SEI

In the 1970s the CMEA countries began to develop numerous mechanisms designed to respond to expanding SEI in fields of mutual interest. Table 5.1 lists the basic factors influencing the integration process during the late 1970s, along with the instruments, forms, fields, and

Fields	Ways of implementation	Domestic adjustments
Energy and raw materials	Bilateral trade	Energy-saving schemes
Agriculture	Pricing mechanisms	Increases in prices for energy and raw materials
Machine building	Settlements in transferable rubles and hard currency	
Other branches		Increased factor productivity
	Commercial and cooperation credits	Reorientation of investments
	Direct involvement in joint projects	Structural adjustments in foreign trade

ways of implementation. The last column mentions the main adjustments required in the national economies for the realization of SEI commitments.

The Basic Factors Influencing SEI

Several basic factors influenced the development of SEI in the 1970s and the early 1980s. Column 1 in table 5.1 divides these between domestic, structural factors, and external ones. The structural factors result from the economic policy conducted during the postwar period. The dependence of the smaller CMEA countries on energy and raw material imports from the USSR is the consequence, first, of a growth strategy based upon industrialization with a priority on heavy industry; second, of a foreign trade policy aiming at self-sufficiency within the bloc. As for agriculture, the present situation can be explained partly by natural endowments but mostly by the fact that agriculture was not a matter of high priority in the growth strategy of the East European countries, and by the failures of the collectivization process. The roots of the technological lag are to be found in weak links between science and industry and in the lack of incentives for innovation at the enterprises level.

These lasting structural factors have in turn been affected by external conditions in the post-1973 period. The oil shocks have created, through their impact on the price structure within the CMEA, a major imbalance in Soviet-East relations. The Western recession limited imports by the smaller CMEA countries. Although the Western sanctions probably did not affect strongly the existing technological gap despite the increased restrictions put on high technology exports to the East, the restrictions certainly did influence the attitude of the CMEA countries as to the reliability of their Western partners in this field.

Let us now discuss how the three structural factors shaped SEI in the last decade. The dependence of Eastern Europe on energy and raw materials supplies from the USSR increased slightly during the period 1973–83 both for oil—mainly through the fact that Romania became dependent on the Soviet Union for oil supplies after 1979—and for gas (Graziani 1983). The deceleration up to 1979, stabilization from 1980 on, and decrease in 1982 of Soviet oil supplies was only partially compensated for by increased gas sales. This dependence on the Soviet Union has not been replaced by an increased dependence on OPEC suppliers. It is true that oil imports have increased from these countries, but not for domestic consumption; the bulk of these imports were reexported in a crude or refined form which might be considered more as a hard-currency constraint than as a true energy constraint.

To cope with this situation, the East European countries have tried both to increase the output of their domestic energy capacities, and to implement energy-saving measures. In the first place, the production of coal and brown coal was pushed forward in almost all countries except Hungary at high costs and damaging effects for the environment. Later on, these countries embarked upon conservation measures and energy-saving schemes for which there is certainly still much room left for improvement, due to their very high level of energy consumption that is in turn related both to the structure of their economy and to the difficulties of internal adjustment through inadequate prices and insufficient incentives (Hannigan and McMillan 1983). In addition to these domestic measures, energy dependence has strongly influenced the instruments of cooperation; the areas considered as main priorities are the development of nuclear power and all the issues linked to the means of implementation such as prices, terms of trade, and imbalances in settlements.

The impact of the two other structural factors has grown since the beginning of the 1980s. The agricultural situation should have led to an intense cooperation between European CMEA countries. In fact, nothing comparable to the European Economic Community (EEC) common agricultural policy emerged. Is it because we are here in the reverse context of a shortage instead of a surplus agricultural situation? The explanations are more complex. A comparison with the energy case gives some clues. Instead of having a clearly cut contrast between one main supplier and a group of buyers as for energy, here all the countries are producers, and they lack self-sufficiency in at least one main sector, crops or animals. All of them seek self-sufficiency through national programs and reforms of agricultural management that differ significantly from country to country. All the countries compensate for their shortages by means of imports, which may be massive as in the case of the USSR, from developed and developing countries. In contrast, agricultural trade has a much more modest share in intra-CMEA trade—about 6 percent—although it is higher for some countries, especially for the three main suppliers, Bulgaria, Hungary, and Romania.

A question that naturally arises is whether the USSR intends to use its leverage as supplier of energy and raw materials to obtain more agricultural goods from its partners. The food program adopted in May 1982 in the Soviet Union outlines a scheme for restoring Soviet agriculture through massive domestic investments and a reform of the management mechanism. Its implementation was not supposed to draw significantly on the CMEA. However, at the CMEA meeting in June 1982, N. Tikhonov stated that "while maximally relying upon our own possibilities, we are hoping that the implementation of the Soviet food program will be helped by a cooperation with the other CMEA countries" (*Ekonomicheskaia Gazeta,* no. 25, June 1982, p. 9). He mentioned the exchange of information on new technologies in the fields of sugar beet growing and processing, fodder production, storage of agricultural goods, as well as a possible participation in building new objects in the Soviet Union.[6] The thirty-seventh session of the CMEA in October 1983 went a step further in recommending measures to stimulate national production in order to increase mutual trade in food products, and this was again repeated in almost the same form in the June 1984 declaration. In addition, as we have seen, the declaration quite clearly linked the increase of Soviet fuel and raw material supplies to a better supply of food products to the USSR.

The technological gap between the CMEA countries as a whole and the West had little influence on SEI until the beginning of the 1980s. In the modernization drive of the 1970s, the East European countries chose to reduce this gap through imports of technology, with an obvious lack of coordination which is now increasingly criticized in Soviet and East European writings (Simai, 1983; and International Institute for Economic Problems of the World Socialist System 1984, p. 11). The Western sanctions and growing export restrictions on high technology exports acted as a spur to closer cooperation in this field, along with a self-restraint in equipment imports linked with the level of indebtedness and the deceleration of growth in Eastern Europe after 1980.

The thirty-sixth CMEA session in 1982 criticized Western sanctions and emphasized the need for cooperation in high technology areas without explicitly linking the two developments. Several general agreements were signed for cooperation in the fields of microprocessor technology, industrial robotics, and microelectronics. The next session, in 1983, stressed the need for cooperation between some countries for the production of equipment needed in fuel extraction. At the 1984 summit the CMEA countries again attacked the sanctions and embargo, then attributed solely to the ruling circles in the United States, in a separate document entitled "Declaration on the Preservation of Peace and on International Cooperation" (Ekonomicheskaia Gazeta, no. 26, June 1984, pp. 6–7). As for the economic declaration, it emphatically insisted upon the need of "a coordinated, and in some fields joint," technological policy. It was announced that a comprehensive program for scientific and technological progress for the next fifteen to twenty years was to be jointly prepared. Following this line, the fortieth session of the CMEA, in 1985, insisted upon the increase of mutual trade in machinery and equipment meeting world quality standards, "which sales are artificially limited by the USA and some other capitalist countries" (Ekonomicheskaia Gazeta, no. 27, July 1985, p. 13).

The need for less dependence on Western technology is increasingly stressed in Soviet literature. A book (Borokh and Glagolev 1984) on "the strategic orientation of cooperation" mentions that coordination of economic and technological policy means, in particular, "the liquidation of unjustified dependence on Western imports" (p.31). It is critical of the previous lack of cooperation in research and development; many specialization agreements resulted in "trade in surpluses," without any "joint elaboration, development, and exchange of modern and high technology: this is why one had to buy many technologies from the West." Still more clearly, O. Bogomolov (1980) writes the following about the development of computer technology: "In creating their own industry for developing modern computer technology, and in implementing it for control of machinery and processing, the CMEA countries cannot count upon cooperation with capitalist countries. The latter, out of military and other considerations, refrain from selling the socialist countries the most modern computers and technologies in these fields. Thus the CMEA countries have no other choice but to secure by their own forces the necessary technological progress in computer production."

All the above-mentioned factors thus point to a strengthening of SEI in the present context. This involves the use of a variety of institutional instruments both multilateral and bilateral. The institutional instruments for promoting SEI were carefully reviewed at the 1984 summit. Table 5.1 divides them into three categories. The five-year "concerted plans for multilateral integration measures" were introduced in the mid-1970s as a new method of coordinating five-year planning, and their most distinct feature was that for each five-year period each member country had to list the relevant provisions in its own national FYP. It soon appeared that this method did not meet expectations (Nyers 1984). The first concerted plan, for 1976–80, was a collection of joint investment projects already decided upon and put together in one document, along with cooperation measures in research and development. The second plan, for 1981–85, was adopted in 1981 after a great delay, "for a whole range of reasons" (Golubev *et al.* 1983, p. 103), the main one probably being the reluctance of the member countries to embark on new joint investments. The content of the plan was a summary of the main projects and activities listed in the two other instruments of cooperation, the target programs and bilateral programs, whose time span coincided with that period. The links with the national planning systems seem to have been rather loose; a Soviet book states that the majority, but not all, of the member states incorporated the provisions of the concerted plan in their own planning (Shiriaev and Bakovetskii 1981, p. 18). The disappointment is seen in the 1984 declaration that states that the coordination of planning will have to be completed "before the beginning of the new plan period," and should be "reflected in the national plans." It had been announced already in 1983 that the 1986–90 plan was being prepared, but nothing had been said about its contents. The fortieth session of the CMEA in 1985 simply mentioned that the drafting of the plan was near completion.

The long-term target programs roughly cover the decade of the 1980s, with a possible extension up to the end of the century. Five are in operation: those for energy and raw materials, agriculture and food industry, and machine building, all signed in 1978; and for industrial consumer goods and transport, signed in 1979. The ranking of these programs reflects the basic factors influencing SEI. The program for energy and raw materials is clearly the most important, with its two dimensions, cooperation—mainly for expanding nuclear power capacities—and structural specialization. The agricultural program represents a new impetus after several years of apparent stagnation. In its initial version, it was mainly a collection of areas of mutual information and research in genetics, breed selection, chemical protection of plants, and technological improvements in agricultural machinery. The only large-scope joint agreements provided for in the program were related to the development of sugar and citrus production in Cuba that were signed in 1981. Already in October 1983 it had been decided to supplement the program, if not to replace it, with a new document entitled "Comprehensive Measures for Improving the Food Supplies to the Population of the CMEA-member States" (Ivashov 1984). These forty-seven measures are comprehensive in their scope and institutional implications. They involve fourteen CMEA organs, including the executive committee, twelve standing commissions, and the Conference of Domestic Trade Ministers. They also require the participation of the two CMEA banks, several organizations such as Agromash, Interchim, and Interneftproduct, that suggest a closer cooperation for supplying the member countries in agricultural machinery and chemicals.

On the whole, available information on the implementation of the other programs suggests no significant progress since 1981.[7]

One may wonder whether the target programs are really meaningful in more than a symbolic sense. It would appear that the third instrument of SEI, the bilateral long-term programs between the USSR and each of the CMEA members, is the most significant. These programs were discussed at bilateral meetings in Crimea during the summers of 1977–79. They include all the measures provided for in the target programs that have an impact on bilateral relations, and they may also include other actions of strictly bilateral interest: "there are no rigid borders between these two forms [multilateral and bilateral] of cooperation. They are flexible and elastic" (Shiriaev and Bakovetskii 1981, p. 190).

In the wake of the 1984 summit, these bilateral programs have all been revamped. On May 4, 1984, the eve of the summit, a new long-term program to the year 2000 was signed between the Soviet Union and Poland. Then followed, on the same terms, agreements with the GDR, October 6, 1984; Hungary, April 1, 1985; Czechoslovakia, May 31, 1985; and more are likely to follow.[8]

Although the communiqué of the 1985 CMEA sessions alludes to bilateral programs being agreed upon between East European countries —some seventeen such agreements are mentioned—the publicity given to those signed between the USSR and its partners suggests a dominant radial profile of SEI centered on the USSR. The content of the target programs is entirely included in the bilateral long-term agreements that, in addition, specify other provisions linked with structural adjustments.

The forms and fields of SEI are closely related. SEI is implemented through joint investments, mainly in the energy and raw materials sectors and through specialization, mainly in the machine building sector. Both forms were specified in the 1971 program. In the mid-1970s, with the launching of the first five-year concerted plan and of the target programs, the joint investment format seemed to have the highest priority. Later on, joint investments were scaled down in favor of a growing insistence upon specialization. However, they have definitely not disappeared.

John Hannigan and Carl McMillan (1981) have clearly analyzed the reasons for the decline in joint investments. The economic difficulties of the CMEA countries and the overall decrease in national investment resources serve as the main reasons for this evolution. In addition, there was pressing need for the Soviet Union to get long-term investment credits from its partners while it was at the same time granting long-term commercial credits for its surpluses in intra-CMEA trade. The measures included in the target programs implied a total cost of 70–90 billion transferable rubles (Golubev 1983, p. 75). According to Hungarian authors, about "20 percent refer to the joint construction of productive facilities or other projects," which would still mean 14–18 billion rubles (Poller and Tesner 1984, pp. 25–26).

Several priority investments are being undertaken. Two nuclear power stations are to be built on Soviet territory, each of 4 billion kilowatt capacity, although both were far from completion in 1985. Electric energy will be carried from these two stations to CMEA countries through two high-voltage lines to be constructed as joint investments. One line, from Khmelnitskaia in the Ukraine to Rzeszów in Poland, had been completed by 1985. The construction of a plant for processing iron ore in Krivoi Rog in the Ukraine is also a joint project. The agreement was signed at the thirty-seventh CMEA session in Berlin in 1983 with Hungary, the GDR, Czechoslovakia, and USSR as partners. According to East European sources, Poland and Romania joined the project later on. Another joint investment project is a new gas pipeline that will increase the transmission capacity to Eastern Europe by about 20 billion cubic meters per year.[9] The agreement was discussed during the 1984 summit and still had not been finalized at the 1985 session of the CMEA.

Thus it seems that high-cost priority projects are pushed forward if and when there are conditions for mutual bargaining. Obviously the partner countries are reluctant to embark upon such ventures, and they do so only if it is the sole way of getting guaranteed supplies. This may explain why in 1985 the CMEA session decided to launch a general program of cooperation for "a rational utilization of material resources" up to the year 2000. It contains over one hundred energy- and raw materials-saving schemes, including recycling of materials as well as substitution measures, with gas and solid fuels being substituted for oil. As we have seen, nearly all the CMEA countries are already intensifying coal production. As for natural gas, the CMEA countries have signed an agreement for cooperation in using it as a fuel for internal combustion engines. This may be an answer to the question whether the CMEA countries really did need such an increase in supplies of gas from the Soviet Union as to justify the building of a new pipeline.

Along with cooperation in the form of investments, specialization is advocated with increasing insistence by the Soviet Union, and it was pushed forward in the CMEA sessions. Two distinct schemes have so far materialized. One of them is related to the energy program. Along with participation in joint projects, and with pressure on East European countries for implementing energy-saving schemes, in the early 1980s the USSR advocated a division of labor that would concentrate on Soviet territory the most energy-intensive production. In 1970 an agreement had been reached for the chemical industry. The first phase of this agreement, now in progress, includes the construction of a large plant processing yeasts out of oil paraffin. The USSR has also committed itself to supply Eastern Europe with ammonia, methanol, and polyethylene in exchange for low energy-intensive chemicals. The total amount of these deliveries should reach for the 1981–85 five-year period 700 million rubles for exports and 750 million rubles for imports to the USSR. This would amount to about 15 percent of the trade in chemicals between the USSR and the other CMEA countries. It is uncertain whether it is possible to go further with such a specialization. The domestic restructuring of industry must now be particularly painful because the CMEA countries have very energy- and material-intensive industrial structures. And for the Soviet Union itself, to increase the output of the energy-intensive sector involves heavy costs in expanding the energy sector itself, although this may also be viewed as a bargaining lever to secure supplies from the most developed CMEA countries. Both the new bilateral agreements with the GDR (1984) and Czechoslovakia (1985) refer to this type of specialization.

The other specialization scheme, agreed upon multilaterally in October 1980, is related to the machine-building industry. This sector has, for a long time, been the object of an interbranch cooperation that appears to have reached a stage of stagnation. The classical examples of this cooperation are those of Hungary specializing in bus production, Bulgaria in electric carts, and Poland in excavators. While these forms are stabilized, there is now a new trend toward developing strategic specialization in seven fields, implying deep intra-branch cooperation: new systems for controlling production processes; machines and mechanisms designed to replace manual labor; mining and excavating techniques, energy-saving machinery and technology; precision metalworking and steel processing equipment; production of universal machines; systems for integrated mechanization of agriculture (Ultanbaev 1983). As may be seen from this list, specialization is directed not toward a specific branch or product but toward a complex group of problems. For instance, the multilateral agreement for cooperation and specialization in robotics gives assignments to each country for the production of different types and parts. This agreement is itself included in priority task number two, the replacement of manual labor, that not only implies installation of robots but a whole set of adjustments in the production processes (Borokh and Glagolev 1984, p. 73). How effective such a method might be is uncertain. Talks with East European economists suggest that it should be more efficient than the joint investment format but also that any real progress implies more direct interfirm relations and considerably expanded monetary mechanisms.

This point seems to be acknowledged, at least in part, in the decisions reached at the 1985 session of CMEA that insist upon industrial cooperation on the enterprise level, although the only general agreement in machine building signed during this session belongs to the usual intergovernmental type. This agreement appears to expand the previously mentioned agreement in robotics to the general field of flexible automated systems. A new CMEA committee, supplementing the three existing ones—for plan coordination, science and technology, and material supplies—was created for machine building. This means that specialization in this sector is to be ensured primarily through coordination on the level of national ministries rather than at the micro level.

The mechanisms of SEI are thus consistently oriented toward a pattern of relations implying both a hardening of the conditions of trade between the USSR and Eastern Europe, and toward domestic adjustments on the side of the smaller CMEA countries. Less certain is whether the Soviet claims for increased and better supplies are real; and what structural adjustments are in fact to be expected.

THE SOVIET REQUIREMENTS AND THE EAST EUROPEAN RESPONSES

One must keep in mind that all intra-CMEA cooperation ultimately results in trade flows. Joint investments or industrial cooperation do not generate capital flows as in a market-type international community, and they only infrequently involve minor manpower flows. Thus the post-1973 changes in SEI have been based on the concept of increased mutual trade, and Soviet requirements for East European participation in SEI have been expressed mainly as conditions for maintaining the existing levels of trade. In turn the desired structure of trade sought by the Soviet Union implies domestic policies that may be unattainable in all or most of the East European countries as well as in the Soviet Union.

The Main Characteristics of Soviet–East European Trade in the 1970s and Early 1980s

Soviet–East European trade in the 1970s and early 1980s was characterized by the following main features:

- prices sharply increased, especially for oil and other carriers after the adoption of the "Moscow formula" in 1975, with prices being modified every year according, in principle, to the average of world market prices during the five previous years;
- given the general trend in energy prices during the 1973 to 1983 decade, the prices for Soviet oil and gas remained well below world prices;
- according to Soviet statistics the much slower increase in prices for manufactured goods brought about a sharp improvement in Soviet terms of trade with the CMEA countries of 43 percent between 1974 and 1983;
- the Soviet Union did not or could not materialize its gains from improved terms of trade by increasing the value of its imports from Eastern Europe at the same rate as the value of its exports. On the contrary, in volume the trend was opposite during the entire 1975 to 1983 period: Soviet imports from the CMEA increased by 2.4 percent annually; Soviet exports by 6.2 percent;
- the Soviet surplus with Eastern Europe, cumulated for the years 1975–83, amounted to 12.8 billion rubles, that is 8 percent of the total Soviet exports for this period. The Soviet Union has granted long-term (ten-year) consolidated credits to cover this debt. In the context of the depreciation of the transferable ruble, related to the movement of intra-CMEA prices, the Soviet Union was a loser in this transaction.[10]

These developments in Soviet–East European trade have aroused the "subsidy debate" initiated by the work of Marrese and Vaňous summarized in this volume. The peculiar situation of the second half of the 1970s, giving the Soviet Union a great potential opportunity for increasing its gains from intra-CMEA trade but not allowing it to take full advantage of this opportunity, had two basic consequences:

- it reduced to practically nothing the significance of prices and monetary incentives, since the debtors do not really have to repay and the creditor cannot use its surplus. It also increased the importance of convertible currency settlements in the CMEA area, which probably now account for 15–20 percent of total settlements, but not to the sole benefit of the USSR; the only country for which precise data are published, Hungary, has consistent surpluses in its hard currency trade;

– it increased the elements of physical bilateralism (structural bilateralism in the terminology of van Brabant) in Soviet–East European relations. The Soviet Union bargains on a country-by-country basis for the supplies that it needs and that the partner may offer; and thus the 1984 declaration is the institutionalization of this process.

The change in world oil prices had no dramatic consequences for this pattern, which is a permanent one. The CMEA price formula probably led in 1985 to a higher price for oil than the current world price. This only symbolically modifies the present situation, because the balance in bilateral trade is not sought in prices but in "nature." Still, this symbolic aspect probably prompted B. Gostev, deputy chairman of the CPSU economics department, to announce at a news conference that "we shall use a method based more on current prices in the world market" *(International Herald Tribune,* June 15, 1984). This led to a great deal of speculation about the pricing formula—a three-year average price formula instead of five and the choice of the lower price between the world and the calculated intra-CMEA price. But the main issue is the level of the Soviet oil supplies, and what shall be asked of Eastern Europe in return.

The same holds true for the reverse case, when the partners of the Soviet Union supply it with hard goods, namely food. This issue is mentioned in the 1984 summit declaration as the need "to secure for the exporters other incentive economic conditions." The intra-CMEA exporters of food products—Hungary, Bulgaria, and Romania—have for many years asked for agricultural trade prices that could be fixed as they are in the Common Market, while the importers have always argued that the world price objectively reflects the international production costs (Matejcek 1984). It has been rumored that a 10 percent increase was agreed upon at the summit, but no evidence to support this has surfaced.[11] More probably, the exporters have obtained some in-kind compensation, or, in the case of Hungary, the guarantee of hard currency payments for food.

The specific features of the present situation within CMEA explain many of the misunderstandings and controversies surrounding the issue of Soviet subsidization of Eastern Europe. Among Western economists concerned with this debate, a number of questions were raised. Among the most important were whether the price structure in Soviet-East European relations implies Soviet subsidies to Eastern Europe, and, if so, what is the amount of the subsidies, or, if not, how should one evaluate the Soviet gains from intra-CMEA trade and what are the trade-offs faced by the Soviets in their trade decisions? More broadly, they asked why the Soviet Union chose to act the way it did toward Eastern Europe in the 1970s and 1980s. When East European economists entered this debate, they clearly stated that from their point of view the issue was quite irrelevant because prices do not really matter in intra-CMEA relations. In their view the whole system of trade and specialization within CMEA is unfavorable to the economic development of Eastern Europe (Köves 1983; and Csaba 1985). Only Hungarian writers have expressed this in Western journals, but their views reflect the attitude in other East European countries also.

The Soviet scheme for structural adjustment reads as follows: the Soviet Union will maintain its supplies of energy and raw materials, with some internal substitutions such as gas for oil; as a condition for this, it is pressing for an overall modernization of the domestic economies of the partner countries, in order to get the goods it needs, modern machinery, high-quality consumer goods, and also food. These requirements look logical. They are repeated and detailed in each of the bilateral agreements signed in 1984–85. But they suffer from major inconsistencies.

The first inconsistency, already noted, is that the present industrial structure in all the East European countries has been shaped according to Soviet dictates since the late 1940s. For Hungary, Tardos (1983) sums up the grievances in the following way: energy-intensive and wasteful industries have been developed to process energy and raw materials obtained from the USSR; a whole set of industries has been created to satisfy the massive requirements of the Soviet market, especially in machinery, whereas the poor quality of this production made it non-competitive on Western markets; this production structure also required heavy imports of semifinished goods from Western countries. In the mid-1970s this structure has been called into question by the energy crisis; all CMEA countries now had to decrease the energy intensity of productions but without allowing existing capacity to remain idle.

It would be simplistic to assume that the Soviet Union is now, or once again, admitting the errors of Stalinist policy and preparing to help its partners to improve their domestic structures. Things are not so simple, in part because the present structures are not easy to alter. First, the development of heavy industry has generated a whole set of lobbies. The politicians serving these lobbies, party members and ministers, still have a major influence in the decisionmaking process and would resist any such shift. The "coal-and-steel community" as this coalition is called in Poland still retains power, including that of allocating investments. The question then arises whether it really is possible to keep heavy industry growing and at the same time to increase investment in modernization. Second, the revised mechanism of cooperation and specialization within the CMEA is supposedly introducing a division of labor where the USSR would develop its energy-intensive production, for instance in chemicals, while other countries would supply it with low energy-intensive, high value goods. But at the same time the CMEA countries are to take part in the development of the energy sector in the USSR, which again implies on their part high material-intensive production. Such is the case for the nuclear power equipment manufactured by Czechoslovakia to meet the needs, first of all, of the USSR and then of the CMEA. The related investments absorb one quarter of the total investments in the machine building sector (Blaha and Tirapolsky 1984; and Fox 1982).

As we have seen, all the CMEA countries are introducing energy-saving measures and signed an agreement in 1985 for cooperation in this sector. Should they succeed in this, their needs in fuel imports from the USSR might be sharply reduced. If so, then costly contributions to energy investments in the USSR do not make sense unless it was assumed from the beginning that energy saving programs would not succeed, which is probably the case.

By basing its future relations with the CMEA countries on a raw materials versus finished goods scheme, the Soviet Union itself is hampering its modernization and its passage to an intensive growth path. True, Soviet writings insist on the need for the USSR to increase machinery exports to the CMEA countries.[12] But if the basic problem of these countries is to step up their exports to the USSR, why should they agree to increase this burden by importing additional quantities of machinery on top of raw materials and energy?

In order to stimulate modernization and innovation, a more flexible domestic economic mechanism is required. This in turn points to the necessity of realizing deep reforms leading toward the strengthening of the market. Wide-ranging changes in this direction might be accepted with reluctance in the Soviet Union. Such changes would also probably entail a revival of market mechanisms within the CMEA. Though advocated by some economists, even in the Soviet Union and in Czechoslovakia, such a revival is not now on the agenda in the CMEA. (Ruzmich 1982; and Grinberg and Liubskii 1985).

The Soviet Union clearly wants the modernization process to be carried out with the least dependence on imports of Western technology. At the same time it wants its partners to meet Western standards of quality. The optimal case would be the export, to the USSR, of high quality goods which would also be competitive on Western markets. To do thus, however, trade with the West ought to be expanded, both on the side of the imports and the exports.

It is very difficult to predict the outcome of these contradictory developments. Reasonably enough, one may expect a growing share of trade with the Soviet Union in the total trade of the East European members of CMEA, along with stagnation of the intra-East European trade as a result of the need to increase exports toward the USSR. As for structural adjustments, they are not really feasible without changes in the economic system. Marginally, the Soviet Union might wish to support the modernization efforts in the most advanced countries such as the GDR, Czechoslovakia, and in some areas Bulgaria, but the very contradictions rooted in the package of the Soviet requirements will probably yield only a slightly improved status quo.

CHAPTER 6

CMEA Institutions and Policies versus Structural Adjustment: Comments on Chapter 5

Jozef M. van Brabant

This rephrased title of the chapter on which I comment is not simply an error or a facetious pun on Lavigne's interesting essay. Although, as on many occasions in the past, I disagree with some of her facts and figures—and I would have put a different emphasis on the interpretation of national, regional, and more general trade policies of the East European countries—there are few statements in the essay with which I fundamentally disagree. However, the dilemma that she poses for the East European members of CMEA provides a solid bone for me to chew on to my heart's desire. The question is whether the East European CPEs in general should have a pronounced preference for enhancing trade with the USSR and market economy partners, to the exclusion of fostering ties to other CMEA or other socialist countries.

I understand Lavigne to have set out the situation thus: realistically speaking, the East European countries can seriously pursue measures to enhance productivity growth only if they intensify their cooperation primarily with the USSR and the developed market economies. These necessary relations will secure for Eastern Europe, in the first instance, predictable import volumes of fuels and raw materials. Ties with the latter group of countries will permit them to offset supply shortfalls in foodstuffs and gradually to close the technology gap. If this interpretation of Lavigne's position is correct, it runs, of course, diametrically counter to what I have elsewhere described as the mainstream policy area for fruitful decisions affecting Eastern Europe's growth potential in the late 1980s and 1990s (Brabant 1987). It also would negate any advocacy of the creation of a central European customs union as the potentially most fruitful institutional form for enhancing cooperation among the active European members of the Council for Mutual Economic Assistance (CMEA).[1]

This volume is not the proper forum for developing my arguments once again ab ovo. However, by commenting first on Lavigne's views on CMEA institutions, policies, and policy instruments and then on her analysis of the need and scope for national and regional structural adjustment, I shall avail myself of the opportunity to restate succinctly my position on the future of socialist economic integration (SEI). In the process, I shall have an opportunity to comment on disagreements with Lavigne as to the achievements of the recent CMEA summit and its aftermath with respect to policies affecting SEI.

GLOBAL RECESSION AND THE CMEA's INTEGRATION MECHANISM

When commenting on the recent economic performance of the CMEA members individually and in concert, it is fair to remind ourselves that the global recession of the early 1980s, while definitely over as far as North America and most of the Far Eastern countries are concerned, is only very slowly being overcome in the European market economies that are the chief Western trade partners of the CPEs. External events and the limping pace of growth attained during the past ten or so years have had a strong impact on feasible levels of economic activity in Eastern Europe, on the formulation of remedial policies, and on the process of SEI. They are also bound to leave a marked imprint on trade and more general economic policies of the CPEs in the years ahead.

It should be recalled at this juncture that the present CMEA institutions, regional policies, and policy instruments have changed little over the past decade or so and most have been in place at least since the early 1960s. That is to say there have been no major changes in integration policies and supporting institutions since the promulgation of the 1971 integration program and the first years of the institution-building euphoria engendered by the debates preceding and surrounding the adoption of that basic SEI document.[2] The severe external shocks and domestic economic disturbances of the last five to seven years cannot but have entailed a deep malaise in intra-CMEA affairs. On that score, I do not differ with Lavigne.

For all practical purposes no new institutions have been created since 1975.[3] The high-level policy meeting of April 1969 was not followed up until the June 1984 economic summit. During the second half of the 1970s it was decided to elaborate target programs and to coordinate medium-term plans more closely, but these instruments as such have not really affected CMEA cooperation in any major way. One achievement of the summit was to enshrine officially the implicit endorsement of dealing bilaterally with the CMEA partners. Although structural bilateralism has been a major force in intra-CMEA affairs at least since the early 1960s, the summit formally recognized the trend to abandon the multilateral SEI approach envisioned in the early 1970s in favor of the more intensive and wider exploration of bilateral relations.[4] The Czechoslovak-Soviet agreement concluded in early July 1984 is a clear-cut practical illustration of this trend.[5]

Policy Issues

Has the concept of SEI been fundamentally altered? Looking back at the integration program, the subsequent policy debates, and council session endorsements, I cannot but deplore the absence of a clear definition of SEI, of the precise goals to be pursued, and of the role of the various policy instruments available to the CPEs. In that context, Brezhnev's suggestions made at the USSR's Twenty-sixth Party Congress in February 1981 are far from new. In fact, Brezhnev was not the first to advocate the convening of an economic summit of party leaders.[6] His was a fairly casual remark in connection with the quite detailed examination of the general state of the USSR's economic cooperation with the world socialist system. This analysis led to the identification of major problem areas that should not be "painted in radiant colors" (Brezhnev 1982, p. 6). Against this backdrop, I find arguments concerning theoretical developments launched by Brezhnev's allegedly new ideas neither very convincing nor illuminating. The only fairly new idea—although it had already been explored in the integration program's section eight—was the advocacy of the creation of joint firms, an elusive concept in any case.[7] The other two topics, the concertation of economic policies and the greater harmonization of economic mechanisms, have been current in CMEA debates at least since the abandonment of the monetary SEI tasks outlined in the integration program's section seven.

Among the two broad documents[8] issuing from the summit, the basic economic one, here referred to as Main Directions, is a carefully worded statement that has two weighty implications: the drift toward the strengthening of structural bilateralism and the adoption of new rules for maintaining a buoyant exchange of fuels and raw materials for manufactures. Otherwise, I cannot find in it any updating of the 1971 document. The concertation issue, which Lavigne discusses in detail, I find largely semantic: greater policy consultation is required in all areas that directly affect intra-CMEA cooperation; but interested members will harmonize their policies, or coordinate their plans if you will, only in areas that have a more indirect bearing on present CMEA cooperation endeavors.[9] Thus, scientific-technical cooperation in new production technologies —for example, the development, testing, and future production of microcomputers—could be a voluntary activity while the coordination of demand and supply of energy would have a more binding character. I therefore do not find it illuminating to identify economic policy with either industrial policy or adjustment of macroeconomic structures as Lavigne does.

Lavigne has a better point as far as the obscurity of the notion of structure of the economic mechanisms is concerned. I would position it primarily in the context of the salient features of the management of CPES rather than in the "harmonization of economic policies." I doubt that suggestions for the synchronization of shadow exchange rates, export incentives, prices, and other such parameters, if made, have ever been seriously entertained for implementation. On the other hand, such topics as the rapprochement in planning and management of foreign trade, economic reforms more generally, and target programming have been singled out repeatedly as key instances for harmonizing the structure of economic mechanisms. I suggest that Main Directions should be read chiefly against that backdrop without searching for any further sinister intents.

On the question of microeconomic integration, I doubt that the complexity of views held in the CMEA can be reduced to that of the USSR versus Eastern Europe. I find it difficult to subscribe to the notion that

Brezhnev was advancing the idea of promoting SEI through interfirm or interenterprise cooperation. From Main Directions, I infer that interenterprise cooperation is being given serious thought as a means of enhancing the implementation of some aspects of types of SEI consented to on various macroeconomic or political levels. This is also the attitude of Czechoslovakia and the German Democratic Republic. For the other CPES, however, the range of desirable forms extends from rigid separation of internal and external markets, as in Romania, to the widest degree of inter-enterprise cooperation, as held by Hungary.

Instruments

The concerted plan in its present form can hardly be considered a new method of coordinating five-year planning.[10] It was a novel way in which to catalog systematically SEI measures that had been agreed upon multilaterally and bilaterally; it may have enhanced the inclusion of these measures in the relevant five-year and annual plans so that proper resource commitments and tradables would be adequately budgeted; and it certainly has called explicit attention to SEI achievements through plan coordination and joint planning. However, as an operational instrument of plan coordination it has been only marginally significant. The concerted plan, in my view, has not failed mainly due to the CPES' reluctance to commit investment resources. Aside from jointly financed projects, each concerted plan contains projects for production specialization, projects for scientific-technical cooperation, and miscellaneous topics including aid to the peripheral CMEA countries.[11] From the very beginning members have found it very difficult to blend the concerted plan with operational trade agreements on the one hand, and each of these with the national medium-term and annual plans on the other. This is probably one of the key reasons why some CPES simply do not even bother to include a special section on SEI measures in their medium-term and annual plans, thus weakening considerably the chances that agreements hammered out at the political level would be formulated concretely and implemented on schedule.

Not much needs to be said about the multilateral target programs because nobody knows exactly where they presently stand. From commentary in the specialized literature, however, it is evident that progress is being made in a few areas of particular interest to CMEA members in view of their current and prospective economic situation, including, for example, nuclear energy generation and transmission.

More important, as could have been predicted in the light of the trade and payments models typical of the CPEs, are bilateral agreements. In fact, it has been crystal clear from the very beginning that target programs would have to pass through several negotiation stages to reach, in the end, what I called the bilateral implementation agreements.[12] It is clear that only a few have been negotiated in the context of the multilateral target programs. The bilateral long-term agreements signed in the last five years or so between the USSR and each East European CPE have, in my view, overtaken the target programs, except perhaps in the few fields for which concrete implementation agreements were signed in 1979–81. Given the USSR's preferred planning instruments and the fact that the CMEA's target programs were preceded by several national target programs in the USSR, it is not surprising that there are apparently no parallel agreements signed among the East European countries themselves. I doubt, though, that the bilateral long-term programs do in fact contain at least all elements of the multilateral target programs. Since they were signed more recently than the target programs, they probably are embedded with a greater degree of realism and hence ignore the optimistic forecasts made for the target programming approach in the second half of the 1970s.

Has the joint investment format for all practical purposes been abandoned?[13] I do not really think so. From an examination of the experiences with the projects coming under the first concerted plan —which was very lopsided as a result of the Orenburg requirements, the discussions of the second concerted plan, and current debates including the summit's deliberations about joint investments—there is strong evidence that joint investments of the Orenburg type will be the exception, if embraced at all, in the future. But that certainly does not mean that the joint financing of investment projects related to SEI, perhaps a better description than joint investments, will be abandoned for the foreseeable future. For one, such investment projects will be decided jointly but they will be financed, in the first place, chiefly by the country where the project will be located. This appears to be the mainstay of whatever projects coming under the target programs are still viable. In this context, the "joint" then necessarily refers to the declared interest of two or more CPEs in obtaining future deliveries of the project's results—hence the trade aspects of SEI investment endeavors that have always been the key element of this form of CMEA cooperation. If the country of location is reluctant to appropriate its own investable funds for the purpose, the CPEs are bound to fall back upon the well-tried methods of "special purpose credits," another description more apt than joint investments. Whether the data cited for the projects cofinanced by the International Investment Bank (IIB) confirm the receding of interest in joint investments is a moot question. The funds appropriated in recent years are not out of line with the experience of the early 1970s if the special circumstances of Orenburg and the turbulent socio-economic environment of the early 1980s are discounted. It is not so much a lack of interest in joint investment as the very extensive gamut of obstacles impeding the effective utilizing of committed funds in trans-ferable rubles and organizational and managerial impediments that ham-pers IIB's further expansion.

One important set of policy variables that the integration program had slated for comprehensive revamping was the financial and mone-tary sphere, including the trade and payments mechanisms directly related to the degree of flexibility in international finance. While a few aspects of tourist exchange rates and related policies were updated, the financial measures introduced in the early and mid-1970s fell far short of what could have been reasonably anticipated. Throughout the crisis years, the established CMEA institutions as well as the individual CPEs did nothing in the financial and monetary sphere that could have eased the external constraints. On the contrary, more and more CPEs resorted to greater bilateralism, especially structural bilateralism. During the preparation of the summit, the role of the transferable ruble (TR), price formation, and international credit received substantial attention. As Lavigne notes, Main Directions has little to say about the matter. But Main Directions does not seem to reflect adequately the issues debated during the summit.[14]

THE MECHANISM OF SEI

The economic mechanism of SEI can be defined as the set of inter-related measures comprising policy instruments, institutions, and behav-ioral rules mobilized to attain some goals shared by the integrating units in harmony with the policies and institutions of the participating countries (Brabant 1980, pp. 231–39). Defined in this way, there would appear to be very few instances in which the changing resource con-straints and capacity limitations for the CMEA as a whole or for individ-ual CPES have affected the SEI mechanism since the promulgation of the integration program. It is undoubtedly true that the sharp realignments of international economic relations in the last ten to fifteen years have been accompanied by mounting pressures for modifying the CMEA's economic mechanism. Apart from a few cases in which well-entrenched components of the SEI mechanism have been streamlined in order to avert the emergence of too great a gap between intra-CMEA and East-West relations, the mechanism as such has remained intact in spite of the promises held out in the integration program and policy discussions thereof. I shall try to show that it is precisely such a fundamental transformation of the SEI mechanism, rather than its fairly simplistic streamlining, that is required at this stage, either to promote regional cooperation, the extension of radial dependence centered on the Soviet Union, or even a shift in East-West trade.

The goals to be served by SEI, apart from the long-term and fundamental ones discussed in the previous section are, of course, a different matter altogether. In this context, alleviating the energy resource constraint has been paramount since the mid-1970s, although it should be recalled that energy costs and availability figured prominently already in the policy debates surrounding the endorsement of Basic Principles.[15] It would be a fundamental mistake, however, to see the energy constraint only from the angle of Soviet supplies, domestic capacity constraints and restrictions, and Soviet price policies in intra-CMEA transactions.

It would appear to be more useful to picture the adjustment problem of the East European CPEs against the kinked-curved supply situation. While a peculiar supply situation for energy, many industrial raw materials, and foodstuffs has been typical of the CMEA during most of the postwar period, it has been sharply magnified, especially for energy, as a result of world price movements. Basically, the net-energy importers face an external supply curve that consists in part of the Soviet TR price supply curve, the Soviet dollar price supply curve, and the rest of the world's supply curve. The real market situation before the oil shock of 1973 can thus be shown in figure 6.1 by the East European demand (D_{EE}^1), the Soviet TR price supply curve (S_{SU}^1), and the world supply curve (S_W^1).[16] With the first oil shock, if anything, S_W^1 moved to S_W^2 while D_{EE}^1 and S_{SU}^1 remained largely unchanged. This created a real gap in required adjustment, indicated in figure 6.1 by CB units, to be worked off variously through mandatory cutbacks in demand, price adjustments, or a combination thereof.

Eastern Europe's demand for oil and global supplies

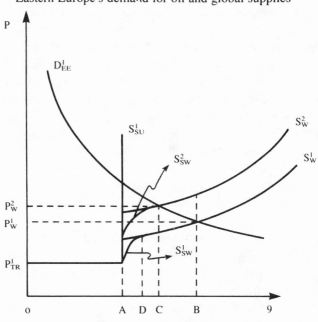

FIGURE 6.1. The first oil shock

With the second oil shock, the reinterpretation of the Bucharest price formula, and cutback in Soviet supplies at TR prices, the market situation changed drastically to something like the supply-demand pattern depicted in figure 6.2: the Soviet TR price curve shifts northwest, implying lower quantities and higher prices, the world's supply curve S_W^3 shifts further north and world prices move to P_W^3.[17] At that level, external deficits are perceived to be unmanageable by CPE policymakers and demand must be reduced further, here indicated by a southwesterly movement of the demand schedule to D_{EE}^2 for a compression of demand by EF. The contraction in affordable supplies from OB units in figure 6.1 to OE units in figure 6.2 illustrates one aspect of the adjustment burden faced by a number of East European CPES.

As shown, world supply at prevailing prices P_W^3 continues to be rather elastic over a wide range, suggesting that in fact the energy constraint is a foreign currency constraint: the East European countries could have procured virtually any realistic amount of oil in world markets had there not been such a sharp gap between the real cost of

Eastern Europe's demand for oil and global supplies

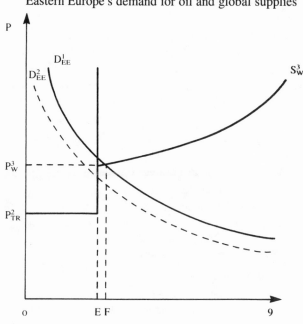

FIGURE 6.2. The second oil shock

imports in TR and dollars, and also had there not been such a pronounced limit on the convertible currency earning ability of the CPES. This may seem like a trivial remark but in fact it is not, as I shall try to show below. Thus, the energy situation has led to two fundamental constraints. On the one hand, there is the adjustment constraint, that is, the material and other resources required to realign production structures to new real relative prices. This could be a temporary measure. Much more fundamental is the constraint on the CPES' capacity to earn foreign exchange. The latter one has now been exacerbated by the apparent summit endorsement regarding the intensification of structural bilateralism.

The second basic constraint considered by Lavigne is the one emerging from the agricultural or rather the foodstuff situation. While from the economic point of view the cause can be reduced to a foreign exchange constraint, too, there is in fact an additional foreign policy component that leads developed and semi-developed countries to seek a substantial measure of foodstuff self-sufficiency for strategic purposes.

In the case of some CPEs, of course, vulnerability to embargoes that can be imposed at will by large foodstuff exporters adds a degree of urgency to ensuring minimum supplies.[18]

The main feature of the agricultural situation in Eastern Europe is not so much that all are producers and none is self-sufficient in both crop and livestock products. The latter is by no means a self-evident proposition. Based on the criterion of being a net exporter of foodstuffs, as distinct from industrial crops, I would argue that at least Bulgaria and Hungary qualify.[19] Measured against their potential, Romania also will have to be included.

In contrast to Lavigne, I do believe that one major objective of the USSR, as it emerges to some degree from Main Directions, is to enhance Eastern Europe's potential to increase food supplies. Aside from energy, foodstuffs is the only target selected for incentive prices as well as joint investments and the proper sharing of the real costs of production from within the region. In other words, there may be a strong trend toward securing greater regional self-sufficiency in foodstuff production in parallel with the USSR's ambitious food program. Lavigne correctly emphasizes that there is no longer any mention of learning from the experiences of the fraternal countries, as Brezhnev and later Andropov repeatedly stressed. However, I doubt that experimentation in agriculture has been abandoned, not only in Hungary but in other East European countries as well.

Once again the technology constraint is, by virtue of there being ample room to catch up with Western technology levels, largely a foreign exchange constraint. The security consideration referred to in the context of agricultural self-sufficiency applies also to some facets of the technology gap. I disagree, however, with Lavigne's contention that the technology gap did not influence SEI until the beginning of the 1980s. There have been several direct as well as indirect feedbacks.

Perhaps the most direct impact has been felt as a result of the request for the "hardening" of intra-CMEA trade that followed upon the surge in East-West transfer of technology in the late 1960s and early 1970s. When these processes came on stream, CMEA partners insisted on acquiring the goods directly or in transformed form. In some instances this transfer was agreed to, only against payments in convertible currency. But a number of CPEs complained that the magnitude of the direct and indirect hard currency components in their intra-CMEA trade had been rising sharply, a factor that may have contributed to the worsening balance-of-payments situation of several CPEs. Another indirect factor has been the ex post realization that the successful transfer of foreign technology usually entails future imports of raw materials and intermediate goods that cannot be substituted without worsening the efficacy of the technology. This embedded structural import demand was one important factor in the difficulties encountered in the late 1970s with containing import demand while trying simultaneously to sustain buoyant domestic output growth. These two, as well as a number of other, consequences of the East-West technology gap have indirectly influenced the policy stance in CMEA-wide scientific-technical cooperation at least in the past decade.

However, the realization that technology levels in East and West have hardly kept abreast has had a significant direct effect on policy stances. In fact, the need to intensify scientific-technical cooperation in both the development and the production phases was a central focus of the debates surrounding the target programs, concerted plans, and other forms of plan coordination.[20] What is comparatively new is the explicit recognition that, as Lavigne notes, the East-West experiments of the 1970s essentially foundered and that there is no reliable alternative to greater regional scientific-technical cooperation under the prevailing circumstances. I believe, as I shall argue below, that in any case there is no alternative, chiefly for balance-of-payments reasons.

REGIONAL INTEGRATION AND
STRUCTURAL ADJUSTMENT

The global recessions of the late 1970s and early 1980s have had a profound impact on the formulation and implementation of short-term economic policies in Eastern Europe. While the recent experiences are bound to leave a marked impression on the molding of longer-term growth policies, economic reforms, and, indeed, integration efforts, I am considerably more skeptical than Lavigne with regard to Eastern Europe's response to the required adjustment policies. I find it hard to subscribe to the notion that the maturation process of structural adjustment policies has already reached its final stages and the East European CPEs are now prepared to implement the adaptations called for by the many years during which reforms have been eschewed. This opinion is most forcefully illustrated by two important developments in the 1970s: the sharp shifts in energy prices relative to manufactures and the volume restrictions encountered in part because of balance-of-payments constraints; and, to a lesser degree, by serious capacity and transportation bottlenecks in the USSR.

One could categorize the scope for structural adjustment in the CPEs into four areas: (i) the alignment of the CPEs with real factor scarcities; (ii) the need to regain a faster growth path through a rapid expansion of factor productivity levels; (iii) the renewal of productive structures in line with the considerable shift in relative trade prices in the 1970s; and (iv) requirements to meet the mounting pressures within the CMEA to expand production capacities, to eliminate bottlenecks, to price goods and services realistically, and to upgrade the technological sophistication of a more export-oriented productive structure. I have argued elsewhere that this is a very ambitious menu whose implementation will take considerable time, even if the present CPE leadership were to decide unambiguously on vigorously pursuing economic policies that foster factor productivity growth; I doubt that this sentiment presently prevails. One way to pursue this course would be to expose the economies to the "economic shock," that is, to create institutions and to set behavioral rules that would induce agents to take real scarcities into account. Given the magnitude of the required adjustment, such a course could only be pursued if the sociopolitical fabric of the CPEs could withstand a sharp cut in living standards through a deep recession. The experiences with the growth deceleration of 1978–82 in a number of CPEs clearly illustrate that, socially and politically, such a course is simply not viable.

The alternative is gradualism: the promotion of the exchange of primary goods for manufactures; the steady upgrading of specialization both by products and technical levels in manufacturing activities; steady increases in regional output levels of foodstuffs; and selective borrowing of technology from the West in combination with growing scientific-technical cooperation within the CMEA as an integral part of production specialization. How does this recipe blend with Lavigne's precepts? She notes that the domestic restructuring of industry should now be particularly painful as most of the CMEA countries have very high energy- and raw material-intensive structures and that the summit participants are now confronted with structural adjustments that will allow them to meet the Soviet needs while pursuing their own economic policy. I find her arguments concerning the Soviet Union's responsibility for the antiquated economic structures in Eastern Europe or the latter's apparent need to maintain too wide an output range far from compelling.

It is undoubtedly true that the CPEs are too autarkic, their production structure is very material-intensive, they lack sophistication in production technologies and products, and that the USSR has for many years been a market willing and able to absorb virtually anything that Eastern Europe has chosen to export. However, East European complacency, lack of strength to test the USSR's tolerance for meaningful economic reforms, and the alleged assigning of CMEA specialization by the USSR under present circumstances are largely excuses that lack a firm foundation in many instances.[21] In the majority of cases, the need for structural adjustments has now built up over a period of nearly twenty-five years; it was evident well before the oil shocks, although the mounting backlog has been considerably exacerbated by the adverse external developments of the 1970s.

Does the building up of bilateral ties with the USSR in conjunction with a rapid expansion of East-West economic ties offer a way out? If the CPES were in a position to divert their trade to the West without incurring severe payments problems, I maintain that they would have realigned their foreign commerce long ago and that there would not be a malaise in the CMEA. It is precisely because of the sharp dichotomy between the fairly insular CMEA market and the high degree of competition in developed market economies and the hard currency markets of developing countries that a sharp and substantial switch to Western markets is simply not feasible in the foreseeable future. Since maintaining steady increases in national output and per capita income levels is the prime legitimation of the CPE political regimes, an alternative to the present moderate growth expansion will have to be found. But it cannot be based either on domestic demand and supply or on an expansion of economic and financial ties with the West. Hence, there does not appear to be a realistic alternative to fostering SEI with great determination.

That, I submit, is precisely the lesson of the summit: to commit the CPES to finding such an alternative economic structure for the sake of restoring buoyant growth. Some useful start may already have been made as a result of the seven or so target areas chosen to date for comprehensive specialization. To the extent that these programs will be pursued against a predominantly economic background they should be welcomed. However, I do not have sufficient details at my disposal to argue the benefits of these activities one way or the other. That the

USSR may have flexed its CMEA muscles a bit more demonstratively than in the past can only be welcomed. After all, had the USSR not been such a complacent market for so long, Eastern Europe would have had to embrace far-reaching structural adjustments much earlier, in any case well before the onset of the oil shocks.

I doubt, though, that the USSR has a ready-made recipe for a feasible SEI strategy. In an earlier essay, Lavigne maintained that the USSR has been using the oil lever to sway its East European partners into adopting the Soviet precept of strictly planned regional economic cooperation, radially centered on the USSR, by means of target programs. (Lavigne 1983, pp. 135ff.) I am glad to learn from her contribution to this volume that she no longer subscribes to this notion, but nevertheless her emphasis on the bilateral target programs is somewhat disturbing.

CHAPTER 7

The Content and Controversy of Soviet Trade Relations with Eastern Europe, 1970–1984

Michael Marrese
Jan Vaňous

INTRODUCTION

Implicit Soviet trade subsidies to the East European members of CMEA are defined as the Soviet Union's opportunity loss as a result of trading at intra-CMEA foreign trade prices (ftps) with East European countries rather than at world market prices (wmps) with the developed West. In this essay our earlier work (Marrese and Vanous 1982a, 1982b, 1983a, 1983b) on this topic is updated and expanded. The third section contains estimates of implicit Soviet trade subsidies to each East European country for the period 1979–84. Moreover, the estimates reported here for 1970–84 are based on a new methodology for revaluing intra-CMEA trade flows of manufactured goods. This essay also addresses some of the controversial issues surrounding Soviet subsidization: anticipated versus unanticipated subsidies; data problems; the nature of bilateral bargaining between the Soviet Union and Eastern Europe; and the interpretation of the magnitude and distribution of subsidies.

The discussion of implicit trade subsidies in Soviet trade with Eastern Europe began with two articles by Mendershausen (1959, 1960) and grew into the Holzman-Mendershausen "price discrimination debate." Mendershausen noted that at the official Soviet dollar/ruble exchange rate, the Soviet Union sold exports at higher prices to Eastern Europe than to Western Europe, and seemed to buy imports at lower prices from Eastern Europe than from Western Europe. Hence the Soviet Union utilized its monopolistic-monoposonistic position to reap the profits accruing to it as a dominant seller and buyer.

Holzman (1962, 1965) criticized Mendershausen's use of unit values of Soviet exports to and imports from Western Europe as proxies for wmps because Western Europe often discriminated against the Soviet Union—by charging higher prices for exports and by means of restrictive policies against imports from the Soviet Union. In addition, Holzman objected to the use of wmps as the proper norm because CMEA was a customs union with price-setting practices different from those of Western Europe's market mechanism.

We have advanced the thesis that the Soviet Union has been subsidizing East European countries by being a net exporter of hard goods (fuels, nonfood raw materials, and, to a lesser degree, food and raw materials for food) at intra-CMEA ftps that are below wmps, and by being a net importer of soft goods (machinery, equipment, and industrial consumer goods) at intra-CMEA ftps that are above wmps. Furthermore, we have argued that the Soviets have transferred the anticipated portion of these subsidies to East European countries in order to secure the allegiance of the political leaderships of these countries. Allegiance includes a range of strategic, political, ideological, and nonmarket economic benefits. We claim that the Soviet Union regards East European allegiance as a substitute for the use of Soviet labor and military hardware in the production of overall Soviet security. The Soviet Union, as the dominant power within CMEA, has the choice of either obtaining East European allegiance through the threat of armed intervention, which is partly dependent on whether Soviet troops are stationed within a particular East European country, or through preferential trade treatment.

METHODOLOGY FOR CALCULATION
OF IMPLICIT TRADE SUBSIDIES

The methodology for the calculation of implicit trade subsidies is described in detail in an appendix available from the authors. The essence of the methodology is to revalue Soviet ruble exports to and imports from six East European countries by aggregating trade flows according to wmps rather than the intra-CMEA ftps that were utilized in the actual transactions. This revaluation is done separately for exports and imports and for each of six commodity categories: investment machinery, arms, fuels, nonfood raw materials, food and raw materials for food, and industrial consumer goods. For each bilateral commodity trade flow a corresponding series of dollar/ruble conversion coefficients is constructed to reflect the relationship between intra-CMEA ruble ftps and East-West trade dollar prices. This involves the collection of the available pairs of intra-CMEA ruble ftps and dollar wmps and their aggregation into dollar/ruble conversion coefficients for the six commodity categories. Such a procedure was followed to produce dollar/ruble conversion coefficients for fuels, nonfood raw materials, and food. In the cases of investment machinery and industrial consumer goods we derive our estimates by means of a unit-value methodology which is controversial when applied to manufactured goods. Only benchmark estimates of conversion coefficients, mostly for 1982, can be thus obtained, and a time series of conversion coefficients was derived by comparing the developments in intra-CMEA ruble ftps—based on official Hungarian and Polish ruble/socialist trade price indices—and East-West trade or world market dollar prices—based mostly on official Hungarian and Polish nonsocialist trade price indices. In particular, faster growth of dollar prices than ruble prices results in an increase in the dollar/ruble conversion rate. Finally, our educated guess is that the dollar/ruble conversion rate for Soviet arms exports to or imports from a particular East European country is twice the corresponding dollar/ruble conversion rate for investment machinery.

Once Soviet ruble commodity trade flows at intra-CMEA ftps are converted into dollars at wmps, the rest of the subsidy calculation is simple. If Soviet ruble trade with a particular East European country is balanced, the implicit trade subsidy measured in dollar terms simply equals the dollar trade surplus calculated as the difference between the dollar value of total Soviet exports and the dollar value of total Soviet imports. However, if the Soviet ruble trade balance with the country is different from zero, then the implicit subsidy simply equals the dollar trade balance minus the dollar equivalent of the ruble trade balance. In order to convert the ruble trade balance into dollar terms, we need a realistic or settlement dollar/ruble exchange rate. For this purpose we use the average dollar/ruble conversion rate for all Soviet imports from a particular country. In other words, we claim that the realistic dollar value of any Soviet ruble trade surplus with a given East European country is the dollar value of a typical basket of East European goods that will be delivered in the future when the Soviet ruble trade credit to that country is repaid through delivery of these goods. As a matter of fact, the dollar/ruble conversion rates for Soviet ruble trade surpluses generally move very closely with official or internal parametric East European commercial dollar/ruble cross-exchange rates, such as those currently in use by Czechoslovakia, Hungary, Poland, and Romania.

ESTIMATES OF IMPLICIT SOVIET TRADE SUBSIDIES TO EASTERN EUROPE FOR 1970–1984

Estimates of implicit Soviet trade subsidies to Eastern Europe measured in current dollars are presented in table 7.1. Three sets of estimates are presented, a baseline estimate, an estimate based on high dollar/ruble conversion rates for manufactured goods, and an estimate based on low dollar/ruble conversion rates for manufactured goods. The purpose of presenting three sets of estimates is to illustrate the sensitivity of these estimates to changes in assumptions with regard to the conversion rates for manufactured goods, which involve considerable uncertainty.

We consider the baseline estimates of subsidies to be the most plausible because they are based on empirically derived conversion rates for manufactured goods. The calculation based on high conversion rates for manufactured goods simply reflects an across-the-board 33 percent increase in all conversion coefficients for the three types of manufactures for all years. Thus it incorporates a higher evaluation of the quality of CMEA-manufactured goods than we estimated empirically. The 33 percent increase leads to estimates of derived conversion rates for investment machinery and consumer goods that we believe are high upper limits. For instance, using the 33 percent increase, the estimated conversion rates for East German exports of consumer goods to the Soviet Union are 1.37 in 1978; 1.47 in 1979; 1.52 in 1980; 1.36 in 1981; and 1.25 in 1982. Compare these figures to the official dollar/ruble exchange rates, which are generally considered to be highly overvalued: 1.47 in 1978; 1.52 in 1979; 1.54 in 1980; 1.39 in 1981; and 1.38 in 1982 (Marrese and Vañous 1984). Finally, the calculation based on low conversion coefficients for manufactured goods reflects an across-the-board 25 percent reduction in these coefficients; it therefore includes a lower quality evaluation than we estimated empirically. Given the empirical foundation of the baseline estimates, the discussion below focuses solely on those estimates. Fortunately the trends described below apply to the alternative estimates as well.

As expected, the baseline estimates of subsidies in terms of current dollars show great variance over time. Their lowest aggregate value was $0.8 billion in 1972 while their peak level occurred in 1981 when they reached $18.7 billion. During the period under study (1970–84), four phases of development in the size of these subsidies can be distinguished. During the first phase, 1970–73, these subsidies averaged $1.1 billion annually, reflecting the last few years of relative price stability on the world market. The fourfold increase in the wmp of oil and the concurrent surge in prices of many primary commodities led to a fourfold increase in the size of these subsidies between 1973 and 1974. During the second period, 1974–79, the subsidies averaged $6.4 billion annually ($5.8 billion if 1979 is excluded), despite the doubling of the ruble price of Soviet oil exported to Eastern Europe in 1975 and steady but smaller increases in Soviet energy export prices in subsequent years. The next round of large increases in world market oil prices, 45 percent in 1979, an additional 65 percent in 1980, and 10 percent in 1981, pushed subsidies to their highest level. During the third phase, 1980–81, the subsidies averaged $18.4 billion annually. Finally, a sharp decline in the size of subsidies occurred during the fourth phase, 1982–84, when their average level declined to $12.1 billion. The dramatic decline in the scale of subsidies in 1982–83 reflected mostly the decline in dollar wmps of oil—1 percent in 1982 and 13 percent in 1983—while the average Soviet ruble export prices of oil to Eastern Europe were rising rapidly, 28 percent in 1981, 41 percent in 1982, 19 percent in 1983, and 8–10 percent in 1984. In this essay the estimate of 1984 subsidies is based on information on trade flows and foreign trade price developments during the first six months of 1984. While analysis of trade data for all of 1984 should not, in our opinion, greatly change the magnitude of the 1984 subsidy estimates, subsidy estimates for 1985 and 1986 are expected to show a further downward slide due to the sudden and severe drop in the world market price of oil that began in late 1985.

The distribution of Soviet implicit trade subsidies among the six East European countries is presented in tables 7.2 through 7.4. In table 7.2

TABLE 7.1. Implicit Soviet Trade Subsidies to Eastern Europe

	In millions of TRs			$/TR conversion rate	
	X (1)	M (2)	TB (3)	X (4)	M (5)
Baseline calculation					
1970	6,063	5,940	122	0.87	0.71
1971	6,195	6,193	2	0.87	0.72
1972	6,703	6,727	−925	0.87	0.76
1973	7,342	7,973	−631	1.12	0.90
1974	8,643	8,434	209	1.83	1.10
1975	11,770	11,111	659	1.42	0.96
1976	12,992	12,055	937	1.32	0.89
1977	15,054	13,670	1,384	1.32	0.93
1978	14,765	14,634	131	1.27	0.93
1979	18,293	17,174	1,119	1.52	1.00
1980	20,621	18,474	2,148	1.91	1.04
1981	23,664	20,131	3,533	1.72	0.93
1982	26,176	23,584	2,592	1.42	0.86
1983	28,922	26,977	1,944	1.15	0.77
1984	32,010	30,000	2,010	1.03	0.70
Calculation with High $/TR Conversion Rates for Manufactured Goods					
1970	6,063	5,940	122	0.94	0.84
1971	6,195	6,193	2	0.94	0.86
1972	6,703	7,627	−925	0.95	0.91
1973	7,342	7,973	−631	1.22	1.10
1974	8,643	8,434	209	1.94	1.31
1975	11,770	11,111	659	1.51	1.16
1976	12,992	12,055	937	1.41	1.08
1977	15,054	13,670	1,384	1.41	1.13
1978	14,765	14,634	131	1.38	1.15
1979	18,293	17,174	1,119	1.43	1.22
1980	20,621	18,474	2,148	2.01	1.27
1981	23,664	20,131	3,533	1.80	1.15
1982	26,176	23,584	2,592	1.49	1.05
1983	28,992	26,977	1,944	1.20	0.95
1984	32,010	30,000	2,010	1.09	0.87
Calculation with Low $/TR Conversion Rates for Manufactured Goods					
1970	6,063	5,940	122	0.82	0.60
1971	6,195	6,193	1	0.82	0.62
1972	6,703	7,627	−925	0.82	0.64
1973	7,342	7,973	−631	1.05	0.76
1974	8,643	8,434	209	1.75	0.94
1975	11,770	11,111	659	1.34	0.82

		In millions of $		
X (6)	M (7)	TB (8)	Adj. (9)	Sub. (10)
5,302	4,191	1,111	71	1,040
5,465	4,482	982	−9	992
5,860	5,781	79	−693	772
8,225	7,190	1,035	−569	1,604
15,825	9,265	6,558	219	6,339
16,655	10,706	5,949	620	5,329
17,172	10,769	6,403	833	5,570
19,825	12,685	7,140	1,282	5,858
21,338	15,457	5,881	120	5,761
27,838	17,137	10,701	1,138	9,563
39,414	19,130	20,283	2,204	18,079
40,714	18,777	21,937	3,200	18,737
37,235	20,216	17,019	2,242	14,777
33,168	20,792	12,376	1,516	10,860
33,153	21,026	12,026	1,427	10,700
5,725	5,006	718	101	617
6,119	5,600	520	4	515
4,388	4,961	−574	−835	262
8,938	8,734	204	−687	891
16,774	11,078	5,697	269	5,428
17,758	12,866	4,892	771	4,121
18,357	13,037	5,320	1,026	4,294
21,263	15,427	5,835	1,587	4,248
23,065	19,114	3,950	146	3,804
29,768	21,024	8,744	1,398	7,346
41,413	23,419	17,995	2,717	15,277
42,521	23,053	19,468	3,932	15,536
38,895	24,856	14,039	2,763	11,267
34,802	25,619	9,183	1,860	7,323
34,798	26,001	8,797	1,743	7,053
4,984	3,579	1,405	48	1,357
5,324	3,994	1,330	−19	1,349
5,464	4,895	569	−586	1,155
7,690	6,031	1,659	−480	2,138
15,110	7,906	7,204	182	7,022
15,828	9,087	6,741	506	6,235

TABLE 7.1. *continued*

	In millions of TRS			$/TR conversion rate	
	X (1)	M (2)	TB (3)	X (4)	M (5)
1976	12,992	12,055	937	1.25	0.75
1977	15,054	13,670	1,384	1.25	0.78
1978	14,765	14,634	131	1.20	0.76
1979	18,293	17,174	1,119	1.44	0.83
1980	20,621	18,474	2,148	1.84	0.86
1981	23,664	20,131	3,533	1.66	0.77
1982	26,176	23,584	2,592	1.37	0.71
1983	28,922	26,977	1,944	1.10	0.64
1984	32,010	30,000	2,010	1.00	0.58

Note: X = exports; M = imports; TB = trade balance; Adj. = dollar value of the ruble trade balance; sub. = implicit subsidy. The above figures may not total exactly because of rounding.

these subsidies are presented in terms of current dollars. In table 7.3 they are presented in terms of constant 1984 dollars. The deflator used in this case was the price index for Soviet imports from nonsocialist countries, which is presented in table 7.5. In our opinion, this deflator measures better than alternative deflators the rise in the real opportunity cost of the potential hard currency export earnings foregone by the Soviets in Eastern Europe. Finally, the subsidy estimates in table 7.4 are presented in terms of their present value in 1984 dollars. For example, the 1970 subsidy figures are discounted forward using the prevailing world market interest rate (LIBOR) reported in table 7.5. The subsidy estimates in constant 1984 dollars in table 7.3 and the present value of subsidies in 1984 dollars in table 7.4 are better indicators of the real Soviet resource transfers to Eastern Europe than are the subsidy estimates in current dollars in table 7.2.

The most interesting finding regarding the subsidies is their distribution among the recipient countries. During 1974–84 the distribution of subsidies stabilized, with East Germany receiving the largest subsidy every year, followed by Czechoslovakia, Poland, Bulgaria, Hungary, and Romania. This ranking correlates significantly with the ranking of the above countries in terms of the strategic, political, ideological, and economic benefits provided to the Soviet Union in the 1970s and during the first half of the 1980s.[1] We believe a country's strategic value to the Soviet Union is measured by geographical location, the presence of Soviet bases and troops, proxy intervention on behalf of the Soviet

In millions of $				
X (6)	M (7)	TB (8)	Adj. (9)	Sub. (10)
16,283	9,068	7,216	688	6,528
18,747	10,628	8,119	1,053	7,066
20,043	12,714	7,329	100	7,228
26,391	14,222	12,169	943	11,225
37,914	15,914	22,000	1,820	20,180
39,359	15,570	23,789	2,651	21,137
35,991	16,736	19,255	1,851	17,403
31,943	17,172	14,771	1,258	13,513
31,919	17,294	14,625	1,189	13,436

Union, effectiveness as an ally against NATO forces, and domestic stability. A country's political and ideological value to the Soviet Union is expressed in part by allegiance in international forums and within CMEA by the support of Soviet policies by the government, media and population, and by successful central planning; and the economic dimension of a country's value to the Soviet Union is related to the provision of technically superior machinery and other needed commodities, plus any contribution to the economic stability of CMEA. It is important to note that the correlation between the scale of Soviet implicit trade subsidies and the provision of nonmarket benefits to the Soviet Union by individual East European countries may require some sort of standardization of the subsidy estimates. In particular, the absolute level of subsidies may be a less important measure of subsidization than the level of subsidies expressed in per capita terms or in relation to aggregate output. (See table 7.6 for these other subsidy measures.)

If the rankings of individual East European countries in the four classes of nonmarket benefits presented in table 7.7 are given equal weight, then East Germany is the most valuable Soviet ally because it has the most important strategic location and strongest economy of all East European countries and ranks second only to Bulgaria in terms of provision of political and ideological benefits to the Soviet Union. The top ranking of Bulgaria in terms of political and ideological benefits provided to the Soviet Union offsets its low strategic ranking—it ranks fourth ahead of Hungary because is has borders with two NATO coun-

TABLE 7.2. Implicit Subsidies in Soviet Trade (in millions of current dollars)

	Bulgaria	Czecho-slovakia	East Germany	Hungary	Poland	Romania	Total
Baseline Calculation							
1970	−4	217	468	106	182	71	1,040
1971	−10	240	439	104	178	41	992
1972	−48	165	416	49	159	31	772
1973	130	309	671	183	295	15	1,604
1974	1,047	1,293	2,070	844	1,038	46	6,339
1975	883	1,167	1,560	557	1,150	11	5,329
1976	809	1,288	1,784	539	1,083	66	5,570
1977	868	1,387	1,952	460	1,110	81	5,858
1978	1,055	1,329	1,867	532	842	137	5,761
1979	1,751	2,026	2,757	1,046	1,804	178	9,563
1980	3,257	4,100	4,774	1,995	3,588	365	18,079
1981	3,352	4,258	4,890	1,992	3,897	348	18,737
1982	2,620	3,289	3,895	1,718	2,943	312	14,777
1983	1,772	2,536	2,860	1,191	2,157	344	10,860
1984	1,744	2,425	2,758	1,246	2,148	379	10,700
Calculation with High $/TR Conversion Rates for Manufactured Goods							
1970	−13	102	313	33	103	78	617
1971	−13	124	270	22	76	36	515
1972	−63	23	256	−51	64	33	262
1973	96	132	432	61	161	9	891
1974	988	1,097	1,769	681	853	40	5,428
1975	818	878	1,129	363	913	20	4,121
1976	718	986	1,358	320	844	67	4,294
1977	730	1,021	1,439	196	763	99	4,248
1978	874	897	1,260	204	429	139	3,804
1979	1,493	1,547	2,067	708	1,348	184	7,346
1980	2,915	3,536	3,918	1,554	2,988	366	15,277
1981	2,951	3,547	3,958	1,477	3,279	324	15,536
1982	2,174	2,487	2,817	1,198	2,294	307	11,276
1983	1,342	1,668	1,753	675	1,570	314	7,323
1984	1,314	1,513	1,643	697	1,542	344	7,053
Calculation with Low $/TR Conversion Rates for Manufactured Goods							
1970	3	303	584	160	241	65	1,357
1971	−8	327	567	165	255	44	1,349
1972	−36	271	536	124	230	29	1,155
1973	156	442	849	275	396	19	2,138
1974	1,092	1,440	2,296	967	1,176	50	7,022
1975	932	1,384	1,884	703	1,328	3	6,235
1976	877	1,515	2,105	703	1,263	65	6,528

TABLE 7.2. *continued*

	Bulgaria	Czecho-slovakia	East Germany	Hungary	Poland	Romania	Total
1977	971	1,661	2,338	659	1,370	68	7,066
1978	1,190	1,653	2,323	777	1,151	135	7,228
1979	1,945	2,386	3,274	1,300	2,147	174	11,226
1980	3,513	4,523	5,416	2,326	4,038	364	20,180
1981	3,653	4,791	5,589	2,379	4,360	366	21,127
1982	2,954	3,890	4,704	2,108	3,431	316	17,403
1983	2,094	3,187	3,690	1,578	2,598	366	13,513
1984	2,066	3,109	3,595	1,658	2,602	405	13,435

tries, Greece and Turkey, and because of its low economic ranking. Overall we rank Bulgaria in second place. Czechoslovakia ranks third overall due to its strategic and economic importance, while Hungary ranks fourth. Even though Poland is third in terms of strategic importance, its low ranking for the remaining three dimensions places Poland fifth in the overall ranking. Finally, Romania ranks last in every single instance and is, undoubtedly, the weakest Soviet ally. This is also reflected in the virtually negligible scale of implicit Soviet trade subsidies granted to this country.

The Soviets are not running some sort of near-perfect scheme for subsidization of East European countries in return for nonmarket benefits. The scheme is extremely inefficient and imperfect but, despite this, the relative distribution of subsidies among individual countries makes a good deal of sense because those countries most valuable in terms of provision of nonmarket benefits to the Soviet Union also receive the largest rewards.

Some economists argue that the high correlation between implicit subsidies and nonmarket benefits is purely coincidental. Instead, they argue, implicit subsidies are related to the particular natural resource endowments of individual countries and historical trade patterns that have emerged over the years (Brada 1985, pp. 85–86). It is true that the country by country distribution of implicit subsidies shows some degree of positive correlation with the relative dependence of individual economies on trade, and negative correlation with respect to the relative degree of natural resource self-sufficiency. In particular, the ranking in table 7.7 of individual East European countries in terms of overall trade dependence in 1983, measured as the ratio of total trade

TABLE 7.3. Implicit Subsidies in Soviet Trade (in millions of 1984 dollars)

	Bulgaria	Czecho-slovakia	East Germany	Hungary	Poland	Romania	Total
Baseline Calculation							
1970	−9	541	1,165	264	454	176	2,589
1971	−26	606	1,108	261	448	102	2,499
1972	−110	380	959	114	367	70	1,780
1973	250	592	1,284	351	566	28	3,071
1974	1,352	1,669	2,673	1,090	1,340	59	8,183
1975	1,030	1,361	1,820	649	1,341	12	6,213
1976	1,008	1,605	2,223	672	1,350	82	6,941
1977	1,022	1,634	2,300	542	1,307	96	6,901
1978	1,185	1,494	2,099	598	946	154	6,476
1979	1,655	1,915	2,605	989	1,705	169	9,037
1980	2,700	3,399	3,958	1,654	2,974	303	14,987
1981	2,782	3,534	4,059	1,653	3,234	289	15,552
1982	2,324	2,917	3,455	1,524	2,611	277	13,107
1983	1,658	2,374	2,677	1,115	2,019	322	10,165
1984	1,744	2,425	2,758	1,246	2,148	379	10,700
Calculation with High $/TR Conversion Rates for Manufactured Goods							
1970	−32	255	780	83	257	195	1,537
1971	−33	314	680	55	190	91	1,298
1972	−145	52	590	−117	148	75	603
1973	185	253	827	117	308	17	1,707
1974	1,275	1,416	2,283	880	1,101	52	7,007
1975	953	1,024	1,317	423	1,065	23	4,805
1976	895	1,229	1,692	399	1,051	84	5,350
1977	860	1,203	1,695	230	899	117	5,004
1978	983	1,008	1,416	229	483	156	4,276
1979	1,411	1,461	1,953	669	1,274	174	6,942
1980	2,417	2,931	3,248	1,289	2,477	303	12,665
1981	2,449	2,944	3,285	1,226	2,722	269	12,895
1982	1,928	2,206	2,499	1,063	2,035	272	10,002
1983	1,256	1,562	1,641	632	1,470	294	6,854
1984	1,314	1,513	1,643	697	1,542	344	7,053
Calculation with Low $/TR Conversion Rates for Manufactured Goods							
1970	8	755	1,453	399	601	162	3,379
1971	−21	825	1,428	416	641	111	3,400
1972	−83	626	1,236	287	531	67	2,663
1973	298	846	1,627	527	759	37	4,094
1974	1,410	1,859	2,965	1,248	1,519	69	9,065
1975	1,087	1,614	2,197	819	1,549	4	7,270
1976	1,093	1,888	2,622	876	1,574	81	8,134

TABLE 7.3. *continued*

	Bulgaria	Czecho-slovakia	East Germany	Hungary	Poland	Romania	Total
1977	1,143	1,956	2,754	776	1,614	80	8,323
1978	1,337	1,858	2,611	874	1,294	151	8,125
1979	1,838	2,254	3,094	1,229	2,029	164	10,608
1980	2,912	3,749	4,490	1,928	3,348	302	16,730
1981	3,032	3,977	4,639	1,974	3,619	304	17,544
1982	2,621	3,451	4,172	1,870	3,043	280	15,437
1983	1,960	2,983	3,453	1,477	2,432	342	12,648
1984	2,066	3,109	3,595	1,658	2,602	405	13,435

turnover valued at prevailing wmps to the dollar value of GNP, reveals the three most subsidized countries, Bulgaria, East Germany, and Czechoslovakia, are relatively open economies while the two least subsidized countries, Poland and Romania, are relatively closed. Only Hungary is an outlier because it is almost as dependent on trade as Bulgaria, yet it ranks fourth in terms of relative subsidy allocation, well below Czechoslovakia.

With regard to the correlation between relative natural resource endowments ranked in table 7.7 and the distribution of implicit subsidies, the picture is more complicated. To the extent that any East European country is relatively self-sufficient in energy and raw materials, implying similarity between the Soviet natural resource endowment and that of the particular country, it is likely to receive smaller Soviet trade subsidies. Relative self-sufficiency in food or excess supply of food increases the probability that Soviet exports of fuels and nonfood raw materials are exchanged for food imported from a particular East European country, thereby typically decreasing the degree of subsidization. In terms of importance, relative sufficiency in energy is considerably more important than self-sufficiency in nonfood raw materials, which in turn is more important than self-sufficiency in food. In our subjective assessment, using the above qualitative criteria, the ranking of East European countries according to natural resource self-sufficiency confirms the expectation that those East European countries better endowed with natural resources tend to be the least subsidized by the Soviets. Again, Hungary is a significant outlier, although it is the second poorest country in terms of its natural resource endowment; it ranks only fourth in terms of relative scale of subsidies.

TABLE 7.4. Present Value of Implicit Subsidies in Soviet Trade (in millions of 1984 dollars)

	Bulgaria	Czecho-slovakia	East Germany	Hungary	Poland	Romania	Total
Baseline Calculation							
1970	−13	773	1,665	377	649	252	3,703
1971	−34	789	1,442	340	584	133	3,254
1972	−147	507	1,280	152	490	94	2,377
1973	381	903	1,958	536	863	43	4,683
1974	2,800	3,456	5,534	2,257	2,774	123	16,943
1975	2,126	2,811	3,758	1,341	2,770	25	12,832
1976	1,821	2,899	4,015	1,213	2,437	149	12,533
1977	1,849	2,955	4,160	981	2,365	174	12,484
1978	2,121	2,672	3,755	1,069	1,692	275	11,585
1979	3,238	3,746	5,097	1,935	3,336	330	17,682
1980	5,380	6,773	7,887	3,296	5,927	603	29,866
1981	4,840	6,149	7,061	2,877	5,627	503	27,056
1982	3,249	4,078	4,830	2,130	3,650	387	18,324
1983	1,942	2,780	3,134	1,306	2,364	376	11,902
1984	1,744	2,425	2,758	1,246	2,148	379	10,700
Calculation with High $/TR Conversion Rates for Manufactured Goods							
1970	−46	365	1,115	119	367	279	2,198
1971	−43	409	886	72	248	119	1,690
1972	−194	70	788	−157	198	101	805
1973	282	386	1,261	179	470	26	2,603
1974	2,640	2,932	4,728	1,821	2,279	108	14,509
1975	1,966	2,115	2,719	874	2,199	48	9,924
1976	1,616	2,220	3,055	721	1,898	152	9,661
1977	1,556	2,177	3,066	417	1,626	211	9,053
1978	1,758	1,803	2,534	410	863	280	7,650
1979	2,760	2,860	3,821	1,309	2,492	341	13,583
1980	4,816	5,841	6,473	2,568	4,935	605	25,238
1981	4,261	5,123	5,716	2,132	4,735	468	22,435
1982	2,696	3,083	3,493	1,485	2,844	381	13,983
1983	1,471	1,829	1,921	740	1,721	344	8,026
1984	1,314	1,513	1,643	697	1,542	344	7,053
Calculation with Low $/TR Conversion Rates for Manufactured Goods							
1970	11	1,080	2,078	571	860	232	4,832
1971	−27	1,074	1,860	542	835	144	4,428
1972	−111	836	1,650	383	710	89	3,556
1973	455	1,291	2,481	803	1,157	57	6,243
1974	2,920	3,849	6,138	2,584	3,144	134	18,769
1975	2,244	3,333	4,537	1,692	3,199	8	15,013

TABLE 7.4. *continued*

	Bulgaria	Czecho-slovakia	East Germany	Hungary	Poland	Romania	Total
1976	1,974	3,408	4,735	1,581	2,842	147	14,688
1977	2,068	3,539	4,981	1,404	2,919	145	15,057
1978	2,393	3,324	4,671	1,563	2,314	271	14,536
1979	3,596	4,411	6,054	2,404	3,970	322	20,756
1980	5,803	7,472	8,948	3,842	6,671	602	33,338
1981	5,275	6,918	8,070	3,435	6,295	529	30,522
1982	3,664	4,824	5,832	2,614	4,254	392	21,580
1983	2,295	3,493	4,044	1,730	2,847	401	14,810
1984	2,066	3,109	3,595	1,658	2,602	405	13,435

The difficulty of deciding whether the distribution of implicit subsidies is mostly determined by the domestic stability of an East European country—and the other nonmarket benefits it offers the Soviet Union—or by its relative endowment of natural resources is illustrated by the fairly strong negative correlation between the two factors. In particular, Romania, which has received the smallest subsidies from the Soviet Union during 1970–84, ranks last in terms of provision of nonmarket benefits to the Soviet Union, but first in terms of the degree of natural resource self-sufficiency. Next Poland, which received the second smallest amount of subsidies, ranks next to last in terms of provision of nonmarket benefits to the Soviets but second to Romania in terms of comparative degree of natural resource self-sufficiency. On the other side of the spectrum, Bulgaria, which was a close second behind East Germany in terms of subsidy receipts, is classed as the second most important country to the Soviets with regard to provision of nonmarket benefits while being at the same time the least self-sufficient of all countries in terms of natural resources. The largest recipient of subsidies in relative terms, East Germany, has been the most important provider of nonmarket benefits to the Soviet Union while ranking ahead of only Bulgaria and Hungary in terms of natural resource self-sufficiency. Hungary alone does not fit the pattern at all. However, the negative correlation between natural resource self-sufficiency and the relative importance of individual countries in the provision of nonmarket benefits to the Soviet Union has not deterred us from emphasizing the key role that nonmarket benefits play in the determination of the magnitude of implicit subsidies.

The key weakness in the natural resource endowment thesis is that it

TABLE 7.5. Deflators and Discount Rates Used in tables 7.6 and 7.8

	Soviet dollar price index for imports from nonsocialist countries		Discount rate (3-Month LIBOR)	
	$1970 = 100$	Inverse of the index $(1984 = 1.000)$	In percentage per annum	Discount factor $(1984 = 1.000)$
1970	100.0	2.490	8.52	3.561
1971	98.8	2.520	6.58	3.282
1972	108.0	2.306	5.46	3.079
1973	130.0	1.915	9.24	2.920
1974	192.8	1.291	11.01	2.673
1975	213.5	1.166	6.99	2.408
1976	199.8	1.246	5.58	2.250
1977	211.3	1.178	6.00	2.131
1978	221.5	1.124	8.73	2.011
1979	263.4	0.945	11.96	1.849
1980	300.5	0.829	14.36	1.652
1981	300.0	0.830	16.51	1.444
1982	280.6	0.936	13.11	1.240
1983	265.9	0.936	9.60	1.096
1984	249.0	1.000	—	1.000

SOURCE: Price index: reconstructed by the authors from official Soviet *Foreign Trade Yearbooks* and official Hungarian and Polish dollar (nonsocialist) import price indices; Discount factor: 3 month LIBOR, annual average figures from IMF, *International Financial Statistics*.

does not explain Soviet behavior at the margin. A good example is provided by the pattern of Soviet oil exports in the 1970s and during the first half of the 1980s. The Soviet Union has been selling relatively underpriced oil to Bulgaria, Czechoslovakia, East Germany, Hungary, and Poland. Romania, the political maverick in Eastern Europe, has repeatedly tried to secure some preferentially priced Soviet oil since the first round of OPEC price increases in 1973–74. Romania became a net importer of oil in 1975, but even at their peak in 1980 these net imports of oil for domestic consumption did not exceed 7.3 million metric tons (mmt), an amount not much over one-half what the Soviets were supplying to Bulgaria at that point. Yet the Soviets have steadfastly refused to sell preferentially priced oil to Romania and at most consented in 1981 to barter 2.7 mmt worth of crude oil valued in hard currency at wmps for a bundle of Romanian exports of food and certain raw materials also valued in hard currency at wmps. The connection between Ceauşescu's independent foreign policy stance and Soviet unwillingness to provide Romania with the trade advantages offered to other East European countries seems highly plausible.

Similarly, Poland was importing about 1.8 mmt of oil on a net basis from nonsocialist countries during 1978–80 for hard currency but was unable to secure additional supplies from the Soviet Union at preferential prices. During this period, Poland was becoming a growing political, economic, and strategic liability to the Soviet Union and Polish-Soviet relations were deteriorating. At the same time, more friendly Bulgaria was reexporting on average 2.4 mmt of Soviet oil in crude or refined form annually during 1979–82. Moreover, in the Polish case the question was how to cover domestic needs, while Bulgaria was able to earn huge arbitrage profits by buying Soviet oil at cut-rate prices for inconvertible rubles and reselling it for hard currency at prevailing wmps.

After the full eruption of the Polish economic crisis in 1980, the Poles were reportedly promised by the Soviets that the Soviets would make up the 2 mmt loss of crude oil imports from the Middle East associated with the Polish shortage of hard currency. The promise was not kept. Subsequently, the Poles were reportedly promised that they would be exempt from the 10 percent cut in oil deliveries in 1982 carried out with respect to the rest of Eastern Europe except Romania. Yet official Polish statistics show that by 1983 combined Soviet deliveries of crude oil and refined oil products were more than 7 percent below the 1981 level. The failure by the Soviets to keep their promises can be reasonably related to the failure of the Jaruzelski regime to satisfy the Soviet expectation of progress in the normalization process.

On the margin the Soviets can and do manipulate the quantities of their energy and other exports as well as the quantities of imports in order to reward a particular country when desirable. Aside from controlling the volume of exports of energy and raw materials, they can reward a country by permitting payment for Soviet exports with a larger share of manufactured goods in Soviet imports from that country. Thus, for example, in 1983 the share of manufactured commodities in Soviet imports from individual East European countries (in ruble trade only) was as follows: East Germany, 88 percent; Czechoslovakia, 86 percent; Hungary and Poland, 74 percent; and Bulgaria and Romania, 72 percent. These shares are the subject of annual Soviet bilateral negotiations with each country and changes in them can have a beneficial or adverse effect on each country's overall terms of trade with the Soviet Union.

TABLE 7.6. Distribution of Implicit Soviet Trade Subsidies in Individual East European Countries and Its Relationship to Provision by These Countries of Nonmarket Benefits to the Soviet Union, 1970–84

	Bulgaria	Czecho-slovakia	East Germany	Hungary	Poland
Cumulative present value of subsidies in millions of 1984 dollars					
Baseline	31,295	43,716	58,336	21,055	37,677
High	26,855	32,724	43,221	13,388	28,419
Low	34,624	51,961	69,673	26,807	44,621
Population in Million (Mid-1984)					
	8.977	15.460	16.699	10.666	36.899
Cumulative per capita present value of subsidies in millions of 1984 dollars					
Baseline	3,486	2,828	3,493	1,974	1,021
High	2,992	2,117	2,588	1,255	770
Low	3,857	3,361	4,172	2,513	1,209
GNP in 1983 in billions of 1984 dollars and GNP per capita					
Billion $	55.5	124.8	159.9	74.1	219.3
Per capita	6,203	8,096	9,574	6,935	5,997
Ratio of cumulative present value of subsidies in GNP in 1983					
Baseline	0.564	0.350	0.365	0.284	0.172
High	0.484	0.262	0.270	0.181	0.130
Low	0.624	0.416	0.436	0.362	0.203

Note: Baseline, high, and low estimates of the distribution of implicit subsidies are based on the respective dollar/ruble conversion rates for manufactured goods. Consequently, the highest esti-

DETERMINATION OF THE LEVEL
OF IMPLICIT SUBSIDIES

In Marrese and Vaňous (1980) we portray implicit Soviet trade subsidies as being determined by the Soviet political leadership's maximization of its utility, a function of Soviet consumption of marketed goods and services and Soviet consumption of unconventional gains from trade, subject to resource constraints. Embedded in the resource constraints is a trade-off between consumption of marketed goods and services and consumption of unconventional gains from trade. Essentially we allow unconventional gains from trade to substitute for marketed inputs in the Soviet Union's production of security and international stature. Thus we employ the notion that intra-CMEA trade can produce positive

Romania	Total
3,846	195,925
3,805	148,412
3,877	231,563
22.630	111.331
169	1,760
168	1,333
171	2,080
113.3	746.9
5,023	6,736
0.034	0.262
0.034	0.199
0.034	0.310

mates of subsidies are based on low conversion rates while the lowest estimates are based on high conversion rates.

externalities for the Soviet Union and implicit subsidies for Eastern Europe.

Yet in virtually all of our work we refer to the bilateral negotiations that determine the anticipated level (defined below) of subsidies. Josef Brada correctly reproaches us for the confusion we have created:

The distinction between seeing subsidies as unilaterally and bilaterally determined is not a trivial one. If subsidies are unilaterally determined by the Soviet Union, then they truly are the outcome of Soviet maximizing behavior and exogenous factors such as the subsidized country's location, political makeup, etc. However, if bargaining is involved then we need to know what it is that the East European countries are trying to maximize and how their bargaining power vis-à-vis the Soviet Union is determined. To put the question more

TABLE 7.7. Ranking of Countries in Terms of Their Relative Importance in Provision of Nonmarket Benefits to the Soviet Union

	Bulgaria	Czecho-slovakia	East Germany	Hungary	Poland	Romania	Total
Strategic	4	2	1	5	3	6	
Political	1	3	2	4	5	6	
Ideological	1	3	2	4	5	6	
Economic	3-4	2	1	3-4	5	6	
Overall	2	3	1	4	5	6	

Ranking of countries according to trade dependence-share of total trade turnover with all countries in GNP in 1983, in percentages (trade flows valued at prevailing wmps in dollars)

	34	21	23	30	12	14	20

Ranking of countries in terms of natural resource self-sufficiency

Energy	6	3-4	3-4	5	1	2	
Raw materials	5	2-3	4	6	2-3	1	
Food	1-2	4	6	1-2	5	3	
Overall	6	3	4	5	2	1	

SOURCE: Subsidy estimates—table 7.4; GNP in 1983—based on estimates prepared by Thad Alton et al., Occasional Paper no. 89 (New York: L. W. International Financial Research, 1985); Country ranking—based on Michael Marrese and Jan Vañous, *Soviet Subsidization of Trade with Eastern Europe: A Soviet Perspective* (Berkeley: University of California, Institute for International Studies, 1983), pp. 68–86.

concretely, why does Czechoslovakia appear much more willing to offer unconventional gains than Romania? Is it a matter of differences between Czechoslovak and Romanian preferences for economic gains versus national autonomy, or does it stem purely from objective factors such as Romania's lack of a border with NATO, or can it be explained by differences in bargaining power? Worse yet, might it not be the other way around, with Romania choosing not to provide unconventional gains simply because its trading needs do not permit it to benefit from CMEA trade as much as does Czechoslovakia? (Brada 1985, pp. 85–86.)

Clarification of the seeming contradiction between unilateral maximization by the Soviet Union versus bilateral negotiations is straightforward. First, the actual determination of the anticipated level of subsidies depends upon anticipated wmps, bilaterally agreed upon ftps, and bilaterally agreed upon quantities to be exchanged. Second, the information needed to employ the maximization problem described in Marrese and Vañous (1980) includes wmps previously forecast by the

Soviet Union and ftps already agreed upon, at least provisionally. The maximization procedure yields a solution to the question facing the Soviets, how much Soviet trade should flow to the developed West at advantageous terms of trade and how much to a particular East European country at disadvantageous terms of trade. Third, this point was absent in our earlier work, the maximization problem is employed iteratively during the bilateral negotiations.

More concretely, the level of anticipated implicit subsidies is determined by the following steps which take place during annual bilateral trade negotiations:

1 Each side engages in private calculations prior to the next round of bilateral interaction.
- Given anticipated wmps, either provisionally agreed upon or anticipated ftps, and some understanding of potential unconventional gains from trade, the Soviet Union determines the exports it is willing to exchange for a specific combination of imports and nonmarket benefits. This is the maximization problem mentioned earlier.
- Given anticipated wmps, either provisionally agreed upon or anticipated ftps, and a perception of its own short-run economic and political situation, which depends partly on the outcome of these negotiations, the East European country determines the exports and nonmarket benefits it is willing to exchange for a specific bundle of Soviet imports.
2 Bilateral interaction.
- The Soviet Union reveals the exports it is willing to exchange for a specific combination of imports and nonmarket benefits.
- The East European country reveals the exports plus nonmarket benefits it is willing to exchange for a specific bundle of imports.
- If Soviet and East European expectations match, then a trade agreement has been reached and the bilateral bargaining ends.
- If Soviet and East European expectations do not match, then haggling commences. The outcome of one round of haggling may be formalized as a change in at least one of the following: ftps, the Soviet understanding of expected unconventional gains from trade, or the East European perception of its own short-run economic and political situation. The process now returns to step 1.

This characterization of bilateral bargaining is consistent with the following common understanding of the interests held by the Soviet Union and Eastern Europe.

Clearly, Eastern Europe cannot do without large transfusions of Soviet energy, but neither can it manage easily on what the Soviet Union is prepared to provide. On past evidence, whatever general commitments the Russians make to supply their allies with energy, they will continue to strike separate deals with individual countries. Their prime minister has already served notice that who gets what depends very much on who is prepared to do what in return. Package deals negotiated in the future, even more than in the past, will depend on an individual country's political loyalty and its active support for Soviet foreign policy in different parts of the globe, as well as its readiness to come up with more cash for joint investment projects in the Soviet Union and with the high quality goods the Soviet economy needs ("Comecon Survey" 1985, p. 13).

Also notice that this picture of bilateral bargaining is founded on the belief that the Soviet Union bases its intra-CMEA trade on factors different from those utilized by an East European country (Marrese 1986). In particular, the Soviet Union has made decisions within CMEA based on its long-term preferences for central planning, superpower status, and a strong Warsaw Pact, as well as on a profound understanding of the principles of international political economy. One such principle is that trade based on comparative advantage leads to a higher level of real national income. This increase in national income can be used for any national goal. The Soviet Union has applied this lesson to trade with, among others, the West, Romania, and Yugoslavia. Another principle is that preferential trade treatment may be extended to a country in exchange for nonmarket military, political, ideological, and economic favors. The Soviet Union has applied this lesson to trade with Bulgaria, Czechoslovakia, East Germany, Hungary, Poland, and Cuba.

The Soviets also understand the advantages to a more powerful country in not altering a weaker country's institutional and production structure so that the weaker country is dependent on trade with the stronger country. For example, in the 1950s the Soviet Union strove to mold East European economies into cheap sources of inputs for Soviet industry and to transform East European nations into strong Soviet allies. As the 1950s progressed it became clear that the Soviet goal of rendering East European economies completely dependent on the Soviet economy at terms very favorable to the Soviet Union was in direct conflict with the Soviet goal of transforming East European nations into allies. Thus the Soviet Union realized that East European allegiance could no longer be secured effectively through threats alone and opted for a new policy that combined trade subsidization with the threats of armed intervention. Since the 1950s, the Soviet Union has attempted to increase Eastern Europe's trade dependence through such means as intra-CMEA product specialization, joint investment programs, and proposals for transnational planning.

East European behavior contrasts sharply with Soviet behavior because East European countries have made decisions about trade and technology that more strongly reflect short-run economic pressures than long-run political preferences. Two reasons stand out. First, East European economies, more dependent on trade than the Soviet economy, have suffered more severely from external shocks. Second, the Soviet Union is dominant in defining the long-term policy of CMEA. For example, East European countries may have some influence over certain characteristics of joint projects and perhaps whether to participate or not, but virtually no influence over which joint projects will be selected. More generally, when preparing for bilateral trade negotiations with the Soviet Union, East European leaders weigh the costs and benefits of more preferential trade with the Soviet Union versus more trade with the West. The costs to an East European country of more preferential trade with the Soviet Union are increased trade dependence on the Soviet Union and diminished national sovereignty. Diminished national sovereignty includes the loss of an independent foreign policy, subordination of the nation's armed forces to the Soviet high command, acceptance of limitations on domestic political institutions and policies, and restrictions on the design and operation of the economy. The costs of more trade with the West are short-term economic losses in the form of initially less favorable terms of trade with the West; the start-up costs of penetrating Western markets with relatively unknown products; and the short-term transition costs of competing on world markets, possibly including bankruptcy and unemployment.

With respect to benefits, more preferential trade with the Soviet Union translates into some combination of implicit subsidies, bilateral deficits in ruble trade, and bilateral surpluses in dollar trade. Such economic subsidization, coupled with the threat of Soviet military intervention, may temporarily solidify the positions of East European leaders. The benefits of more trade with the West are derived from increased exposure to the competitive pressure of the world market that could lead to increased efficiency and access to new technology and managerial techniques. These benefits can be realized only after a long time lag, during which the transition costs will fall most heavily on the political leaders who have made these decisions.[2]

Because of the way in which prices and trade flows in intra-CMEA trade are negotiated, subsidies have an anticipated and an unanticipated component. Although the concept of an anticipated subsidy is quite simple, it is difficult to quantify. Under the less than realistic assumption that the quantities to be exchanged determined during bilateral negotiations in period t-1 are actually exchanged, the anticipated subsidy is the amount that the Soviet Union would transfer to a particular East European country if the wmps anticipated by Soviet decisionmakers for period t were realized in the same period.

Since bilateral negotiations occur annually and the Soviets do not adhere to the intra-CMEA price-formation formula during actual intra-CMEA price setting (Hewett 1984d), a change in the anticipated component of implicit subsidies reflects new information obtained during the preceding year. In particular, any change in the anticipated subsidy is some combination of: (a) a conscious decision by the Soviet Union to alter the extent to which it affects a country's political-economic stability; (b) a Soviet desire to change the magnitude of nonmarket benefits received; (c) the bargaining skills of Soviet negotiators who downplay the importance of the nonmarket benefits offered by any single country and remind the East Europeans that certain nonmarket benefits may be obtained by pressure as well as through subsidies; and (d) the bargaining skills of East European negotiators who stress the fragility of political-economic stability in their country.[3] Notice that reason (a) implies that the conscious decision is made after the unanticipated change in factors influencing events in the country being subsidized. Any unanticipated subsidy reflects the opportunity cost of deciding on the quantities to be traded before wmps and the political-economic stability of the East European country are known. An unanticipated subsidy is the cost of engaging in forward contracting.[4]

If we assume the quantities agreed upon during the annual bilateral negotiations are delivered, then an equation defining the anticipated subsidy as the amount that the Soviet Union would transfer to a particular East European country if the wmps anticipated by Soviet decisionmakers for period t equal the prevailing wmps in the same period is easily constructed.[5] The unanticipated subsidy is the estimated implicit subsidy minus the anticipated component. Since we have no reliable information on how the Soviets form price expectations, table 7.8 contains three possible decompositions of the subsidy estimates into anticipated and unanticipated components.

Decomposition 1 is based on the notion that Soviet negotiators anticipate that the dollar/ruble exchange rates in every commodity category of exports and of imports equal the corresponding actual dollar/ruble exchange rates for year t-1. Thus Soviet negotiators anticipate that wmps will move from t-1 to t in exactly the same manner implied by the movement of the bilaterally agreed upon ftps. Decomposition 2 assumes that Soviet negotiators anticipate that the dollar/ruble exchange rates equal the product of the corresponding actual dollar/ruble exchange rates for t-1 times an adjustment factor based on one-half of the change in dollar/ruble exchange rates between t-2 and t-1. Thus Soviet negotiators anticipate that wmps relative to bilaterally agreed upon ftps will shift from t-1 to t at one-half the magnitude that occurred from t-2 to t-1. Decomposition 3 assumes that Soviet negotiators anticipate that the dollar/ruble exchange rates equal the product of the corresponding actual dollar/ruble exchange rates for t-1 times an adjustment factor based on one-half of the change in dollar/ruble exchange rates between t-1 and t. Thus for decomposition 3 we assume that Soviet decisionmakers always anticipate the correct direction of changes in wmps relative to bilaterally agreed upon ftps, but are able to predict only one-half of the magnitude of the changes.

Table 7.8 reveals that for each decomposition the anticipated component exhibits an upward trend over time. The unanticipated component takes on its largest positive values during and immediately following large upward shifts in the wmp of either energy or raw materials (1970, 1973, 1974, 1979, and 1980) and takes on its largest negative values during the years that changes in the intra-CMEA ftps of energy follow earlier changes in the corresponding wmps (1975, 1981, 1982, and 1983). For most years of each decomposition, the magnitude of the anticipated component is much larger than the magnitude of the corresponding unanticipated component and, while the magnitudes of the unanticipated components may be extremely large in any given year (1974, 1975, and 1978–83), over a period of time they tend to cancel each other out, a result of the ways in which expectation-formation is

TABLE 7.8. Anticipated and Unanticipated Components of Implicit Subsidies Measured in Millions of 1984 Dollars*

| | | Decomposition 1 | |
Year	Actual subsidy	Anticipated subsidy	Unanticipated subsidy
1962	630	707	−77
1963	251	588	−337
1964	435	99	336
1965	928	526	402
1966	1,080	917	163
1967	1,095	1,211	−116
1968	1,470	1,183	287
1969	1,517	1,520	−3
1970	2,589	1,142	1,447
1971	2,499	2,564	−65
1972	1,780	2,056	−275
1973	3,071	1,600	1,471
1974	8,183	2,282	5,901
1975	6,213	12,809	−6,596
1976	6,941	7,086	−145
1977	6,901	7,925	−1,024
1978	6,475	8,181	−1,706
1979	9,037	6,223	2,814
1980	14,987	9,295	5,692
1981	15,553	18,759	−3,206
1982	13,107	20,069	−6,962
1983	10,165	16,074	−5,909
1984	10,700	12,314	−1,614

SOURCE: Table 7.3. Marrese and Vaňous (1983b), table 2, p. 38; table 26, p. 122; table A−6, p. 171. Vaňous and Marrese (1984), table A−2, p. 183; table A−14, p. 196.

*In order to transform from 1984 dollars to current dollars multiply each row by the following factor: 1962 = 235/630; 1963 = 96/251; 1964 = 173/435; 1965 = 369/928; 1966 = 434/1,080;

modeled. For instance, one measure of the extent to which anticipated diverges from actual is calculated by dividing the summation of implicit subsidies into the corresponding summation of each anticipated component for the periods 1962–69, 1970–73, 1974–79, 1980–81, and 1982–84. The results are reported in table 7.9.

The steady growth of anticipated subsidies over a period of time can be explained by changes in a number of factors. First, since the mid-1970s, there has been a steady increase in both Soviet-American

Decomposition 2		Decomposition 3	
Anticipated subsidy	Unanticipated subsidy	Anticipated subsidy	Unanticipated subsidy
1,174	−544	654	−24
1,205	−954	422	−171
403	32	283	152
1,108	−180	715	213
1,016	64	994	86
1,387	−292	1,147	−52
1,805	−335	1,335	135
2,153	−636	1,496	21
1,358	1,231	1,404	1,185
2,334	165	1,759	740
3,029	−1,249	1,368	412
2,632	439	1,887	1,184
3,813	4,370	4,780	3,403
24,490	−18,277	8,693	−2,480
6,341	600	6,290	651
8,906	−2,005	6,683	218
10,510	−4,035	6,359	116
7,370	1,667	6,467	2,570
11,599	3,388	11,256	3,731
24,526	−8,973	16,188	−635
19,875	−6,768	16,042	−2,935
15,457	−5,292	12,591	−2,426
12,277	−1,577	11,016	−316

1967 = 427/1,095; 1968 = 555/1,470; 1969 = 585/1,517; 1970 = 1,040/2,859; 1971 = 992/2,499; 1972 = 772/1,780; 1973 = 1,604/3,071; 1974 = 6,339/8,183; 1975 = 5,329/6,213; 1976 = 5,570/ 6,941; 1977 = 5,858/6,901; 1978 = 5,761/6,475; 1979 = 9,563/9,037; 1980 = 18,079/ 14,987; 1981 = 18,737/15,553; 1982 = 1,477/13,107; 1983 = 10,860/10,165.

and global tensions. Soviet-American relations deteriorated steadily with the introduction of the Jackson-Vanik amendment in 1974, the Soviet invasion of Afghanistan in 1979, the failure to approve the SALT 2 agreement in 1980, growing Soviet interference in Polish affairs (1980–81), the introduction into Europe of cruise and Pershing 2 missiles (1983), and the Soviet destruction of the KAL airplane (1983). In addition, global tensions were heightened by developments in Iran, Iraq, Lebanon, Nicaragua, El Salvador, and Grenada. Other incidents

TABLE 7.9. Ratio of Anticipated to Total Subsidies

	1962–69	1970–73	1974–79	1980–81	1982–84
Decomposition 1	0.91	0.74	1.02	0.92	1.43
Decomposition 2	1.38	0.94	1.40	1.18	1.40
Decomposition 3	0.95	0.65	0.90	0.90	1.17

also prompted the Soviet Union to be more suspicious of the West as a supplier of both high-technology items and, to a lesser degree, grain. An additional humiliating event was the refusal of Western countries to attend the 1980 Olympic Games in Moscow. These developments led to a growing Soviet appreciation of and reliance on the military, political, ideological, and economic advantages of maintaining a strong alliance with Eastern Europe.

The second factor was a major change in Soviet and Western defense doctrines as both began to stress the increased probability that any future conflict between the major powers would more likely be conventional rather than nuclear in nature. This led to a renewed Soviet awareness of the strategic value of a defensive corridor between the Soviet Union and Western Europe.

The third factor was the increasing cost of using the stick. It may well be that the Soviets learned a lesson from the 1968 invasion of Czechoslovakia. In addition, given the growing labor shortage in the Soviet Union, they faced increasing opportunity costs of stationing Soviet troops in Eastern Europe rather than having those troops engaged in either civilian or productive military activities such as construction or harvesting in the Soviet Union.

The fourth factor was the weakening of Soviet hegemony over Eastern Europe, during the second half of the 1970s in the case of Romania and Poland and in recent years over Hungary and East Germany. In some sense, certain aspects of East European allegiance were more available for "open bidding," which in turn led to an increase in their procurement cost. As the West was bidding with attractive credits and prospects of improved trade relations, the Soviets countered with an increase in preferential trade treatment. The fifth factor, closely related to the fourth, was the growing neutralism on the part of East European countries. The Soviet propaganda about the dangers of nuclear warfare backfired, and in order to secure continued support of Soviet hard-line positions in East-West relations, the Soviets were compelled to sustain large-scale economic aid to Eastern Europe.

Last and most important, the deterioration in East European trade, both with the Soviets from 1975 on as well as with the West from 1973 on, and East European difficulties associated with their hard currency debts from 1980 on made it imperative that the Soviets support East European governments or face increased probability of widespread political upheaval throughout Eastern Europe.

One may ask why, given the crude nature of the subsidization system, the Soviets simply do not make lump-sum payments to East European countries for nonmarket benefits. The reason is that Soviet compensation of East European countries for military, strategic, political, and ideological nonmarket benefits has to be hidden from the public because of conflicts between governments and populations. The Soviet government does not want its population to be fully aware that Eastern Europe is being subsidized for three reasons. First, Soviet propaganda proclaims the strength of international socialist cooperation. Therefore, it would seem unnecessary to compensate Eastern Europe for friendship which should be forthcoming freely because of shared beliefs and values. Second, the Soviet people might be angered if they realized that East European living standards, higher than those of the Soviet Union, are being further bolstered through subsidization. Third, even if the Soviet political leadership were to explain to the Soviet population why it is necessary to exchange economic aid for various nonmarket benefits, the Soviet population's taste for maintaining an empire differs from that of the Soviet political and military leadership. Moreover, the Soviet population has been thoroughly indoctrinated over the past forty years with the notion that the people of Eastern Europe love the Soviet Union because of its role in the liberation of Eastern Europe from fascist rule and because the Soviet Union provides protection to Eastern Europe from the West. Under such circumstances, it would be difficult to understand why Eastern Europe should not compensate the Soviet Union for the military protection it provides to Eastern Europe instead of the Soviet Union compensating Eastern Europe for its allegiance.

At the same time East European governments do not want their populations to know that national sovereignty is being sold to the Soviet Union. The surrender of national sovereignty includes the loss of any independence by most East European countries in the conduct of foreign policy, subordination of their defense to Soviet commanders, acceptance of absolute limitations on domestic political institutions and policies, as well as on the design and functioning of their economic systems. It is hardly a surprise that East European governments rarely make it clear to the population how dependent their economies are on trade with the Soviet Union or how advantageous or disadvantageous intra-CMEA trade actually is. In fact, few efforts are made by the government officials in these countries to dispel persistent widespread rumors circulated among the population about Soviet exploitation of East European economies through trade, and there is evidence that some of these rumors can be traced to government officials. Such a strategy makes sense because it leads the population to believe that certain domestic economic difficulties are due to Soviet exploitation rather than the sheer incompetence of indigenous economic and political bureaucracies. Therefore it deflects potential criticism by the population from the domestic to the Soviet government.

Interestingly enough, the Soviet government does not counter the popular East European perception of Soviet exploitation of Eastern Europe. In a recent internal memorandum, a Soviet economist complained about the way this issue is handled by the Soviet government:

> Soviet economic assistance is rendered in two forms. Part of it—credit and official aid—is officially transacted and accounted for, that is, it is "open."
>
> However, a considerable portion comes in the form of "hidden" subsidies. These are in fact gifts from the Soviet Union which are neither officially recognized nor accounted as such in trade agreements or any other documents. This undocumented, "hidden" aid assumes many forms, and occurs practically in all spheres of cooperation: in foreign trade, in scientific and technical cooperation, in hard-currency credit relations, and in joint construction projects.
>
> Notably, the press in the USSR and the CMEA countries, as well as documents published by Communist and other official organizations, report almost nothing about Soviet economic assistance to the socialist countries, and even less about its second form—the officially unrecognized "hidden" assistance, which in most cases is not accounted.
>
> For comparison, it should be pointed out [that] the U.S. publishes data in current prices on all forms of economic assistance it gives to other countries, a considerable portion of which it can represent in the politically advantageous form of "gifts." American aid receives much media coverage, and to some extent, the U.S. is able to capitalize on it politically. (Text from a confidential Soviet source.)

Other forms of hidden Soviet aid to Eastern Europe exist beside implicit trade subsidies, though these are not discussed in this essay. The Soviets can provide additional aid to East European countries through subsidization of ruble trade credits and certain other services, or through subsidization of hard-currency credits. Another form of Soviet aid is the willingness to purchase certain commodities from East European countries for hard currency and incur deficits in hard-currency trade with these countries, which have to be settled in cash, that in turn can be used to service East European financial obligations to the West.

A Sea of Controversy

The difficulties associated with interpreting the significance of implicit subsidies are natural given the amount of guesswork that accompanies Western analysis of CMEA. In general, statements concerning the preferences, goals, and status of CMEA-member countries are based on speculation, as are statements about the actual proceedings of bilateral bargaining. Likewise, analysis of CMEA institutional characteristics, trade flows, terms of trade, and overall efficiency is solid, but analysis of trends that have recently emerged or may emerge in the future remains speculative.

Given the uncertain nature of commentary about CMEA, it is useful to present a variety of perspectives concerning Soviet-East European trade. Crucial aspects of the official Soviet perspective include the claim that major conflict is absent among CMEA countries because of socialist solidarity, a rejection of the principle of comparative advantage because of the market chaos it would create, and a belief in economic integration based on mutual profitability and coordination of economic plans. This perspective fails to explain: (1) the publicly articulated arguments between net exporters of hard goods and net exporters of soft goods concerning intra-CMEA pricing policies; (2) the fact that intra-CMEA trade transacted in transferable rubles (TRS) between any two East European countries has exhibited balanced trade both in hard goods and in soft goods, yet such a pattern does not characterize Soviet bilateral trade with most East European countries; (3) price discrimination within CMEA; and (4) the slow pace of general socialist economic integration among CMEA countries as measured by coordination of national plans, technology transfer, product specialization, and joint investment projects (Marrese 1986, pp. 317–18). On the positive side, it does draw attention to the importance that all countries place on avoiding the chaos that short-lived, sharp fluctuations in wmps could cause if these fluctuations were introduced instantaneously into their domestic economies.

The customs union perspective, derived from strictly economic reasoning and presented most thoroughly by Holzman (1962, 1965), is based on the idea that CMEA is rational in promoting trade among its members and restricting trade with nonmembers. Brada's recent summary of the customs union perspective is particularly relevant to our discussion:

The most obvious consequence of the formation of a customs union is the increase in intramember trade relative to trade with the rest of world. More important from our standpoint is the fact that, if the resource endowment of the integrating countries differs from the endowment of the rest of the world, then relative prices within the union will differ from relative prices on the world market.

This divergence between intra-union and world-market prices affects the distribution of the gains from trade among the integrating countries. Compared to the distribution of such gains at world-market prices, integration will increase the proportion of gains obtained by those integrating countries that have abundant endowments (relative to other integrating countries) of the input that is scarce (relative to the rest of the world) within the union. Conversely, those integrating countries that are abundantly endowed (relative to other integrating countries) with the factor that is abundant (relative to the rest of the world) in the union will receive a smaller share of total gains than they would receive under free trade.

The reason that countries join customs unions even though they may be forced to trade with other members at terms of trade worse than those prevailing in their trade with nonmembers is that they expect the gains generated by the increase in the volume of their trade with other members will offset the losses resulting from lower terms of trade. Thus even though a customs union redistributes gains from trade among members, the welfare effects of integration should not be viewed as a zero-sum game. Depending on the nature of the union and the characteristics of the member countries, it is possible that all members, even those whose terms of trade deteriorate, may benefit (Brada 1985, pp. 87–88).

From the Soviet perspective, a truly accurate understanding of the static and dynamic benefits and costs of CMEA as a customs union requires an in-depth comparison of either the "pre-CMEA" tariff-trade-production structure of the Soviet Union or some hypothetical tariff-trade-production structure with the tariff-trade-production structure of the Soviet Union since CMEA's inception. Some brief observations indicate that since the early 1960s the economic rationale for Soviet participation in CMEA is virtually nonexistent.[6]

Trade creation, a beneficial effect, and trade diversion, a potentially detrimental effect, are measures of the static impact of the formation of a customs union. Trade creation could be large if, before integration, the actual output patterns of the integrating economies were similar as a result of protective tariffs. With the elimination of these protective tariffs, it may prove rational for integrating economies to specialize within the customs union along the lines of comparative advantage. If such specialization occurs, trade between member countries will increase.

Trade diversion is detrimental if the increased trade among member countries siphons trade away from the world's low cost producers, who are not members of the customs union, toward relatively high-cost producers who are members of the customs union. Clearly if member countries of a customs union are among the most efficient producers in the world, the detrimental consequences of trade diversion are minor. Dynamic gains related to the formation of a customs union include economies of scale, the stimulus of competition, and incentives for greater investment.

Because the Soviet Union is a large net importer of manufactured goods from Eastern Europe, the static rationale for Soviet participation is weak. It is true that substantial trade creation has occurred between the Soviet Union and Eastern Europe and that both sides have benefited through conventional gains from trade. However, the detrimental effects of trade diversion may well outweigh the benefits of trade creation because East European countries are not among the world's low-cost producers of manufactured goods. Moreover, the quality of CMEA manufactured goods is poor.

The dynamic picture is even more discouraging. Pecsi (1983) notes that incorrect investment decisionmaking, faulty policies with regard to capacity utilization, insufficient specialization, lagging technological cooperation and exchange, and poor incentives to increase productivity characterize CMEA. A dynamic rationale for membership in such a customs union is nonexistent either for the Soviet Union or for Eastern Europe.

Putting aside our disagreement with the advocates of the customs union perspective, it is interesting to note that some of them have not challenged our subsidy estimates, only our interpretation of them. For instance, Brada (1985, p. 88) claims that our estimates of implicit subsidies represent "an excellent measure of the amount of gains from trade that are redistributed among integrating countries because they do trade at terms of trade that differ from those prevailing in the world market."

Marer, on the other hand, challenges the validity of the subsidy estimates themselves.

Three sets of factors account for the large discounts on East-bloc exports of manufactures to the West. One is the poor quality of the East's products. A second is the systematic shortcomings of Eastern export pricing: exporting on the basis of plan directives, which reduces the flexibility required to obtain the best price; preference for barter and compensation deals inconvenient for the Western partner, who therefore pays a low price for such products; and hard-currency balance-of-payments pressures, which often force Eastern countries to make drastic price concessions. The third set of reasons for Eastern export price discounts is Western discrimination—whether in the form of high-tariff or non-tariff barriers to CMEA goods.

Since Marrese and Vanous argue that a portion of Soviet subsidy arises because the Soviet Union pays more for imports from Eastern Europe than it would have to pay if the same goods were purchased from the West, the correct dollar opportunity cost is not East-to-West export but East-from-West import prices. If the Soviet Union imported the same manufactured goods from the West, it would not be able to obtain as large discounts as when the East exports to the West because the second and third sets of discount factors would be absent. In missing this point and assuming that they can substitute East European export prices for Soviet import prices to value Soviet purchases from Eastern Europe, Marrese and Vanous introduce a significant upward bias into their calculation.

There is an even more fundamental criticism of their subsidy computations. Just because an East European machine or consumer product is not of the latest Western design—that it is not equipped with the ultimate series of gadgets, does not have all the assortment, packaging, and other convenience features that characterize the most modern Western products—does not mean that the Soviet importer of these goods provides a subsidy to Eastern Europe equivalent to the Western quality discount. There must be many instances where the East European products are as, or even more, suitable to Soviet conditions than the most modern Western counterparts (Marer 1984, p. 177).

The essence of Marer's first argument is that because of West European trade discrimination against CMEA-manufactured goods, the correct dollar opportunity cost for manufactured goods is based on East-for-West import prices, not East-to-West export prices. Marer's claim is weak for several reasons. First, the CMEA generally does not import the same type of manufactured goods from Western Europe that it produces domestically. For example, automobiles are both imported from Western Europe and produced in the CMEA, but the quality differential is so great that a dollar unit value based on East-from-West import prices is not comparable to a ruble unit value based on intra-CMEA trade. The CMEA simply does not import from Western Europe the type of automobiles that it produces. However, East-to-West export prices can produce a reasonable comparison of a dollar unit value with a ruble unit value because Western Europe imports automobiles that are produced and traded within the CMEA.

Second, Marer neither offers evidence that such trade discrimination occurs nor estimates the quantitative impact of trade discrimination. In addition, he fails to mention a factor that may more than offset any upward bias imposed by Western trade discrimination, namely, that East European nations tend to export a higher quality composition of products to Western Europe than to the Soviet Union. In our work we analyzed commodities and partner Western markets in an effort to minimize the presence of both the upward bias, trade discrimination, and the downward bias, higher-quality goods going to Western Europe. For those who strongly believe that the upward bias dominates, we offer estimates with high dollar/ruble conversion rates for manufactures; for those who strongly believe that the downward bias dominates, we offer estimates with low dollar/ruble conversion rates for manufactures.

It is reasonable to ask why Marer does not simply use the estimates based on high conversion rates. Marer rejects all such estimates because they are based on a "realistic or settlement" dollar/ruble exchange rate that we estimate. Marer, on the other hand, advocates the use of the official Soviet dollar/ ruble exchange rate in the subsidy calculation We strongly disagree with his selection because the official exchange rate is strictly an accounting device that has no decisionmaking or policy role on the enterprise, ministerial, national, or CMEA level.

Koves (1983) notes that the controversy surrounding the subsidy question has obscured two crucial pillars of the East European view of their trade with the Soviet Union. First, Koves argues that for whatever reason the Soviet Union has been encouraged to become a net exporter of hard goods and a net importer of soft goods vis-à-vis Eastern Europe, and Eastern Europe has been forced to develop its economic structure according to the Soviet specifications of the 1950s and 1960s. This has proven to have long-term detrimental consequences for Eastern Europe's trade with the West. Second, Köves points out that when Marrese and Vaňous refer to Soviet willingness to engage in trade subsidization, they insufficiently emphasize that Eastern Europe suffered from deterioration of its terms of trade vis-à-vis the Soviet Union throughout much of this period. Dietz (1986) provides a detailed accounting of this deterioration in terms of trade.

CONCLUSION

We have argued that the Soviet Union has been subsidizing East European countries by being a net exporter of fuel and nonfood raw materials at prices below corresponding wmps and by being a net importer of manufactured goods at prices above corresponding wmps. We have shown that the total real value and and the real anticipated component of these implicit trade subsidies have grown over time. We believe that the Soviet Union trades with Eastern Europe at such disadvantageous terms of trade in order to secure the allegiance of individual East European countries.

Because so much uncertainty surrounds analysis of CMEA, perspectives that differ from our own and our reactions to them have been presented. We readily admit that no single perspective completely explains Soviet-East European trade since 1970. For instance, given the Soviet Union's observation of events in Poland during 1977 and 1978 and the statements of Polish leaders about the severity of that situation, our perspective of Soviet behavior fails to explain the decline in real implicit subsidies to Poland during 1977 and 1978. More recently, the sudden and sharp decline in the wmp of oil since late 1985 has jolted Soviet–East European trade relations. Future research will determine how well the perspectives mentioned in this chapter are able to explain Soviet-East European trade during the transition to a lower real wmp of oil.

PART IV

Participation in the Larger World Economy

CHAPTER 8

Centrally Planned Economies in the IMF, the World Bank, and the GATT

Paul Marer

INTRODUCTION

In the early postwar years, and well before CPEs became a significant factor in the international economy, the Western countries had established three international economic organizations (IEOs)—the International Monetary Fund, the World Bank, and the General Agreement on Tariffs and Trade (GATT)—to help manage economic interdependence between nations. Although at that time it was hoped that membership in these IEOs would be universal, the participation of CPEs was, and has remained, controversial. From the point of view of the West, the dilemma is this: is it in the political and economic interest of the IEOs to encourage the membership of CPEs in these organizations, and if so, can a CPE system be made compatible with the market-oriented rules and operations of these organizations? There is a parallel dilemma for the CPEs: is it in their political and economic interest to seek membership and, if so, what systemic and policy adjustments would be required to obtain the benefits of membership?

While these fundamental dilemmas have remained the same ever since the three IEOs were established, the political and economic circumstances in which these issues have been considered and decided have changed a great deal. The purpose of this study is to describe and assess the postwar history of CPE relations with the IMF, the World Bank, and the GATT, and to examine the substantive economic issues that arise in connection with CPE membership in these organizations.

Section 1 summarizes the purposes, the main institutional features, and the operations of the IMF, the World Bank, and the GATT in order to provide a common understanding of the possibilities and limits each IEO has in its dealings with its members, since this has direct implications for its dealing with CPES. Section 2 reviews CPE relations with the three IEOs during the postwar period. Section 3 examines the main substantive issues that arise from the systemic differences between CPES and the market-oriented rules and practices of the IEOs.

1. EVOLUTION, ORGANIZATION, AND OPERATIONS OF THE THREE IEOs

Origin and Purpose

The origins of the IMF, the World Bank, and the GATT can be traced to the traumatic experiences of the Great Depression. The practices of that period, namely, competitive currency devaluations, multiple exchange rates, exchange controls, import restrictions, and bilateral trade agreements, disrupted international trade and reinforced the effects of the Great Depression. Therefore, the overriding economic objective for the postwar era was to reconstruct a multilateral system of world trade and payments to prevent a repetition of the interwar mistakes. Three cooperating IEOs were created: the IMF, to promote currency stability and a system of international payments; the World Bank, to help reconstruct war-ravaged countries and to develop the economies of poor nations; and an international trade organization, to set rules of conduct for international trade and investment.

The IMF and the International Bank for Reconstruction and Development (the World Bank) were formed at the 1944 conference of forty-four nations at Bretton Woods, New Hampshire; their charter became effective at the end of 1945. After lengthy negotiations, a charter for an international trade organization (ITO) was drafted at the 1948 conference in Havana, Cuba. The document covered not only commercial policy but also such issues as employment, economic development, state trading, cartels, and intergovernmental commodity agreements. But the U.S. Congress did not approve the charter because by the late 1940s the country's attention had shifted from the goal of global multilateralism to Western Europe's economic distress and to the spread of communism in China and Eastern Europe. The adverse effects of the failure of the ITO were mitigated by the rise to prominence of the General Agreement on Tariffs and Trade (GATT), an almost casual off-shoot of an international conference held in 1947 in Geneva to consider the draft charter of the ITO. The GATT, strictly speaking, is not an IEO but an international agreement on codes of conduct on commercial policies and a forum for negotiating multilateral reductions of trade barriers. In many ways, however, it does function like an IEO.

Membership and Decisionmaking

International Monetary Fund. Membership in the Fund is open to every state that controls its own foreign relations and is able and willing to fulfill the obligations of membership contained in the Fund's Articles of Agreement. Each member has a quota, based on the relative importance of its currency in international transactions; the exact size of the quota is negotiated. A member's quota is equal to its subscription in the Fund. Voting power and maximum access to the financial resources of the Fund are directly related to the size of quota.

The senior decisionmaking body is the board of governors. It consists of one governor appointed by each member; the person is usually the country's minister of finance or the head of its central bank. The board is responsible for the admission of new members, the determination of quotas, and certain other matters; all other powers are delegated to the executive board, in practice the most important organ of the Fund (Edwards 1985, p. 28). The executive board has twenty to twenty-two executive directors, partly appointed and partly elected, and the managing director who chairs it. Both boards use a system of weighted voting. Each member has an allotment of 250 votes plus one vote for each part of its quota equivalent to special drawing rights (SDRs) 100,000. The basic allotment recognizes the sovereign equality of states and thus strengthens the voting position of the smaller members. The variable allotment recognizes differences in financial contributions, "to ensure the cooperation of those members that account for the greater part of international trade and financial transactions" (Hooke 1982, p. 17). At the end of 1984, the United States had approximately 19 percent of the 930,000 total votes. Governors and executive directors cast as a unit the number of votes allotted to the members that have appointed or elected them, but this does not prevent them from stating the positions of individual members of their group during the discussion. Most decisions taken by the two top bodies, including the decisions to admit new members, are adopted by a simple majority of the votes cast (Gold 1974, p. 468). For more important decisions, a larger majority is required: 70 percent to resolve such operational issues as rates of payment and charges on the acquisition and use of Fund resources; and 85 percent to decide, for example, changes in the structure of the Fund, changes in quotas, and broad policies on the allocation of SDRs. Thus, the United States alone or, when voting together, the members of the European Economic Community (EEC), or the developing countries, have veto power. In practice, formal votes are rarely taken; in most cases, decisions are arrived at by consensus. However, decisions usually take cognizance of the distribution of voting power among members.

Since the founders of the IMF believed that decisions on membership might be affected by political considerations, they gave the final say to the board of governors. Procedures leading to membership are usually conducted contemporaneously in the IMF and the World Bank (Gold 1974, p. 29). Upon receipt of a formal letter of application, a committee of five or six executive directors is appointed to obtain relevant information, to conduct the negotiations, and to make a recommendation to the executive directors when a full agreement is reached with the applicant on all issues. The executive directors usually approve the report and submit a resolution to the board of governors, where a simple majority of the votes decides the outcome. To become a member, an applicant must accept all of the obligations under the IMF charter, without reservations or interpretations.

A member may withdraw from the Fund voluntarily, or the Fund can compel a member to withdraw for failure to perform its obligations. Three members, Poland, Cuba, and Indonesia, have withdrawn voluntarily, although Indonesia and Poland have since rejoined. Only one country, Czechoslovakia, has been compelled to withdraw (see the next section).

Forty-three of the forty-four countries represented at the Bretton Woods conference became founding members or joined the IMF soon thereafter; the USSR was the single exception (Gold 1974, pp. 13–18); Poland, Czechoslovakia, and Cuba left the Fund subsequently. By 1986 membership in the Fund had grown to 151 and included all the industrial market economies except Switzerland, most less-developed countries (LDCS), as well as a few CPEs in Asia, Africa, and Europe. Concerning the policy of the Fund on admitting new members, Sir Joseph Gold—who has been associated with the Fund since 1946 and served as its general counsel from 1960 until 1979—states that the Fund has been guided by an unformulated policy of readiness to accept as wide a membership as possible (Gold 1974, p. 474).

World Bank. The World Bank was established at Bretton Woods as a sister organization to the Fund. A requirement of membership is that the country be a member of the IMF, but IMF members are not obligated to join the Bank. In 1987 the memberships of the two organizations were identical. The World Bank, too, has a board of governors, an executive board, and a system of weighted voting. The responsibilities of the president of the Bank who, by convention, is an American, are similar to those of the managing director of the Fund who, by common agreement, is always a European.

The World Bank comprises three institutions, the International Bank for Reconstruction and Development (IBRD), founded in 1945; the International Finance Corporation (IFC), set up in 1956; and the International Development Association (IDA), established in 1960. Although legally and financially these are separate entities, the facilities and some of their staff are shared. A majority of the countries that belong to the IBRD are also IFC and IDA members. The IFC assists the economic development of LDCs by promoting the growth of their private sectors and by helping to mobilize domestic and foreign capital for this purpose. IDA provides development assistance to the poorest LDCs on concessionary terms.

The General Agreement on Tariffs and Trade. The GATT is not legally an international organization; nevertheless, in practical terms, the GATT has evolved into an IEO. Powers normally granted to an IEO are vested in the contracting parties—the signatories acting jointly—and these contracting parties are the senior organ of the GATT. Each contracting party (analogous to the term "member") has one vote. Decisions are taken by the majority of the votes cast, unless otherwise provided; for admitting new members, a two-thirds majority is needed.

Other bodies have been set up by the contracting parties including: (1) The council of the GATT, made up of representatives of all GATT members. It has broad powers, and its actions require a majority vote.

A member adversely affected by a council decision can appeal to the contracting parties. (2) The consultative "group of eighteen," composed of high-level officials of countries representative of membership; it prepares the groundwork for decisions by the council or the contracting parties. (3) Special working groups to examine and make recommendations on specific issues. These bodies, together with the secretariat, which is affiliated with the United Nations (because legally the GATT is not an IEO), are referred to as the GATT organization.

The GATT agreement became effective in 1948 with a membership of twenty-three industrial countries. By September 1986 there were ninety-two contracting parties, accounting for more than 80 percent of world trade. In addition, some thirty other countries also apply GATT rules in their trade. The most notable exception is the Soviet Union.

Operations

IMF. The IMF has three main functions: (1) to administer a large pool of monetary assets and to issue SDRs to members; (2) to administer codes of good conduct regarding currency and other matters; and (3) to provide the machinery for consultation and collaboration on international monetary problems.

The Fund has a pool of monetary assets, composed of national currencies, gold, and special drawing rights (SDRs). National currencies are acquired mainly from quota subscriptions. Until 1970, 25 percent of a member's subscription was paid in gold, 75 percent in their own currency.

Since then, new members pay 20 to 25 percent in the convertible currencies of other members, as prescribed by the Fund. Periodically there is a general quota increase. The Fund has the authority to augment its resources by borrowing, but so far it has borrowed only from member governments and Switzerland (Driscoll 1984, p. 29). The Fund has substantial gold holdings, although since 1970 one-third of its gold holdings have been sold, with the proceeds used to create a trust fund to help LDCs.

Since 1969 the Fund has been authorized to issue SDRs, a composite reserve asset allocated to members in proportion to quotas. It is an asset to its holder and a liability of the SDR department of the Fund, and thus indirectly of all the participants in the department. Its worth derives from the member countries' willingness to accept it and to use it; its value is determined daily as the weighted average value of the currencies of the five largest trading countries.

The Fund's pool of monetary assets is revolving. The first 25 percent of a member's quota can be borrowed automatically, but as the amounts requested become larger, the Fund will provide them only with conditionality. Since countries tend to turn to the Fund for relatively large loans only when alternative sources have been, or are about to be, exhausted, and since it is not the Fund's mission to provide long-term development assistance, the Fund must ensure that the borrower will be able to repay the loan within a few years. Conditionality is a tool to encourage the borrowing countries to implement policies that will reestablish their creditworthiness; it also enables the Fund to try to prevent countries from increasing trade and payments restrictions during payments difficulties.

The policies a member intends to implement in order to have access to the Fund's resources under conditional (standby) arrangements are described in a letter of intent to the Fund, containing a summary of the borrower's economic policy objectives and the measures being adopted to achieve them, the so-called adjustment program. The program reflects the outcome of the negotiations on the terms under which the money committed will be available; it imposes no contractual obligation on the borrowing country, only on the Fund. If the country meets the terms agreed upon, the Fund will be obligated to the phased release of the money committed. But if the country deviates from the agreed program, there is no breach of its international obligations. This arrangement "protects the member from the charge that it has subjected important areas of policy to the legal authority of the Fund" (Driscoll 1984, p. 39). Noncompliance with terms cancels the country's right to further disbursements and starts new consultations. If the areas of noncompliance are small, a waiver may be approved; if substantial, a new program will have to be negotiated. Only if no agreement is reached will the drawing rights remain suspended (Edwards 1985, p. 268).

Since excess domestic demand is frequently an important cause of payments difficulties, its elimination is a focus of most adjustment programs, typically by restraining bank-, budget-, or foreign-financed spending. Other elements in the program are intended simultaneously to decrease domestic demand and increase the supply of exportables: by raising real interest rates to promote saving and to discourage wasteful investment; increasing the prices of subsidized goods and services, which reduces budget deficits and fosters more efficient resource allocation; and currency devaluation.

Fund programs generally specify quantified targets, called performance criteria, such as ceilings on the expansion of bank credits and limits on external borrowing. If external payment arrears are outstanding, their reduction or elimination is usually required.

Another important IMF function is to administer codes of good conduct regarding exchange rate practices and convertibility. The Fund requires that payments for trade in merchandise and services that, together with certain other transactions, comprise the current account in the balance of payments, take place freely and that balances arising out of current account transactions, held by nonresidents, be freely convertible into other currencies. Members must eschew restrictive bilateral and regional payments arrangements and maintain a uniform exchange rate. It is the obligation of all countries to work toward convertibility. The status of those that have succeeded is recognized by their formal acceptance of the "code of conduct" obligations of Article 8 of the IMF agreement. The essence of this code is that a country will not introduce restrictions and practices that will make its currency inconvertible. IMF approval may be sought and granted for temporary exceptions, justified by severe balance-of-payments pressures. Countries whose economies are not sufficiently strong to make their currencies convertible can avail themselves of transitional arrangements permitted under Article 14. This code permits a member to maintain the restrictions it had in place when it joined the Fund and to adapt them to changing circumstances. But even under Article 14 countries may not introduce new restrictions, or reintroduce restrictions that had been eliminated, without the Fund's approval.

In 1961 the major West European nations became Article 8 countries; in 1964 Japan joined the group. By 1986 sixty-one members, including all the industrialized countries, had accepted Article 8 status and obligations, while eighty-seven members, including all the CPEs that were members, were availing themselves of the transitional arrangements under Article 14. In practice, the transitional status Article 14 has meant that existing payment restrictions could be retained for a period of undefined duration.

Until the early 1970s the IMF promoted the fixed exchange rate system, but the inexorable buildup of currency pressures in the 1960s and early 1970s led to its demise. Since the Fund was powerless to prevent this, it had to change the rules. Since 1973 de facto (de jure only since 1976), members have been free to choose their exchange rate arrangements; they may peg the value of their currency to that of another currency or some composite of currencies, adjust currency values according to a set of indicators, or permit exchange rates to be determined wholly or partly by market forces. However, the Fund continues to exercise surveillance over the exchange rate policies of members so as to ensure that they refrain from manipulating exchange rates to gain unfair competitive advantage, intervene in their exchange markets if necessary to counter disorderly conditions, and in their intervention policies take into account the interests of other countries.

Perhaps the most essential provision of a code of good conduct is the obligation to consult and collaborate with the IMF. Consultation includes the provision of information: the willingness to explain policies and their intended effects; the willingness to engage in a mutual assessment of policies and their effects; and willingness to receive advice from others, but without a duty to follow it (Edwards 1985, pp. 570–71). Consultation is exceedingly important because it yields important benefits to the membership as a whole. The IMF and the World Bank accumulate a great deal of knowledge about the economies of member countries. For many small nations, the IMF and the World Bank may be the only institutions able and willing to marshal the expertise needed for an independent, in-depth analysis of the country's economic situation. One step in the iterative cycle of consultation is sending missions to the country, where discussions are held with experts, possibly including those who are not government officials. Consultation permits outsiders to comment on a country's policies and thus influence its actions. Consultations may be a time when a country's policies are given a careful internal review that otherwise may not take place. It may also identify shortcomings in statistical information, gaps in the authorities' knowledge about their own economy, or the poor training of a country's personnel; countries may feel compelled to take actions to rectify matters. Fund recommendations during consultations may make it possible for the authorities to persevere with sound policies in the face of domestic or external pressures to abandon them. The large amount of statistical data and information that the Fund and the Bank collect, standardize, and make available is a public good. Analyses based on these data may reveal emerging problems that can trigger collective action to prevent them from developing.

Hence, the importance of countries who observe the code of good behavior regarding consultation, including the provision of accurate data. Consultations may yield benefits that are independent of the actual influence the Fund and the Bank may have on the policies of members.

The third major function of the Fund is to provide machinery for members to consult with each other and to collaborate on international monetary matters. The Fund has played an important and substantially positive role in this area, in spite of the policy paralysis that in recent years has often characterized the actions of important member governments.

World Bank. The World Bank's main mission is to promote the economic development of its poorer member countries. It administers a pool of resources for the benefit of members, but it obtains and allocates them differently from the means used by the IMF.

Quota subscriptions by member governments serve principally as the base on which the Bank borrows on the international capital markets. Only 10 percent of the quota is paid in; the additional 90 percent is callable, for the protection of the Bank's creditors, in the unlikely event of defaults by the countries to which the funds it borrowed are loaned. The Bank's ability to provide growing amounts of finance on attractive terms and its firm policy against rescheduling give it leverage that it has used to ensure that its loans will be serviced.

Although lending for reconstruction formally ended in 1955, loan disbursements to developed countries continued until about 1967 (Ayres 1983, p. 3). Thereafter, the World Bank has loaned only to LDCs to promote economic development. The Bank channels funds to member governments (or requires government guarantees) in the form of medium- and long-term loans; the typical term is twenty years. Because the Bank borrows on approximately the same terms as the United States government and pays no dividends on paid-in capital—many LDCs would have no access to private capital markets on comparable terms—Bank loans in fact contain substantial grants to the recipients. For this reason, and because the Bank also administers the IDA—which provides soft loans to the poorest countries—the Bank is also a development agency. In fact, its Articles of Agreement require that loans be made only to members that cannot obtain development finance on reasonable terms on private capital markets. But since "extent of access" and "reasonable terms" are not precisely measurable, the Bank has relied since 1973 largely on dollar per capita GNP as a proxy for the level of development to identify the countries in which it will finance projects. In 1973 the threshold level was $1,000 in 1970 prices; in 1980 the equivalent was $2,650 in current prices, after adjusting for inflation and exchange rate movements.

An important advantage of membership is that only suppliers from member countries are eligible to bid on Bank-funded projects. The Bank thus also promotes international trade; the industrial countries are the main suppliers of the technology and hardware.

The Bank both helps form and reflects prevailing thinking about how economic development can be promoted most effectively by external finance. Before Robert McNamara became president in 1968, lending was predominantly for infrastructure. Thereafter, many social service projects to help the basic needs of poor people also were funded. In the past decade roughly 30 percent of lending has been for agricultural and rural development projects. Prior to 1979 the Bank often insisted upon borrowers making changes only in policies that bore directly on the projects financed. Since 1980 the Bank has been involved in developing and supporting programs of "structural and sectoral adjustment," providing support to the economy to assist it with its balance-of-payments problems. Since the IMF, which used to provide only short-term balance-of-payments finance, has begun recently to provide medium-term facilities also, the distinction between the lending operations of the two organizations—including the concept of conditionality —has become less sharply drawn. A further reason for this convergence is that as the debt crisis deepened, the Bank's seal of approval, like that of the IMF, became important to commercial banks, both generally and specifically, in connection with the recently instituted cofinancing program under which the World Bank and commercial banks jointly finance projects.

These developments have led to closer formal cooperation between the Bank and the Fund. This includes not only the exchange of information, but also occasional participation by officers from one institution in the missions to member countries that are led by the other institution. Although the Bank and the Fund continue to apply their own criteria in appraising requests for assistance, on occasion the Bank has indicated that it would like the prospective borrowing country to accept the standby program recommended by the Fund. On other occasions, the Bank, at its own initiative, has required a letter of intent stating the policies the country intends to pursue (Edwards

1985, p. 48), thus, in effect, engaging in conditional lending.

The Bank promotes policies that help create and maintain a favorable investment climate and strong balance of payments: fiscal and monetary probity; getting prices right or removing the obstacles to their free-market determination; levying realistic user charges for certain public services to control waste; positive real interest rates to encourage savings and limit uneconomical investments; wage increases that do not outrun gains in productivity; a sound currency that is not overvalued; prudent liberalization of trade policies; and debt management that strengthens creditworthiness. At the sectoral and micro levels it assists countries in determining their current and prospective comparative advantage, advises policymakers to shift resources into those sectors, and evaluates the soundness of projects that it is asked to, or that it may suggest that it might help finance.

How much influence the Bank has in these areas and in particular countries is difficult to say. The more a country depends on the Bank for external finance and the more the Bank lends with conditions attached, the closer its influence will be to that of the IMF providing loans to countries in similar circumstances.

GATT. The major difference between the GATT and the two international financial institutions is that the GATT does not gather and distribute funds. The main similarities are that the GATT also administers a code of good conduct and provides a forum for international collaboration.

The activities of the GATT fall into two main categories: bargaining over tariffs and nontariff barriers (NTBs); and settlement of disputes involving members.[1]

Since 1948 when the GATT had been put into operation, seven tariff conferences have been held to negotiate mutual tariff concessions. Agreements to reduce rates, or to bind them against any further increase, cover products that make up more than half of world trade. At tariff conferences, negotiations on lowering tariffs on individual commodities are conducted bilaterally between countries that have especially strong interests in the outcome. While negotiating, each party is aware that other members are also negotiating and that the results of those negotiations will accrue to their benefit. This is accomplished because the results of the rounds of bilateral negotiations are not finalized until all of them are gathered into a single master agreement that all participants sign. In this way all the concessions in the master agreement apply to trade among all GATT members. Most countries grant MFN status automatically to all GATT members; other nations, including the United States, may grant MFN status to certain countries only after a bilateral trade agreement has been negotiated. The essential principle of the process of bargaining over the reduction of tariff and nontariff barriers (NTBS) is *reciprocity*.

Since 1965 the GATT has recognized the special needs of LDCs by authorizing members to give trade preferences to them without reciprocity. Although there is a general agreement among eighteen developed countries about which products to include, which countries are to be the beneficiaries, and how the generalized system of preferences (GSP) is to be administered, each industrial country may have its own rules about granting GSP status to certain countries and implementing its program.

The GATT charter promulgates a code of good conduct regarding such widely used NTBS as quantitative restrictions. The GATT secretariat has compiled more than 800 specific kinds of NTBS, grouped into five broad categories (F. Root 1984, p. 324): government participation in trade (e.g., export subsidies, procurement, countervailing duties); customs and administrative entry procedures (e.g., classification, valuation, customs formalities); standards and packaging regulations; specific limitations on trade (e.g., export restraints, licensing); and charges on imports (e.g., prior deposits, variable levies). The relative importance of NTBS has grown in recent years because tariff levels have declined and because as protectionism has increased, it has often taken this form. Recognizing the need to reduce NTBS, the seventh (Tokyo) Round, held during 1975–79, negotiated codes covering the first three categories. Especially important is the subsidies/countervailing duty code, which prohibits outright export subsidies in manufacturing and primary mineral products, suggests procedures to determine injury resulting from subsidies, and regulates the imposition of countervailing duties designed to offset them.

The GATT allows a member to withdraw or modify tariff concessions granted if, as a result of the concession, there is such an increase in imports as to cause—or threaten to cause—serious injury to domestic producers. This provision used to be called the "escape clause" provision. When a member wants to apply this clause, it must consult with the supplying countries to try to agree on remedies. If no agreement can be reached, the supplying countries can withdraw "equivalent" concessions previously granted. In practice this code has often been circumvented. Therefore, there is a growing need for a code on safeguards generally. A main issue in the negotiations is whether safeguard action should be taken on a multilateral basis, or whether a protective measure could be taken that would affect only imports from the country actually causing injury.

A significant activity of the GATT is its role in the settlement of trade disputes between members. Although there are justified complaints from time to time about the inability of the GATT to enforce its rules and rulings, the contribution of the GATT lies in its role as a forum for frank discussion between member countries. International meetings sponsored by the GATT have helped to breed a common international viewpoint on trade policy. Hence, member governments take the GATT into account when contemplating measures to protect their balance of payments (F. Root 1984, pp. 320–21). The new (eighth) round of trade negotiations launched in September 1986 in Punte del Este, Uruguay, is the most ambitious undertaking in the history of the GATT because it has placed on the agenda virtually every concern of the contracting parties.

2. HISTORY OF CPE MEMBERSHIP IN INTERNATIONAL ECONOMIC ORGANIZATIONS

IMF and the World Bank

In May 1944 the United States invited forty-four governments, the original signatories of the Declaration of the United Nations, to send representatives to a conference at Bretton Woods to discuss the founding of the IMF and the World Bank. The invitees included the USSR, Czechoslovakia, Poland, and Yugoslavia, but of course only the USSR was a CPE at the time. Many representatives, including those of the United States and the United Kingdom, argued that a place should be found for the USSR and for "state-controlled economies" generally. The 1942 draft of the White Plan, which argued the position of the United States, suggested that no restrictions as to membership should be imposed on the grounds of a country's economic system; that, in fact, because the conduct of international commerce is so completely under the control of the government in a socialist economy, there is all the more reason to attempt to obtain their cooperation under the aegis of IEOs. The White Plan then noted, prophetically (quoted in Gold

1974, p. 130): "Furthermore, no one can know what direction some of the smaller liberated states will take in the shaping of their economic structures. There is likely to be, during the next decade or two, a variety of economic systems and it would seem desirable that these should not be discouraged from cooperating with the others so long as they are willing to agree to conduct their international economic affairs in accordance with the principles acceptable to the United Nations." These sentiments were still echoed in 1946 by John Snyder, secretary of the treasury and chairman of the board of governors of the IMF, at the first joint annual meeting of the Fund and the Bank: "Cooperation in the economic world is no less important than cooperation in the political world. It is essential to the peace and prosperity of all nations that they operate under the same fundamental rules in their business dealings with one another. The characters of the Fund and the Bank are drawn broadly enough to encompass various types of economic and trading systems" (quoted in Gold 1974, p. 130n).

The USSR participated in the negotiations leading to the establishment of the Fund and the Bank. The Soviet Union's political perspectives and positions during those early years are elaborated in publications authored by Lavigne (1978), the United Nations (1986), and Assetto (1988). The final articles of agreement of the IMF adopted some Soviet recommendations and accommodated certain of its objections. The USSR wanted a formula that would increase its voting power to at least 10 percent of the total (Gold 1974, p. 133). The conference gave the USSR the third largest quota, 13.64 percent of the total subscription, giving it 12.37 percent of the total voting power. One reason for the USSR's interest in having at least 10 percent of the voting power may have been the provision recommended in an early draft of the IMF charter that gave each member having at least 10 percent of aggregate quotas a veto over Fund decisions to change the price of gold (Gold 1974, p. 133). Ultimately, a 20 percent share was (since 1978, 15 percent is) required for such a veto (Article 4, section 7).

In the end, the USSR did not become a member because by the end of 1945 the frictions between East and West that developed into the cold war had begun to assert themselves.

Czechoslovakia, Poland, Yugoslavia, and Cuba, which at the time the IMF and the Bank were founded were not CPES, were founding members. Poland's departure from the two IEOS can be traced to a deterioration in East-West relations. In 1946 Poland requested a large loan for the reconstruction of its coal industry from the World Bank. Negotiations on this loan continued until mid-1948 when Poland refused participation in the Marshall Plan and sided with the USSR on various cold war issues. In 1948 the U.S. executive director of the Bank stated that the United States would not grant export licenses for the equipment that Poland would purchase with the loan and that the United States would vote against the loan (Mroczkowski 1988). Thereafter, Poland's relations with the Bank and the Fund deteriorated and, in March 1950, Poland withdrew for political reasons. Poland's letter of withdrawal alleged that the Bank and the Fund had failed to fulfill their duties and had become submissive instruments of the United States.

In 1954 Czechoslovakia was compelled to withdraw, although it insists that it did so voluntarily. After 1949 Czechoslovakia ceased to supply information and did not respond to requests for consultation. On June 2, 1953, the Fund received a cable from the State Bank of Czechoslovakia, informing it that on May 30, 1953, the par value of the Czechoslovak crown had been appreciated in terms of gold and that its exchange rate vis-à-vis several currencies had been changed as part of a monetary and economic reform. Since these measures had been carried out without consultation with the Fund, a lengthy legal skirmish ensued. The U.S. executive director took the position that Czechoslovakia failed over a period of years to perform the minimum obligations required of a member and therefore should not be allowed to continue in good standing. The representative of Czechoslovakia argued that the country had every right to change its exchange rate since this did not affect its international transactions, and that discriminatory actions that the United States had taken against Czechoslovakia forced it to cease providing information for national security reasons. In November 1953 the executive board declared Czechoslovakia ineligible to use the resources of the Fund. The consensus was that a member's refusal to supply information and consult made it impossible for the Fund to understand its economy, which made it logical that it should not be eligible for loans.

In June 1954 the U.S. executive director recommended that, in view of Czechoslovakia's continued failure to fulfill its obligations, it be asked to withdraw. For almost a year Czechoslovakia fought the interpretation on which the recommendation was based. It is not clear whether Czechoslovakia, the only CPE in the Fund and the Bank at the time, wanted to remain a member or simply wished to avoid the opprobrium of expulsion. There was broad consensus that Czechoslovakia had failed to live up to its obligations and had fallen short of the cooperation that it could have offered, even on the basis of its own assumptions, but there was considerable disagreement about what to do. Some were inclined to give weight to the claim of national security since the same reasoning was accepted for other members in other contexts. Others doubted the wisdom of requiring withdrawal because circumstances might change and enable Czechoslovakia to cooperate with the Fund in the future. On September 28, 1954, the board adopted a resolution asking Czechoslovakia to withdraw as of the end of the year. Subsequently the Fund advised all members that Czechoslovakia's withdrawal had taken effect as of December 31, 1954. Czechoslovakia continued to contest the legality of the action well into 1955. On May 4, 1955, Czechoslovakia withdrew from both organizations and considers that its memberships ceased as of that date (Gold 1974, chapter 16).

About a decade later Cuba, which in the meantime had become a CPE, left the organization. In 1963 the executive directors requested a formal reply from the Cuban government as to why the country was seriously delinquent in fulfilling its obligations to the Fund. Specifically, the amounts Cuba had borrowed in 1958 remained unpaid for five years, the maximum period under the Fund's policies on the use of its resources; Cuba had not paid in its share of the general quota increase in 1959; it stopped furnishing economic information after July 1961; and it appeared to be applying, without consultation, exchange practices for which Fund approval was required. Cuba did not reply to numerous inquiries on these matters. But just before a meeting of the executive directors, scheduled to declare Cuba ineligible for Fund resources—a step likely to have been followed by a request for Cuba to leave the organization—Cuba withdrew, effective immediately, on April 2, 1964 (Gold 1974, pp. 342–44).

Yugoslavia, a founding member whose economy was centrally planned only during 1950–51, has remained a member and has exercised its rights and obligations continuously.

China was a founding member, but when the mainland became communist the Republic of China (Taiwan) continued to represent the country until 1980, even though the People's Republic of China did make representations in the early 1950s to take over the seat.

The 1980 Brandt Commission Report (p. 202) concluded that the Soviet Union and the other CPEs decided either not to join or subsequently to sever their links with the IMF because of their dissatisfaction with:

(1) the procedure adopted for allocating votes among members;

(2) the obligation to provide such economic information as national gold and foreign exchange holdings;

(3) the requirement to transfer a portion of their gold and foreign exchange to an institution located in the United States;

(4) conditionality on balance-of-payments credits.

A Soviet economist, discussing why most CPEs have not taken part in the IMF, mentioned all of the above points and added one further reason:

(5) that Article 8 of the IMF charter obligates members not to limit foreign exchange payments and transfers on their current account, a requirement "totally unacceptable to the socialist countries with their state monopoly of foreign trade and monetary operations and other economic administrative principles . . . (Fomin 1978, p. 106).

The gradual improvement in East-West political and economic relations that began during the second half of the 1960s, and the increasingly divergent ideological, political, and economic developments in what the West once viewed as the monolithic Soviet bloc, contributed to a gradual change in the attitudes of some countries on both sides. In 1972, Romania became a member. Vietnam took over South Vietnam's membership in 1976. The People's Republic of China replaced the Republic of China (Taiwan) in 1980. In 1981 Hungary applied and became a member in 1982. Poland also applied at the same time, but its application was held in abeyance for several years, at U.S. insistence, following the imposition of martial law in Poland. After a great deal of political maneuvering, Poland was readmitted to the IMF and the World Bank in June 1986. Laos, Cambodia, and North Yemen —countries that have CPE-type economies—are members also.

In the summer of 1986 the Soviet Union put out feelers about the possibility of joining the IMF, the World Bank, as well as the GATT (for details, see Marer 1986b). Subsequently, in an interview given by D. V. Smislov, deputy director of the Institute of World Economy of the Soviet Academy of Sciences, he elaborated on the USSR's position. From *Heti Vilaggazdasag,* Budapest, September 6, 1986 (in Hungarian):

Q: Our journal reported that the Soviet Union wishes to join the GATT. Is the USSR also reassessing its relationship with the IMF and other international financial organizations?

A: It is undeniable that our assessment of international economic organizations has changed since the Twenty-seventh Party Congress. The Central Committee report stressed, for the first time, the emergence of global economic integration and interdependence. This requires a new approach on the part of the USSR, not only regarding international economic organizations but also concerning important developments in the world economy. A broad debate has begun about these issues among our experts. In spite of this—in the short run—I don't foresee the possibility that we would join the IMF and the World Bank. This has several obstacles. The USA, which continues to exert a large influence in the IMF, does not favor USSR membership, is concerned about the ideologization of debates, about the slowdown of procedures. The IMF in turn is afraid that the USSR, being a planned economy, will plan year after year a balance-of-payments deficit, and will ask the IMF to finance it. We on the other hand don't want to accept economic policy advice with IMF loans. We also believe that the IMF's market-centered ideology is inappropriate. Thus, it is our feeling that under present conditions, the Soviet Union would have difficulty realizing its interests. But in the end, much will depend on the general political atmosphere. It that were to improve, numerous opportunities would arise for creating linkages, even to achieve monetary cooperation.

GATT

The Soviet Union did not participate in the negotiations on the ITO or the GATT. The agreement to establish the GATT was signed in 1947. In 1955 the Soviet Union, probably in response to a temporary improvement in East-West relations, recommended that the charter of the by then defunct ITO be ratified, although it did not express an interest in joining the GATT. The ITO had been conceived as a UN organization with universal membership, whose charter had adopted a general solution for state-trading countries, and thus the Soviets could support it. By contrast, the GATT was composed mostly of the industrial Western countries. It was clear that if they were to agree to the affiliation of a CPE, it would be under special arrangements on a country by country basis so that, in effect, CPEs would have second class status (Kostecki 1978, p. 8). These considerations notwithstanding, some East European countries began to express an interest in the GATT in the mid-1950s.

The establishment of the European Economic Community in 1958 undoubtedly played a role in the emerging East European interest in the GATT. The countries wanted to be in a better position to parry the adverse impacts of EEC policies, such as those in agriculture, and to reduce Western quotas on imports from Eastern Europe. As it turned out, the EEC was unwilling to make a firm commitment to abolish those restrictions. Members did agree to their gradual reduction, but implementation has been slow (Orr 1981).

The East European countries also obtained fewer concessions from the United States than they hoped. Since 1962 congressional legislation has prevented the United States from extending unconditional MFN treatment to the East European countries except for Yugoslavia and (with an interruption between October 9, 1982, and February 19, 1987, during which sanctions were imposed) Poland.

The issue of reciprocity, discussed in greater detail in section 3, is the main problem posed by the accession of CPES to the GATT. The agreed solutions represent compromises that both sides consider less than perfect. Czechoslovakia was a founding member of the GATT, but was not then a CPE.[2] Its terms of accession have not been subsequently renegotiated. During the early 1950s the United States protested the fictitious nature of that country's tariff concessions and, on that basis, in 1954 it renounced unilaterally its agreements. The complaint brought by Czechoslovakia before the contracting parties was dismissed without investigation on the grounds that the issue was a political one, and thus outside their jurisdiction. Although since then the United States and certain other countries have discriminated against Czechoslovakia, the country has continued to take part—with a very low profile—in the activities of the GATT and has generally refrained from attacking it openly, on ideological grounds, as frequently practiced by some other CPES. During the Kennedy Round, Czechoslovakia offered to increase its imports from the GATT members by 30 percent over five years in exchange for a removal of quantitative restrictions, but the offer was not accepted. Market economies desiring to improve commercial relations with Czechoslovakia rely mainly on bilateral agreements (Kostecki 1978, pp. 23–25). Cuba's case is somewhat parallel to that of Czechoslovakia, except that Cuba places its complaints against U.S. discrimination in the context of its developing country status.

Yugoslavia, not a CPE but a "socialist" East European country, obtained observer status in the GATT in 1950 when it was still a CPE. As it moved away from central planning, its relations with the GATT intensified and in 1958 it became an associate member. In 1962, after Yugoslavia introduced a tariff system, abolished multiple exchange rates, and simplified controls on trade, it became a provisional GATT member. The chief obstacle to full membership was its inability to bring the average level of tariffs down to acceptable levels; large disparities between domestic and world prices required tariffs as high as several hundred percent. After its 1964 "market socialism" reform, however, it became a full member (Kostecki 1978, pp. 25–27).

In 1957 Poland and Romania became observers. At that time it was hoped that economic reforms in Poland would decentralize its economy sufficiently for tariffs to become an effective trade control instrument. In 1959 Poland requested full membership, but because several GATT members argued that Poland was not in a position to assume the obligations of full membership, it became an associate member. In 1960, immediately after Poland's associate membership in the GATT came into force, the Eisenhower administration granted it unconditional MFN treatment on the basis of Poland's status in the GATT.

At the same time the United States, Canada, the United Kingdom, Japan, and other members of the "anti-EEC front" (Kostecki 1979, p. 29) have shown a great interest in freeing Poland from the discriminatory regime maintained against that country through the EEC's extensive system of quotas on goods imported from Poland and the other CMEA countries. According to some observers, the EEC's aim is not so much the protection of sensitive sectors, but rather the maintenance of a trade-policy leverage on the socialist countries of Eastern Europe. The United States and other distant countries are against the EEC's discriminatory regime because it impairs their ability to penetrate the markets of the CMEA countries under conditions of a multilaterally applied regime of MFN. Accordingly, the United States and its allies in the GATT were not happy when Poland gave in to the EEC by accepting a clause by which the EEC would eliminate the restrictions "after a period of transition," to be defined later. In 1965 Poland was admitted to participate in the Kennedy Round and in 1967 became a full member of the GATT, formally pledging to increase the value of its imports from GATT members as a group by not less than 7 percent per annum. The weakness of the formula for Poland is that is does not take account of its balance of payments, which prevented it from fulfilling this obligation during the early 1980s. This provided the legal justification for the United States to withdraw MFN status for Poland as part of the sanctions it imposed after martial law.

Romania became an observer in 1957 and a full member in 1971. Recognizing the pitfalls of the Polish formula, and benefiting from its

LDC status and political capital in the West, it simply assumed the obligation to increase imports from GATT members as a group at a rate not less than its planned growth of total imports. The intention of the contracting parties was to make it difficult for Romania to reorient its trade to non-GATT members. The Protocol on the Accession of Romania was very sloppily drafted; one of several reflections of this is that it did not provide for means of controlling the fulfillment of this obligation.

Romania's stance vis-à-vis the EEC's discrimination was similar to that of Poland. The Romanians accepted that an increase in EEC import quotas can be regarded as evidence of trade liberalization, thereby handing the Community an instrument of trade-policy leverage.

Hungary's 1958 efforts to establish contacts with the GATT were rebuffed for political reasons, but in 1966 it became an observer and in 1973 a full member. In its application Hungary claimed that since its 1968 economic reforms it had relied largely on tariffs to control trade. Several GATT members noted, however, that the effectiveness of its tariffs could be weakened by quotas, the presence of many monopolies on the domestic market, and restrictions on free price formation (Kostecki 1979). After difficult negotiations, Hungary acceded to the GATT on similar terms as market economies, not because all members were convinced that Hungary had a viable domestic market mechanism, but to reward and encourage the significant steps it had taken in that direction.

Upon Hungary's application, its economic management system was subjected to more than a three-year examination. The outcome was that Hungary was not asked to modify any element in its existing economic system, though the GATT secretariat noted that it was not passing "any judgment on the effectiveness of Hungarian tariffs as a trade policy instrument" (Nyerges 1976, p. 138). To be sure, the significance of Hungary's accession on terms similar to those of market economies is that the maintenance of GATT conformity represents a significant pressure on Hungary to develop, or at least to maintain, its economic reforms.

Hungary's Protocol of Accession gave the country the right to maintain her existing regulations on trade with the socialist countries, namely, that Hungary does not apply tariffs to goods imported from them. The purpose of this exemption was not to allow discrimination in favor of CMEA trading partners but a recognition that intra-CMEA trade is conducted at fixed prices and is regulated by quotas, not tariffs. At the same time Hungary insisted on, and received in its Protocol of Accession, a straightforward and unconditional pledge by the Common Market that its discriminatory quantitative restrictions (QRS) against Hungary would be eliminated. Since the EEC was not prepared to set a target for their elimination, the agreed text called for their "progressive elimination" (Nyerges 1976, p. 141).

One conclusion that can be drawn is that the various compromise solutions on the basis of which the above CPEs have been admitted to the GATT do not provide them with the same legal protection in concrete situations as that which is available to those other GATT members that joined via the normal mutual granting of MFN status. The reason for the special status of the CPEs is that, with the possible exception of Hungary, they are unable to offer to the other members full and reciprocal MFN treatment (Bolz and Pissulla 1986).

In 1967 Bulgaria and in 1982 China became observers. In 1984 China signed the Multifiber Agreement that functions under the auspices of the GATT. On July 15, 1986, China formally applied to resume its membership in the GATT, in keeping with the increasingly important role it has assumed in world trade since implementing an open-door policy in 1979. Its request to resume membership was based on its earlier status as one of the original contracting parties in 1947. Whether or not China can reactivate its former membership or must join as if it were a new member is a legal question that remains to be addressed. Extensive consultations will be required to determine the obligations China must agree to conform with GATT rules. In one possible scenario China would become an associate member by the end of the 1980s and a provisional or full member by the early 1990s (United States International Trade Commission 1987, pp. 42–43).

On September 8, 1986, Bulgaria submitted its application for accession to the GATT, stating (GATT 1986, p. 2) that "[T]he economic and trade policy instruments being introduced at present within the context of the general evolution of economic policy in Bulgaria correspond to the basic principles and objectives of the General Agreement and thus ensure the effective participation of Bulgaria as a contracting party to the GATT."

The attitude of the USSR toward the GATT also has changed. Until the early 1970s it opposed the GATT because—as an exporter of energy and raw materials, and as a large country that could obtain trade concessions through bilateral agreements—it did not perceive many advantages to membership. Viewing the GATT as an imperialist institution that was dominated by the United States, the USSR originally gave strong support to the more democratic institution of the United Nations Conference on Trade and Development (UNCTAD), an organization it helped to establish. During the late 1970s the USSR softened its ideological opposition to the GATT and reexamined pragmatically its economic interest in membership, apparently concluding that it would not be worthwhile to abandon its practice of preferring bilateral over multilateral trade negotiations.[3]

During 1986–87 the Soviet Union assessed anew its policies toward participation in IEOs and appears to have concluded that its strategic as well as economic interests would be better served by offering cooperation. Although an outsider can only speculate on what the Soviets might be thinking, Soviet interest in having a say in the formulation of new rules, in reaping the benefits of multilateralism, and a more positive posture toward domestic economic reforms that might be supported by the requirements of membership in such IEOs as the GATT, are the presumed reasons for the recent change in Soviet policy toward the GATT.

In a letter delivered to the GATT secretariat on August 15, 1986, the Soviet Union formally requested to participate in the new, eighth round of GATT negotiations that were to commence in September 1986 in Punta del Este, Uruguay. The letter stated that the Soviet Union wished to participate in order to obtain the experience necessary to decide whether to seek accession to the GATT. The letter referred also to the new regulations on trade that were being drawn up and mentioned prospective changes in the Soviet foreign trade regime (United States International Trade Commission 1987, p. 47). This may be reported as an indication that the Soviet leadership regards membership in the GATT as a useful tool to implement market-oriented economic reforms.

The Soviet request was taken up at the GATT ministerial meeting in September 1986. Although the ministers did not act formally on the Soviet request, their declaration amounted to a rejection. The United States reportedly took the lead in drafting the declaration. Therefore, it is especially worth noting that in March 1987 Deputy Secretary of State John C. Whitehead said: "We would like to see the Soviet Union become a member of the IMF, the World Bank, and the GATT" (*New York Times*, March 6, 1987).

3. COMPATIBILITY OF CPE SYSTEMS
WITH OPERATIONS OF THE IEOS

The IMF, the World Bank, and the GATT were established to serve the needs of market economies. The compatibility of their rules and operations with the economic system features of Soviet-type central planning are questionable. To probe this question, five system-compatibility issues that bear most directly on CPE membership in the IEOS issues are examined: the convertibility provisions of the IMF and the inconvertibility of CPE currencies; the ability of the CPES to make the required financial contributions; the special problems of measuring the level of development of CPES to determine their eligibility to use World Bank resources; designing programs to help ensure the appropriate use of Fund and Bank resources; and obtaining reciprocity for trade concessions granted to a CPE.

Convertibility

There are many different concepts of convertibility, depending on whether the conversion is into another currency (financial convertibility) or goods (commodity convertibility); who has the right to make conversion, a foreign holder of funds (external convertibility) or a domestic resident or organization (domestic convertibility); and which items in the balance of payments can be converted freely (current- versus capital-account items are usually differentiated). In CPES, a further distinction must be made between three kinds of currencies: the transferable ruble used in intra-CMEA transactions; cash and savings deposits in the hands of consumers that command goods and services on consumer markets only; and bank balances of enterprises that generally do not command goods and services, including labor, unless they have first been allocated to the enterprise by the planners (Allen 1980).

In the IMF the concept of external financial convertibility for current account transactions, as specified in Article 8, is the most relevant one, although the statement in section 2 that "no member shall, without the approval of the Fund, impose restrictions on the making of payments and transfers for current international transactions," requires both external and domestic financial convertibility. External financial convertibility requires that a foreign resident may acquire and hold the domestic currencies of trade partner countries. Such convertibility does not exist in any CPE, even though all CPE currencies can be converted by certain foreign residents for certain purposes, such as tourism.

Achieving commodity convertibility requires not only giving up compulsory plan directives, but also altering other features of the system, such as the arbitrary nature of domestic prices and the monopoly over foreign trade that blocks direct access by foreigners to producers of exports and users of imports (Holzman 1974a, p. 144).

Thus, while the currencies of most market economies—even those that do not have financial convertibility—have a high degree of commodity convertibility, the general absence of commodity convertibility is a distinguishing feature of CPE currencies.

In principle a CPE could introduce financial convertibility without commodity convertibility by allowing nonresidents to hold its currency. The value of such holdings would have to be guaranteed in terms of designated convertible currencies or gold. In any event, evidence shows that financial convertibility is easier to introduce where a large measure of commodity convertibility is already present (Allen 1980, pp. 142–43); having sufficient reserves and a strong balance-of-payments position are of course also important.

The inconvertibility of CPE currencies may be an obstacle to the membership of CPEs in the Fund on the conceptual level, but not at the practical level. According to the Articles of Agreement, a member must pledge to move toward the convertibility of its currency. CPEs, especially those not contemplating comprehensive, market-type reforms, cannot make such a pledge. Nevertheless, at the practical level, the convertibility obligations need not be a stumbling block. The Fund long ago reconciled itself to allowing developing countries to retain the transitional escape clause of Article 14 indefinitely. The basic purpose that convertibility was intended to support, namely, to provide the financial preconditions for multilateral trade, is adequately served by the convertibility of a limited number of currencies of the industrial countries that serve as vehicle currencies for other countries.[4]

Financial Contribution

The national currencies subscribed by the members constitute a large part of the basic pool of permanently available revolving funds. The IMF provides much of its financial assistance by selling the currencies of members in exchange for the borrower's own currency. Until 1969, only convertible currencies could be designated usable, so that, by definition, CPEs, had they been members, could not have made a contribution to the pool of loanable funds over and above the 25 percent of their quota payable in gold or convertible currencies. The 1969 second amendment to the Articles made it possible for the Fund to designate as "usable" any currency it holds. A number of essentially inconvertible currencies have been considered usable when the Fund judged the countries that issued the currencies to be in sufficiently strong balance-of-payments and external reserve positions. In such cases the Fund must work out appropriate conversion arrangements with the country whose currency is so designated (Chandavarkar 1984, p. 28). The real issue, therefore, is whether there is anything about the economic system of CPEs that makes it unlikely that they will ever be in a sufficiently strong balance-of-payments position for their currencies to be considered usable.[5]

Which CPE Is also an LDC?

An important issue when a CPE wants to borrow from the World Bank is its level of economic development. Only members classified as LDCs have access to World Bank loans. Each of the four CPEs that have joined since 1972, Romania, China, Hungary, and Poland, was so classified. That Hungary was placed in the LDC category generated some controversy.

Finding the appropriate exchange rate to convert GNP in local currency to dollars for the purpose of ranking a nation in terms of development level is problematic. The Bank relies on its member countries' prevailing and, for most countries, largely market-determined exchange rates as convertors because they are available for practically all countries on a timely basis. There are special difficulties when such computations have to be made for CPEs. Many CPEs employ a plethora of exchange rates and exchange rate type coefficients, largely for accounting purposes.

Using the Hungarian official exchange rate to convert GNP in forints to dollars yields a 1980 per capita GNP of about $2,000, an implausibly low figure that reflects certain peculiarities in Hungary's domestic price system, the method of establishing the exchange rate when the NEM was introduced, and the effects of a series of devaluations to improve its balance of payments (Marer 1981). Per capita dollar GNP computations for the same year based on the estimated purchasing power parity (PPP) of the Hungarian forint yield around $6,000 (Alton 1985). A team of experts commissioned by the World Bank to evaluate alternative approaches to estimating the dollar GNPs or CPEs concluded that a third approach, yielding a 1980 per capita dollar GNP of $4,400, was the most plausible one (Marer 1985a, 1985b).

When Hungary joined the World Bank in 1982, the Bank decided to accept the per capita dollar GNP based on Hungary's official exchange rate. The decision prompted questions by members of Congress (Lewis 1984), U.S. government agencies, and the media about why the Bank accepted Hungary's official exchange rate, which yielded such a low estimate and qualified Hungary for loans. The Bank's indirect reply was that as long as the official exchange of a member is "not exceptionally far removed from the rate effectively governing foreign payment transactions," the Bank prefers to accept it because that convertor is applicable, with the least controversy, to the currencies of most of its members (Baneth 1985). A further consideration was whether a CPE should be singled out for possibly less advantageous treatment than the many LDCs that share with CPEs such system features as currency inconvertibility and a great deal of government control in exchange rate determination.

While some of the controversy on whether a CPE should be considered an LDC and thus be given access to Bank resources may be motivated by ideological or political considerations, the origin of the controversy lies in the determination and role of exchange rates in CPEs. Although substantial uncertainties surround the computation of the dollar per capita GNPs of the market economies as well, the Bank's approach when applied to market economies is more defensible, operationally and politically, because their exchange rates are at least partly market determined, than when it makes a similar decision for a CPE.

Independent of the merit of any decision the Bank makes on computing the per capita dollar GNP of CPEs, the controversy generated may impair the credibility, and thus the organizational effectiveness, of the institution. This may be one of the intangible costs of the membership of CPEs in the Bank.

IMF and World Bank Programs for CPEs

An important issue on the compatibility of CPE systems and Fund and Bank operations is designing adjustment programs for such economies. To improve the balance of payments of any country, there must be a reduction in domestic "absorption" (investment, consumption, or government expenditures), a transfer of resources from less to more productive uses, and a switch from the nontradable to the tradable sector. Dealing predominantly with market economies, the Fund has developed a set of policy measures that, when tailored to the circumstances of a country, yield improvements in the balance of payments. In CPES, for systemic reasons, these same policy measures often do not work as expected.

For example, to reduce domestic absorption, Fund programs focus on restrictive money and credit policies. But owing to the soft budget constraint of CPE enterprises and to the forced savings of the population, tighter control over money and credit may not constrain expenditure as expected (Wolf 1985a). Even if inter-enterprise credits are indeed cut—so that effective excess demand in the enterprise sector is eliminated by imposing economy-wide ceilings on credits and subsidies to enterprises—the authorities, intolerant of bankruptcies and even temporary unemployment, may tax the unprofitable firms to subsidize the inefficient. This means that credit ceilings, aside from possibly not having much effect in the enterprise sector, will not have the beneficial microeconomic effects that would be desirable on efficiency grounds (assuming that the relative price structure is at all rational). The details of this issue are discussed by Wolf (1985a, 1985b). In CPES, administrative intervention is more likely to be effective in restraining domestic demand.

To improve the general efficiency of the economy Fund programs typically rely on market mechanisms, such as adjusting the relative prices of tradables to reflect prices on the world market, and raising interest rates to improve the efficiency of investment allocation. But in CPES, such measures often do not work as intended. Given the soft budget constraint on enterprises and the policies against open unemployment, CPES are less flexible than market economies. Investment decisions are made less on the basis of expected rates of return and more on a mix of social, political, economic, and bureaucratic considerations.

The Fund's preferred instrument to encourage switching of demand into tradables is exchange rate depreciation. In a traditional CPE enterprises producing exports and using imports are insulated from the external sector and they will not feel the impact of a devaluation. Even in a reformed CPE like Hungary, where enterprises do feel the impact, relatively little is known about their responses to price signals. Moreover, it is one thing to increase the supply of products to be marketed for convertible currency and quite another to actually sell them on the world market. Finally, the extent to which these economies have the ability to substitute domestic production for convertible currency imports in response to price signals is also questionable (Holzman 1979, pp. 78–79).

One consequence of this situation is that even though recent Fund programs in Romania, Hungary, and Yugoslavia have been associated with considerable improvements in these countries' balances of payments, it appears that, in varying degrees, most of the improvements were brought about by administrative restrictions on imports and mobilization of exports rather than improved efficiency, even though improving economic efficiency is one of the objectives of Fund and Bank programs. Direct administrative intervention was strikingly the case in Romania, as detailed by Pissulla (1988). One problem with excessive reliance on administrative measures is that they typically undermine sustainable improvements in the balance of payments.

Reforms that introduce market mechanisms in CPES might increase the relevance of standard IMF programs. At the same time, because there are differences among these reform programs, understanding how modified CPES like Hungary and China function, and designing appropriate programs for them, is difficult. The Fund is aware of these problems and has initiated research to improve its understanding of these economies (Wolf 1985a, 1985b).

All CPES, like many LDCS, are in structural disequilibrium, a term indicating that a disproportionate share of a country's products cannot be sold readily on world markets and that there is excessive waste of inputs. Improved efficiency requires that the Bank's evaluation and financing of investment projects should be tied to reforms in the economic system and to changes in investment policies. But it is not clear whether this kind of conditionality is acceptable to the authorities in CPES. The Bank, too, faces difficult operational problems in providing structural assistance and advice to CPES. For example, in deciding on the investment projects that it should endorse or fund, it has to deal with arbitrary domestic prices and systemic inflexibility. Evaluations are further complicated by the fact that investment projects often use inputs from and sell a portion of output to the CMEA market, an arrangement the functioning of which is not well understood.

An even more basic issue is whether the Bank should evaluate the entire investment strategy of a CPE, or whether it should focus only on investment decisions at the margin. For example, should the Bank take as given the planners' projections of future energy requirements based on the existing structure of production—in which case the Bank's concern would be the choice between alternative energy projects—or should the Bank try to convince the country to alter its production structure? Investment choices have political implications because some choices promote trade with the CMEA, others with the West. As the contrast between the experience of Hungary and Romania shows (Pissulla 1988), how much conditionality the Bank is willing to insist upon and how much will be accepted and implemented depends very much upon the coincidence of objectives between the member country and the advising agencies. A similar situation exists, of course, in Bank and Fund relations with many LDCs.

Reciprocity for Trade Concessions

When the GATT considers the accession of a CPE, a key issue is whether a CPE can offer meaningful reciprocity for tariff and nontariff concessions. Several interrelated issues are involved. GATT rules require governments to control trade only indirectly, through tariffs rather than through quantitative restrictions. Since the essence of central planning is detailed prescription of production and trade, the foreign trade regime of a CPE is not compatible with GATT rules.

A more practical concern is whether a CPE can offer any kind of trade concession that will reduce the protection of its domestic industries. When a market economy reduces tariffs, domestic producers face increased competition from increased trade, but only if individual firms are free to choose between domestic and foreign suppliers. Since such is not the practice in CPEs, tariff reductions will not expand trade.

A frequent alternative, as pointed out earlier, is a quantitative commitment by the CPE to increase imports in return for trade concessions. This solution has limitations in theory as well as in practice. If an agreement is negotiated bilaterally, the bilateral increase in trade may be largely at the expense of other nations. This would be contrary to the nondiscrimination clauses of the GATT (Holzman 1974a, p. 162). A preferable solution is to multilateralize the import commitments by setting a global quota of purchases from all GATT members, with the distribution of trade determined by commercial considerations. This was proposed in 1945 as the most equitable way of reintegrating the USSR into the international trade network (Gerschenkron 1945).

This solution was used by the GATT to admit Poland and Romania. In addition to the practical problems already noted in connection with the Polish agreement, a more general problem is that the intended trade-expansion effect may be distorted by the nature of central planning. Since planners control the composition of foreign trade, global import commitments may be fulfilled by concentrating imports on a few GATT members, such as those with a CPE system. Thus, there is no assurance of the nondiscriminatory treatment provided for in the general agreement. Market economies often also discriminate, but discrimination by CPEs is less transparent and therefore less remediable.

4. Conclusions

Three IEOs were established after the Second World War to promote a multilateral system of world trade and payments and international cooperation on economic issues. Although the three IEOs have distinct roles, their functions sometimes overlap and at other times are complementary, resulting in cooperation among them. For example, because a country's trade practices can impede Fund policies on payments and exchange rates, the GATT prohibits members from taking exchange actions that frustrate the intent of the IMF, just as the Fund and the Bank advise members to observe the GATT code. The Fund and the Bank also cooperate closely to ensure consistent advice to members.

Incorporating CPEs into the operations of these IEOs presents problems that arise from the systemic features of central planning. These systemic features are in certain ways similar to those of many LDCs; comparisons are especially apt between certain LDCs and those modified CPEs that have introduced significant economic reforms. The basic similarity is that very imperfect market mechanisms operate in both. Financial markets are often at infant stages of development, which calls into question the feasibility of depending heavily on financial instruments for influencing economic performance; many prices are arbitrary and inflexible, which calls into question reliance on market-mechanism incentives; and severe structural disequilibria are often present which, together with the problems in the financial and price mechanisms, cast doubt on the effectiveness of currency devaluations to improve the balance of payments. Currency inconvertibility is also a common feature that results from all the foregoing factors.

That there exist significant similarities between certain LDCs and

CPEs may help the IEOs to solve some operational problems that arise when CPEs become members. Arrangements with LDCs may be considered precedents to justify often uneasy accommodation that must be made with individual CPEs on particular issues. Also, the experience gained in dealing with LDCs may be relevant to CPEs.

This study has noted the increasingly divergent ideological, political, and economic trends among the CPEs and examined the impact of such trends on their attitudes toward membership and on their ability and willingness to cooperate with the IEOs. The interests of the West regarding membership by CPEs is an important issue also, but is not dealt with in this chapter. If the IEOs wish to promote the purposes for which they were established, they should try to convince both the more traditional as well as the modified CPEs to reform their economic systems. The ability of the IEOs to succeed in this endeavor cannot be guaranteed any more in a CPE than in any other country. Only when the authorities of a country are themselves convinced of the advantages of reform and of cooperation—and have a firm commitment to such a course—are the prospects of meaningful external influence assured. The willingness of a CPE to cooperate with an IEO on such terms should thus be the principal consideration for Western policy toward CPE membership in IEOs.

PART V

Economic Systems and Reforms

CHAPTER 9

How to Create Markets in Eastern Europe: The Hungarian Case

Márton Tardos

There have been many assessments of the development of the Hungarian economy, which openly broke with the traditional central planning in 1968, and in general the tone of these assessments has been positive. Basically two conclusions emerge from these analyses. First, it is clear that the Hungarian economy has made great strides toward satisfying the market demands of the members of society since the introduction of the New Economic Mechanism (NEM) in 1968. But the change has been incomplete, leaving considerable room for further improvements in the efficient utilization of economic resources and in the ability of the system to adjust to changing market demand.

I will not recount here the familiar two-decade long history of the NEM. This study explores two issues only. The first concerns the nature of the relationship between the system of the Hungarian economic mechanism and models used in economic analysis of socialist economies. The second relates to the identification of the most important social and economic conditions that must be changed in order to create a successful socialist market economy in Hungary.

THE MODELS OF THE SOCIALIST ECONOMY AND THE HUNGARIAN NEM

Before 1917 two extreme images of socialist economics emerged in debates about socialism. The adherents of socialism envisaged an economy operating on the basis of the social ownership of the means of production as an ideal image of organized harmony, transcending individual and social conflicts of interest, and, therefore, being the opposite of the anarchic system of individual interests based on capitalist private ownership. Critics of socialism expected it to collapse after the abolition of the private ownership of the means of production because of the lack of information required for the central guidance of society and the implementation of organized harmony. The socialist debate of the 1930s and the appearance of the Lange-Lerner model can really be viewed as offshoots of this not very practical controversy.

But what is most important about centralized socialism and the decentralized vision of Lange-Lerner is not what divides them, but what they have in common. Both the centralized model of the socialist economy and the Lange-Lerner model, which sets only prices and producer behavior, correspond closely to the traditional model of general equilibrium. They differ from the general model of equilibrium of the capitalist market economy only in that the latter does not need a center at all while the model of the socialist economy is only viable if it has a center, with the special knowledge and ability to make optimal decisions for production and distribution or to set optimal prices.

In fact, the countries that adhere to the concepts of socialism—and have implemented the nationalization of the means of production —consider neither complete centralization of decisions nor the concept of price determination derived from consumer preferences as applicable to their activity on the practical plane. Traditional central planning evolved after nationalization as a pragmatic expansion of the centralized hierarchy of state bureaucracy to the economy. This is a practice many have tried to characterize (Medvedev 1983; Brown and Neuberger 1968; and Bornstein 1977). The system that evolved and developed historically amidst different national circumstances is built on the following general characteristics:

1 The state administration gains a dominant role through the large share of state ownership.

2 The activity of the economic units is directed by government administration and the party apparatus using the directive elements of central planning—target setting and central allocation of resources—to coordinate enterprise activities with the national economic plan.

3 The role of the monetary system is to finance the plan. The system requires price and income regulation that makes it possible to cover the costs incurred in implementing the plan. Producer prices approximate costs of production and consumer prices diverge from producer prices to reflect state preferences. The harmonization of supply and demand is not a prime task of the price system (Bornstein 1978). Credit allocation is accommodated to the national plan.

4 The incomes of citizens are derived from activities of centrally regulated organizations. Remuneration for enterprise management and employees, as well as financial incentives of an egalitarian nature, are defined in the plan.

There are many ancillary features associated with traditional central planning in addition to these four. Among the most important are:

- forced economic growth, often leading to open neglect of quality.
- strong uncontrolled state preferences that distort the pattern of resource allocation.
- the insulation of the economy from the noncontrolled external world economy.
- stable prices over long periods.

The system of traditional central planning had worked acceptably when economic growth was attainable by increased employment and investment, accompanied by a decreasing share of consumption in a utilized national product. Moreover, growth was a consequence of the extensive use of the abundant natural resources and of overutilization of the inherited infrastructure. As these reserves were exhausted, the modification of the system of management assumed increased urgency.

In general, the response to the increasing importance of quality over quantity led to efforts to modify some of the less essential features of the economic system while retaining its main characteristics. Measures were taken to reduce the separate levels of the multidimensional hierarchy of government management. The reduction in the number and authority of ministerial bodies, enterprise mergers and the establishment of large corporations can be viewed as forms of administrative decentralization that differed significantly from nation to nation. The large companies, associations, and corporations appearing as legal entities were less dependent on government administration for detailed directions regarding their operations than they had once been. The number of plan indices was reduced, but so was their tautness, and the need to adhere to them under all circumstances.

Also it became clear that a concentration of resources aimed principally at the implementation of one or two central targets was not viable, at least for two reasons. First, the utilization of industrial inputs by the priority sectors requires complicated interenterprise relations of the sort that cannot be built up even within a huge corporation. Second, satisfactory incentives for workers require that the supply of commodities corresponds to the effective demand of wage and salary earners. The consequences of ignoring these considerations can be seen in the political and social crisis in Hungary in the 1950s traceable in part to efforts to create "a land of iron and steel."

Simple recognition of these two factors alone leads to a growth in the number of tasks that must be solved in an organized way by the central plan. This, in turn, creates extreme difficulty in enforcing production development preferences, meaning that the ability of central management to establish priority sectors is reduced (Medvedev 1983).

The desire for insulation from the effects of international trade has lost a great deal of its significance in the Soviet Union and Eastern Europe since it has become clear that domestic resources are insufficient to attain economic policy goals. It has been recognized that exploitation of all opportunities, including the utilization of the gains from the international division of labor, is required. A somewhat more realistic set of exchange rates was introduced in most CMEA economies to make enterprises sensitive to import costs and export revenues. This reduced the insulation of the economy from foreign markets—although changes in the foreign trade system did not go very far in the majority of the countries because of insufficient conditions in CMEA trade and because of limited opportunities in East-West trade, primarily as a consequence of insufficient production of high-quality exportables in CMEA.

Some endeavour was made for a more active use of money and for a price system that expressed more directly the costs of production and scarcities. In almost every CMEA country the interest rate took on a more important role and taxes were levied on mineral resources. The subsidization of consumer prices was reduced. In the meantime, the

TABLE 9.1. Distribution of National Income by Forms of Ownership (in percentages)

	1960	1970	1978	1982	1983
State /1/	67.4	70.7	73.2	68.4	67.3
Cooperative /2/	17.0	23.6	21.3	23.6	23.2
Ancillary farming of members of agricultural cooperatives /3/	4.2	5.2	4.3	4.7	4.1
Ancillary farming of employees /4/	6.6	3.1	3.3	3.8	4.4
Private sector /5/	9.0	2.6	2.2	4.2	5.1
Private activities $/6/ = /3/ + /4/ + /5/$	19.8	10.9	9.8	12.7	13.6

SOURCE: *Statistical Yearbook 1983, KSH*, Budapest.

supply of high-priced luxury consumer goods was increased in order to diminish the accumulated money balances of the population.

Thus it can be concluded that the centrally planned economy using traditional methods proved to be quite flexible from the point of view of less essential features, even if it did not undertake to make fundamental changes in the four basic characteristics that were specified as essential.

But Hungary's reform in 1968 was at least intended to be the exception. The NEM sought to alter the four basic characteristics. I turn now to a discussion of what in fact did occur.

The Dominance of State Ownership

After 1968 it was emphasized in Hungary that state and cooperative ownership were equivalent in status and that, in addition, output produced by private producers had a long-term role to play in the satisfaction of overall demand. Yet for the first ten years of the NEM—up to 1978—there was a clear increase both in the share of state ownership in national wealth and of the state sector in the production of national income, at the expense of both the cooperative and the private sectors (table 9.1). The only place an opposite trend existed was in the ancillary farm business in agriculture.

The cooperative sector began its relative growth after 1978, followed by the growth of the legal private sector after 1982. However, the changes have not reached a real turning point in either case. The private sector's presence is significant only in the sphere of commerce and in some service activities. In 1984 the private activities—in which we include the ancillary farms of the members of agricultural cooperatives and of state employees, the workers' associations, and craftsmen —produced 15 percent of gross domestic product (GDP). The ratio is much less than it was in 1960, but 50–60 percent more than the lowest share of 1963–64.

As far as private activity is concerned, it should be noted that statistical figures can, of course, only cover activity for which licenses have been granted and taxes levied. Domestic and foreign observers of the Hungarian economy alike are of the opinion that the growth rate and spread of private activity in Hungary are far in excess of what can be followed in statistics, which means that its role in the output of the economy is more significant than indicated by the data. Taking into account these unreported activities may raise the share of private activity to about one third of the whole. Even this estimate does not alter the conclusion that the dominance of the state sector did not begin to diminish until 1972, and the changes after 1978 have only slightly modified the proportions. The cooperative sector regained its lost share only after 1972.

The potential to mobilize unutilized capacities and improve economic performance by integrating private economic activity with the remainder of the economy has not been fully exploited. Part of the problem is income controls on state and cooperative firms that suppress incomes there. On the other hand the incomes, partially illegal, of private activities in industry, construction, and services are rather high.[1] This leads to a segregation of the labor market between a high wage private sector and a low wage state and cooperative sector that diminishes the productivity of the state and cooperative sector. Furthermore, the development of *legal* private activities is constrained by vigorous taxation, by the uncertainty of the future, and by the undeveloped credit conditions that exacerbate the lack of a suitable supply of private capital goods for private activities.

The Autonomy of Enterprises

The elimination of target planning in 1968 promised significant changes in the role of the party and government in enterprise management. It was generally recognized that the most important success indicator of enterprises would be profit. However, the control of enterprise activity remained the task of the government and party apparatus, even though it was not linked to the fulfillment of state plans. Although enterprises were formally liberated from target planning, many other institutional devices for controlling their activities remained. The government and party appointed and confirmed the positions of the most important managers of the enterprises and made the decisions on material and moral rewards to managers. In deciding on these rewards profit was one, but not the most important, sign of success. Other criteria included supply to the domestic market, increasing exports, and the avoidance of social conflicts such as tension over wages and conflicts of interest among manager groups within the enterprise. These often proved more important than even transitional losses, not to mention the return on enterprise capital. These criteria, which are inconsistent with profit maximization, were allowed to operate since the financial institutions neutralized the consequences of economic success and failure in the financial results of the enterprises through their tailor-made channels of credit and subsidy, as we shall see later on.

An important role was also played by the party and government in influencing the formally independent cooperatives. The direct approval of the regional party bodies was required for the manager elected by the cooperative members. The incomes of cooperative managers depended not only on decisions by the membership and the elected bodies of the cooperative, but also on the regional cooperative organization, County-level Cooperative Association (MESZOV), which was formally intended to protect the interests of the cooperative, but in reality acted in many respects as the representative of the central and regional organs of power. This practice was expanded in the 1970s when central authorities ordered mergers against the will of the members. Because of the explosion in mergers of agricultural and industrial cooperatives it became commonplace for several villages to operate a single agricultural cooperative. The result was a weakening of personal contact between members and leaders, making it impossible for the members to assess the activity of the cooperative and difficult for them to control elected bodies.

Restrictions on cooperative autonomy also manifested themselves in the systematic repression of the industrial and service activities of agricultural and agriculturally based cooperatives. The rural cooperatives could earn a significant profit if they used a part of their buildings for industrial activity. This profit often compensated them for losses caused by low agricultural prices, and these profits were generally used to finance agricultural investments. However, it happened that cooperatives had to reduce industrial and service activities that were generating these profits because local party and state organs deemed the migration of manpower from industry to the farms as unfavorable and wanted it stopped ("A szovetkezeti . . . ," 1984). Finally, the economic decisions of the party and government bodies also retained the restrictions on private output.

The Financial System

Most of the changes promised by the NEM were in the financial sphere. After 1968 the role of financing was no longer to serve the needs of the national plan, but rather to ensure economic rationality. Profits became the basis of enterprise decisions. When selecting among production, sales, and investment possibilities the enterprises would have to decide according to profits. Credit financing of enterprises should consider the expected return of capital. According to the established guidelines the redistribution of income between enterprises and the central bodies should take place on the basis of uniform rules valid for all enterprises. The uniform system of credit and income regulation could be violated only by state preferences proclaimed in advance.

In other words, the new financial system promised a continuously increasing freedom of decision for enterprises, and although the real changes introduced were not as radical as had been promised, they were not insignificant. The autonomy of enterprises increased meaningfully when it came to preparing their own plans; and the objective of bargaining between the different levels of the economic hierarchy changed. Formerly, in bargaining about the plan, the center made high demands and offered few factors of production while the enterprises did the opposite. After 1968 the bargaining focused on financial conditions. The new object of bargaining differs from the old one in that it does not touch on the concrete tasks and conditions for production, sales, and investment. Basically, decisions in this sphere are left to enterprise managers who must use their rights to make decisions not only in harmony with profitability considerations and the return to capital invested, but also in harmony with the fulfillment of expectations of the centralized hierarchy. In fact, the reforms did result in a shift in central decisionmaking power to fiscal and monetary authorities. However, because of restricted trust in markets, this has not led to a significant reduction in regulation. Instead, the central administration has regulated the system on a firm by firm basis.

The result is a complex web of regulations that have had the effect of placing central organizations, not the market, in the position of deter-

TABLE 9.2. Distribution of Major Control Components*
According to 294 Regulations

	Leveling		Neutral	Differentiative**		Total
	Supporting low-efficiency companies	Penalizing high-efficiency companies		Supporting low-efficiency companies	Penalizing high-efficiency companies	
Price control/67/	14.9	11.9	16.4	23.9	32.9	100.0
Income control/155/	33.6	11.6	15.5	25.8	13.5	100.0
Credit control/22/	4.6	4.5	4.6	5.0	36.3	100.0
Wages control/50/	36.0	14.0	24.0	18.0	8.0	100.0
Total /294/	27.6	11.6	16.3	25.8	18.7	100.0

* Galik, 1983.
**Regulations do actually exert influence toward the differentiation of incomes.

mining winners and losers. Table 9.2 summarizes some of the results of a ministry of finance study of the effects on the variance of enterprise profitability of 294 regulations in the area of pricing, income, wages, and credits. Of the 294 regulations, 39.2 percent have the effect of reducing intra-enterprise profitability levels, either by supporting low-efficiency companies or penalizing high-efficiency companies. Only 16.3 percent are neutral. The remaining 44.5 percent of the regulations increase profit differentiation, but even here the consequences are uncertain since it is central authorities that are designating winners and losers.

Furthermore, these 294 regulations are only a portion of the interventions through which the central authorities determine winners and losers. During the last seventeen years central authorities have:

- modified regulations on price calculation regardless of market changes;
- rescheduled loans for current assets and investments;
- canceled taxes;
- granted wage preferences;
- granted special state subsidies to some and then withdrawn them from others;

- imposed an obligation to generate special reserves;
- collected company funds, primarily obligatory reserves;
- forced mergers.

Out of fear of the insolvency of companies, central organizations actually agreed to increase producers' prices and, in addition, they were forced to grant special tax exemptions and to grant subsidies and credit allowances.

This shows clearly that state interventions constraining enterprise autonomy are not accidental in the NEM, but rather a conscious effort to control the system through preferential fiscal and monetary policy and by other governmental means.[2]

This situation has created a duality of goals such that, although the enterprises have had to pay much more attention to their revenues and costs, they have had to achieve these financial results in a way that avoided any sharp conflict with the nonfinancial expectations of the party and state bodies. The way out of this contradictory situation was facilitated by the fact that, despite government declarations, neither prices nor the rules for income redistribution among enterprises were stipulated clearly. Bargaining with the state administration over financial conditions has nearly always led to a compromise guaranteeing enterprise survival, even with no more than moderate effort.

Very often enterprise managers are insulted by what has been said about the significance of financial bargaining because it ignores the managers' efforts to organize production and to adjust to market conditions.[3] Obviously, an enterprise that does not produce or does not solve technical problems well will not be successful no matter how well it manages financial bargaining with the state administration. The real issue is one of proportion. Bargaining about state regulation may offer big gains, and therefore the manufacture of obsolete products at high cost—or the use of production technology that may appear advanced from a technical viewpoint but that is not profitable—cannot be precluded as possible sources of enterprise profits.

The Status and Income of the Citizens

Although the reason for introducing the NEM was that the incentives for managers and workers were considered insufficient, the changes in this respect are insignificant. Citizens have obtained new options for employment and income acquisition only in the nonregulated sphere of the economy or in the so-called second economy. In the socialist sector, in state and cooperatively owned enterprises, the only change was that profitability took the place of plan fulfillment in the determination of enterprise income.

Traditional central planning made managers' incomes dependent on plan fulfillment and on many other success indicators that changed from year to year. Initially, the NEM shifted to a system based on base salaries augmented by profit sharing. Later, the system was changed and the basic salaries and profit sharing of managers were augmented by bonuses linked to fulfillment of certain conditions aside from profits. But despite constant pragmatic changes, the system was unable to adequately reward successful managers, or even to alter the undesired outcome that the growth of managers' income was below the average for all incomes.

Management's ability to adjust compensation to workers was also severely constrained under the NEM for a number of reasons. Under the NEM the main function of enterprise personal income regulation continued to be the maintenance of equilibrium between the purchasing power of the population and the supply of consumer goods. This, at times, took the form of a limitation on the average wage level that an enterprise could pay, which acted as an incentive to retain cheap manpower. At other times the limits were on the total wage fund of an enterprise, which led to wage increases or manpower reductions, even if the labor market did not require such. Perhaps the most significant, positive development under the NEM was that, over a long period, enterprise wage payments came to be restricted by prohibitive progressive taxes that were less of a disturbance to economic operations than the direct and rigid limits used earlier.

Nevertheless, the payable wage and income have remained an earmarked cost that is given to the firms. And the egalitarian traditions in income distribution among employees are so strong that the actual wage distribution has been even more equal than required politically. The complaint of managers has been that they could stimulate greater efforts of a narrow strata only by special allotments and by overtime pay. For the bulk of the workers the wage compensating their forty to forty-two hours working time has reflected neither the quality nor the intensity of their work. These conditions have contributed further to unsatisfactory work, to hidden unemployment, and to low productivity.

The wasteful wage expenditure and the shortage of labor in state and cooperative firms are products of rigid wage control. The improved satisfaction of demand has been to a great extent due to the auxiliary sector where incomes are less controlled. For trade unions and party organizations this has the especially favorable consequence that, not only have commodity supplies improved, but those who combine legal and illegal activities in the auxiliary sector are not dissatisfied with their income even in the period of real wage decreases.

The Need for Further Changes

In general, the experience in Eastern Europe suggests that a modification of the traditional system of central planning, without changing the basic characteristics, can be partially successful by diminishing shortages, by avoiding the most striking imbalances of supply and demand, and by exploiting economies of scale resulting from mergers.

Although the improvement is able to compensate for the exhaustion of the sources of growth it is advantageous for the functioning system in two respects:

- On the one hand, the change does not affect the fundamental features of the centralized hierarchic structure of economic management. It only reallocates decisionmaking power, in some cases only formally, from the top echelons of the hierarchy to lower ones.
- On the other hand, the modification of the system, based on the realization that the center is not able to regulate directly the full range of social and economic activities in harmony with the social needs, does not openly contradict the goal (that legitimizes the system) of overtaking the developed countries. The expectations of the modified system in this regard are based on the economies of scale to be achieved in the large, modern firms created through mergers.

At the same time the analysis of the Hungarian experience suggests that the deeper reform of traditional central planning—encouragement of cooperatives, significant diminution of constraints on private activities, abolition of target planning and the official system of centralized resource allocation, while strengthening the regulatory role of money —did mobilize meaningful new forces and did improve the supply situation. But even that change was not enough to counteract the exhaustion of resources and the deterioration of the external market conditions.

The critical point is that the profit motive of enterprises was eliminated by central intervention especially after 1972. The reform did not alter the fact that property rights to the enterprises remained in the branch ministries. Because of the lasting dependence of enterprises on the central management the latter easily resorted to traditional means —using property rights as an excuse—to compel enterprises to fulfill central requirements and desires without the need to apply the methods of directive planning. On the other hand, the state budget was used to relieve the market pressure upon the enterprises.

It might be concluded, therefore, that the abolition of the property rights of the branch ministries and the reduction of subsidies might alone lead to an efficient, regulated market. No doubt the critical comments concerning the practice of property rights and the firm-discriminative financial intervention—called by Kornai "paternalism" (Kornai 1980a, p. 19)—refer to substantive problems. Nevertheless, the question remains open as to what can be expected from a change in the property rights of the branch ministries and from the abolition of the firm by firm discrimination while keeping other parts of the economic system of 1968 unchanged.

In fact, the abrupt elimination of paternalism under current circumstances would lead directly to serious or even unbearable disturbances.

– A great share of enterprises—not 5–10 percent but rather 40–50 percent—would go bankrupt.
– The profitable enterprises would increase wages by unjustified amounts and would start investments with dubious returns.
– The redeployment of the assets and employees of the bankrupt firms would take time, and shortages would increase.

The reform program cannot start with such a plan because of the social consequences of these disturbances even if the assumption is reasonable that the change will lead later on to good results. In searching for an answer to why such strong limits exist to a reliance on markets in Hungary, it is necessary first to understand how market systems differ from the Hungarian system.

TRADITIONAL MARKETS VERSUS THE NEM

The key feature distinguishing the market model from the NEM is the reliance on a self-regulating mechanism to achieve a harmonization of supply and demand. The market model I am using here is not the idealized vision from the nineteenth century of perfect competition, but rather the mixed economy where, although the state and large oligopolies play significant roles, all actors have to prove themselves on the market. Such a market economy generally operates as a combination of different markets, the market for goods and services, the markets for labor, capital, and land, and the market of money, all correcting each other.

In market economies these markets are interrelated with and influence each other. Changes on commodity markets are accompanied by changes on factor and money markets. The producer encounters the expected price of labor and capital when making a decision about the utilization of his savings or mobilizing new capital. If the company's development does not make it possible to recover expected labor and capital costs, the firm would not only cease seeking outside resources but would also consider investing its own internal savings outside the company.

Companies operating with decreasing profits or temporary losses have significant possibilities for adjustment. They can adjust to the conditions of the labor market, laying off some of the workforce and possibly raising wages for those who remain, without having to pay new taxes. Similarly, the company does not lose links with money and capital markets even under deteriorating economic performance. Should it be able to convince partners of the expected profits of a proposed investment, it may even obtain new capital. Company bankruptcy is a threat. However, it occurs only if all else fails, and it is the socially most expensive version of economic adjustment.

The management system of the Hungarian economy established in years 1966–68 has acknowledged self-regulation with respect to commodity markets, only to a degree limited by price administration not only for officially controlled commodities but also for the range of commodities with so-called flexible prices. Regarding capital and labor markets, the system gives ground to self-regulation to the extent that a share of profits (achieved on the commodity market) is available for investment (also augmented by amortization funds) and wage increases.[4]

This apparent coherence is less rational than first appears. In accordance with the logic of the system, profitable companies have used available sums for wage increases, even if such increases were not justified by labor conditions. Net profits and retained amortization have been used for company investments, based on the logic of the system, regardless of the conditions for investment at the company. In addition, companies have had the opportunity to apply for new loans indepen-

dently of expected returns. Investment over-expenditures have been rational from the companies' viewpoint because performance was judged
not by returns on utilized resources and achieved profits, but according
to whether domestic supply of commodities was satisfactory and exports
were increasing, both requirements easier to meet with larger capacity.
In addition, companies having high profits who chose not to invest
were required to deposit them with the National Bank of Hungary at
low real interest rates.

Possibilities for the utilization of net profit outside the companies
have been extended since the second half of the 1970's through licensing joint ventures and later by the bond sales. At the same time company management made use of the possibilities only when it facilitated
the company's growth.

The lack of an efficient monetary and capital market has generated
even more severe problems when company profits were low or profits
were succeeded by temporary losses. In such a case, in harmony with
the rules, the company was unable to increase wages even if economic
conditions required it, and as a result it began to lose labor. Insignificant
or decreasing profits have resulted in similar difficulties for investment.
Thus, a company not exceeding the limits of the regulation was not able
to initiate new investment projects, whatever efficient opportunities for
development were offered.

In sum, there is no feedback from factor markets toward commodity
markets in the NEM, nor is there a relation among factor markets. Furthermore, economic management works with methods that restrain the
distribution of enterprise incomes and turns their utilization to a forced
path. This does not mean that there is absolutely no feedback from
factor to commodity markets, only that such feedback is not realized
through price movements and adjustments to prices. If, for instance,
investment is more profitable than projected, it is not expressed in the
revaluation of capital but only in the growth of company profits. This
extra profit leads to wage increases, possibly unrelated to conditions on
labor markets. In the opposite case, when the actual yield of investments is less than planned, wage increases are severely constrained.
Manpower in this case either leaves the company or wage costs are
increased. The effect of a nonprofitable investment further damages the
position of the company through the capital and money allocation mechanism. As a result of less successful investment, the company's capital
value will be not less than its accounting value, however it will experi-

ence insolvency for lower than planned returns, thus eliminating the possibility of obtaining new loans without state promotion. In this way the company becomes defenseless.

It is therefore characteristic of the NEM that while companies may prepare production, sales, and investment plans on their own, nevertheless their tolerance of unplanned change in the environment, or of a deterioration of their performance, is minimal. Any change in external conditions, or in their ability to perform, makes them dependent on the benevolent support of central organs.

ARE BANKRUPTCIES THE ANSWER?

Frequently the solution proposed to the contradictions of the NEM —both in government declarations and in the statements of many economists—is a hardening of the hitherto soft budget constraints within which Hungarian enterprises operate. This approach, based on Kornai's (1980a) analysis in *Economics of Shortage*, has intuitive appeal. Put simply, the proposition is that the bankruptcy laws be enforced. Nevertheless, there are a number of reasons why in fact it is not, by itself, a feasible or advisable approach to solving the problems inherent in the current economic system.

Bankruptcy performs two positive functions in a society: on the one hand, fear of bankruptcy and the force of survival may serve as a significant impetus for change. On the other hand, bankruptcy and the related devaluation of company assets, along with the rearrangement of production structure, can facilitate the necessary adjustments. However actual bankruptcy, and the related sociopolitical tensions, are helpful only as a final argument in the process of adjustment. Bankruptcy cannot be the fundamental means of adjustment in any system. Capital, labor, and money markets take the bulk of the adjustment, with bankruptcy as a last resort.

An economic situation where the exclusive and major method of adjustment to the uncertainty of the economic system is bankruptcy leads to a large, and socially unacceptable, number of bankrupt companies. Yet, in view of the lack of capital, money, and labor markets in the NEM, and the elimination of state intervention, bankruptcy would have to be the major means of automatic adjustment in each case where the company was unable to remain on the narrow path of growth, determined by financial conditions in accordance with central requirements.

In the system of the NEM, not only those companies generating sustained social losses (incomes less than current costs) would go bankrupt. In addition, those enterprises would fail which are in a much better situation, but still face worse conditions than are considered acceptable by the economic regulations (Tardos 1980).

This suggests that before bankruptcy laws are enforced, a number of other changes in the NEM must be introduced. Certainly the approach to economic control would have to change. To control companies in a uniform way, more flexible prices are required, rather than the cost-plus pricing system of the NEM, so as to better adjust to changes in demand and supply. The need for a change in these conditions is generally accepted; however there is very little progress. Regulations apply to all firms and branches, and an elimination of bargaining (a normative approach to Hungarian terminology) is generally considered in Hungary to be rational from the point of view of efficiency. But its effect on income differentiation of companies and individuals is viewed as intolerable.[5] Such a regulation requires that the rule according to which domestic prices cannot be raised above the level of import prices, converted at a realistic exchange rate plus a tariff, should be enforced for all companies, and not only in the case of companies unable to satisfy domestic demand for their products. It should also apply to those companies that are not in a position to fully utilize their capacities owing to an inability to efficiently increase exports, but whose products are in demand on the domestic market.

A further impediment to the successful utilization of bankruptcy as an adjustment mechanism is the lack of free, mobile, capital assets in the system. This is not a result of the shortage of capital, but rather of the centralization of free enterprise earnings. Only capital necessary to implement economic objectives acceptable to the center remains with the enterprises.

The question of investments is a delicate one for the center. It was, and up until now is, considered as a sound argument, based on information about the efficiency of money and capital markets in developed countries, that enterprise autonomy concerning investment decisions should be restricted. If a firm is seeking to make investments leading to major changes in its production pattern then, the argument goes, it should do so only under strong central control.[6]

That policy led to a large tax burden on enterprise income and to credit lending and subsidization based on the enterprise plan backed by central authorities. It left out of consideration both the expected rate of return and the financial pressure if an appropriate rate of reform is not obtained. The practice based on these assumptions has created its own winners and losers. The main victim has been society because the new practice, in spite of the promises, was unable to suppress the demand for investment capital, or to halt the erosion of working capital.

The absence of a genuine labor market, along with the prevailing attitude of managers that they need not economize wage costs as they do any other item of expenditures, impedes the enforcement of bankruptcy. Yet neither the workers nor the enterprise administration are prepared for the appearance of an open labor market and of conflicts between management and employees. And the change would surprise social and political organizations such as the communist party and the unions even more.

Without efficient money and capital markets it would be possible to manage a national economy well only if the efficiency of taxation, subsidization, and granting of preferential credit by the state was up to that of money and capital markets, and if the centralization of income and subsidization did not damage enterprise behavior on commodity markets. But such levels of efficiency cannot be reached. Therefore, if an economy wishes to achieve meaningful success with a regulated market, then it needs not only commodity markets but a more developed self-regulating system of labor, money, and capital markets than exist under the NEM.

Among the beneficiaries of a constrained market system we can find those organizations, such as the planning office and branch ministries, that have been able to keep more power than justified in the new situation because of the enforcement of state preferences; or those, such as the treasury, the National Bank, and the State Development Bank, that have reinforced their position. The situation is ambiguous from the managers' point of view. On the one hand, their security is consolidated because the moral risk of developments is shared with the state administration. This is especially true when state organs initiate or require the development, but fail to grant the needed and claimed amount of money. Here the state accepts the odium of failure. On the other hand, the situation has deteriorated for managers, because there are no unambiguous criteria for successful achievement. Enterprise success is sometimes more the consequence of the goodwill of the state administration than of managerial work. The vagueness of managers' standing has increased through the often unreliable partnership of the state organs, characterized by the withdrawal of credits, or the unexpected modification of credit conditions or the rate of interest.

Finally, the substitution of administrative control for money and capital markets has led to the improper use of assets by the enterprises. They have sought to increase production and sales, leading to financial results acceptable to the state administration, rather than seeking to maintain and increase the value of their assets. There has been no possibility for entrepreneurial behavior, focused on the value of assets, because the manager has not been able to obtain capital when he required more money than the current net income of the firm could finance. And for firms where net income has exceeded the amount of investments, promising good recovery in the firm itself, there has been no, or hardly any, possibility for investing it elsewhere.

Is There any Feasible Solution under Socialism?

After these statements, the first question that remains open is whether, without capitalist property rights and in a situation where management cannot be directly controlled by the owner, an established system of incentives, set with the aim of maintaining and increasing the value of assets, can be strong enough for efficient control of the economy? (Szego 1983, 1984.)

This is a legitimate concern. The experience of the East European countries that have undertaken economic reforms is not promising. The managers, not only in state companies but also in cooperatives and in Yugoslav labor managed firms, often make ill-considered decisions without sufficient concern for the long-term effects on asset values or the profitability of the firm.

Even in capitalist corporations, stockholders encounter difficulties in controlling management. Nevertheless, stockholders generally can ensure that the enterprise management has to seriously consider issues such as the value of assets, the levels of profits, the value of shares, and the size of dividends. If managers are harming the owners' interests, they might be replaced.

The failures in socialist economies in this respect should not be regarded as inevitable because we have had, as yet, no cases where the state has set the return to capital as the prime objective. Similarly, the members of the cooperatives and the labor managed firms have not made a stand from a property rights point of view. At most they have sought to assert their interests as wage or income earners.

Furthermore, there are many examples of rational economic management without pecuniary interest under suitable institutional conditions. Several managers have identified themselves with enterprises even if the success of the latter influenced only slightly their incomes. There is no reason to believe that only a strong pecuniary interest may produce such identification. There are many successful state firms in other Western countries working with the aim of maintaining and increasing the value of assets, for example, Renault in France. If society is able to recognize the importance of the capital interest in the market sector of the economy, not including the sector of public services, and is able to enforce it, then managers of enterprises will submit themselves to the requirement of the capital return.

Such a conclusion implies that the evaluation of state firms should be based neither on production nor current profits, but rather should consider the value of assets. This means that every state firm has to declare not only the profits attained but also the change of the value of its assets. Among other things the change in the value of assets provides information about its expected profits. The introduction of this well-tried technique means that management must account for the difference between the accounting value of assets, which are based on investment expenditure and amortization, and the value of assets as measured by expected profits. On the basis of this calculation, they have to explain their plans for the reconstruction, closing, and sales of workshops, or they have to propose other investments in or outside the enterprise.

Those enterprises that have to admit that not only is the value of their property less than the accounting value of assets, but also that their expected profits are not enough to cover the requirements of their creditors, will be forced to declare themselves bankrupt. Such a system of capital accounting will help in the institutional control of management. Business rationality could be improved even more if enterprises pay dividends to their employees and grant them some measure of control over management (Kotz 1984; Adamecz and Komlos 1984; and Rott 1984). If most of the enterprises were to be reorganized into stockholding companies and the purchase of stock by other business units were possible, then the market value of a firm's stock will provide additional control on the performance of management since poorly managed firms could be acquired by better firms.

The second unanswered question is whether it is possible for a socialist state—with a one-party system that represses capitalist property rights—to establish developed, regulated market relations in which labor, money, and capital markets function. Such a change can be realized only if economic coercion for increased efficiency is accepted by central organs. But this approach must be supported by different social strata as well. Finally, the social groups not linked to the old institutions must be able to enforce their will.

Economic coercion together with institutionalized representation of political interests of different social strata can induce the party and state hierarchy to make broad changes in economic institutions. Among such changes would be some in contradiction with the inherited image of socialism: the multi-sectoral nature of ownership—state, cooperative, and private; and the functioning of labor, money, and capital markets. But these changes are not in contradiction with the nonexploiting concept of socialism.

It cannot be denied that the value system of the political leadership —inherited in part from central planning—and its desire to retain the traditional means of using its power, works against such a change. The conservatism stemming from these sources can be defended by pointing out the real difficulties of implementing a market-oriented policy. During the transformation toward a demand-oriented, regulated, and developed market economy, the danger of inflation, of partial commodity shortages, of extreme income differentiation, of unemployment, and of insolvency of the National Bank, all increase.

Because of the ambiguity of the center's power, in such a system it has to be stressed that "developed market" cannot mean here anything other than a regulated market. To achieve all this, the socialist state must try to fulfill more efficiently those economic functions that it has not properly performed in the past. Instead of regulating the activities of individual units, it must deal with questions such as: aggregate demand management; the balance between revenues and expenditures of the state budget; the development of the banking system to make it capable of financing efficient business actions; market regulations to ensure that firms do not misuse their monopoly power; the development of the tax system to constrain disparities in personal incomes; and the reallocation of budget expenditures to reach harmony between infrastructural services and social demand. Moreover, the state has to ensure that business does not neglect long-run, technical development and should maintain equilibrium between export revenues and import expenditures.

WHAT IS HAPPENING AFTER 1984?

After the introduction of the NEM, the new system of management flourished in 1968–72, after which followed a period of hidden recentralization and increasing indebtedness during 1973–78.

In 1979 a new reform-oriented period started. The policy that limited the extent of the recentralization of 1973–78 was not able to neutralize the effects of the deterioration of the foreign economic environment through foreign borrowing. The accumulated volume of external debt and the increasing difficulties caused by the break in credit acquisition created a pressure for a new economic strategy (Nyers and Tardos 1979, 1984). The strategy in this period, without openly saying so, consisted of two steps: consolidation that aimed at the rearrangement of credit relations, and the departure on a new development path.

The first step, whose effects were evident in 1979–84, is reflected in a significant deceleration of production growth, in administrative restrictions on imports and in the development of small-scale business activities. These changes were accompanied by the elaboration of the conditions for a general market-oriented development. Hungarian membership in the IMF, the renegotiations of loans with the international banking community, and the production of an export surplus instead of the increasing indebtedness—primarily with the convertible currency area—produced the conditions for the transition into the second phase.

The framework for the second phase was established by the central committee decree of the Hungarian Socialist Workers' Party (HSWP) in April 1984 and with a new wave of legislation thereafter. In 1984 fifty-eight new or modified laws and rules were issued to deal with the questions that had previously been unanswered by the NEM.

The modest importance of the changes of 1984–85 are evident first of all in the fact that the policymakers emphasized that, contrary to the suggestions of some economists (Bauer 1984), no other policy initiatives were undertaken as the current correction of the 1968 reform process started. This attitude, which de-emphasized the significance of the changes, can be deduced from the fact that in the official documents there were no hints regarding the failures in economic management after 1972. Moreover, in the resolution of the thirteenth congress of the HSWP that followed the April 1984 Central Committee session, neither the notion of the reform, nor even the modification and development of the economic control system, were mentioned. Ferenc Havasi, secretary of the Central Committee, in his speech considered the changes already implemented and those planned to be sufficient for generally desired developments. The resolution of the congress mentioned only the requirement of faster development. Meanwhile, the Hungarian mass media often was devoting attention to the fact that other socialist countries, such as the GDR, Czechoslovakia or the USSR, were not carrying out market-oriented economic reforms, or even contemplating such reforms, and that these countries had come out from the standstill or recession of 1980 by increasing the requirements and rigors of planning.

Second, the extent of the changes can be judged by making a survey of the modification in the regulations of enterprise autonomy and finances. The most substantial change carried out was in the application of property rights of state enterprises. There was no change in the status of the state enterprises supplying public goods and in a small number of other very important enterprises and trusts. For the latter, the property rights remained in the hands of state or of local councils.

The property rights to smaller enterprises delivering goods to the market were given to the general assembly of employees of such enterprises. The property rights of bigger enterprises were placed in the hands of the enterprise council (EC). The council consists of two parts, delegated managers and representatives of the employees. The general assembly, or the EC in the community enterprises, appoints the general manager and makes decisions about important development plans in agreement with the local authorities and branch ministries.

These new measures reflect a weak response to three related positions that have emerged in the debate on how to reform the management of state property. Some have advocated the formation of labor managed enterprises, allocating all property rights to the employees. Others have suggested a corporate solution according to which the control of the management should be allocated to a tripartite council consisting of the management representatives of state and social institutions, and representatives of the employees. Finally, some have argued for a competitive system of businesslike independent institutions that would control the enterprises only from the viewpoint of the return to capital. The experts behind the different suggestions were for a final solution based on the experiences with all the above-mentioned methods.

The practice currently evolving, while a constrained step toward self-management, has retained possibilities for formal and informal state intervention in the decisions of the firms and in capital allocation. Control over the return to capital remains a task for the future. The most appealing aspect of the new regulations is the step toward institutional autonomy of state enterprises. But they have not established conditions either for the creation of a capital market or for the resolution of conflicts between the interests of labor and state planning. Therefore they leave open the possibility that after some transitional disturbances, the management will not be satisfied with the situation because of the contradictory requirements of production growth put on them by government organs and of the financial pressure for achieving an acceptable return to capital. Moreover management's independence in decisionmaking will be constrained not only by the remaining government controls but also by the income-oriented supervision of labor.

Labor is also unlikely to unambiguously favor the new regulations. Labor will probably not try to act as property owners, even though that is formally the position they hold due to nationalization. Instead, they will try to improve their position as employees by influencing wages and working conditions. But in this respect the formation of new institutions may lead to dissatisfaction. The election of directors in 1985 makes it very likely that the new form of property rights will offer mainly some formal rights for the employees that in practice may lose their economic content.

Finally, it is likely that these changes, which may satisfy neither managers nor workers, also will not be satisfactory to the state. The changes are not sufficient to reverse the existing disadvantageous trends. The compromise among the short-run interests of the state bureaucracy for uninterrupted commodity supply and export growth of unprofitable goods, the objectives of managers, and income increases of workers thus may be attained at the cost of state, or social, property. An extreme, but not rare, example of such a compromise is when workers remain employed in state firms offering lazy work for low but secure wages, while holding a second job or fulfilling private orders during the official working hours, possibly using the materials of the firm. Such behavior is accepted by the enterprise management because in this way it can prevent a decrease in manpower, which is a condition for growth of the firm, and for the fulfillment of government requirements concerning sales on domestic and on export markets, without creating a conflict over wage regulation. The change in the property rights of state enterprises cannot be considered a success unless similar tendencies are prevented by vigorous efforts of management and the bodies supervising it.

The second substantial change introduced in 1985 was in finance. Concerning fiscal policy, the main requirements during the preparatory work were a reduction of profit taxes and the liberalization of administrative income or wage control. Many new regulations appeared which reallocated these taxes. The profit tax was diminished and the centralization of the amortization was abolished, whereas formerly 40 percent of amortization went automatically into the state budget. The very profitable enterprises have a possibility for almost avoiding the prohibitive tax on wage increments by paying a very high flat tax on wages.

But the newly introduced taxes, such as the property tax and the investment tax, have neutralized the abolition of the old ones at least from the point of view of the state budget. Thus the tax burden on enterprises has remained as oppressive as before. As a consequence, a substantial portion of the enterprises supplying goods demanded by the market cannot realize a profit at the existing prices, or their profit is insufficient to finance investments demanded by the market. They have three options for survival: price increases, tax exemptions, and in some cases stopping production. It seems almost certain that they, as before, will prefer hidden price increases and bargaining about their taxes, because open price increases and stopping production run contrary to government expectations.

Aggregate demand management has remained out of control during the changes in 1985 but the government possesses strong formal and informal power, called "market supervision," to make enterprises fulfill their requirements even if that causes losses. So long as government intervention is able to prevent the stoppage of deliveries and open price increases, government control is forced to bail out enterprises in the interest of their survival. To expect improved efficiency and more industrious business from enterprises that depend so intensively on the state budget is an illusion.

The ambiguous modification of the Hungarian economic system in 1985 clearly proves the difficulties of implementing sweeping reforms toward efficient markets in Eastern Europe. A change requiring substantial structural transformation in social power by giving free possibilities for formulating and asserting the will of different social strata is not easily acceptable, either for the leading bodies or for the population used to certain privileges of the present situation such as easy jobs and good paying secondary occupations.

Concerning the future prospects of the NEM, or more generally of market socialism, we may expect further continuous trials. It must be recognized that only a full scale transformation can lead to a socialist economy that can offer more to the citizens both in terms of self-accomplishment and in terms of the satisfaction of their needs from their incomes (Pokol 1985). Moreover, only such a transformation may lead to a stable interrelation between state and population that could be viewed as a real political consensus.

CHAPTER 10

The Politics of Creating Efficient Markets in Socialism: Comments on Chapter 9

Ellen Comisso

I agree with Dr. Tardos's characterization of the Hungarian economy and his proposals for creating efficient markets. My main reservation is simply that it is not clear to me why political leaders with the power to satisfactorily answer these questions would want to do so, particularly insofar as what he describes as the four necessary features of a planned economy not only perform economic functions but also serve as the bases on which these same political leaders acquire and exercise political power itself. Bearing this in mind, most of my comments on the essay will center on what kind of domestic political arrangements could complement efficient markets under socialism.

I question Tardos's observation that the lack of integrated markets in Hungary creates a situation in which enterprises either do not see existing opportunities or have no interest in exploiting them. It is unclear whether such behavior is due more to the absence of interconnected markets or to two related but separable phenomena, the lack of markets and regulatory obstacles. To give an example, a textile firm briefly considered building a garage in Budapest in view of the parking problem there, but was deterred from doing so for fear of ministry disapproval and the political controversy in which it could get embroiled. Here, the problem was not that the firm did not see a market opportunity, but that regulatory obstacles stood in the way of exploiting them.

In Hungary the distinction between the lack of interconnected markets and regulatory obstacles may not be a major one, since both are present and clearly reinforce each other. However, it seems to me that these are potentially two different barriers to entrepreneurial behavior on the part of the firm, as can be seen in nationalized enterprises in Western economies. In such cases, one finds interconnected markets, but firms are often deterred from exploiting them by political considerations. For example, Elf Aquitaine's attempt in 1979 to buy a controlling share in an American company was halted by Giscard d'Estaing's election campaign. If this is so, it would seem that the task in Hungary is more complex than that of creating efficient markets; it involves creating an appropriate mode of regulation as well.

I concur with Tardos's analysis of the origins of the "expansion drive" in enterprises, that is, that it originates in the center and derives from the conditions under which political leaders achieve positions of power rather than being an inherent characteristic of the firms. Two kinds of evidence support this view. First of all, it is unclear why firms are willing to conform to cues from the center during downturns in the investment cycle or how the center is able to gather the political force to engineer a downturn at all if firms have an autonomous interest of their own in expansion. Second, the political behavior of Hungarian firms does not support a view that sees them as autonomous organizations with their own interests. Rather, they behave very much as they are described by Tardos: as creatures of the center's will, entities whose objectives are defined outside the organization itself and whose interests consist in satisfying the often contradictory expectations located both above them in the ministries and alongside them in the party. Soft budget constraints in this context serve to facilitate political control of the economy, control which may or may not promote expansion. On the one hand, "slack" within the firm serves à la Cyert and March as a side payment on the conflicting forces that define enterprise objectives. On the other, since budget constraints are soft, enterprises have no reason or incentive to resist changes in policy and expectations affecting their operations or to organize coalitions to influence overall policy directions. Thus, we find a pattern of firms exhibiting a lack of real combativeness and even interest in general economic policy combined with feverish lobbying in bureaucratic corridors for individual exemptions, exceptions, and the like in order to meet current expectations.

For example, in Hungary the chamber of commerce has to be given the task of organizing enterprises to express their opinions on economic policy; in Western countries, in contrast, chambers of commerce are formed by the firms themselves, who are anxious to press their views and interests on policy makers. Another suggestive example is the textile industry's virtual lack of opposition to 1971 legislation encouraging young mothers to stay home with infants, a serious blow for an already labor-short industry. Such political passivity can be contrasted with the periodic mobilizations of the American textile industry each time raising the minimum wage is considered by Congress.

Significantly, the limited evidence available suggests that nationalized firms in the West exhibit patterns of political behavior similar to those in Hungary. For example, the French steel association felt its relationship with the government had changed much more after the 1978 nationalization than with the election of a socialist government in 1980. With nationalization, the industry lost its interest in partisan politics, the area in which general policy directions are determined and an area in which the privately owned steel industry had traditionally played a very active role. Instead, after 1978 it no longer mattered whether the government was left or right. Consequently, the steel association no longer took political stands (prise de position) on economic issues. Moreover, the government no longer dealt with it politically as an industry representative, preferring to deal individually and bureaucratically with each steel company, much in the Hungarian manner.

It would appear, then, that the consequence of state ownership everywhere is to deprive firms of autonomous interests, to eliminate them as genuinely independent political actors, and to confine their relationship with government to lobbying in ministerial offices to acquire the means needed to satisfy the political expectations conveyed to them. If this picture is correct, it implies that the economic success of a Renault or an Elf Aquitaine is not due only to objective institutional arrangements, but also to the subjective politically determined objectives they are given. If so, a major cause of the more entrepreneurial economic behavior of Western state-owned firms may be the fact that Western political leaders derive political benefits from an efficiently operating nationalized sector whereas Hungarian leaders do not.

To continue this line of thought, it follows that the key question facing reform efforts in Eastern Europe is not only what to do or what changes to make in the institutional arrangements affecting the economy. In addition, one must also supply political incentives for leaders to make such changes and pursue policies consistent with them. Otherwise, leaders seeking power and influence will necessarily act in ways directly counter to what economic reform prescribes, as they did after the NEM. A realpolitik approach to economic reform in Eastern Europe, therefore, would not necessarily eliminate political control from the economy. Rather, it would center on creating political incentives to make it in the interest of political elites to exercise control in a way that is conducive to micro- and macroeconomic efficiency.

This is not a very simple task, and may well be an impossible one, as political leaders everywhere are neither primarily interested in economic efficiency nor very skilled at achieving it. In Western systems, the presence of electoral competition combined with the substantial political clout of a large private sector with "real" interests forces political elites to take account of macroeconomic efficiency in the economy and microeconomic efficiency in nationalized sectors; being forced to defend their position in an open and competitive international economic system pushes in the same direction.

Yet the situation need not be a hopeless one for Hungary. For one thing, some fiscal decentralization, allowing county governments to receive a centrally determined share of the profits generated by firms within the region, would give regional leaders in an interest in both the profitability of firms in the area and in breaking up some of the mammoth monopolies whose operations are dispersed throughout the country. Moreover, if local party elites gain increased discretion over the allocation of this new source of local revenue, they would be better able to accomplish their social welfare tasks by influencing the local government's policies rather than by intervening directly in enterprise decisions —assuming that central party directives pushed them toward this and rewarded them accordingly. The experiences of Yugoslavia and China in this respect do suggest that increased fiscal discretion does indeed make local political elites much more anxious to stimulate the local economy and much less interested in simply hooking local ventures onto central projects; the latter has been the practice in Hungary and in the 1970s was a strong political factor abetting economic centralization. Nevertheless, at least the Yugoslav experience should serve to caution us that local fiscal autonomy alone is not sufficient to create efficient markets and competition; the center itself must be strong and firmly committed to this goal as well. If it is, maintaining democratic centralism and discipline in the HSWP might well be an organizational advantage rather than a threat to economic decentralization.

A second possible scenario for reconciling continued political control of the economy with the use of market mechanisms and expanded enterprise autonomy rests on what would be a persisting need for regulating enterprises even in the presence of interconnected domestic markets. That is, industrial structure is always more concentrated and monopolistic in small countries than in large ones, for well-known economic reasons. In the West the solution has been to encourage foreign competition, but Hungary's balance-of-payments situation and CMEA's inability to reduce barriers to cross-national competition make such a response there unlikely. Without it, however, the ability of market forces to control economic activity will necessarily be weak and this, in turn, implies that economic rationality itself would require supplementing market controls with political ones.

One form such controls could take is administrative: ministries enforce a set of rules, adopted by Parliament, on enterprises. Nevertheless, the experience of Western countries with nationalized enterprises suggests that purely administrative controls based on legislated rules are either ineffective or have undesirable consequences on enterprise behavior because the entrepreneurial function cannot be routinized sufficiently to fit the categories prescribed by fixed regulations. Hence, it makes sense to supplement market and bureaucratic controls with more flexible and less legalistic political supervision. With the latter, enterprises can depart from the rule of law to pursue opportunities the economic environment presents because a politically responsible agent is answerable and can take responsibility for violations of the letter of the law on behalf of its spirit.

To whom ought such political overseers be accountable? In a pluralistic system, they are accountable to spontaneously organized social forces, as is the case with the various regulatory boards established at federal and state levels in the United States. There, the exercise of discretion over economic actors reflects the claims of relatively narrow, partial interests varying from consumer groups and environmentalists to unions and lobbies created by the very enterprises these boards are assigned to regulate. Moreover, both the "logic of collective action" and the American practice makes precisely the firms being regulated able to exert the strongest and most effective pressures on their nominal controllers.

In a Leninist system, in contrast, political controls on economic actors and bureaucratic agencies are exercised by party officials ultimately accountable to the national party leadership. Thus, they have an incentive to make interventions in economic decisions that reflect national priorities and claims. In practice, these priorities have often made little economic sense, but in theory, they could be quite rational if national political elites chose to make them so.

Recent changes proposed in Hungarian ownership structures would assign regulatory functions performed by ministries to special boards while giving the ministries' former ownership functions to the enterprises. In such a context, political control over the economy could be centered on framing and applying the regulatory constraints articulated at the board level rather than through direct intervention in the firm. In this scenario, enterprise and local cadres could continue to exercise influence in the firm, but their tasks would be confined to ensuring compliance with higher-level constraints and promotion opportunities for cadres would be based on their efficacy in doing so. At the same time, higher-level leaders would retain their discretion over appointments where board membership is concerned. Rather than pushing the party out of the economy, which will not happen in any case, an attempt would be made to capitalize on the organizational advantages a Marxist-Leninist party offers to enhance the efficacy of regulatory structures — through reduced vulnerability to partial interests—that would be required in any case.

Yet a third strategy for giving political elites a greater interest in economic efficiency is an electoral one, as exemplified in the recent, "contested" parliamentary elections in Hungary. Here, one might expect that to the degree the broader population benefits from increased economic efficiency and the wider use of market mechanisms, limited electoral competition would give it the opportunity to reward political elites associated with such policies and punish those who are not. Hence, the forces favoring "efficient markets" will be strengthened by their ability to win contested elections. Moreover, if reform advocates find themselves on weak grounds within the HSWP, they will be able to rally Parliament to their defense.

Although there are many reasons that make the introduction of contested parliamentary elections a most welcome political development in

Hungary, forwarding the cause of economic reform may not be one of them. For one thing, political power remains a monopoly of the HSWP, and as a nonparty state organization, Parliament does not share it. Thus, the mere fact that individual parliamentary delegates now stand in contested elections does not by itself alter the essentially marginal importance of Parliament as an institution in the contemporary Hungarian power structure, as the brevity of time during which Parliament convenes indicates.

Certainly, an activated Parliament may exert greater surveillance over the activities of the executive branch of government by, for example, calling ministers to account in question-and-answer periods. But to the degree parliamentary representatives do keep ministry officials accountable, the actions the latter will be accounting for will not concern the discretion that officials have exercised in the course of carrying out laws Parliament has passed on its own initiative. Rather, they will be called upon to explain their bureaucratic implementation and interpretation of guidelines and policies the HSWP has formulated for both executive and legislative branches of government alike. In effect, then, Parliament will constitute simply another check on the way in which state administrators implement policies made outside Parliament itself.

Meanwhile, should maverick deputies attempt to use parliamentary immunity to make Parliament a source of power and policy independent of the HSWP, one can imagine two consequences. On the one hand, the experiment with limited electoral competition may simply be abandoned altogether; to quote my colleague, Gary Jacobson, "Why won't it be like Egypt? They allowed an opposition to run candidates in the election, and then when they didn't like the results, they got rid of it." On the other hand, such attempts, if unchecked, could create a kind of dual power situation that would endanger the position of everyone in the HSWP, including reformists. For this reason, no intraparty group, least of all reformists, is likely to rally Parliament to its defense.

Further, the political imperatives confronting individual MPs in Hungary are first and foremost to keep local constituents happy. In some cases this may mean support for efficient markets, but in all cases it will mean lobbying with national bureaucracies for local privileges: as every American congressman knows, first he brings the "pork" home, and only after the water project or defense establishment in his district is secured does he worry about excessive government spending.

In Hungary such localistic tendencies may even be more pronounced among independents than among establishment candidates, since the former do not have the resources of a national organization behind them in parliamentary electoral campaigns. Consequently, their political future is even more dependent on the resources they can extract from national authorities for local purposes. By the same token, they are not subject to the discipline a national party can normally impose on its members by virtue of its control of the party label on the ballot.

At the same time the dependence of individual representatives on bureaucratic favors for their districts may impair the ability of Parliament to exert control on how government officials carry out even the policies the HSWP formulates.

The French experience is instructive in this regard. As in Hungary, a large portion of the most significant actions the government takes are accomplished through administrative decrees that do not require parliamentary consent. Legislation is basically prepared by the government, which effectively controls proceedings in both houses: the success rate of amendments moved by opposition deputies between 1958 and 1979 in France was insignificant. Parliamentary sessions are short, deputies receive relatively low financial compensation, have little interest in extending their stay, and receive rather restricted staff support, while legislative committees are so large their effectiveness as organs of control is impaired. Moreover, the French constitution bars parliamentary initiatives that would decrease government revenues or raise state expenditures, and if the budget submitted by the government is not approved within ninety days, the cabinet can enact it by ordinance. Moreover, the severe constitutional limitations on the deputies' role as lawmakers and watchdogs of the executive are complemented by the presence of a highly centralized state administration able to regulate local matters in great detail. Not surprisingly, a deputy's day-to-day activities consist less of preparing and debating legislation, calling ministers to task, or even reading speeches into the parliamentary record than of visiting with officials in the state bureaucracy to remind them of his locality's needs and explaining the complexities of administrative processes to mystified constituents.

Certainly, the eclipse of the legislature as a check on the executive branch has not progressed nearly so far in the United States or even in the parliamentary system of Great Britain. Yet the ways in which both the American and British legislatures differ from the French are also ways in which they differ from the Hungarian system, suggesting that the Hungarian MP is likely to find him/herself in a situation quite similar to that of his/her Parisian counterpart. That is, in the United States, Congress has maintained its active role thanks to the constitutionally prescribed separation of powers that is absent in all parliamentary systems. And in Britain the House of Commons continues to exert some control over the executive, thanks to the presence of a cohesive opposition party anxious to seek out opportunities to challenge the ruling party's control of government on the basis of national policies. And in neither the American nor the British case are local authorities as dependent on the central government for the revenues and permission necessary to undertake actions of their own choosing as in France.

In Hungary, however, the distribution of legal authority between national Parliament, state bureaucracy, and local governments is much closer to the French model. Furthermore, the government will automatically command a majority within Parliament while there certainly will be no opposition party seeking to challenge it on the basis of national issues. Indeed, precisely because independents cannot form an opposition party whose platform would address national questions, the tendency for district elections to be fought out purely on the basis of local issues and personalities will be strengthened. As a result, leaders with a genuinely national political profile and constituency may well be at a disadvantage although the name recognition factor that is often a critical determinant of voters' preferences in nonpartisan elections may compensate somewhat. If so, this hardly bodes well for reform advocates, who tend to be based more in national government and party bodies than in regional organs.

Nevertheless, if an electoral strategy by itself may not lead to a satisfactory answer on the part of the Hungarian government to the questions Tardos raises, the possibility of using it is a far from trivial development. While limited competition for parliamentary offices may not have a major effect on the power of Parliament per se it can have an impact on the distribution of power within the HSWP. To the degree that who participates in policy formation and party committees has a critical impact on what policies are chosen, the inability of certain party leaders to win a local election may well reduce their political value within the HSWP itself. Likewise, elites within the HSWP who have been edged out of important party positions may be able to use electoral campaigns to stage a political comeback, as György Aczél may well contemplate. In this sense, parliamentary elections may have a real and important impact on the use of power in the HSWP, although whether that impact will be to forward the cause of economic efficiency and reform is an open question.

Yet one can imagine other, perhaps more efficacious, strategies for using limited pluralism to enhance the cause of economic reform and give leaders political benefits from the pursuit of economic policies that contribute to efficiency. Such a strategy would seek to institutionalize a limited, controlled, and "reversible"—and therefore politically acceptable in the Hungarian context—political pluralism through the mass organizations, rather than through the Parliament.

Currently, mass organizations in Hungary operate according to the traditional Leninist "transmission belt" formula. Their leaders are approved for the offices they hold by the party. Thus organizations tend to represent their leaders rather than vice versa, and the leadership itself answers to the HSWP whose policies it implements within its respective organization. In effect, the leader of a mass organization finds his real constituency in the HSWP, not in the members of the association he directs and consequently, when leaders of mass organizations take a political stand on an issue, it reflects neither their organization's interest nor that of its members—who have no means to keep leaders accountable in any case. On the contrary, such stands reflect the political interests and orientations of the party-approved leaders themselves, and it is articulated within the party rather than outside it.

All politically recognized social interests in Hungary currently have this form of political representation: workers have unions, women have a women's association, young people have the Communist Youth Organization (KISZ), even enterprises have the chamber of commerce. Moreover, each organization has a monopoly on representing individuals eligible to join it. Hence, while no student is required to join KISZ, there is no other student organization in which to enroll; although workers need not join existing trade unions, there is no alternative union to which they may turn. Partly because of their monopolistic position, such organizations of social "representation" act more to control and manage their members than to voice their demands, participating in the definition of members' "objective" interests within the HSWP much more than articulating and mobilizing their subjective interests outside it.

One can, however, imagine an alternative mode of political representation for recognized social interests that would simultaneously reinforce the HSWP's hegemonic political position, allow it to take the real preferences of mass organization members into account, and perhaps therefore create political incentives for adoption of policies more conducive to economic efficiency. Such a mode of political representation would be a nontraditional variant of the transmission-belt pattern. That is, rather than establishing *one* transmission-belt organization that monopolizes all representation in a sphere of social life, the HSWP could set up *several* transmission-belt organizations that would compete for members within a single jurisdiction. Such a model of interest representation would be similar to what now prevails in France or Italy: several farm associations compete for peasant members in France or Italy; and the jurisdictions of the three main trade union federations in Italy overlap. Yet, whereas in France or Italy each competing interest association is either formally or informally linked to a different political party, in Hungary, all interest associations would continue to be tied to the HSWP. Thus their leaders would still be approved for their positions by the party and would consequently remain accountable to it. Likewise, they would continue to implement party directives within their own organization, since their ability to retain their positions depends on doing so. In short, what is being proposed is a modified transmission belt formula, not a vehicle for establishing organizations able to mobilize interests independently of the HSWP, as was the case with Solidarity in Poland.

Nevertheless, if transmission-belt organizations must compete for members, leaders would have an incentive to use their discretion in interpreting directives in ways that would maximize their organization's following. Moreover, insofar as mass organization leaders have a major voice when the HSWP adopts directives that apply to their own functions, such leaders would have a reason to use that influence on behalf of expanding and retaining their membership—as opposed to simply equating their own views and interests with those of a captive following.

The broader population would still be prohibited from forming its own organizations, but it would be able to shift support among party-approved rivals with at least slightly different bases of appeal. Hence, if efficient markets would benefit concrete social interests, those interests would at least have some way of rewarding leaders and organizations accordingly.

Let us now consider how such an innovation could happen. The existing mass organization leaders would reject any proposal to break up their organizations: given actual power configurations in the HSWP, one can hardly imagine three competing trade union federations coming into existence in the immediate future. However, one can imagine such an experimental form of representation being introduced for *new*, politically recognized social interests that are currently not covered by the existing network of mass organizations: namely, the various small ventures that have sprung up in Hungary since 1982, and the new economic contract work associations (ECWAS) in particular.

Significantly, small ventures are once again becoming an object of political controversy in Hungary, as evidenced by the debates in the 1985 party congress and the adoption of new measures, including a 10 percent surtax on the formation of ECWAS, designed to prevent unfair competition. And once again, the contribution the various small ventures make to economic efficiency and flexibility is inversely correlated with their political strength. Precisely for this reason, reform advocates within the HSWP have apparently begun to consider a way to supply them with political representation in either an existing or a new secondary association.

Such representation could take the form of the traditionally monopolistic transmission-belt organization or it might take the less orthodox form of competing transmission-belt organizations advanced here. In either case, political representation would certainly help institutionalize small ventures and ECWAS as permanent fixtures of the Hungarian economic scene. But how they are institutionalized may vary a great deal depending on what mechanisms for representation are instituted.

If small ventures and ECWAS become members of a monopolistic transmission-belt organization its leaders will be committed to the expansion of, say, ECWA activity in Hungarian firms, since their influence will depend on the size and strategic value of the activities for which they are responsible. Moreover, such a leadership will have clout where it counts, in the HSWP. Insofar as the propagation of ECWAS and small ventures is part of a broader reformist program, such an organization would signify that at least some elements in the political elite would directly benefit from its adoption.

On the other hand, one can also expect such a leadership to be accountable to the HSWP and its top echelons in particular, and not to its own members. Hence, it would regulate and routinize the formation of small ventures, despite the fact that such bureaucratization need not be in the interests of those participating in ECWAS or small ventures and indeed, is antithetical to the entrepreneurial functions reformers intend them to perform. The activities of the cooperative association in the great Hungarian merger movement of the 1970s supply ample precedent in this regard. Moreover, if a single monopolistic association incorporates all forms of new ventures it will also tend to ignore and/or discriminate against ventures formed outside the politically strategic socialist sector. Within the socialist sector one would expect to see an expansion of the use of ECWAs as regularly established collective teams/ work brigades along with an atrophy of ECWAs as spontaneous, in-house entrepreneurs. From that, it would be a small step to regulating the incomes ECWA members generate and receive as well, and the traditional enterprise hierarchy will simply assert itself in a new form.

In contrast, if there were competing transmission-belt organizations, they would have the same incentive to generalize ECWAs to the labor force in the socialist sector and extend the operation of small ventures outside it that a single, monopolistic representative would have. Nevertheless, several competing organizations, each catering to a somewhat different clientele, would have neither the temptation nor the ability to impose a uniform model on all units. Instead, each would have an incentive to lobby for small venture forms that reflect the particular exigencies of its own constituency. Moreover, members will join voluntary associations based on the selective benefits it provides as well as the collective benefits it offers or the general policies it advocates. Hence, organizations anxious to expand their membership would have an incentive to advise and participate in the formation of ECWAs and small ventures at the grass roots, so to speak, providing would-be entrepreneurs within and outside of the socialist sector with an institutional ally whose political interest lies in making their ventures successful, rather than in regulating them in conformity with its own institutional profile. The presence of such an ally could be critical should opposition from enterprise hierarchies or local officials emerge.

Ironically, the reason why establishing competitive transmission-belt organizations for small venture participants may be possible is precisely because of the political opposition they have generated. Much of the resistance to small ventures is undoubtedly from sources who see monopolistic organizations as strong entities; but this opposition would presumably be less threatened by an arrangement that permits controlled competition among political representatives in the small-venture sector than by one that sets up a new single mass organization or reallocates power within an existing association to give small ventures a larger voice. Since the opposition would see competing organizations as politically weaker, it could support the introduction of nontraditional transmission-belt representation on those grounds. As for the party as a whole, part of the appeal of such an experiment is the fact that it is easily reversible; such organizations and their leaders would remain accountable to the HSWP, and if the party is dissatisfied with their performance, organizations can be amalgamated as easily as they are established, and leaders can be transferred as easily as they can be appointed. Meanwhile, however, if new organizational elites can translate the aspirations of their members into a viable political program, then the support of a nonorthodox Leninism may well begin to appeal to other mass organization leaders as well.

Finally, it must be noted that a more accurate reflection of real social interests need not necessarily translate itself into increased political benefits for elites who favor the widened use of genuine market mechanisms in Hungary. In a society where virtually all personal income is a return to labor, pressures for maintaining permanent full employment, for example, may be even stronger than they are now. Likewise, there is no reason to think that competing transmission-belt organizations will not strive to block economic liberalization measures that endanger their members any less than monopolistic organizations have succeeded in blocking reforms that endanger their leaders. Yet, to the degree it becomes more difficult to reconcile social interests politically within the HSWP, party leaders may seek to find a more neutral allocator of resources: the market itself. In this sense, bringing interest conflicts into the HSWP rather than restricting its ability to arbitrate them (that is, the thesis that the party should be moved from the economy) may give leaders a real incentive to create efficient markets, as they would become vital for maintaining the party's own position in the Hungarian political system.

In making these modest proposals I take my cue from Jonathan Swift; I neither expect them to be taken entirely seriously nor am I particularly committed to defending them. I suggest them less as realistic solutions than as illustrations of the way in which one can think about the problem. For a political scientist the challenge is less one of designing an efficient economic system per se than of proposing an efficient economic system that will provide the political benefits that will induce leaders to adopt and implement it. If economic reform is conceptualized as a purely economic task or as a program to take power away from political elites, it is difficult to see why they would support it. In contrast, if nondestabilizing changes in political institutions serve to complement reforms in economic structures such that not only enterprises but political elites as well derive benefits from good economic performance, the possibility of a nonreversible economic reform is a real one. Such incrementalism may not transform society from the object to the subject of collective choices, but to the degree society's economic interest could be better articulated and satisfied the change would be significant.

CHAPTER 11

Comments on Chapter 9

Paul Marer

Tardos's insightful and complex essay about Hungary's reform experience since 1968 can be summed up in two statements. First, reality has been quite different from the NEM blueprint. The blueprint envisioned that enterprises would have a great deal of autonomy over the composition of current production and inputs, the distribution of output, and replacement investment, and that enterprise decisions would be guided by market forces as reflected by profits. The authorities would guide market forces by means of general rules concerning the formation of prices and wages, and by taxes, subsidies, interest rates, credits, exchange rates, and tariffs. These so-called economic regulators would become the new instruments of central planning. More direct controls would be maintained over new investments and trade with CMEA partners. In reality, however, enterprises and cooperatives have remained, in many respects, under direct central government and party control, even though the instruments of control have changed. Flexible compulsory plan directives were replaced by more, but often still enterprise-specific, rules and by bargaining about their application.

Second, the most important reason why the NEM blueprint did not operate as envisioned was that a sufficiently strong market mechanism was not created. While market relations were developed quite extensively in agriculture and in the consumer sector, in the enterprise sector their emergence was hindered by the highly concentrated structure of industry and construction, and by the almost complete absence of import competition. The development of a labor market where wage rates would approximately equate the supply and demand for labor was hindered by the absence of a countervailing power among the owners of capital who in any case may not have had sufficiently strong interest in profits to resist the always strong pressures for wage increases. The development of a market for real assets, where value would be based not on costs but on the expected rate of return, was prevented by the lack of institutions that would fulfill the functions of a stock market by revaluing real assets continuously. Finally, the development of a market for financial capital was hindered by the monopoly banking system and by financial intermediation that had to be carried out almost exclusively through the state budget.

Under these circumstances the authorities have had no alternative but to step in and somehow try to simulate through numerous and frequently adjusted rules and regulations what competitive markets would achieve if they existed. This is why many prices continue to be set administratively, why complicated rules determine whether and how prices can be changed by firms, why there exist very complex rules about the formation of wage funds, and why there is continued strict control over average wage increases. Enterprises continue to depend on the authorities for new investment in part because, given the arbitrary elements in prices, wage rates, exchange rates, taxes, subsidies, and asset values, it is not always clear that a loss-making enterprise is a truly unprofitable producer. Moreover, given the highly concentrated production structure and the absence of import competition, allowing any of Hungary's large firms to go bankrupt would create major supply bottlenecks, to say nothing of the social and political problems of dealing with sudden large pools of unemployed workers. Consequently, although the economy has become subject to some degree of influence by market forces, the authorities will not allow large enterprises that lose money year after year to go bankrupt. Tardos concludes that in spite of Hungary's notable economic achievements, the many remaining problems are rooted not in the soft budget constraint facing enterprises but in the fundamental design of the economic system.

During the last few years I have studied extensively Hungarian reforms (Marer 1985b, 1986a) and I agree fully with Tardos's reasoning and conclusions. Therefore, I would like to add only a few comments, oriented toward the future. Since about 1979, when Hungary began to face severe problems in the balance of payments, whose roots I and many economists in Hungary have traced to the remaining inefficiencies of the system (Marer 1986b), a consensus has been developing in Hungary that no significant and sustained improvement in economic performance is likely without further fundamental reforms in the economic mechanism. The emergence of this consensus is important because it is necessary though not a sufficient condition for continuing the reform process.

Sustained improvements in economic performance will require the favorable resolution of three sets of interrelated problems, namely: the willingness and ability of the authorities to change permanently certain economic policy characteristics of traditional central planning; to move from the present stage of trying to simulate a market mechanism through administrative rules to a stage where much greater scope is given to genuine market forces; and to reconcile the operation of a domestic market mechanism and foreign trade with CMEA partners.

Regarding the first problem, the traditional tendency of planners to push growth rates and to undertake or approve large investment projects beyond feasible levels is an important cause of shortages and problems in the balance of payments. Those problems, in turn, make it more difficult even for partial reforms to have the desired impact on performance and also impede the introduction of further reform measures. During the first eleven years of the NEM (1968–78), there was a great deal of tension between traditional economic policies and the reforms (Marer 1986b). Only when the convertible currency balance-of-payments constraint became binding around 1979 were growth and investment rates significantly reduced. The question for the future is whether, once the payments balance is reestablished, the authorities will return to traditional economic policies and thus continue to impede the operation of the system and the introduction of new reforms.

Commitments to certain social goals, first and foremost full employment and relative price stability, also stand as obstacles to economic efficiency. This is especially true during a transition period from an administratively planned to a more market-oriented economy; once a well-functioning market mechanism has been created, unemployment and inflation are likely to be less severe problems than they could be during the current transition period.

A further aspect of economic policy that hampers economic efficiency is the lack of a dynamic industrial strategy, one that would help move the country closer to its potential comparative advantage and would help close its growing technological gap vis-à-vis the West, the NICS especially. There is much talk but little action on industrial policy. Although there seems to be a consensus that a larger share of total industrial investment should be devoted to improve manufacturing, such resources continue to be used to secure the energy and raw materials Hungary needs to utilize the existing and excessively energy- and material-intensive production structure. The explanation of this paradox apparently lies in the power of the heavy industrial lobby and the fact the economic policies and the economic system are mutually determined.

Regarding the economic system, Tardos reasons brilliantly about the need for, and the difficulties of, modifying the system so that sufficient power and the right incentives are given to persons or institutions that would represent the interest of capital, but without leading to the emergence of large capitalist owners. Such a mechanism is essential for developing a well-functioning market for labor as well as one for real assets. Such markets are preconditions for improving resource allocation, especially investment, which has remained the Achilles' heel of the economic system. The reforms currently being introduced, creating workers' councils at small firms and management boards with worker representation at large ones, are important experiments in this direction, but they alone are not likely to achieve all that is needed.

The other essential precondition for developing a genuine market is to open up the economy to more domestic and, especially, import competition. The importance of the latter is not stressed sufficiently by Tardos. It is erroneous, in my view, to reason that imports cannot be allowed in more freely because of the tension in the balance of payments. Rather, the causation runs the other way. Because so many producers cannot get the right kinds of imports and do not face import competition they cannot be competitive on the world market. This is especially true in manufactures that require sophisticated technology and components. Insufficient export competitiveness, in turn, is the main reason for the tension in the balance of payments.

The third dilemma is posed by Hungary's large trade with the CMEA.

The regional trading system operates through bilateral trade agreements that specify the quantities and prices of the goods to be traded. Each state then requires its enterprises to fulfill those agreements This arrangement provides scant incentive for firms to become more competitive, and indeed assured and profitable access to the relatively soft CMEA markets—where firms do not face competition, do not engage in real marketing, and do not control the prices and the quantities traded—is one of the reasons why Hungarian firms have been losing competitiveness on world markets with their manufactures. More generally, it is difficult to get enterprises to operate under one kind of system when they sell to one market and under another system when they sell elsewhere. Thus, there is a need to create a bridging mechanism between Hungarian firms and the state trading entities of other CMEA nations. The essence of such a mechanism would be to make intra-CMEA trade agreements obligations of the Hungarian state, not of enterprises, and then finding market-type incentives to motivate enterprises to fulfill them.

During the last two decades Hungary has pioneered the attempted reconciliation of central planning as a process with the introduction of a market mechanism in order to improve the efficiency of the centrally planned system. It has done so under very difficult regional and global circumstances and without being able to depend on the experience of any other country with implementing such a transformation. At the same time a consensus is now emerging that further fundamental reforms are needed. While outstanding Hungarian economists like Tardos have diagnosed the problems and are offering logical prescriptions on how to improve the system, it is the political leadership that must decide whether and how to implement them. The pressure on the leaders to introduce further reforms comes from the political imperative to improve economic performance. The many constraints on reforms are rooted in ideological, political, economic, bureaucratic, and foreign policy considerations, as Tardos also indicates. The outcome is difficult to predict, except to say that, even in Hungary, the issue of economic reform will certainly remain on the agenda.

CHAPTER 12

Soviet Central Planning: Probing the Limits of the Traditional Model

Ed A. Hewett

Over the last half-century the most impressive aspect of the performance of the Soviet economic system has been its ability to resist several concerted efforts to change it. To be sure, there have been a myriad of changes in various aspects of the system; it is not precisely the same system it was fifty years ago. But, as systems go, it does not differ fundamentally from the original version of the 1930s.

While there has never been an effort at a truly comprehensive reform of the traditional system of central planning in the Soviet Union, certainly the reforms introduced in 1965 had important elements of such a comprehensive approach. Those reforms had no lasting impact on the system. The partial reform program of 1973, aimed at streamlining the system that supervised industrial production, led to changes that were ultimately of minor, if any, significance to the functioning of the system. The July 1979 decree was virtually stillborn.

Despite these disappointing results, Soviet leaders talk almost constantly of the necessity of changing the system, and the sources of their dissatisfaction with the system have not changed noticeably over time. This persistent concern about the performance of the system, combined with an apparent inability to construct an effective program to alter it, has led to what Berliner (1983, p. 350) has called a "routinization" of the process of altering the system. Now, every five or six years, in rough synchronization with the preparation of the next five-year plan, new reforms are introduced. Mikhail Gorbachev, building on the legacy of Andropov's brief tenure as general secretary, is mounting yet a new effort at reform. How "routine" it will be only time will tell.

Gertrude Schroeder (1979) has characterized this constant, inconclusive bickering between the system leaders and the system itself as a "treadmill of reforms." The point is well taken, but incomplete. Western specialists on the Soviet economy share the treadmill with Soviet leaders, and are running just as hard as they to get nowhere. Year after year Western analysts of the Soviet economy write of the need, even the urgent need, to reform the Soviet economic system. Yet most years nothing happens, and in those years when something happens, it turns out to be of little lasting importance.

The two other consistent phenomena of the last two decades have been a secular decline in national income growth rates and an increasingly serious deterioration in important exogenous factors, in particular demographic factors and diminishing returns in resource extraction. It is an unchanged system, combined with a consistent deterioration in macroeconomic performance, which keeps Soviet leaders on the treadmill and keeps Western specialists trotting along with them.

That impressive display of the system's ability to avoid change, even in the face of growing pressure from deteriorating economic performance, raises a logical question. Is there any reason to suppose that the future will not replicate the past? Things have gone on this way for several decades, why not several more?

The easiest, but least satisfying, answer to this question is that because of the continued deterioration in economic performance Soviet leaders will eventually be compelled to admit the logic of comprehensive economic reforms and change the system. That is reminiscent of Arthur Okun's tongue-in-cheek dictum to economists: "If you must make a forecast, either give a date or give a number, but never give both." Observations about the inevitability of genuine economic reform in the Soviet Union are probably correct, but not terribly illuminating. If Western specialists have any grasp whatsoever of the dynamics of this system they should be able to be somewhat more precise than that.

Yet, is it possible that it is asking too much to go beyond that? An intellectually satisfying theory of the evolution of the Soviet economic system would require not only a thorough comprehension of the interactions between economic performance and the economic system, but also a comprehension of the political forces arrayed for and against systemic change and their interaction. The complete theory of systemic change in the Soviet Union awaits a new Marx to outline the dynamics of this derailed revolution, more closely resembling state capitalism than any form of "socialism" that Marx would have recognized. Are those of us who study the Soviet economy doomed, while awaiting this new Marx, to play a part somewhat analogous to that Utopian socialists played in the nineteenth century, outlining a different future for Soviet socialism without any but the vaguest notion of how or when the system might proceed from here to there? Is our vision so blurred, our understanding so poor, that we can do no more?

I honestly do not have a definite answer. My purpose in this essay is to develop a framework for thinking about the future of the system, which is primarily useful for identifying the types of information we need in order to form expectations about the future of the Soviet economic system which both say something substantive and have a date.

The year 2000 is used as a convenient date. Although the year 2000 sounds far away, it is not. If I had been writing this essay in 1970, I would most likely have been impressed with the need to fully implement and move beyond the 1965 reforms in order to forestall a further decline in economic performance that, if it occurred, would have created political problems for Soviet leaders. Now, over fifteen years later, it would appear that the point on the link between system stability and performance would have stood the test of time, but the predicted political consequences are nowhere to be seen. It is useful to remember that when peering fifteen years ahead. It is plausible that in the next fifteen years successive Soviet leaders will continue their efforts to change the system with no notable success, that economic performance will deteriorate further, but that successive leaderships will somehow manage to contain the political consequences.

On the strength of historical precedent, this is a perfectly reasonable prediction for the next fifteen years. Moving away from this prediction, say to one that foresees substantial system change, can only be defended in light of compelling evidence that the future simply cannot replicate the past.

This essay constitutes a search for that evidence. I begin by looking at the past in an effort to understand why this system has remained essentially unchanged despite efforts to change it. I then turn to the future to apply the lessons of the past to the task of outlining the likely future course of the system. In the end I talk of probabilities, not certainties, and the conclusion I reach is that Soviet leaders are most likely not yet through in their search for the limits of the traditional model, nor does it appear that they have reached those limits.

This chapter was completed when Mikhail Gorbachev was at the beginning of his second year as general secretary, and in the midst of defining through speeches and decrees the changes he wishes to introduce in the economic system. I will not attempt here to characterize what he is doing; the focus here is rather on setting a context within which it is possible to understand his policy measures and systemic changes as they unfold.[1] To the extent I discuss Gorbachev's views or measures introduced since he assumed office, it will only be to illustrate the continued validity of observations relating to leaders and periods preceding him.

TERMINOLOGY

Before proceeding to a discussion of the evolution of the Soviet economic system in the past and the future, it is necessary to be clear about terminology. The basic concepts involve varieties of economic reform, and policy change within an unchanged system. However in both cases there is ample room for confusion, which it is best to try to minimize at the start.[2]

The Concept of Economic Reform

Economic reform means a change in a country's economic system, a *re*formation of the system. Because the term "economic reform" covers a very broad range of phenomena—from reforms in only one part of the system to a massive overhaul of the entire system—it frequently is preceded by an adjective: "radical" reform, "real" reform, "partial" reform, "comprehensive" reform, or "fundamental" reform. It is, in fact, an imprecise term and one must be careful when using it that its meaning is as clear as possible.

That is all the more important because there are many options open to leaders for improving economic performance that involve changing policy without changing the system. A change in investment strategies or policies on technology imports, or priorities for the allocation of scarce materials among competing users all may affect economic performance even though the system remains unchanged. Here leaders seek to achieve their goals not by altering the system but by using it to improve economic performance.

Leaders surely do not envisage their options under artificially simple categories such as "policy changes" and "system changes." They are seeking ways to improve economic performance that are politically acceptable, but that have some effect; and they almost always decide on a combination of measures that fall into both categories. All of the major efforts to improve economic performance in the Soviet Union and Eastern Europe have involved a combination of new policies and some change in the system. Granting that reality is not neatly divided up into these two categories, it is still useful to keep them in mind for reasons that will be discussed below.

A final point about economic reforms that, while obvious, still deserves to be stressed, is that they are not an event, but a series of events. Every reform has a stage of debate, preparation, and (possibly) experimentation that lasts at least several years. Every reform will have a general legal decree or decrees (the date of which confers the label—for example, the 1965 reforms), followed by a long implementation stage during which detailed decrees implement the general decrees. The implementation stage can stretch out for some years, both by design—as the reforms are set to be phased in gradually—and also because the opposition is strong enough to successfully engage in delaying tactics. In most reforms the implementation stage shades into a retrenchment phase in which the decrees, as implemented, are reversed, either de jure, or de facto. It is this typical dynamic of reforms which makes the analogy of a wave so apt.[3]

In order to define the various types of reform and policy changes I begin with an "unreformed" system, and then define which systemic changes constitute "radical" reforms, and which do not. For the properties of the unreformed system I begin with Bornstein's (1977, pp. 103–4) list of nine essential characteristics of the traditional Soviet (Stalinist) economic model which I will refer to simply as the traditional model. I have combined the list into four general system characteristics:

1 The state owns the means of production, and property incomes automatically revert to the state. Individual incomes are essentially limited to wages and salaries.
2 Economic administration is hierarchical with decision-making concentrated at the top. The production and distribution of goods and services are planned in detail in physical units. Capital formation and utilization are controlled by the center, as are the important labor force variables.
3 Prices, and therefore money, are passive, supporting, rather than influencing, centrally determined plans for resource allocation.
4 Throughout the system the emphasis is on the fulfillment of quantitative targets.

These four characteristics summarize the unchanged skeleton around which the Soviet economic system has existed for the last half century. They are mutually linked in many complex ways. Passive prices and centralized economic administration reinforce each other. Because prices only reflect costs of domestic production and not the demand for the product or the potential profits involved in exporting or importing it, central planners must directly control the production and distribution of key goods and services. Enterprises, even if they were inclined and able to make their own decisions on inputs, outputs, and sales cannot be trusted to do so because domestic prices are potentially quite misleading.

Centralized economic administration and the quantitatively oriented incentive system complement each other. Because the central authorities plan in terms of physical quantities—and the realization of those plans is the responsibility of the ministries—it is necessary to have an incentive system which induces managers and workers to give highest priority to the quantitative portion of their plans. Changing the incentive system (say to encourage firms to produce high quality products; or encouraging them to save on energy and material inputs, even if outputs suffer somewhat) will clash with the remainder of the system unless, simultaneously, the criteria are changed by which ministries are judged.

A radical (or comprehensive) reform of the traditional system alters most of the system's fundamental characteristics—changing the nature and responsibilities of the economic hierarchy, the price system, and the incentive systems of intermediate and primary economic units. The 1965 reforms were the closest approximation to radical reforms in the postwar period, but they still fell far short of the mark.[4] A partial reform seeks to change only some of the characteristics of the system. The decree on associations in 1973 could be construed as an effort to reform the hierarchy, without in any significant way altering the price system, the incentive system, or the form of ownership.[5]

Because of the logical interconnections among the elements of the traditional system, the presumption should be that unless there is a compelling evidence to the contrary, partial reforms will ultimately fail. An attempt to alter the quantitative orientation of incentives for enterprises, without at the same time altering the quantitative targets given to ministries (that flow from the material balance system), is unlikely to succeed as long as ministries retain their considerable influence over enterprise management. An attempt to reduce central control over economic activity without simultaneously increasing the reliance on a flexible price system responsive to supply-demand pressures will lead to distortions in resource allocation that eventually will bring about a recentralization, or further reform.

In this essay the word "reform," without adjectives, simply signifies a change in the system, whether partial or radical. This differs somewhat from the way the Soviet literature and leaders now discuss the issue of system change. The word reform went out of vogue in the aftermath of the discussions preceding the 1965 reforms. It would now only be used in the context of a discussion of what in the terminology of this essay would be called radical reforms. Instead, most Soviet leaders and most economists discuss the further perfection (dalneishee sovershenstvovanie), improvement (uluchshenie), or restructuring (perestroika) of the system. These are different words for partial reforms, a point emphasized by the fact that both the leadership and economists who write on the system divide the system into several components: the system of management, which encompasses the economic hierarchy supervising resource allocation; the planning system, which generates the decisions enforced through the hierarchy; and the economic mechanism itself that apparently refers to the role of economic levers (prices, interest rates, incentive systems). Andropov, in the last speech attributed to him, in December 1983 mentioned the need to introduce improvements in all three of these areas, bringing them together under the general rubric of the ". . . complex further perfection of the entire mechanism of management." (Andropov 1984, p. 5). Mikhail Gorbachev has, from the very beginning of his administration, regarded economic reform as one of his highest priorities, and he has gone so far as to reintroduce the term "radical reform" into public discourse on the system.[6]

Policy Changes versus Economic Reforms

Economic reforms—partial or radical—are not the only possible measures available for responding to unsatisfactory economic performance. Economic leaders have at their disposal an entire continuum of measures ranging from doing nothing to radical reform. At one end of the continuum, only a little beyond doing nothing, are policy measures designed to use the existing system to change performance. Such measures are constantly being introduced in all socialist countries: new bonus schemes to encourage the introduction of new products, or to stimulate increases in the export of manufactured goods; selective imports of technology intended to accelerate technical change in a particular industry; new rationing schemes for the distribution of scarce materials; new programs to develop domestic production of advanced technologies and special bonuses to producers of new products or products that can be exported for hard currency. They are the first resort of the leader who is dissatisfied with some particular aspect of economic performance, and who quite naturally feels that if incremental policy changes can improve performance without changing the system, then that is preferable to reforming the system.

Farther toward the right are major policy changes, such as a significant change in the investment's share in GNP, a change in the sectoral structure of investment, or possibly a change in the priorities for investments within sectors. Another measure that fits in the category of major policy changes would seem to be Gorbachev's (previously Andropov's) discipline and anticorruption campaign, a major effort to improve the operation of the system without changing it.

Policy changes are a constant feature of the Soviet approach to managing the economy, as one would expect them to be. Partial reform efforts occur with much less frequency, usually the result of cumulative dissatisfaction with the results of policy changes. Leaders will always try to deal with a problem in economic performance first by changing policies, only resorting to reforms when it is clear that policy changes within the existing system will not have a sufficient impact.

It is clearly in this realm of policy change that Soviet leaders have considerable room for maneuver that, if used skillfully, will allow them to minimize the need for economic reforms. To take but one example, consider the problems in the Soviet oil industry in the 1970s. When it became clear in the mid-1970s that the oil industry would have increasing difficulties in meeting output targets, the options included reforms in that industry that could have effectively improved its performance with a lag; reforms or policy changes in the rest of the economy to reduce demand for oil; or policy changes in the oil industry designed to increase oil output without significantly altering the system. The latter path was chosen and considerable new inputs were diverted from the remainder of the economy to the oil industry. The results were at least temporarily satisfactory, albeit expensive.[7]

The many similar examples one could cite suggest a view of Soviet planners in which the norm is firefighting through policy changes designed to deal with particular symptoms, interrupted periodically by efforts at partial reform of those parts of the system that are producing some of the hottest fires. In predicting the future of the Soviet economic system one must try to balance a healthy respect for Soviet planners' skills as firefighters with a sober analysis of the types of fires they are likely to face in the future and their ability to deal with them.

IMPEDIMENTS TO REFORMING THE TRADITIONAL MODEL

Recent Soviet economic history suggests that there must be formidable barriers to reforms of the traditional model. Three broad categories of impediments seem possible, and each probably plays some role in the final outcome. Soviet leaders themselves are one possible impediment to change in the system. The fact that they have introduced reforms on several occasions in the past, and are now doing so again, does not in any way represent proof that they are committed to the process of reform, in particular to implementing reforms. At the extreme one might hypothesize that Soviet leaders are acting like politicians in many countries, devising programs for change in order to cultivate the appearance of actively seeking to deal with a politically sensitive problem.

A second likely source of impediments to change is the central management hierarchy: the state committees, the ministries, and the intermediate authorities under them; and the local party committees. These are the powerful institutions in the traditional model, and reforms could significantly alter the distribution of power among them, and between them and the primary economic units in the system. Their vested interest in the traditional model, and their necessary role in administering any changes to it, constitute an obvious incentive and opportunity for obstructionism.

The third likely source of impediments to change is the population itself. In the antiseptic language of economists, reforms alter the way in which resources are allocated. But some of those resources are people, accustomed to the benefits and costs of the traditional model. While workers or managers might, as consumers, wholeheartedly support the goals of reforms designed to improve the quality, mix, and even quantity of goods supplied for consumption or goods moving in intra-industry transactions, at the same time they will probably seek to avoid the new mix of benefits and costs those same reforms would bring to their personal activities in the work force. The dual character of individuals in society, as consumers and as producers, can result in dual positions on the same reform.

The Leadership as an Impediment to Reform

It is difficult to discuss in any specific way the views of the leadership about economic reforms in the Soviet Union over a period of several decades. The composition of the leadership has changed over time, the collective wisdom in leadership circles concerning what is wrong with the economy and what can be done about it may also have changed, and the problems they are facing have grown more challenging over time. Still there are several generalizations that seem consistent with the behavior of Soviet leaders in the last several decades.

First, it seems implausible that the few Soviet leaders who have attempted to change the system in the last two decades were, or are, insincere in their professed desire to pursue partial reforms. In each case—1965, 1973, 1979, and 1986—the evidence suggests a sincere effort to construct and introduce reform programs affecting important fundamental elements of the system. While the importance of being seen to act should not be dismissed, it would not appear to have been the main motive.

There are two other ways in which Soviet leaders could more plausibly be regarded as an impediment: through their unwillingness to persist during the implementation of the reform; and through their naivete about the possible efficacy of partial reforms in an interconnected system. It is difficult for an outsider to follow the implementation of a reform program, not just in the Soviet Union, but in any socialist country. In Hungary, for example, a country in which much more information is available to the outsider than is the case in the Soviet Union, it is still impossible to construct more than a fragmented picture of how vigorously the government and the party are acting to firmly support the principles of a reform during the stage of implementation.

The problem here is what I have called elsewhere the "battle over exceptions" (Hewett 1981, p. 521). In the discussion of the general principles of a reform, enterprise managers and their ministries may remain silent, or even speak out in support of those principles. But when the actual decrees are issued and new procedures come into effect that tighten up expectations for the performance of individual enterprises and ministries, the pleas for exceptions begin to flow to the center. Many enterprise directors, while supporting the general principles of the reform, argue that in their particular case an exception is justified (usually the continuation of a subsidy). These battles occur in the halls of the ministries, planning authorities, party headquarters, and the like. They are not, for the most part, reported in the press; hence the difficulty for an outsider to follow them. Yet it is precisely these battles that are critical. It is not the eloquence of declared reform principles, but rather the tenacity with which they are defended in the aftermath of the declaration, that determines the ultimate fate of a reform initiative.

It is in this phase of every reform wave that it is usually compromised, with the tacit approval, or at least the conscious resignation, of political leaders. This apparent unwillingness or inability of leaders to persevere in the implementation phase is presumably one impediment to reforms.

Soviet leaders have also created problems for themselves in their almost cavalier disregard for the interconnections in the system. Historically, one of the most important interconnections that has been inadequately addressed in reform efforts in the Soviet Union has been the distribution of authority and responsibility up and down the economic hierarchy. In the 1965 reforms, the July 1979 decree, and the Gorbachev reforms one common thread is the attempt to increase both the autonomy and responsibility of enterprises (or production associations) while leaving essentially unchanged ministerial responsibility and authority. Yet the center clearly still judges ministries in terms of the collective performance of their enterprises and, of most importance, including the output of major products. In that situation the ministry is impelled to interfere in the enterprises' activities. Although the law may formally limit the number of obligatory plan indicators a ministry can impose on the enterprises under its supervision, the ministry still has considerable resources available to influence enterprise managers. On the basis of the right to hire and fire managers, set their bonuses, and offer or withhold favors, ministries can easily resort to informal means of supervising enterprise activities (for example, letters, "instructions," phone calls, and visits). The only effective way to reduce ministerial interference in enterprise decisionmaking is to change the success criteria for ministries, emphasizing aggregate measures of sectoral performance, and dropping all detailed performance criteria. That, in turn, probably means discontinuing the material balance system as it is presently operated, and a similarly dramatic change in the material-technical supply system.

The tension between the price system and the fluctuations in enterprise autonomy is another area in which insufficient attention is given to interconnections. If enterprises are given more autonomy, and incentives are structured in such a way that enterprises will seek to minimize the costs while producing goods in demand, then obviously the price system must accurately reflect the relative value to society of various products. Barring that, the enterprise is bound to go wrong, which will call forth corrections from above, which will eventually lead to a constriction of enterprise autonomy.

The leadership's failure to take interconnections in the traditional system into account seems a fairly clear impediment to the realization of reforms. This does not necessarily mean that in the Soviet Union there are no economists, including those who advise leaders, who understand the interconnections and the need to design reform programs that respect them. On the contrary, there are economists in the Soviet Union who fully understand the problem; but they, like their Western counterparts, find it difficult to push a logically coherent reform package through the bureaucratic process—now routinized—that generates reform programs.

The Management Hierarchy as a Source of Impediments

The central management hierarchy is clearly an important source of impediments to reform in the Soviet Union. I define this hierarchy to include the ministries and their intermediate authorities, the state committees, and the local party organizations (in particular the obkomy and gorkomy) that are so deeply involved in the supervision of economic activity by primary economic units and local planning authorities.

Each of the three reform efforts since 1965 has had as a major goal the reduction in arbitrary and frequent external interference by ministries and intermediate authorities in the detailed operations of enterprises. And in each case the ministries have successfully reestablished whatever powers they lost at the time the reforms were introduced. The reductions in obligatory plan indicators for enterprises introduced in 1965 were reversed by the early 1970s as the ministries reestablished their authority over enterprises. The effort, beginning in 1973, to shift some of the decisionmaking power residing in ministries and enterprises to the production associations was successfully resisted by the ministries from the beginning. The final results were little more than a formal unification of various enterprises in production associations. The 1979 reforms, with an emphasis on norms in place of detailed intervention by ministries in the affairs of enterprises, were virtually still-born due, in part, to opposition from the management hierarchy. The Gorbachev reforms are, again, seeking to reduce excessively detailed interference in enterprise operations.

This reluctance of ministries to relinquish power in part reflects a natural bureaucratic urge by each ministry to protect, and if possible expand, its authority over economic activity. That urge is surely abetted by the fact that the center has not significantly changed over time the implicit success indicators for ministries. For these two reasons, reforms—as they have historically arisen in the Soviet Union—would appear to be almost unambiguously a threat to ministries. The improved economic performance that might result from successful economic reforms could well show up in improved qualitative, but not quantitative indicators, which would be good for the economy but of little help for the ministry. Problems in economic performance stemming from difficulties in enterprises working under the new system could be blamed on the ministry. It is, therefore, no surprise that the ministerial system in the Soviet Union is an important impediment to the implementation of reforms.

Local party organizations may present similar problems. We know from the seminal work of Hough (1969), and more recent work (see Grossman 1983) that party organizations at all levels, but particularly the oblast' and city level, play a major role in resource allocation decisions. First secretaries at this level are judged by economic performance in their area. Inevitably they are drawn into solving procurement problems, lobbying for particular investments, supervising enterprises in trouble, or pushing for the fulfillment of key plan indicators at important enterprises. Local party organs are so deeply involved in the administration of the economy that national party leaders are concerned that they are neglecting political work, a concern reflected in Konstantin U. Chernenko's repeated calls for party officials to involve themselves less in the day-to-day economic affairs of enterprises in their area, leaving those activities to the local governmental authorities (the gorispolkomy and obispolkomy).[8]

Reforms that seek to enhance the autonomy of enterprises must inevitably affect the rights of party organizations to intervene in local affairs. From the local party organizations' point of view the problems are similar to those faced by ministries. If the first secretaries of the obkomy and gorkomy are to be judged after a reform by precisely the same performance criteria as before, then they have no incentive to leave things alone and see how it goes. In addition, there is good reason to believe that after years of deep involvement in enterprise affairs, party committees will find it difficult to convince themselves that it is wise to allow enterprises to operate without supervision.

All of this suggests that party committees are also a potential source of impediments to the implementation of economic reforms. However there is very little evidence on that one way or the other. Unlike the ministries, where there have been obvious cases of resistance to reform efforts, I know of no major case in which party committees have been accused of impeding the implementation of a reform program. That may simply reflect my ignorance of the right literature, but for now I leave the party committees in the category of simply a suspect.

The Population as an Impediment to Reforms

The Soviet population at large may be one of the most important sources of impediments to economic reforms, although to document that would be virtually impossible because there is very little evidence on the matter. The issue here is not so much partial reforms directed at a particular sector, or a particular characteristic of the system—although opposition from the population can arise there; rather the issue is of much more interest in the case of radical reforms.

There are only two broad groups of individuals in the Soviet Union who might feel a priori that they would have a decent chance to benefit from the introduction of a radical reform: the very young and the very old, who are primarily consumers, and not part of the active labor force;[9] and the rest of the population, the majority, for whom radical economic reforms are in each case a mixture of potentially large benefits and costs with varying degrees of uncertainty attached to them.

For the working-age population, the benefits are probably clearest for them in their role as consumers. They could legitimately expect that the quality, quantity, and assortment of consumer goods would improve dramatically. Nevertheless, even here there would be significant uncertainty on the price side, for a radical reform would mean a price system in which relative prices would change significantly at first, and frequently thereafter. Consumers in the system would trade uncertainty in consumer goods supplies for uncertainty in the price of a more certain and diverse flow of goods. Either way they face uncertainty on their real incomes, but under the reformed system they might find that uncertainty even more unsettling.[10]

But it is in the workplace that the working-age population would find life revolutionized in a reformed system. Consider the blue-collar worker first. Under the traditional system he has a guaranteed job, and can easily find another should he or his employer grow dissatisfied with the current situation. His income is predictable, very closely related to his profession, and very loosely related to his performance at work. Under the reformed system the demand for labor in the country as a whole would probably decline; and the wage spread among individuals within factories, and between factories, would dramatically increase. Workers in general would find conditions on the job more demanding. If they could not respond to those tougher conditions, they might find themselves with considerably lower earnings and in the extreme case without a job. Any general secretary who chooses to implement a reform that actually gives enterprise directors the right to hire and fire workers, and the right to freely set their wages relating to performance, will find it very tough to sell workers on the idea.

Factory managers would also in many cases have serious concerns about the consequences for them and their factory of a reform. Factories in the USSR face uncertainty in procuring productive inputs, and in the constantly changing plans they receive from above, that have both become the hallmarks of the traditional model. Managers do not like those uncertainties: they complain about them incessantly and the leadership has on several occasions sought to deal with them in the course of introducing a reform program. A radical reform would remove much of the uncertainty in those two areas. Ministries would lose their authority to control enterprise economic activities in any detail, so the uncertainty of frequent and sometimes arbitrary changes in plans would be gone. Inputs might still be difficult to procure, but an active price system would reduce shortages more quickly and efficiently than Gosplan and Gossnab ever could.

It is the new uncertainty brought about by the radical reforms that would, a priori, be of concern to enterprise managers. Under a reformed system the success of an enterprise, and possibly even its survival in its current form, would depend on a market evaluation of enterprise activities. It would no longer be a matter of satisfying a relatively small and familiar group of administrative superiors and party officials, all of whose addresses and phone numbers are in the manager's card file (if not his head). Rather it would now be a matter of satisfying thousands of customers, involving totally different approaches than the enterprise was accustomed to using. In the traditional system the plan indicators and the implicit preference of supervising authorities formed the objective function on which the manager kept his eye, all of which were only loosely linked to product quality and genuine customer satisfaction. In the new system product quality and fickle markets would be the sole determinant of success or failure.

I do not know how many factory managers and workers, if given the opportunity, would vote in favor of a radical economic reform in the Soviet Union, and obviously that opportunity is not imminent. Clearly the most competent and energetic factory managers and workers would welcome radical economic reform, and there may be many of those in the Soviet Union. On the other hand, there are two groups likely to oppose reforms. The strongest opponents will be those most clearly protected by the old system: incompetents, those who have little desire to work hard, or old workers who fear that their skills will find no application in the new system. A second, presumably larger, group would seem to be those workers who are neither the best nor the worst: they are competent and work hard enough. For them, there must be tremendous uncertainty about how they will fare under the new system. That uncertainty may cause many of them to oppose a radically reformed system, preferring the currently flawed system for one whose flaws are yet to be discovered.

Common sense, and the experience of Hungary, suggests that while it might be possible to introduce a radical reform, it would prove devilishly difficult to implement. Every factory manager would set to work on an elaborate justification for special treatment for his factory and his labor force. His gorkom or obkom first secretary would enthusiastically support him. And the arguments would frequently be compelling. As Egon Neuberger (1968) reminded us some years ago, the legacies of traditional central planning are indeed formidable, including many enterprises full of human capital that would prove useless in a market economy without retraining and physical capital that should be scrapped. The transition to a reformed system would raise difficult dilemmas for the leadership in choosing between equity and efficiency. In this situation the political leaders would be hard pressed to stick to the reform program; indeed it might be the height of political folly to do so.

Political Considerations against Economic Reform

These impediments to economic reform add up to a considerable political case against any radical reform and many possible partial reforms. Soviet socialism has at its core, in doctrine and in fact, extraordinary job security, the appearance of price stability (which is not too far from the truth) and a relatively egalitarian income distribution—at least in ruble terms. Partial reforms that might affect one or another of these three fundamental system features would change the character of socialism for the population in ways that could undermine whatever support the party has. A price reform that dramatically altered relative prices would create uncertainty about individual real incomes. A reform in the wage system in the direction of increased inequality linked to variations in individual work performances would be perceived virtually as a revolutionary change from the system now in place.

A radical reform would simultaneously threaten job security, price stability, and the income distribution, particularly during the early transition stage. As Berliner (1983, p. 372) notes, the transition to a radical model would create enormous economic rents that some firms and individuals could capture, along with the concomitant large incomes. Such disparities in income and wealth would be a political shock to a society that has grown used to relatively flat income and wealth distributions. Simultaneously with increased uncertainty about the size of their incomes, the population would also wonder about the security of their current jobs and the prices they would be facing on consumer markets. Radical reform would, for the population, be tantamount to a revolution, in this case a revolution from above.

It is possible that political leaders, if they carefully plot their strategy, can sort out ahead of time the groups who will be most opposed to the reform, the issues that are likely to be the most controversial, and diffuse both of them. This was surely one of the most interesting points of recent writings by Zaslavskaia in which she cautions her readers that successful reform (she calls it restructuring the system) ". . . is possible only on the basis of using a thought-out social strategy, which simultaneously activates the participation of the groups interested in changing the current productive relations, and blocking the actions of groups capable of interfering with those changes."[11]

But there are limits to how much political neutralizing of reforms is possible without altering the fundamental character of the reform program. A reform which seeks to harden the budget constraint for enterprises, but is implemented with so many exceptions that in fact the enterprise with the hard budget constraint is the true exception, may be politically popular. But its popularity comes at the cost of the reform itself; it becomes yet another formalistic, but essentially empty, alteration in the system. To make a radical reform politically palatable in the Soviet Union could destroy it, which is the reason that one can convincingly argue that radical reform will not soon be introduced into that system.

The Impetus for Reform

Juxtaposed with the political considerations that ultimately impede the introduction and implementation of reforms in the Soviet Union are the strong political considerations that argue for doing something. The dissatisfaction Soviet leaders have with economic performance stems from a long list of problems that have characterized Soviet economic performance over the last quarter-century: a secular decline in national income growth rates; the chronic tendency of enterprises to ignore customers' needs, and to be concerned only with the center's needs; low quality, outmoded manufactured commodities; the willingness of enterprises to accept very high production costs in the process of fulfilling output plans; the tendency toward autarky in mid-level portions of the hierarchy (departmentalism, regionalism); low rates of technical change; low labor productivity; and chronic problems in the supply of critical consumer goods (housing, food). Those familiar with the debates of the 1960s, who are also following the debates of the 1980s, will be struck by the relatively close correspondence between the basic themes in both periods.

However, the underlying issues have changed somewhat in the years since the debate leading up to the Kosygin reforms. In the first half of the 1960s GNP growth rates were averaging 5 percent per annum; in the early 1980s the average was roughly 2 percent.[12] This is consistent with trends in the rest of the developed world.[13] Nevertheless, it is worrisome to a leadership that has openly set itself a task of surpassing, rather than mimicking, the performance of Western economies.

The economy is at a significantly higher stage of development now than it was a quarter of a century ago. Per capita GNP in 1980 was 1.8 times larger than in 1960; per capita consumption was 1.6 times larger (U.S. JEC 1982, pp. 72–73). The entire system is far more complex than it was at the beginning of the 1960s. Products are more numerous and more sophisticated now than they were several decades ago. As a consequence it is increasingly difficult to control effectively production through the traditional Soviet model. The population is better educated and more sophisticated (as workers and as consumers) than it was then.

For these reasons some of the long-standing problems may seem more urgent to Soviet leaders now than in the past and some new problems are emerging. During his brief tenure in office Andropov devoted substantial attention to the economy. In the process he provided a valuable glimpse at the Politburo's views on the nature of Soviet economic problems. His first major policy speech after Brezhnev's death began with, and devoted considerable time to, a detailed discussion of economic problems. It is in that speech that he invited a full-scale debate on the economy (Andropov 1982a): "In general, comrades, there are many pressing problems in the economy. I have, to be sure, no prepared prescriptions for their resolution. But it falls to all of us—the Central Committee of the Party—to find answers. I wish to emphasize that these questions are of the highest order and of vital importance for the country. By deciding them successfully, the economy will continue to advance, and the welfare of the population will increase."

In Andropov's and Gorbachev's speeches, and in the debate on the economic system that has continued since 1983, several aspects of economic performance have clearly emerged as sources of concern to the leadership, and to the majority of economists, whatever their position might be on reforms of the economic system.

FIGURE 12.1. National Income Growth Rates in the USSR: 1960–1982

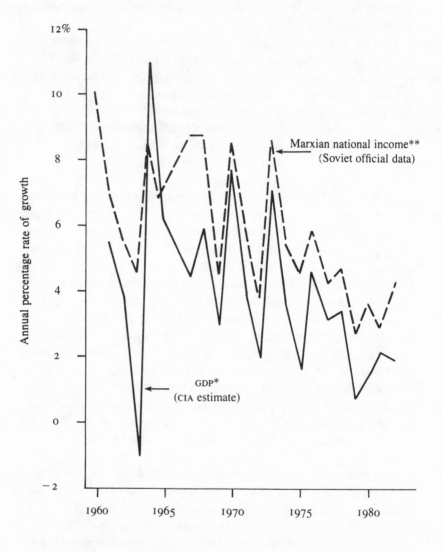

*CIA estimates of Soviet GDP growth rates, where GDP is valued at estimated factor cost. CIA, *Handbook of Economic Statistics*, various years.

**Soviet official data on the growth rate of Marxian national income, which is the value added in the production of material goods and services in support of material goods production, *less* depreciation. USSR, Central Statistical Office, *Narodnoe khoziastvo SSSR: statisticheskii ezhegodnik* (Economy of the USSR: Statistical Yearbook), various years.

Falling National Income Growth Rates

This is a long-standing theme in the list of problems with the Soviet economy, and one can understand why from the summary of growth rate trends in figure 12.1. Two data series are shown here: the CIA's estimate of Soviet GDP growth rates, weighted by estimates of 1970 factor cost; and the official Soviet data on the growth of produced national income. Both series show an unmistakable secular decline in national income growth rates. CIA estimates of the growth rates are always lower—which probably has to do primarily with the exclusion of services from the Soviet data—and sometimes differ significantly in the year-to-year trends they depict, particularly in the latter half of the 1960s. But the two data sets agree that there has been a secular decline in Soviet national income growth rates, with a very sharp dip in the 1970 to 1981 period.

Soviet leaders most frequently discuss their concern about falling growth rates in terms of falling rates of growth of labor productivity as if there were a distinction between falling national income growth rates and falling growth rates for labor productivity. But in fact when an economy is at full employment, fluctuations in national income and in labor productivity are very closely correlated. Whether one talks of national income growth rates or growth rates of labor productivity, the underlying concern of the leadership is that increases in the efficiency with which productive factors are used in the system are currently insufficient to generate the growth rates they—as politicians—are striving to achieve in order to meet important needs in defense, consumption, and investment.

Macroeconomic Imbalances

Although Soviet economists do not typically think in terms of aggregate demand and supply, it is useful to consider a number of the concerns they voice about the economy in terms of a perceived imbalance between the major components of aggregate demand and the commodity supplies available to satisfy those demands. The most visible concern here relates to a perceived imbalance between consumer incomes and the supply of consumer goods and services. These issues were discussed frequently during the latter years of the Brezhnev period and have continued to be a major theme to the present.

The general concern here is that somehow enterprises usually find a way to fulfill or over-fulfill the planned level for wage funds, even though they frequently under-fulfill output plans. In the aggregate this leads to a split between factor incomes and the value of products generated with those incomes. In the consumer goods sector in particular it is the conventional wisdom in the Soviet Union (difficult for an outsider to verify) that the incomes consumers would like to spend (in the terminology of the disequilibrium macro models, "notional" demand) considerably exceed the supply of consumer goods. This leads to inflationary pressures to which retail prices do not respond, which implies either involuntary savings or purchases of less-preferred goods.

Andropov was quite frank in his discussion of this issue, telling the workers at the Sergo Ordzhonikidze machine-building factory in Moscow during his visit there in February 1983 that "miracles, as they say, do not happen in the world. You yourselves understand that the state can provide commodities equal only to those produced" (Andropov 1983b, p. 3). What has worried the leadership for some time is that because workers are increasingly aware of the fact that the incomes they receive will be difficult to convert into goods, the incentives to work harder in order to earn bonuses are deteriorating.

The disjuncture between the aggregate demand for investment goods and the capabilities of the construction and machine building industries may be an even more serious symptom of macroeconomic imbalances. Enterprises and ministries have, to use Janos Kornai's (1980b) phrase, a virtually insatiable "investment hunger" that reflects the security they enjoy on a protected domestic market overseen by a very forgiving government hierarchy. It falls to Gosplan to curb that hunger by choosing among the far too ambitious list of project proposals that percolate up from the ministries. In 1982, to give but one example, the ministries and other departments proposed to Gosplan 2000 investment projects with a budgeted value of at least R3 million each. Gosplan's departments for the various sectors cut that to 600; a final review reduced it to 385 projects (Baryshnikov and Galakhov 1982, p. 26).

But that is only the first chapter of the story. Ministries and enterprises —veterans of this game with the center—have learned over the years to submit project proposals that significantly underestimate what they know will be the final cost of the project. After the project is accepted they gradually raise the estimated cost to what they knew all along it would be. During FYP X, when capital expenditures on projects in process rose about 1 percent per annum, their estimated costs were rising 6.9 percent per annum, which simply means that gestation periods were lengthening as the total cost of projects was revealed to the center (Kirichenko 1982, p. 63). This excess demand for investment goods appears in the system as a dispersion of the resources of the construction industries among an excessively large number of projects. That creates a strong sellers' market for construction services, machinery and equipment, and construction materials, all of which undermines measures designed to encourage those in charge of investment projects to increase pressure on contractors to finish projects on time.

Finally, it is probably the case—although it cannot be documented—that the defense sector is constantly putting demands on the economy that exacerbate disequilibria in markets for investment and consumer goods. In effect, defense is part of the general excess demand for national product, although its high priority probably means that civilian sectors bear a disproportionately large share of the burden of the disequilibrium.

One would think, in theory, that the traditional Soviet model would at least allow the center to exercise tight control over aggregate consumer incomes and aggregate investment expenditures. In fact, the center has only partial control over total wage payments, and only very weak control over the investment process. This fundamental weakness of the center in controlling aggregate demand may reflect a general characteristic of the traditional Soviet model wherever it is applied.[14]

Microeconomic Imbalances

Consumer Goods. Microeconomic imbalances in the supply of consumer goods have existed in the Soviet economy for all of its history. Two broad areas of particular concern to the leadership for obvious political reasons are food and housing. Both are highly visible and important components of living standards; and in both cases there are chronic problems. In the case of food, recent Soviet leaders have all expressed forcefully a perception that it is politically and economically important to improve the performance of the agricultural sector and the industries that produce food products. This is the purpose of the food program introduced in 1982 under Brezhnev and a subject of sustained leadership attention since then.

The chronic housing shortage is a constant concern to Soviet leaders. It is a problem that will only be resolved through commitments of new resources and innovative approaches, both of which have been under consideration for some time. Andropov (1983c, p. 4) suggested that in solving the housing problem one tactic might be to distribute new housing on the basis of workers' performance. Chernenko obviously regarded housing as one of the most important problems facing the leadership, to which he was willing to respond not only with more resources, but also with some rather startling ideas by Soviet standards (Chernenko 1984c, p. 4): "The housing problem is far from solved, and we will seek new ways to improve living conditions. This will involve not only the means of the state. Possibly it will be necessary to move more boldly in also expanding cooperative and individual bases of construction (applause)."

In addition to these large and obvious areas of concern, there are more general problems with a wide range of consumer goods and services produced in quantities or qualities insufficient to meet consumer demands. Enterprises are producing goods that allow them to fulfill the output (now sales) plan with minimum pain, irrespective of their customers' needs. Many goods produced are of such poor quality, or are otherwise so unsuitable, that the trade organizations or consumers reject them. Andropov (1984, p. 4) noted, for example, that of consumer goods intended for sale in 1984, trade organizations rejected 500,000 televisions, 115,000 radios, 250,000 cameras, 500,000 watches, and 60,000 refrigerators. Some of these amounts are surprisingly large relative to 1983 output (presumably the relevant year for comparison), representing 5.8 percent of television production, 1.2 percent for radios, 6.2 percent for cameras, 0.7 percent for watches, and 1.1 percent for refrigerators.[15] And it is likely that a significant proportion of the goods trade organizations do accept are either rejected by, or far from satisfactory for, consumers. At the same time high-quality consumer goods are in quite short supply and that, combined with the general excess demand for consumer goods, provides fertile ground for speculators.[16]

Aside from the general disequilibrium in consumer goods' markets, the fact that many of the goods produced are unacceptable to consumers is yet another factor weakening the impact of bonuses offered to workers in exchange for a greater quantity or quality of work effort. Although numerous measures have been introduced to improve the quality and quantity of consumer goods, it is clear that there are no quick fixes. And as Soviet consumers grow more sophisticated, so do their quality demands, a point about which the current leadership is well aware.[17]

There is a circular relationship here that complicates matters. One of the reasons for inadequate consumer goods' supplies is poor incentives for workers to work harder and better than they do now. Yet the difficulty with improving incentives for workers is that the deficits on consumer goods' markets weaken the effectiveness of financial bonuses as an incentive to work harder. Possibly it was the difficulty of this problem that led Andropov to indicate that it would be sensible to link the distribution of apartments—the most obvious example of a consumer good in short supply—to how a person works at his or her job (Andropov 1983c, p. 4).

But that is a one-time shot that will not solve the need for incentives capable of eliciting a sustained improvement to the quality and quantity of the labor input. The long-term fix will have to address the supply of consumer goods as a whole.

Material Inputs and Intermediate Products. Intra-enterprise economic relations are also characterized by widespread imbalances, and these have probably grown more severe since the mid-1970s. There are the well-known problems with shortages of steel; shortages of some forms of energy; many bottlenecks in transport, especially railroads; and a general shortage of labor. All of these shortages seem to lead to a considerable, and growing amount of unused industrial capacity (Rumer 1982; and Andropov 1984).

Unlike the microeconomic disequilibria in the consumer goods' market, there seems to be a consensus among Soviet economists and the leadership that the problem here is more on the demand than the supply side. As R. S. Belousov (of the Central Committee's Academy of the Social Sciences) noted at a recent debate on the economic system, the problem is not insufficient production of metal, coal, gas, and so on. The problem "first of all, is the low efficiency in the utilization of those resources, which is manifested in the very high norms for expenditures on final production . . ." (Belousov 1983, p. 23).

Excessively High Input Demands

In part, this phenomenon is considered a major source of microeconomic imbalances. Enterprises' well-known propensity to hoard labor has led to labor shortages that in turn lead to new factories operating at under full capacity due to insufficient labor supplies. This is an economy that produces and uses an extraordinary amount of steel per dollar of GNP, which leads one to suspect that it is high demands for steel rather than inadequate steel supplies that explain recent shortages in that sector.

Nevertheless, the input demands are also an issue in their own right. The problem that has increasingly come to concern Soviet leaders is that, even in areas in which there are no current shortages, the investment requirements associated with maintaining (and in many cases increasing) supplies of raw materials and energy are growing much more rapidly than total investment resources available for the economy. This constrains investment in other sectors, and ultimately constrains the growth of per capita consumption.

The energy sector provides an excellent example here as a major, although not the only, source of concern to the leadership. During 1976–80, in comparison to 1971–75, investment in the economy rose by 29 percent, while investments for fuels rose 47 percent; and investment expenditures on oil and gas pipeline construction rose 135 percent. Energy production rose at 4.2 percent per annum during 1976–80, down from 5 percent per annum in 1971–75 (Hewett 1984b, table 4.8).

For 1981–85, when total investments grew at half the rate of 1976–80 (18 percent in 1981–85 relative to 1976–80), and investments in industry rose 20 percent, investments in energy rose 45 percent. The result was that energy, which accounted for 13 percent of total investment during 1981–85, took 27 percent of the increment to investment during that period. Yet, even with that high priority, total energy production grew 2.4 percent per annum, down from 4.2 percent in the preceding five-year plan (*Narkhoz* 1985, pp. 53, 364, 367).

These are disturbing trends for the leadership. Energy production growth rates are falling rapidly despite very generous investments. Meanwhile investments in other sectors (including presumably parts of industry) are growing very slowly; and in some sectors investments must be falling (schools, roads, housing, and service establishments are all likely candidates).

Similar trends are appearing in other sectors supplying the system with the raw materials. The general problem is that for all primary products and fuels, increasing investments are necessary simply to *maintain* output as the quality of mineral and fuel deposits falls, and as their distance from the center of industrial activity rises. And the front-end investment costs associated with sustaining or increasing output of those goods is probably rising even more rapidly than total marginal cost, an important point for a country that accepts no direct foreign investment, and that makes light use of world capital markets. It is for this reason that the excessively high demands for inputs have become a major concern of the leadership.

Low Rates of Technical Innovation

In the traditional Soviet system enterprises have little incentive to introduce innovations, either in the production processes they utilize, or in the products they produce (the two are frequently inseparable). In an economy in which the growth rates of both the labor force and the capital stock are falling, it is only through technical change that national income growth rates can be sustained at historical levels. Furthermore, many of the microeconomic imbalances are in reality excess supplies of low-quality goods, alongside excess demands for higher quality goods, and technical change is the major means by which that problem will be resolved.

Inter-Connections

These problem areas represent the major ways in which the performance of the economy has been a disappointment to Soviet leaders. They are interconnected: slow growth is explained by the existence of the other four factors; and each of those last four factors serves as one explanation for the existence of the other three.

It is tempting to summarize the concerns of the Soviet leadership by combining all of them into a concern about growth rates (whether of national income or labor productivity), but that would be an oversimplification. Two other themes emerge frequently in discussion of concerns over economic performance. First, there is the chronic tendency of Soviet enterprises to produce manufactured goods that are not only way below quality norms established by manufacturers in Western countries, but even way below the minimal standards of potential Soviet purchasers of the products. If the Soviet economy could achieve a perceptible increase in the quality of manufactured goods' output, even without any change in the output growth rates, Soviet leaders would probably consider that an improvement in economic performance. If the quality improvements came in consumer goods, then consumer satisfaction would rise, an important political consideration. And quality improvements in goods produced for industrial use would aid technical progress, and therefore support further quality improvement, as well

—possibly—as increases in manufactured goods' exports. These latter developments should eventually influence growth rates, but that would not occur immediately.

Second, there is the much broader issue, which lies underneath several of the concerns listed above, that in the traditional Soviet model the attempt to centrally monitor and control much of economic activity can result in the absence of the effective control over the variables of most importance to planners. It is rather extraordinary that in a Western economy with a well-coordinated fiscal and monetary policy, the resulting control over the level of investment is probably far more effective than it is in the centrally planned economy in which planners attempt —and fail—to control every single investment project. If Soviet leaders could enhance their control over the system—even without immediately achieving an increase in growth rates—they would surely regard that as an improvement in the performance of the system.

The System and Economic Performance Problems

The performance of any economy is the outcome of interaction among exogenous, systemic, and policy factors. It is important in analyzing the performance problems discussed above to try to sort out which factors might play the most prominent role in which problems, and for two reasons. Falling growth rates in the Soviet Union certainly reflect in part the natural effects of diminishing returns and a population growth slowdown that might have occurred no matter what type of economic system was allocating resources in that country. If exogenous factors are the major reason for the growth slowdown, then reforms offer no quick panacea, although they might moderate the rate of decline.

Furthermore, if, say, insufficient investment allocations are an important contributor to the housing problem, then that is a matter that a policy change could address without any reforms. That is not to say that reforms in the construction industry would not also improve matters, but they are not the only way in which leaders could improve performance.

In order to think as carefully as possible about the evolution of the economic system over the rest of this century—and the options Soviet leaders have—it is useful to at least try to form an impression of the relative importance of systemic, policy, and exogenous factors in each of the economic performance problems outlined above. Any rigorous treatment of this issue would require a separate paper; and this is only intended to sketch the broad outlines of what the answer might look like.

Declining Growth Rates. Exogenous factors obviously played a major role in the decline in growth rates. Increasing factor costs in extractive industries must explain a significant proportion of the fall in factor productivity in the Soviet Union in the last two decades. Falling population growth rates, and the fact that a significant proportion of additions to the labor force are concentrated in areas with relatively little industry and infrastructure, also were a factor.

Not all the exogenous factors were negative. The windfall terms of trade gains of the 1970s allowed the Soviet Union to import machinery, equipment, and food worth several tens of billions of dollars gratis, without having to export a single ruble's worth of national income (Hewett 1983). That in itself must have had some positive effect on growth rates.

These exogenous factors aside, a good case can be made for the significant contribution of the system and economic policy to the slowdown in economic growth, resulting from the way they have dealt with deteriorating exogenous factors. Because this system exerts virtually no pressure on enterprises to economize on inputs, the growth of economic activity in the Soviet Union has been associated with a disproportionately higher growth rate in the demand for, and therefore the production of, raw materials and fuels. This is obviously the case with fuels. In 1980 the Soviet Union consumed 2.5 times the amount of energy per dollar of GNP as was consumed in the EEC. Its energy/GNP elasticity stayed well above unity in the 1970s when Western countries were showing elasticities well below one-half (Hewett 1984b, chapter 3). It can surely also be documented for key raw materials and semifabricates. It is no longer a source of pride, and rightly so, to the Soviet leadership that the Soviet Union is the largest producer of steel in the world.

This tendency toward excess consumption of key raw materials and fuels has accelerated the shift eastward in the production of those commodities, which in turn has accelerated the rate at which returns have diminished in extractive industries. That is certainly a contributing factor to the growth rate slowdown.

A second way in which the system may contribute to the growth rate slowdown is through the link between consumer goods' supplies and labor productivity. Since the second half of the 1970s the Soviet leadership has shown a consistent concern that inadequate consumer goods' supplies were partly responsible for the low and falling growth rates of labor productivity. To the extent that is true, these particular imbalances may be contributing to the growth rate slowdown, although to substantiate that, one would have to show that the shortages had grown worse in the last decade and a half (likely, because of the growing sophistication of consumers), or that workers had become more attuned to the problem of converting their wages to goods (unlikely).

Other microeconomic imbalances may also have contributed to the growth rate slowdown, particularly in the late 1970s. Bottlenecks in transportation, steel, and energy supplies are all likely candidates for causes of the growth slowdown in the second half of the 1970s, and all are reflections of problems in the system.

The contributions of policy to the growth rate slowdown are less easy to trace, but no less real. The policy emphasizing investment in energy has diverted investment from other sectors where capital productivity was far more favorable and would probably have contributed to a more rapid growth of GNP (not only because of differences in capital productivity, but also because of longer lags in the energy sector). Even with the system and exogenous factors constant, this investment policy is itself contributing to the slowdown in growth.[18]

There are many other ways in which policy decisions may have had an effect on growth rates. In fact most major policy decisions by Soviet leaders should have some growth rate implications. But the point has been made, and I will not pursue it further here.

Macroeconomic Imbalances

Where there are macroeconomic imbalances, system and policy seem to share the credit. It is surely the fault of the system that enterprises feel unconstrained in their demands for new capital. Considerably harder budget constraints that would automatically come through economic reforms are the logical panacea here. The same is true of the excess demand for consumer goods. Enterprises, again because of soft budget constraints, are perfectly happy to pay workers whether or not their products are salable.

It is important, nevertheless, to keep in mind the possible role of policy here. The decision by Soviet leaders to give defense industries a very high priority and heavy industry the next highest priority has in itself, independently of problems generated by the system, contributed to macroeconomic imbalances in consumer goods' production. And the mismatch between real wages and available consumer goods' supplies in part reflects a primarily political decision by Soviet leaders that nominal wages, but not prices, will rise.

Microeconomic Imbalances

Here, also, system and policy both play a role. The system is primarily responsible for the low quality of many consumer goods and services. Aside from the charitable inclinations of selected enterprise directors, there is no reason to expect enterprises in this system to be overly concerned about satisfying their customers. The same applies to the quantity of consumer goods, and the mix.

Still, policy considerations are potentially important here also. Low-quality consumer goods may in part reflect the low priority for light industry in materials acquisition, the relatively low wages paid—as a matter of policy—to workers in light industry, and the scarcity of capital needed for innovation in processes and products. Clearly in an area such as housing, where there is direct competition between resources devoted to housing and resources devoted to other investment projects, the policy on dividing those resources is an important determinant of the final outcome, regardless of the nature of the system.

High Demand for Inputs and Low Rate of Technical Change. Here the system would seem to be the major, almost the sole, source of the problem. In the case of input demands it is primarily the soft budget constraint for the enterprise that permits, even encourages it to pay scant attention to the costs of production. The excessive use of steel, of other raw materials, and of energy are among the hallmarks of the traditional model and a direct result of the incentives embedded in the core of the model.

Low rates of technical change are likewise directly attributable to the system. This is a system that discourages innovation, not as a matter of policy (on the contrary), but as an outcome of the system itself. "Why are the achievements of science and technology introduced into production at an unsatisfactory rate?" asked Andropov. Because "first of all . . . our work directed at improving and restructuring of the economic mechanism, forms and methods of management, lagged behind the demand inherent in the achieved level of material-technical, social, and spiritual development of Soviet society" (Andropov 1983a, p. 13).

THE SOVIET ECONOMIC SYSTEM
AT THE END OF THE CENTURY

Can the next fifteen years be a replay of the last fifteen? Is it possible that in the year 2000 the Soviet economic system will, in its essentials, resemble today's system? And if that is the case, how will the system be performing in the problem areas discussed above?

The exogenous variables with a major role in determining Soviet economic performance are likely to deteriorate for the rest of this century relative to the preceding several decades. Labor force growth rates will continue to fall. The costs of raw materials and fuels' extraction will continue to rise. What will happen to Soviet terms of trade is difficult to predict. However, a prudent Soviet planner would not count on terms of trade in the rest of this century any better than the Soviet Union had in the 1970s.

The international political environment would also seem to be deteriorating, at least in ways of importance to the Soviet economy. Another round of the arms race—very likely even if U.S.-Soviet relations improve—means continued high demands on the economy to support modernization and innovation in Soviet military capacities. Eastern Europe's economic future is sufficiently unpromising that at the very least the Soviet leaders will probably find it difficult to decrease subsidies to its allies, and it may face difficult choices in which it either increases subsidies, or takes its chances on East European economic and political instability.

The preferences of the population itself are in some ways an exogenous variable for the system, and one whose development is increasing the tasks the system must resolve. The educational level, sophistication, and living standards of Soviet citizens continue to rise, and so also would one expect a constant rise in citizens' standards regarding the performance of the system.

All of these exogenous variables are moving in a direction that challenges the ability of the system to cope. The system is operating on a moving target; and an unchanged system working on steadily deteriorating exogenous variables is hardly a system with a bright future.

The critical question is whether Soviet leaders have reached the limits of the traditional model. Is it now the case that they have exhausted all of the potentially effective partial reforms and policy changes available to them, and that their only options in the face of deteriorating exogenous factors are to change the system, or do nothing, which would threaten the very foundations of their power trying to defend it. We can count on Soviet leaders to search for new reforms and policy changes. But will they look in the right places, and is there anything there to find?

I think they may well look in the right places and also that there may be something there. Andropov's fifteen months in office provide interesting, although hardly unambiguous, testimony on this. During that short time there were no reforms in the system, but there were some policy changes. Most notably Andropov began the process of bringing new, younger people into positions of power in the administrative apparatus; and he instituted a serious discipline campaign. Both obviously had a positive effect on the morale of the population, and it is not implausible to argue that some of the growth rate acceleration of 1983–84 reflects positive results of those policies.

Now Mikhail Gorbachev has moved ahead in the same tradition. Generational change moves rapidly as he presses forward with a campaign to enhance discipline and streamline the bureaucracy. What long-term effects these measures may have is hard to say, but it does seem worth considering that by merely revitalizing the leading cadre of the Soviet economy even the traditional model could work better.

There are also ways in which new policies could act to slow the decline in growth rates. Even within the traditional system, a serious commitment to increased energy conservation (backed by new investment funds available for energy-saving technologies and a firm commitment by planners and the party), combined with a decline in investments in energy production, could have positive effects on the growth rate (Hewett 1984c). To the extent the housing problem is one of investment priorities, the old system could implement new priorities and increase the rate at which apartments are added to the stock. The food program, now in its third year, is more policy than system change, and may bring some improvement in agricultural performance.

Each of these possibilities has two things in common. They do not require any change in the system. And political leaders are fully aware the possibilities exist.

There are also partial reforms that might work, and that could be designed in a way to limit contradictions with the traditional system. The Shchekino method is a good illustration. By giving enterprise directors more authority over how they manage their labor force and what they pay them, incentives are strengthened to economize on labor and as a result effective labor supplies would expand. To be sure, this would have to be handled very carefully vis-à-vis local party organizations (which could be counted on to effectively represent workers' interests) and the ministries. But the experiments here suggest that this is a workable approach, and Gorbachev's reforms are carrying the conditions of the experiment to all of industry. Brigade methods for organizing labor, if handled properly (*and not formalistically*) hold similar promise.[19]

A vigorous leadership, bent on exploring possibilities for policy changes and partial reform that would retain the essentials of the system but improve its operation has, it seems to me, a chance of a perceptible improvement in performance. It would be nothing spectacular, but possibly enough to muddle through.

If this indeed occurs, then fifteen years from now the system will look much as it does today, differing only in matters of policy and possibly some systemic features that are not fundamental to the system. It is conceivable that under this scenario, performance would stabilize and not continue to deteriorate; depending on the policy decisions, some of the microeconomic imbalances could be substantially narrowed (food and housing). There would still most likely be chronic problems in the supply of high quality manufactured goods that would still be below what planners desired. But it would be turning in an acceptable performance, comparable to that of the mid-1980s.

But suppose that developments are not so favorable, and that economic performance continues to deteriorate, possibly with negative national income growth rates in some years (although it is hard to see how that could consistently happen with a growing labor force and growing capital stock, however slowly both may be growing). Is that a politically acceptable outcome for the population? No one really knows. Growth rates in the late 1970s and early 1980s were very low in the Soviet Union, low enough that it would have been reasonable to expect some political signals from the population. Yet nothing of the sort occurred. It is possible that the Soviet consumer, already exhibiting his patience, still has reserves there, particularly if the leadership exploits them with skillful use of real or imagined external threats. But it is unlikely that Soviet leaders want to test the patience of their population in this way, which is why they can be counted on to search for ways to invigorate the old system.

All of this suggests that it is certainly possible that at the end of the century the Soviet system will be much as it is today. It might even be the most likely outcome. To say something more precise it would be necessary to actually try to connect up the major possibilities for partial reform and policy change with economic performance possibilities. This is beyond what I was able to do for this essay, so I leave it in this vague formulation.

CHAPTER 13

Economic Reform and Foreign Trade in Poland

Urszula Plowiec

For a medium-sized country such as Poland the foreign sector plays a critical role in the broader process of economic development. This essay examines in some detail the evolution, over the past thirty-five years, of the relationship between the Polish economic system and the development of Polish foreign trade.

The first section of the paper briefly considers three relatively distinct periods in Polish economic history: (1) a period of relatively centralized planning and management (1950–65), when the basic institutions of the Polish foreign trade system were set into place; (2) the years 1966–70, which were characterized by several partial improvements in the foreign trade system; and (3) the period 1971–81, which witnessed the partial implementation of various parametric methods of management in the Polish economy and in foreign trade.

The economic crisis that engulfed the Polish economy in the late 1970s spurred a widespread discussion of the need for further reform of the Polish economic system. In the second section of the essay some of the more striking effects of the crisis on Poland's external economic relations are briefly reviewed. This is followed by a discussion of the basic principles of the Polish economic reform blueprint that was worked out in the course of 1980–81 and legislated in 1981–82.

The implementation of the economic reform through 1985, its implications for Polish foreign trade in that period, and the prospects for the future, are discussed in some detail in section 3.

1. CENTRAL PLANNING AND PARTIAL REFORM, 1950–1981

Strict Methods of Central Planning and Management, 1950–1965

A system of central planning and management of the Polish economy and Polish foreign trade had been shaped by the end of the 1940s. In 1949 the Ministry of Foreign Trade (MFT) was established and all state-owned foreign trade organizations were to be subordinated to it. Beginning in 1950 central plans for foreign trade were worked out and specified as directives for the different branch ministries, the obligatory branch associations, and, as worked out by the MFT, for the individual foreign trade organizations (FTOS). The FTO directives were broken down by country and commodity, and were expressed in terms of physical units. Quarterly plans were also elaborated. At that time all the efficiency calculations regarding foreign trade were made at the central level.[1]

Under the reform of the monetary system in October 1950 the value of the Polish zloty was established at 0.222168 grams of pure gold. This in effect pegged the zloty, given the existing gold parity of the dollar, at 4.0 zlotys per dollar. This official or external exchange rate, however, was not related to the real domestic zloty cost of acquiring dollars through exports. Foreign trade prices converted into zlotys therefore had no economic meaning, and domestic producers therefore had no need to know these prices.

The FTOS operated as buyers or sellers for their own accounts. They bought commodities for export and sold imported goods domestically at fixed domestic prices. The differences between these domestic wholesale prices and the foreign trade prices converted into *deviza*, or external zlotys, were automatically subsidized (taxed) by the state budget by the "special account of budget differences." The FTOS were therefore directly accountable financially to the budget, although their commissions were determined by the MFT as a percentage of their foreign trade turnover. Under this system foreign trade transactions had no direct influence on either domestic producers or users of goods produced abroad. Foreign trade was carried out by a small number of FTOS (as few as twenty at one point). The range of products traded by each was strictly determined, and as a rule, export and import activities within an FTO were strictly separated. This system essentially reduced the role of foreign trade to importing those goods deemed necessary for fulfilling the central plans, and to exporting usually "forced" surpluses in order to pay for these imports. The cold war climate prevailing at the time reinforced this tendency toward autarky, at least insofar as trade with the convertible currency area was concerned.

There was some relaxation in this system in the late 1950s and early 1960s. At the same time that foreign trade developed at a faster pace, some branch committees were formed that brought together FTO and industrial managers, and some industrial enterprises and cooperatives obtained licenses to carry out export operations. During this period some new coefficients of export efficiency, based on various "partial" criteria, were established as obligatory analytical instruments. These coefficients included the financial indicator of export efficiency (KWF), which compared the foreign and domestic prices of exported goods; the last-phase export efficiency coefficient (KWN), which compared the cost of processing of a given product, expressed in zloty, with the net price in foreign currency; and the coefficient of material intensity for exported goods (Trzeciakowski 1978, pp. 41–47). These coefficients had the common feature of circumventing the distorting effects of the official, or deviza exchange rate, by comparing world market prices directly with domestic prices or costs.

Beginning in 1959 a new price coefficient was used in foreign trade, based on the average zloty cost of acquiring dollars through exporting. This coefficient, set at twenty-four domestic zlotys per deviza zloty, affected the size of the so-called budgetary differences for particular FTOS, but it did not influence any other sector of the economy.

*Partial Reform of the Foreign Trade
System, 1966–1970*

The second half of the 1960s saw more significant, although still only partial, improvements in the Polish foreign trade system. The need for these changes became increasingly apparent as the number of items traded rose, and the share of processed goods in exports and the number of trade partners also increased. Beginning in January 1966 the central foreign trade plans were expressed in deviza zlotys rather than in physical units. The branch ministries and the MFT became responsible for plan fulfillment. This increased the latitude for decisionmaking among the industrial enterprises and the FTOs, but it also increased the role played by the branch ministries in foreign trade.

With this greater freedom for decisionmaking, the enterprises and FTOs needed some criteria for making rational decisions. It was at this time that the current export efficiency calculus was first used. Beginning in July 1966 enterprises were expected to optimize their shadow profit in the export of processed goods using calculated shadow exchange rates, shadow export prices, and shadow costs. The optimization process was based on the construction of comprehensive models, encompassing both exports and imports, and deriving from the global plan model (Trzeciakowski 1978, chapters 6–8, 9–12). The necessity for calculating these shadow profits arose from the distorted system of producer prices: it was realized that the above-mentioned efficiency coefficients could no longer be used, if the interests of the enterprises were to be coordinated with those of the economy as a whole.

A special fund, derived from the central budget, was formed as a percentage of shadow profit and used to stimulate producers and exporting enterprises to obtain higher export prices and to reduce domestic costs. Producers and their subcontractors participated in 95 percent of this fund, while FTOs obtained the remaining 5 percent.

This export efficiency calculus and the system of rewards based on shadow, or "constructed," profit demonstrated that despite the passive financial system, and the organizational separation of producers from exporters, there were strong economic links between them. Because any two partners were assigned to one another, the producer and exporting enterprise found they had a common interest in attempting to optimize exports, in terms of both country and commodity composition. This experiment also showed, however, that an economic calculus based on prices not used in the actual financial settlement between producers and exporters could only be a temporary expedient. The coexistence of two parallel price systems could not be maintained. By the end of the 1960s enterprises allegedly were seeking to maximize calculated profits by reducing calculated costs of export production through an understatement of the corrective coefficients applied to producer prices.

The second half of the 1960s also witnessed the use of a shadow exchange rate and actual foreign currency prices to determine the financial (not just the constructed) results of two large industrial associations that grouped together the pharmaceutical and shipbuilding enterprises respectively. These profits directly affected employee remuneration and allocations to investment funds in these industries. These experiments also provided the opportunity to evaluate the actual merits of alternative enterprise taxation schemes (Trzeciakowski 1978, pp. 172–82). Nevertheless, they also showed the necessity of ensuring the connection between the financial system and a system of calculated prices, and also the tendency of such pilot industries to become export enclaves, rather than integral connections between the domestic and foreign market.

One achievement of this period was the general acceptance of the use of shadow exchange rates for both the convertible and clearing-agreement trading areas. The differences in the shadow exchange rates between the two currency areas did not correspond to the differences in the deviza zloty price of the dollar and transferable ruble (TR), respectively. In general, the domestic zloty cost of one dollar, relative to the domestic zloty cost of one TR, was determined by three factors: (1) the different commodity structure of Polish exports to the two areas, (2) the different price structures prevailing on the two markets, and (3) the inconvertibility of the TR. It should also be mentioned that the shadow exchange rates used in this period had a submarginal character; that is, they were below the marginal rates that would have equalized imports from and exports to the respective currency zones. The marginal rate was rejected mainly because of the conviction that it reflected the costs of incidental, rather than basic transactions. In any event, use of the submarginal rates permitted, to a large extent, the optimization of exports.[2]

Partial Implementation of Parametric Methods, 1971–1981

By the beginning of the 1970s there was already the quite common conviction in Poland that the sources of extensive growth were exhausted, that the economy could gradually be shifted to an intensive development strategy, and that the latter would be facilitated by a more rational development of foreign trade. The transition from extensive to intensive growth, however, required a consumer-oriented strategy and, as was later demonstrated, really substantial changes in the way the entire economy functioned.

As a result of political changes in 1970–71, only two of the major modifications in the foreign trade system that had been envisioned actually materialized. The first change involved the introduction of "transaction" prices into the foreign trade sphere. These prices, which were expressed in zloty by multiplying foreign currency prices by the appropriate coefficients, replaced the previous fixed domestic prices in the financial settlements between producers and importers or exporters. These coefficients were in effect submarginal exchange rates based on the domestic cost of exports. During the 1970s nearly all exports were realized on the account of producers, but were actually sold by the FTOs on a commission basis. Thus the producers had an interest in directly comparing domestic and transaction prices. Imports, with the exception of fuels and basic raw materials, were now sold by the FTOs to domestic producers and other users on the basis of transaction prices that fluctuated with changes in foreign currency prices. The import prices of consumer products and other processed goods, however, were also subjected to turnover taxes and, beginning in 1976, to import duties.

The domestic prices of fuels and basic raw materials were fixed for the periods 1971–75 and 1976–81. These products were therefore subject to price distortions that tended to increase in the course of these five-year periods. This insulation of domestic users of imported raw materials and fuels from the influence of changing world market prices made it more difficult to adjust to the explosion in world energy prices. In response, the government required these users to employ shadow price techniques in their production, investment, and trade decisions; a windfall profits tax on exports based on these subsidized imports was also imposed.

Although export profits had a parametric character, in that they were based in part on transaction prices, profits from domestic sales of domestic output were calculated at producer prices that were shaped according to a cost-plus formula. Yet both sources of profits were added together in the calculation of an enterprise's overall profit, on which employees' remuneration was partially based. In effect, this meant that there were disincentives for exports, because it was easier to increase profits by sales on internal markets subject to excess demand than by increasing exports on highly competitive foreign markets. As a result, export growth took place mainly on the basis of central directives that were expressed in terms of deviza zlotys.

The second major change involved the organization of foreign trade. In the original reform blueprints worked out in the late 1960s large or specialized industrial firms were to have acquired direct foreign trading rights. It was thought that by setting up their own export activities these firms would be better able to adjust to the special and changing requirements of foreign buyers of processed goods. In the new socioeconomic reality that emerged at the beginning of the 1970s, and particularly as a result of the growing importance of industrial lobbies in Poland, the branch ministries were able to acquire twenty-five of the forty FTOs, including most of those dealing with processed goods. These twenty-five FTOs accounted for 60 percent of foreign trade turnover in 1971. Although the administrative supervision over many FTOs was changed, producers were once again separated from foreign buyers.

The opinion that came to prevail in Poland was that changes in the economic mechanism should be introduced only step by step. An important change was the replacement of "gross" measures of enterprise evaluation, such as the value of sold production in domestic prices, by "net" measures such as the volume or rate of profit. Indeed, it had been demonstrated theoretically that, using the model of current optimization of the economy, realization of final demand at minimum cost is equivalent to using a partial criterion of profit maximization (Trzeciakowski 1978, chapter 6). Only under special circumstances would maximization of value added yield results equivalent to profit maximization. In practice, however, it was decided that industrial enterprises should maximize value added, as this was seen as parallel to the concept of national income. The theoreticians recognized that this value-added criterion was not perfect, but it was nevertheless viewed as superior to a gross measure.

In 1973 the WOGs, of "large economic organizations," each of which included a number of industrial plants, began to shift to the value-added maximization criterion. Both the wage and salaries fund and the investment fund depended on value added (Gliński 1973). The WOGs therefore had more autonomy with respect to setting wages and salaries than did other industrial units. They soon encountered various difficulties, however, both in dealing with partner organizations that still operated on the basis of incentive-passive principles, and with their superior ministries that still relied primarily on plan directives. The predominance of the annual plans gradually weakened the incentive-active principles of the WOGs and at the end of 1975 this innovation was discontinued. Certain FTOs, trading in chemicals, industrial plants, aircraft, and nonferrous metals, had also been operating on the incentive-active principles, but after some years they shared the fate of the WOGs.

These changes in the incentive mechanism were only partial in nature and this, together with the reversion to previous economic policies, represented a major shortcoming of the management system in foreign trade in the 1970s. Moreover, the export incentives were relatively weak and there was a lack of progress in rationalizing the structure of imports. The exchange rate policy, and therefore the structure of transaction prices, was inflexible and inadequately reflected the changing situation in foreign trade. Whatever changes in transaction prices that did occur did not affect the value of sold production (expressed in domestic wholesale prices) that was the main success indicator for most industrial firms. The impact of transactional pricing on the structure of production and domestic prices was therefore negligible, or at best delayed.

By the end of the decade it was clear to most economists that partial reforms of the late 1960s and early 1970s had not been successful. The rich experience of this period had demonstrated that experiments targeted only for individual sectors of the economy (whether in foreign trade in 1966–70, in the pharmaceutical and shipbuilding sectors in 1967–70, or the WOGs in 1973–75) were only condemned to failure if the rest of the economy continued to function under the old incentive-passive system. Sooner or later the system of central directives would reassert itself because every economic system has its own logic and inertia. Small changes in the economic mechanism can only be effective temporarily. Indeed, they may help foster the illusion that the economy is functioning in a better way, when in fact its management is deteriorating. By the late 1970s and early 1980s, and especially in 1980–81, intensive efforts were resumed to draw up a plan of comprehensive reform for the Polish economy.

2. THE POLISH ECONOMIC REFORM BLUEPRINT

The Impulse for Reform

The direct impulse for accelerated efforts at formulating a comprehensive economic reform was of course the economic crisis that had

TABLE 13.1. Main Indicators of the Polish Economy,
1971–85 (Percentage change from preceding year
at constant prices)

	1971	1972	1973	1974	1975	1976	1977
National income (generated)	8.1	10.6	10.8	10.4	9.0	6.8	5.0
National income (distributed)	9.8	12.7	14.3	12.1	10.9	7.0	2.7
Output of socialized industry	8.8	10.2	11.0	11.3	11.0	8.3	6.3
Total agricultural production	3.6	8.4	7.3	1.6	−2.1	−1.1	1.4
Exports	6.2	15.5	11.6	12.3	8.3	4.4	8.0
Imports	14.0	21.8	22.8	14.9	4.4	9.6	−0.1
Social productivity of labor^a	6.9	8.6	9.0	8.2	8.3	7.7	5.0
Productivity of fixed capital^b	1.8	3.8	3.0	1.0	−1.1	−2.6	−4.3
Technical equipment of labor^c	4.9	4.6	5.9	7.1	9.4	10.6	9.7

SOURCE: 1971–1980: Rzadowy Raport o Stanie Gospodarki published by *Trybuna Ludu*, July
1981, table 1; 1981–1985: own accounts on the basis of data published in *Rocznik Statystyczny
1985*, table 105, and *Rocznik Statystyczny 1986*.

engulfed Poland by the end of the 1970s, and that was soon transformed into a political and social crisis. The essence of this crisis was
the growing disproportion between the objective potential of the Polish
economy (large industry, abundant raw materials, a large and highly
qualified labor force) and its low level of efficiency. In the 1970s the
productivity of Polish labor amounted to no more than 25–30 percent
of that of the industrialized nonsocialist countries. Living standards
remained relatively low and did not match either the objective possibilities or the aspirations of Polish society. This in turn caused rising
tensions, conflicts, and the political-social crisis.

These difficulties resulted above all from the failure of the Polish
economy to create sufficient incentives for efficient work and the full
utilization of the factors of production. Moreover, the economic system
did not ensure employees the satisfaction of participation in management; this was particularly important for the more ambitious and creative individuals. The system was rigid, bureaucratic, and steered largely
by means of administrative orders and prohibitions. It led to a waste of
human energy and the absence of initiative.

These problems were reflected in the substantial deterioration of the
main economic indicators, particularly in the latter half of the 1970s.
(See table 13.1) After peaking in 1973, the growth rate of the social

1978	1979	1980	1981	1982	1983	1984	1985
3.0	−2.3	−5.4	−12.0	−5.5	6.0	5.6	3.4
0.7	−3.4	−5.9	−10.5	−10.5	5.6	5.0	3.8
3.6	1.9	−1.2	−11.4	−2.5	6.2	4.9	4.1
4.1	−1.5	−10.7	4.0	−2.9	3.3	5.6	0.8
5.7	6.8	−4.2	−19.0	8.7	10.3	9.5	1.3
1.5	−0.9	−1.7	−16.9	−13.7	5.2	8.6	7.9
3.3	−1.5	−4.0	−11.8	−2.4	6.8	5.7	NA
−5.6	−9.6	−11.0	−15.0	−7.2	3.4	2.8	NA
9.5	8.9	8.0	3.7	5.2	3.3	2.4	NA

[a] Value of national income (generated) per capita of employee.
[b] Value of national income (generated) per zloty of fixed capital.
[c] Value of fixed capital per employee.

productivity of labor (the value of national income produced per capita) continuously declined and turned negative in 1979. This happened despite the rapid growth of the capital stock—the value of fixed capital per employee grew at an increasing rate in the first half of the 1970s, peaking in 1976 but it was still growing at a rate of almost 10 percent a year as late as 1978. This was linked, of course, to the buildup in debt to the West. The rate of growth of productivity of fixed capital became negative in 1975 and declined at a greater rate each year thereafter. By 1981 the amount of unfinished construction was so large that if it were all to be completed, it would consume the total planned investment outlays of the 1980s. The experience of the 1970s conclusively proves that a policy of rapid investment growth cannot be an adequate substitute for economic reform.

In 1981 the economic situation continued to deteriorate, accompanied by a spiraling inflation. The agreements signed on the Baltic Coast and in Silesia between the workers and the government envisioned a rise of nominal wages in circumstances that actually suggested the need for their reduction. It was estimated that only 80 percent of the population's money incomes could be met with supplies of consumer goods at the then prevailing prices. These prices that were arbitrarily fixed and left unchanged for years required huge budget subsidies and failed to

TABLE 13.2. Polish Debt and Debt Service, 1971–84
(in Billions of U.S. Dollars)

	1971	1972	1973	1974	1975
Exports to market-economy countries	1.5	1.8	2.5	3.9	4.4
Imports from market-economy countries	1.4	2.0	4.0	6.0	7.4
Trade balance	0.1	−0.2	−1.5	−2.1	−3.0
Gross debt [credits received long-, medium-, short-term][1]	1.1	1.2	2.6	5.2	8.4
Debt increase[1]	—	0.1	1.4	2.6	3.2
Principal payment and interest paid[1]	0.3	0.3	0.4	0.9	1.4
Debt service ratio [as percent of exports][1]	20.0	16.7	16.0	23.1	31.8

[1]Data concerning 1981–84 are not comparable to the previous years because of restructuring of debt and debt service obligations.

[2]If one takes into account arrears in interest payments in 1983–84, the global debt in 1983

ensure profitability for a sizable percentage of all enterprises. In 1981 industry as a whole ran a deficit.

Beginning in 1974 the rate of growth of distributed national income declined each year and turned negative in 1979. The national income in 1981 in constant prices was only 81 percent of its 1978 level. All this occurred despite growing imports from and trade deficits with the West between 1972 and 1980. This experience teaches another lesson: that credit-financed imports cannot be an adequate substitute for economic reform. By 1975 Poland's debt service exceeded 25 percent of convertible currency exports, which is commonly considered a measure of maximum prudent external indebtedness. (See table 13.2.) With the continuing increase in debt, and the abrupt rise in world market interest rates after 1979, by 1981 the hard-currency debt service amounted to 110 percent of Poland's convertible currency export revenue. In sum, by the end of the 1970s, Poland had become a country in which there was a fundamental incoherence between the level of development of the production forces and the productive relations.

The Logic of the Reformed Model

The logic of the reformed model of a socialist economic system, the necessity for which became even more apparent in the above circum-

1976	1977	1978	1979	1980	1981	1982	1983	1984
4.5	5.1	5.7	6.6	8.0	5.5	5.0	5.4	5.9
7.5	7.1	7.6	8.8	8.8	6.2	4.6	4.3	4.5
−3.0	−2.0	−1.9	−2.2	−0.8	−0.7	0.4	1.1	1.4
12.1	14.9	18.6	23.7	24.1	25.5	24.8	23.7^2	22.7^2
3.7	2.8	3.7	5.1	0.4	1.4	−0.7	−1.1	−1.0
1.9	2.8	4.3	6.2	8.1	3.7	2.2	2.1	1.7
42.2	54.9	75.5	93.9	101.2	67.3	44.0	39.0	28.8

would amount to $26.4 billion and to $26.8 billion in 1984.
SOURCE: Own calculations on the basis of data published in various issues of *Rocznik Statystyczny, Finanse, Życie Gospodarcze*, and other publications.

stances, may be analyzed in terms of three elements of an economic system: planning, economic guidance, and organization.

With respect to *planning*, central plans cease to be the main instruments of management in the reformed model and are obligatory only for the government. Enterprises operate according to their own plans and the necessary linkage with the central plans is ensured by prices, taxes, and other financial norms, as well as by contracts with the state and other enterprises. The enterprise plans are aimed at maximizing net measures, such as profit or value added; thus their financial plans are determining and do not simply reflect, passively, a predetermined level and structure of production, as under the classical centrally planned system.

The system of *economic guidance* becomes in the reformed model the main instrument of the central authorities. Commodity prices are parametric and originate either from domestic or external markets. Exchange rates become the basic parameters determining the level of exports and imports. The economic calculus carried out by the enterprises constitutes the basis for rational decisionmaking and in principle leads firms to optimize the adopted net measure. The enterprises themselves determine the level and structure of their production and employment, their wage and salary funds, the level and sources of material inputs, and investment outlays. Foreign trade activities are integrated with the domestic economy, and this "open economy" policy means

that foreign trade influences the level and structure of domestic wholesale and retail prices.

Regarding *organizational* structure under the reformed model, only
two levels of decisionmaking are required—there is no longer a need
for branch ministries or other intermediate levels of administration.
Functional ministries and the banking system take on a fundamental
importance in the regulation of the economy. Legal agreements become
the main elements in the relations between enterprises and foreign trade
rights are extended to producing enterprises and to other legal entities,
as well as to the FTOs.

The main virtues of the reformed model are the significant increase
of the role of economic calculus in the decisionmaking process, a greater
degree of worker participation in this process, the greater adaptability
of the economy to a changing external environment, and the possibility
of an enduring export orientation of the economy. The main shortcoming of the model, from the standpoint of classical socialist thinking, is
that equality of opportunity and increasing differentiation of people
replaces the principle of equality of incomes.

If the political will exists to pass from the classical to the reformed
model of the socialist economy, the main problem that still exists is
how to move from a nonparametric to a parametric price structure. The
necessary condition of autonomous enterprise decisionmaking is the
objective character of prices. If this condition is not met, enterprises
cannot be counted on to make decisions that are consonant with the
interests of the national economy as a whole. If this condition is not
satisfied, the idea of economic reform may be discredited.

Basic Principles of Poland's Economic Reform

The reform blueprint developed in the course of 1980–81 was a
comprehensive undertaking aimed at ensuring the rational operations
of economic units at all levels and releasing their sense of responsibility and initiative. The improvement of the foreign trade system was an
important element of the reform and was closely intertwined with the
proposed changes in other spheres. The initial legislation regarding the
principles of the reform was passed in September 1981. Most of the
legal foundations of the reform, however, were legislated by the Sejm at
the end of February 1982, although some of these provisions did not
come into force until after the suspension of martial law in July 1983.

According to the law on planning, Poland's economy was to be a "planned economy based on a system of socioeconomic plans actively shaping economic development, using the market mechanism" (*Dziennik Ustaw*, no. 7, 1982, section 51). Central plans were now to have strategic and informative, rather than operational, functions. The implementation of the strategies designed by the central plans was to be left to the decisions of the individual economic units, which were not to be directly controlled by means of quotas and directives from above. The necessary links between the autonomous plans of enterprises and the central plans were to be ensured by: contracts concluded by state agencies with these firms; contracts between enterprises; price, income, finance, and tax policies and instruments; the exchange of information between the central authorities and enterprises in the course of elaborating plans; and in special circumstances (such as national disasters, national defense, and the fulfillment of international obligations), by imposing obligations on firms.

The law on prices introduced three categories of price: (1) *official* prices, for basic consumer goods and important industrial inputs, as well as for basic products procured from the agricultural sector; (2) *regulated* prices, for standard products, imported means of production, and commodities distributed by state agencies; and (3) prices that were to be *freely determined* in agreements between buyers and sellers. The main objective of this law was the introduction of rules shaping prices and their flexibility (*Dziennik Ustaw*, no. 7, 1982, section 52). General rules, applying to each price category, were that prices should converge on their market-clearing levels, and that official and regulated prices of exported or imported means of production should be formed on the basis of average prices realized in hard-currency trade multiplied by the proper exchange rate (i.e., transaction prices). As a temporary measure, however, regulated prices could be formed either as transaction prices, or as prices based on justified processing costs increased by a 10 percent profit norm.

A new exchange rate system was introduced at the beginning of 1982. The separate deviza and internal exchange rates were folded into uniform commercial exchange rates, one for the dollar area (at an initial rate of eighty zlotys per dollar) and one for CMEA trade (sixty-eight zlotys per transferable ruble). These exchange rates were meant to be submarginal rates in the sense of ensuring the profitability of about three-quarters of all exports.[3] The basic rate for the clearing ruble was set at the same level as the zloty/TR rate, and was to be applied in settlements of bilateral transactions with socialist countries that are not members of the CMEA. In settling noncommercial payments, the exchange rates for particular currencies of the socialist countries were applied pursuant to multi- and bilateral agreements with those countries. The retail price reform of 1982 (see section 3) necessitated upward adjustments of the noncommercial exchange rate to reflect the diminished purchasing power of the zloty.

The commercial exchange rate for the dollar determined the zloty price of other convertible currencies on the basis of cross rates. The principle of flexible rates, applied by Poland since 1978, was retained. In effect, the current dollar rate was adjusted depending on the weighted basket of convertible currencies, each of which accounts for not less than one percent of current account convertible currency transactions. Since the beginning of 1982 the zloty has been devalued several times; as of September 1, 1986, the commercial rates were 200 and 95 zlotys per dollar and TR, respectively. In actuality, the same exchange rate was used for noncommercial as well as commercial transactions in convertible currencies; in other words, the exchange rate with this payments area was a uniform one. Foreign trade planning and profit calculations, as well as official foreign trade statistics, were now all expressed consistently in terms of domestic zlotys.

Economic activities in Poland are carried out by three types of enterprises: State-owned (accounting for 70.8 percent of national income in 1982), cooperatives (9.2 percent), and private activities (20 percent). Large industrial units, construction, transport, and communications remain in the domain of state-owned firms. There is a significant cooperative sector in trade, while small-scale production is dominated by cooperatives and private enterprise. The reform blueprint covered all three areas, but its main provisions had to do with the state-owned enterprises.

The reform concept rested on three principles: enterprise self-dependence, self-financing, and self-management (*Dziennik Ustaw*, no. 24, 1981, section 122). Enterprise self-dependence, or autonomy, meant that the enterprise was to set its own production targets, decide on its own investment projects, determine its sources of supply, its level of employment, and the amount of its remuneration.

Self-financing meant that, just as in the market economy, the existence of the enterprise, as well as the living conditions of its employees, was to depend on its profitability (*Dziennik Ustaw*, no. 7, 1982, section 54). After deducting its income tax, the obligatory deduction for the reserve fund, and for the State Vocational Activization Fund (PFAZ), the enterprise was to be free to divide its profit between the investment fund, the wage fund, and other purposes. The income tax depended on the size of the enterprises's profit in relation to its processing costs. The enterprise was also subject, however, to a tax on turnover, a property tax, and a tax on the wage fund. The concept of bankruptcy has also been incorporated into law (*Dziennik Ustaw*, no. 36, 1983, section 165).

Enterprise self-management meant the participation of workers in managing the enterprise (*Dziennik Ustaw*, no. 24, 1981, section 123). In enterprises employing less than 300 workers, the key issues facing the firm were to be decided by the entire work force at a general meeting, or at a meeting of delegates elected by secret ballot. These issues would include the adoption of the enterprise's statute, the distribution of profit, an annual evaluation of the workers' council, as well as the approval of the long-term plans of the enterprise. A fifteen-member workers' council, elected for a two-year period, was to be the organ of self-management. It was to have the responsibility of ratifying all the decisions of crucial importance for the enterprise, with the scope determined by general legal principles.

In enterprises of crucial importance for the country—railroads, airlines, and certain industrial enterprises—the director was to be appointed by the founding body (usually the supervising ministry) that represents the state. In the majority of enterprises, however, the director was to be appointed, on a competitive basis, by the workers' council. The founding body, as well as the workers' council, had the right to launch a justified protest against decisions appointing or recalling the director. If the other side was not in agreement, the case could be brought to court.

All these enterprises remain, of course, the property of the state. According to Article 3 of the law on state-owned enterprises, the enterprise "manages the property set aside to it and that which it acquires, which is part of the national property." The state authority, through its representatives, is to undertake control functions vis-à-vis the enterprises.

In the preparation of the reform blueprint it was intended that ultimately convertible currencies acquired by exporting enterprises would be sold to the banking system at the new official exchange rates (Plowiec

1982). At the same time importers would be able to purchase convertible currency from the banks as well as to apply for credits at domestic and foreign banks. These rights were included in chapter 9 of the law on the financial system of the state-owned enterprises, but they could not be implemented during the economic situation prevailing in Poland in 1982. Instead, producers of goods exported to the hard currency area, and associations of producers or FTOS acting on behalf of producers, were authorized to apply for hard currency retention quota accounts (Plowiec 1982). The retention quota concept was envisioned by the authors of the reform as the first step toward convertibility. (See section 3 for more detail.)

Under the reform blueprint the banking system had a new role of great significance for enterprises. Previously the banking system played the role of an automatic supplier of money for the implementation of the plan and, in fact, it was subordinated to the Ministry of Finance. According to the new banking law (*Dziennik Ustaw*, no. 7, 1982, section 56), banks were now to be autonomous organizational units, having legal status and operating in accordance with banking law and statutes. If an enterprise could not demonstrate to a bank its ability to repay a bank loan, the bank would simply refuse to extend it credit. Of course the objective was not to dissolve immediately any enterprise that could not prove its ability to repay its obligations. Indeed some rescue measures were foreseen, such as development of a program aimed at improving the efficiency of the enterprise and temporary receivership. Nevertheless, enterprises that would not be able to become profitable in the near future would have to be dissolved.

The principle of enterprise self-dependence, or autonomy, implies a number of changes in the organizational structure of the Polish economy. These changes are complex and will have to be introduced gradually. The first major step, implemented as early as July 1981, involved the organization of the governmental economic administration. Eleven branch ministries were merged into six; further changes were envisioned that would merge the remaining branch ministries into only one or two ministries.

The second step involved the liquidation, beginning in January 1982, of obligatory cartel-like industrial associations that grouped enterprises according to branch or territorial criteria (*Monitor Polski*, no. 32, 1981, section 286). The continued obligation of enterprises to join such an organization was envisaged only for certain branches that were considered to be of crucial importance for the basic economic interests of the state. Enterprises in other branches, however, were permitted voluntarily to form sectoral associations, although these may only be servicing rather than supervising bodies. At the same time, according to the law on state-owned enterprises, firms could conclude agreements that established mixed enterprises with a foreign unit or with a cooperative organization. Moreover, they were permitted to undertake activities in fields that were not explicitly provided for in their founding acts. This may permit some undermining of monopolistic positions.

According to the law on licenses to carry out foreign trade operations (*Dziennik Ustaw*, no. 7, 1982, section 59), foreign trade rights could be granted not only to FTOs subordinated to the MFT, but also to any legal entities or individuals that hold licenses to undertake production, service, or trade operations. These foreign trade rights, granted by the MFT, could be full licenses or limited to operations in a particular market, related to definite contracts, or to a particular period of time. Foreign trade licenses could not be granted, however, for trade in goods that were considered to be of basic importance to the national economy, particularly because the transaction prices of basic raw materials and fuels traded with the socialist and nonsocialist countries were significantly differentiated.

To apply for a foreign trade license, an entity was expected to meet some basic requirements. Specifically, at least 25 percent of its production should be exported, or its annual exports should exceed one million zlotys. It should also be able to demonstrate that it has adequate personnel, an appropriate organization, and sufficient technical after-sales service capacities to engage in the activities envisaged by the license.

The foregoing law introduced the possibility of breaking the monopoly positions of the FTOs. Moreover, as a producer was no longer to be arbitrarily assigned to a particular exporting organization, the legal and economic relations between the two partners might be more flexible.

3. IMPLEMENTATION OF THE REFORM, 1982–1985

The economic reform was initiated under conditions of an acute crisis that was only aggravated by the sanctions imposed on Poland by the Western countries. Especially damaging were collective credit restrictions that made it very difficult to secure certain supplies for the national economy, including feedstocks and foodstuffs, as well as industrial inputs. Despite the difficulties, it was believed by the Polish government that it would be a serious mistake to postpone the reform until more advantageous conditions emerged. The population would view such a postponement as a first step toward giving up the reforms altogether. The government believed that it could not frustrate the awakened hopes. From both a social and political point of view it was deemed better to run the risks associated with the introduction of a reform in such a dire economic situation (Bobrowski 1982).

Since the beginning of 1982 central directives and prohibitions in planning have in principle been abolished. Enterprises have elaborated their own plans and acquired greater freedom in shaping their own employment, wage structure, and internal organization. Nevertheless, shortages of domestic and imported raw materials had earlier necessitated the introduction of various provisional measures. So-called operational programs imposed various restrictions on trade in materials that were in short supply, on some semifinished products, and even on some final products (*Monitor Polski*, no. 32, 1981, section 287).

At the same time the operational programs ensured a privileged material supply for the production of goods considered as absolute necessities, including staple foodstuffs, medicines, toiletries, and clothing. There was great pressure from enterprises to be covered by those programs; as a result, they were inflated and an excessive number of "priorities" appeared. It has been estimated that the sixteen programs in force in 1982 encompassed sixty percent of industrial production, including production for export. By 1983 the number of operational programs had been reduced to six, and they accounted for only 20 percent of industrial output; in 1984–85 there were only four operational programs.

In 1983 government contracts, foreseen in the law on planning, were introduced in order to ease bottlenecks in the production of some raw materials, semifinished products, and consumer goods, as well as to induce some structural changes in production. These orders constituted about 3 percent of the value of industrial production. The system of government contracts was expanded in 1984, with additional objectives being to achieve some important targets with respect to research and development and to complete various construction projects (*Monitor Polski*, various issues). In 1984 these contracts encompassed 111 products and materials as well as fifty-three central investment projects. This contrasted with thirty materials and ten projects in 1983. Some economists suggested that the number of contracts already meant that there were too many priorities (*Życie Gospodarcze*, no. 11, 1982, p. 2). The role of government contracts increased in 1985. They now encompassed 106 products and materials, seventy-six central investment projects, and some important areas of research and development. Government contracts became the main tool for realizing central economic priorities. Because of the high degree of concentration in production, government contracts are partially awarded at open auctions, and may involve state-owned, cooperative, or private enterprises. These contracts are treated preferentially in the aquisition of supplies.

Substantial reform of prices has already occurred, but the process of fully adjusting wholesale prices to domestic costs and to the structure of foreign trade prices will take a long time. On January 1, 1982, new wholesale prices were introduced for raw and semi-processed materials and as a result the gap between the true costs of production and the level of prices was narrowed. The new level of prices was 3 to 3.6 times higher than the earlier level, and this significantly diminished the aggregate losses suffered by industrial enterprises. Although official prices of fuels and raw materials were systematically corrected during the 1983 to 1985 period, the new producer price system is still quite distorted, and is being criticized for its failure to promote exports and to discriminate against inefficient imports.

There have been two basic deviations from the exchange rate principles embodied in the reform blueprint (Foreign Trade Research Institute 1983). One departure was the establishment of a de facto exchange rate 40 percent lower than the basic commercial rate insofar as setting the official prices of basic raw materials in 1982 was concerned. Second, the commercial rate actually corresponded to the average zloty cost of earning foreign exchange, rather than the envisioned submarginal rate that was to ensure the profitability of 75–85 percent of exports. During 1982–84 the domestic cost of earning one U.S. dollar in exports was growing because internal wholesale prices were increasing at the same time that export prices in dollars were falling and because the structure of exports was changing. Consequently, export efficiency deteriorated and successive devaluations of the zloty did not offset this deterioration. These deviations tended to create disincentives to export and to restrain imports. In order to place exporters and producers for the domestic market in a comparable position, the government has applied a price equalization mechanism that brings the de facto exchange rate for producers of exportables and for exporters to a slightly more realistic level.

As noted in section 2, the concept of the retention quota account was envisioned as the first step toward convertibility and was introduced to enable enterprises producing for export to acquire imported inputs independently of the central import fund. This was thought to be necessary to diminish the export disincentives that always exist when there is excess demand on the domestic market for producers' goods. The retention quota rate depends on the degree of import intensity of production for export, except that the import of basic materials is not included in this calculation. In 1985 the maximum percentage of convertible currency export revenue that might be retained could not exceed 50 percent. The MFT established this quota rate on an individual basis for those enterprises holding foreign trade concessions, as well as for enterprises with annual exports in excess of $15 million. For all other firms, the rate is fixed by groups of enterprises.

Once the retention quota rate is fixed, the enterprise opens a banking account at the Bank Handlowy in a currency specified by the firm. Foreign currency obtained under this scheme may not be traded, but may be used solely by the owner of the account or may be ceded to subcontractors that are supplying the components necessary for such export production. The account may only be used to acquire necessary inputs, and may not be used to import luxury goods that could be resold on the domestic market at windfall prices.

In order to ensure uninterrupted production, pending the acquisition of export proceeds, an enterprise is entitled to obtain temporary credits from the Bank Handlowy or, in exceptional cases, and with the consent of the Ministry of Finance or the MFT, from foreign banks or enterprises, respectively. Holdings in an export retention quota account also give the holder the right to purchase from the Bank Handlowy any convertible currency at the prevailing exchange rate.

The export retention quota mechanism is a part of the general system for supplying enterprises with sufficient foreign currency to maintain their production. It is also believed that this mechanism will help persuade producers of the basic truth that if one wants to import, one must export. Nevertheless, the mechanism is criticized because the maximum retention rates are quite differentiated and because this differentiation is based on the present import intensity of export production, not necessarily on its efficiency.

The Polish economy entered 1982 with a huge inflationary gap. Permitting prices to clear markets in general would have led to an unacceptably steep increase in the price level. At the beginning of 1982 about 50 percent of commodity turnover was allowed to take place at *free* prices. In the course of the year these prices rose appreciably, in some instances as the result of enterprises taking advantage of their monopolistic positions. Highly progressive income tax rates on enterprises were insufficient to discourage such practices. As a result, the scope of *official* prices had to be temporarily broadened beyond the original plan. In 1982 the share of total turnover of intermediate goods realized in free prices was 75 percent, in 1983 it diminished to 55 percent, but it rose in 1984 to 63 percent. Other steps were also taken to reduce the rate of open inflation. Raising the free prices of intermediate goods was banned beginning with the second half of 1983, except in those cases in which enterprise costs had increased as a result of official action, such as increases in official prices of other intermediates or of transport services. Since the beginning of 1984 nominally *free* prices may be temporarily frozen by the authorities, and for some commodity groups price increase ceilings were introduced. These measures were accompanied by the introduction of a flat rate income tax (60 percent in 1984 and 65 percent in 1985) on all enterprises. This change was positive and encouraged the growth of production and profits in 1984.

An active policy in agriculture in 1981–84 improved incentives for private farming activities. With this policy the incomes of farmers grew more rapidly than those of the urban population. In February 1982 steep increases in retail prices of food and fuels were introduced, although these measures were partially offset by higher money wages and other compensations that caused nominal personal incomes to rise by 66 percent. Retail prices for products sold by state-owned and cooperative shops increased by 109.4 percent in 1982. In 1983 these prices rose on average by another 22.1 percent, but this increase was roughly matched by a rise in personal incomes of 22.3 percent. In 1984 the growth of personal incomes (18.9 percent) outpaced the increase of retail prices for goods and services (14.7 percent). A substantial decline in the real income of the population usually breeds considerable popular dissatisfaction with the government. The problem was intensified in

Poland in 1982 because it occurred during the period of martial law and the opponents of reform eagerly interpreted this decline in the living standard as the cost of reform, whereas in fact it reflected the cost of the economic crisis.

Aside from the manipulation of the structure of enterprise income tax rates as an anti-inflationary instrument, the government also has imposed special taxes to finance the State Vocational Activization Fund. In 1982 this tax was geared to the average wage increase granted by an enterprise, but it failed to enforce more rational employment and thereby raise labor productivity. In 1983–84 the tax was levied instead on the growth of an enterprise's total wage bill, and this helped to stimulate productivity. In 1984 this tax was made more progressive than before and the ceiling on the portion of the wage fund free from taxation was lowered. It is expected that this change will help to raise productivity and to limit the growth of the wage fund.

Central distribution encompasses basic fuels, raw materials, and even some machinery and equipment, particularly that imported from the nonsocialist countries. There was some central distribution of materials in 1982–83 (Monitor Polski, no. 37, 1983). Materials were distributed by special procurement units, whose role in the purchasing operations of enterprises is obligatory. In 1984–85 central distribution as such (i.e., by administrative rather than legal relations) was terminated, but these materials continue to be bought—by producers from procurement units whose role is still obligatory—on the basis of the previously concluded agreements. It has been estimated that the guaranteed supplies for units executing operational programs and government contracts in 1984 accounted for 40 percent of the total value of intermediate goods' deliveries; in 1983 in some sectors it encompassed as much as 90 percent (e.g., imports of shoe leather from the nonsocialist countries). (Życie Gospodarcze, no. 11, 1984, p. 2.)

Enterprise self-management activities were suspended for the entire period of martial law (Dziennik Ustaw, no. 32, 1981, section 185). In the course of 1983–84, however, workers' councils were gradually established, and by the end of 1984 councils were operating in 87 percent of those state-owned enterprises that were entitled to have such councils (Życie Gospodarcze, no. 47, 1984). It is generally believed that self-management is derivative of enterprise self-dependence; the greater the autonomy of an enterprise, the greater the scope for self-management. The law that shifted decisions on wages from the central planners to enterprise managers has contributed significantly to the enhancement of self-management.[4] By the middle of 1985 this new system of wage determination by enterprises was applied in 50 percent of all enterprises supervised by central founding bodies.

Numerous examples of reform can be found in agriculture. These include the new policy that attempts to ensure that all sectors of agriculture can freely make output and investment decisions and that they will have equal access to credits and equal treatment with respect to credit terms, equal access to agricultural inputs, and equivalent opportunities for selling their products. In July 1983 the Sejm introduced the so-called peasant provision into the constitution that grants the highest legal status to family-run farms and ensures that they will be a permanent element of the Polish socioeconomic system. Private purchases of land from the state land fund increased in 1982–84, but beginning in 1983 the rate of increase declined because of higher land prices and the increased relative profitability of leasing of land. Farms of up to 100 hectares are now allowed, contrasted to a maximum of only 20 hectares in earlier years. The average size of private farms has been increasing; at the present time there are more than 1,000 private farms consisting of 50–100 hectares. As a result of these trends, the share of private farms in total agricultural output rose from 76.9 percent in 1980 to 80 percent in 1982.

Various restrictions on artisans and shopkeepers have also been removed under the reform. Such enterprises can now employ up to fifty employees. The easing of restrictions encouraged growth in private sector employment, at the same time that employment in the economy as a whole was declining.

An important achievement of the reform has been the increased freedom of enterprises to acquire much needed convertible currency. By the end of 1984, 2,188 or one-third of all enterprises had opened retention quota accounts. Among the industrial enterprises, the share of firms holding such accounts was much larger. In 1982–84 the average rate of retention of export revenues was 20 percent. At the same time imports financed by these accounts increased from 2.8 percent of total hard currency imports in 1982 to 14.2 percent in 1984. It would appear that these retention quotas are on the whole rationally utilized and that they give enterprises an incentive to maintain exports despite strong excess demand pressures on the domestic market.

Beginning in the second half of 1982 state-owned enterprises that did not have retention quota accounts, and yet wanted to develop production capacities for nonluxury consumer goods or export production, were permitted to take part in convertible currency auctions organized by the Bank Handlowy. Any enterprise could buy up to $100,000 at the official commercial exchange rate. If a winner, the enterprise was required to deposit for two years an amount in zlotys exceeding three times the value of the purchased foreign currencies, without interest. These fairly harsh conditions, however, resulted in only ten enterprises applying for such purchases in the first year of operation of the plan. The regulations were liberalized somewhat at the end of 1983 (cooperatives were allowed to apply, the deposit obligation was reduced to one year, and its amount was reduced to two times the value of currencies purchased), but this did not induce many more applicants.

At the end of 1983 socialized as well as private enterprises producing for export to the convertible currency area gained the right to apply for hard currency credits from the Bank Handlowy for the import of materials needed for current export production, and for spare parts, machinery, and equipment for its development (*Dziennik Ustaw*, no. 56, 1983, section 249). In the former case these credits are granted for one year, and in the latter case for up to two years. These credits are as a rule supported by foreign borrowings of the Bank Handlowy, and therefore their costs are high (LIBOR plus bank spread and servicing fee). The credits are to be repaid from the retention quota account or, if it amounts to less than 15 percent of the enterprise's export revenues, from 50 percent of these proceeds. The high costs of these credits, combined with the uncertainties faced by the enterprises as a result of frequent changes in the economic system, have meant that these credits have only a negligible importance in financing imports.

In general, the incentives for export development are still inadequate and it is still easier for importing enterprises to obtain hard currency from the central fund than to earn it. With continuing excess demand pressures on the domestic market, due to an inflationary gap or inflationary overhang or both, it is necessary either to establish very strong incentives for export development (e.g., export premiums for workers and managers—although these tend to be inflationary), or to reduce the constraints on export development (e.g., the list of centrally financed imports should be reduced and the users of imported materials should have to pay for them out of their own export earnings).

The year 1985 saw some positive changes aimed at developing small export-oriented investment projects. According to the new legal provisions foreseen in the resolution of the Sejm on the credit plan for 1985 (*Monitor Polski*, no. 29, 1984, section 193), economic units undertaking export-oriented investment projects with rapid recoupment may obtain income tax relief amounting to 20 percent of the costs of these investments, a priority on zloty investment credits, and a preferential interest rate on these credits. If the cost of the investment projects does not surpass 500 million zlotys and the period of realization is less than three years, the firm may obtain income tax and amortization tax relief up to 50 percent of the value of the projects. Moreover, it can also obtain additional resources from the special fund of the Ministry of Foreign Trade and from its corresponding FTO. It is expected that the small restructuring fostered by these policies will bring expanded exports of processed products over a two- to three-year period.

Under the reform the banks became responsible for monitoring the actual economic situation of the enterprises. In 1982 the banks were able to evaluate—by means of their new credit granting procedures —the economic health of 3,200 enterprises. This exercise revealed that 700 enterprises were subject to potential bankruptcy. This process of evaluation continued in 1983–84, and as a result credits to some enterprises were restricted, while for others credits were extended only on the condition that the enterprises accept a specific recovery program acceptable to their bank. Between the last quarter of 1983 and the end of 1984 there were 143 cases of establishing a specific recovery program and eleven cases of temporary receivership. As a practical matter, however, enterprises that are members of voluntary industrial associations may be subsidized by the association, or they may receive subsidies from the Ministry of Finance. This makes it difficult in reality to easily identify the weaker enterprises, although in 1984 one construction firm went bankrupt and was dissolved.

Some of the organizational changes foreseen in the reform blueprint have already been achieved. In 1982, 400 obligatory associations of enterprises were liquidated (those in the mining industry were retained), and the intermediate level of management was abolished. At the same time, however, voluntary associations were established, which accounted for about half of the employees of enterprises belonging to the former obligatory associations. It was widely believed, therefore, that these new associations would function very much in the same manner as their predecessors. This situation arose partly because when the self-management organs were suspended with the onset of martial law, directors of enterprises did not have the strength to oppose the pressures coming from the directors of the old obligatory associations, who very often had also become the directors of the new associations. Gradually, however, the situation has been changing. In 1983 there existed 169 associations (including 45 that were obligatory), while in 1984 there were 162 (including 36 obligatory associations). At the beginning of the reform period the main function of the associations was to ease the problems that enterprises had in the acquisition of intermediate goods or in their relations with the central authorities. More recently, however, enterprises stress the growing importance of the associations in facilitating the exchange of information and joint research and investment projects. Participants in a given association, however, still tend to belong to the same rather than to several different industrial branches.

It is possible that these new associations may function quite differently once the rationing of energy and raw materials is terminated and after further reforms of the central administration take place. As long as the branch ministries are retained, they will support the old functions of the associations of enterprises. It might be pointed out that beginning in 1986 the fees for maintaining the associations will have to be subtracted from enterprise profits, rather than being added to their costs; this may induce the enterprises to review the usefulness of these associations.

There have been positive changes in the organization of foreign trade activities, although they are smaller than initially expected. In 1982 the MFT granted one hundred ten additional licenses to engage in foreign trade; sixty-one of these were given to artisans and shopkeepers, thirteen to small socialized enterprises, and thirty-six to an assortment of other firms, including construction enterprises. In 1983–84 a further seventy-nine licenses were granted for foreign trade. Newly licensed units accounted for 6.8 percent of total exports and 2.5 percent of total imports in 1984. That only this many new licenses have been granted demonstrates that despite the possibility of abolishing the FTO monopolies, the majority of producers preferred to continue to trade through the specialized export-import enterprises. In 1982, 60 percent of total Polish exports were transacted on the account of FTOs (Michalski 1983). Exports sold on the account of the FTOs tend to be more profitable than direct exporting for several reasons. The specialized FTOs often face lower transaction costs and most producing enterprises lack employees with professional experience in foreign trade. Moreover, at the present time many producers may be served by the same FTO for both exports and imports, and it is possible to establish a special office within the FTO to handle both kinds of transactions for a given large producer.

The idea of transforming state-owned FTOs into joint-stock companies owned by one or more industrial firms and the state treasury, represented by the MFT and holding at least 51 percent of the shares, is gaining support (*Dziennik Ustaw*, no. 31, 1982, section 170). Joint-stock companies may realize exports on their own account or on the account of producers. This type of operation might ensure closer contacts between producers and exporters and might make it easier for producers to adapt to the changing needs of foreign customers. By the end of 1984 twenty-five joint-stock companies, established mainly by groups of enterprises producing processed goods, were operating and accounted for about 60 percent of Poland's foreign trade turnover.

4. CONCLUSIONS

Socioeconomic reform is a gradual process. The more difficult the economic situation, the more drawn out this process must be because it will occur with less consistency. In the Polish case both the internal and external environment has not favored reform; nonetheless the decision was taken to proceed. Economic reform was begun in a period of acute economic crisis, characterized by sharp internal and external disequilibria. In this situation the fundamental objective was to reduce, by any means, the imbalances on the market for basic consumer goods. At the same time the suspension in 1982 of reforms involving self-management also meant that the reform as implemented was inconsistent with one of its three underlying principles. As a practical matter, therefore, the full process of reform did not begin until martial law was lifted in mid-1983. It is therefore too early to assess the effects of reform.

Until now the main achievements of the reform are the abolition of central directives, the reform of retail prices, the introduction of economically meaningful exchange rates, greater autonomy, self-management and self-reliance of enterprises (including that relating to wage determination), the new functions of the banking system, and substantial changes in the interrelations among enterprises. Coincident with these achievements, Polish national income grew by 6.0 percent in 1983, social productivity of labor increased by 6.8 percent, and real income per capita ceased falling.

Shortcomings in the implementation of the reform to date include the unstable taxation system for enterprises, insufficient reform of wholesale prices, an overvalued zloty, and inadequate shifts in the structure of production and investment outlays. As a result, there has been insufficient growth of profitable exports of processed goods to the convertible currency area. Many economists believe that the main shortcoming of the reform has been the inability to develop strong incentives aimed at raising labor productivity. The dilemma of efficiency versus equality has not been clearly resolved in favor of the former, and there is a continuing hesitation in economic policy—particularly in the wake of the sharp decline in the living standard of the population that occurred in 1981–82. The government is permanently under strong egalitarian pressures that have been reinforced as a result of the establishment of the new unions. Consequently, although the reform of the economy is progressing, it would be difficult to affirm that the reform process has already passed the critical point after which the return to the previous system would be impossible.

This is not to say that some improvement has not occurred in foreign trade. In 1982–84 export volume increased to both currency areas and the convertible currency trade balance was in surplus in 1982–85 for the first time since 1971. These export results were mainly the result of increased sales abroad of coal and raw materials, however, and not of increased exports of processed goods. At the same time, hard currency imports, despite rapid growth in 1983–85, were still well below their 1978 level in volume terms. These foreign trade developments are of course only partially the result of the economic reform. The decline in imports from the nonsocialist countries, which is the main reason for the improving trade balance, has limited the expansion of exports, due to shortages of imported intermediates. Polish exports have also been adversely affected by Western tariff and nontariff barriers, increasing competition on Western markets from highly indebted developing countries, the climate caused by the sanctions applied against Poland by the United States and other NATO countries, and by a lack of strong export incentives within Poland itself.

The economic reform was unfortunately formulated without giving a high priority to export development. At the present time, because of the extraordinarily difficult balance-of-payments situation and the exhaustion of possibilities for further reduction of imports, the basic assumptions of the reform need to be reexamined. This is particularly so because the domestic environment of excess demand serves as a disincentive to exports, and indeed is perhaps the main obstacle to export development.

It should also be recognized, however, that rapid development of exports of processed goods can only be rational, from the standpoint of the national economy as a whole, if exchange rates are near their equilibrium levels and if the prices of exported, imported, and exportable goods are based on the transaction prices of goods traded with the nonsocialist countries. This is the sine qua non of rationality in foreign trade. Some of the facilities created by the reform to spur export development (such as the hard-currency retention quota accounts, expanded foreign trade rights, and tax incentives for exports) do favor the expansion of exports, but not necessarily their rational development. Required are distinctly export-oriented investment decisions (at the expense of all other types of investment projects) and systemic changes oriented toward efficient exports. There must be further devaluations of the zloty and changes in the wholesale price structure in the direction of the structure of world market prices. Because of Poland's huge external indebtedness and fundamental dependence on imports from the hard currency area, it is condemned to an open economic policy. At least for the foreseeable future there is no better, more rational choice.

CHAPTER 14

Changes in the Polish Foreign Trade System and Adjustment: Comments on Chapter 13

Zbigniew M. Fallenbuchl

At the end of her essay Professor Plowiec rightly points out that, as the result of the accumulated heavy external debt, the Polish economy has become an open economy. This has created a special need for far-reaching changes in the Polish foreign trade system and adjustment. Professor Plowiec describes very well what happened in the past in Poland when it seemed that the role of foreign trade was going to be revised, that the strategy of development would become more outward looking, and that some significant economic reforms in the foreign trade sector and in the whole economy would be put into operation.

The present economic reform program has been much more complex than all the previous attempts. It is supported by legislation and by frequent assurances from the leaders that they are going to proceed with it. However, the actual working of the economy and economic policies that are being followed suggest that, unfortunately, history seems to repeat itself again. At least this is what has happened so far. Whatever the reasons, some of which may be valid, there is a sharp difference between the theory and the practice of the present economic reform. Professor Plowiec stresses the former and does not emphasize sufficiently strongly the difference between the theory and the practice, although she clearly states that many aspects of the reform have not yet been implemented.

Some systemic modifications have, indeed, taken place. However, as Professor Plowiec points out, the original reform program, which was formulated and adopted in 1981 to be introduced in 1982, did not take the openness of the economy as a starting point and was rather limited in its provisions concerning foreign trade. The systemic modifications that have actually been implemented are even more limited than the original program, especially in the field of foreign economic relations.

It appears that no significant systemic adjustment to a changed economic situation has taken place. Therefore, the process of macroeconomic and structural adjustments still depends, to a considerable extent, on the mechanism that is typical for a command economy rather than on any alternative mechanism. Indeed, it is when the macroeconomic structural adjustments are examined that the limited nature of the actually implemented reform becomes evident. Professor Plowiec does not discuss this aspect very thoroughly. I shall, therefore, try to supplement her essay in this respect.

When in the middle of the 1970s a serious balance-of-payments deficit appeared and hard currency indebtedness was rapidly growing, the authorities had at their disposal only the very limited adjustment mechanism of a centrally planned economy. In the absence of a meaningful rate of exchange and a system that could respond to changes in it, they had to depend on a discretionary commercial policy of import cuts and attempts to stimulate exports by administrative commands, and on a discretionary reduction in domestic absorption (Holzman 1974a, chapter 4). A reduction in imports and the policy of pushing exports at any price, both effected in a highly centralized administrative manner, resulted in an adverse impact on aggregate supply. This impact was magnified through the operation of Holzman's (1974a, chapter 5) bottleneck multiplier. When the gap between imports and exports started to decline in 1977–79, the greater inflationary pressure appeared on the aggregate demand side. The gap between aggregate demand and aggregate supply at the full capacity level of national income (the maximum level of real income that could be produced with the restricted supply of imports) was widening. For political reasons the authorities continued increases in nominal wages, despite growing shortages of consumption goods. Cuts in investment, effected by highly centralized administrative methods, were to adjust domestic absorption. The reduction was not sufficient, however, and a mix of open and suppressed inflation appeared (Wernik 1984).

Some structural adjustments also were attempted with the help of administrative measures. The authorities tried to redirect output to export and for the domestic consumers' market, creating considerable dislocations when, for example, some intermediate goods were exported instead of being delivered to the producers of final goods, some of them potential exporters themselves. The short-term measures could not be supplemented by long-term structural adjustments because of a drastic decline in investment outlays and a large number of unfinished investments.

In 1982 the reform was introduced. Because the economy was paralyzed in the months following the imposition of martial law in December 1981, no results could have been expected from the reform in 1982. Starting with 1983, however, there should have been some impact of the reform on the way in which the external and internal disequilibria were handled. So far there does not seem to have been any noticeable change in this respect.

A heavy dependence on discretionary commercial policy has continued. Drastic cuts in imports and some improvements in exports resulted in a positive balance of visible trade in 1982–85. The increase in hard-currency exports after 1982 was achieved mainly by expanding the export of fuels, raw materials, and foodstuffs—all in short supply in the domestic market and having limited possibilities for expansion and, except for agriculture, highly capital and energy intensive. Exports of metallurgical products, chemicals, and food and agricultural products increased; but the export of these products can be expanded with the help of centralized administrative methods. The reform has not been applied in coal mining and is very limited in other sectors producing primary goods (Jeziorański 1984). Even in agriculture, state procurement depends not only on increased prices, but also on the linked sales of agricultural inputs (fertilizers, pesticides, and coal can be obtained only if certain commodities, mainly grain, are delivered), and bureaucratic interference continues (Consultative Economic Council 1984). On the other hand, the industries in which the reform should have given the best results have not been able even to maintain their exports to the West. Between 1981 and 1984 the hard-currency earnings of the engineering industry declined from $1,665 million to $1,259 million, of light industry from \$424 million to \$311 million, of the wood and paper industry from \$205 million to \$177 million, and of the mineral industry from \$83 million to \$72 million. In 1985 hard-currency exports declined by 3.6 percent. This decline well illustrates how vulnerable exports still are.

The role of the exchange rate was supposed to alter under the reform and a series of devaluations should have taken place. It appears, however, that the system is still unable to utilize the rate of exchange in the adjustment process (Ledworowski et al. 1984; Michalski et al. 1983; and Consultative Economic Council 1984). At the beginning the prices of basic raw materials were calculated at a different rate of exchange and a mainly administratively effected price reform, therefore, did not eliminate price distortions. "Transaction prices" are used only to a limited extent and the majority of prices are calculated on a cost plus basis. The enterprises sell exportables at the domestic prices to the foreign trade organizations (FTOs) and are not interested in obtaining licenses to export directly to the foreign markets. The price equalization system has been maintained and the FTOs are compensated from the state budget for their losses. Administrative methods are used to stimulate exports (Consultative Economic Council 1984). Most of them are on a selective basis, subject to the usual administrative process of bargaining and lobbying. The partial retention of hard-currency earnings is based on import intensity and discourages its reduction. Various incentives, such as tax deductions, are based on the quantity of export and not on its profitability. The majority of imports are centrally administered and allocated, like many domestic materials, according to the planners' priorities. The Consultative Economic Council (1984, p. 6) has pointed out that "the corrections of the system of the functioning of the economy which were introduced from January 1, 1984, did not change the existing system of very ineffective export inducement" and, "for this reason, it is necessary to continue to use various ad hoc administrative measures and to effect a fundamental modification of the system in the future."

The positive visible trade balances reduced aggregate supply, since they were achieved mainly by a reduction in imports and at the same time increased inflationary pressures. A reduction in domestic absorption has become even more necessary. Consumption was reduced in 1982 as the result of drastic price increases. Real incomes declined but increases in prices did not induce increases in output, except in agriculture with respect to products other than meat. The idle cash balances in the hands of the population have continued to grow. To eliminate their excess money holdings it would have been necessary to increase expenditures either by increasing the volume of goods and services or to further increase prices. About three-quarters of total increases in wages were effected centrally and were unrelated to greater economic performance. Subsidies for food have been maintained. Credits to households are granted at a rate of interest lower than that on savings deposits and there has been a rapid expansion of net credits. There are many inconsistencies in the price and income policy by which the authorities have been trying to control expenditures on consumption.

The state budget has continued to create a strong inflationary pressure. Deficits exceeded planned deficits in 1982, 1983, and 1984. Subsidies, which it has not been possible to eliminate because of price distortions, represented 46.9 percent of total budgetary expenditures in 1982, 40.6 percent in 1983, 40.3 percent in 1984, and still represent 38.4 percent in the 1985 budget (Zdyb 1985).

The authorities have very little freedom to maneuver in effecting structural adjustment. Contrary to expectations, it was not possible to substitute imports from the CMEA countries for imports from the West, and the size of the negative balance of visible trade with the socialist countries was smaller than planned in 1982, 1983, 1984, and 1985. No planned changes in the structure of production occurred in 1983 and 1984. It has been easier to expand the production of producer goods than consumption goods and exportables. It is difficult to adjust the structure of supply to the required structure of demand—a typical problem of a centrally planned economy.

Producer prices cannot be used to help structural adjustment. Originally 35 percent of their prices were fixed, 15 percent regulated, and 50 percent were contractual, that is, freely determined. However, this last group has been subjected to increasing controls. They have to be based on "justified costs" that are to be determined by authorities for every enterprise. There is clearly a regress in this field (Jeziorański 1984; Kalinowski and Karpiński 1984; and Zdyb 1985).

So far "changes in the wage policy have been small and insignificant" and "completely insufficient from the point of view of the principles of the reform: the autonomy, self-government and self-financing of the enterprises" (Jozefiak 1985a). At the same time the experience of the early 1980s has demonstrated once again that administrative methods are unable to solve the problem of irrational and excessive employment in various sectors of the economy (Dach 1984). There is still a lot of unnecessary labor hoarded by the enterprises because the low wage bill, the cost-based formula for price determination and the rule of justified costs make it possible for enterprises to obtain permission to raise prices to the level that covers the cost of all unnecessary labor that, in the opinion of the enterprise, may one day become necessary. The introduction of the partial obligatory use of labor exchanges has only aggravated the situation, as the enterprises are afraid that it may not be easy in the future to obtain authorization to hire more labor (Dach 1984).

While excess labor is hoarded by numerous enterprises, shortages of labor are felt by others. This prevents structural changes, as do the shortage of investment funds, continuation of unfinished investments, and insufficient funds for modernization and expansion of financially successful enterprises. Gross investment has been reduced to the point that real depreciation is not being covered and negative net investment has appeared, unfortunately not in those sectors that should be reduced in size (Misiak 1984).

There is practically no link between the profitability of an enterprise and its ability to finance its expansion. The banking system allocates credits, taking into consideration the centrally determined priorities—as expressed in operational programs, government procurement contracts, and pressures from the branch ministries, and the intermediate administrative level formed by the new associations (Jeziorański 1984).

So far the authorities have not been able to effect any visible structural changes. They are, however, preparing to undertake them as soon as it would be possible to expand investment outlays. Unfortunately, it appears that they intend to implement structural changes again from above on the basis of what the central planners believe the new industrial structure should be, instead of permitting it to emerge from below with the help of microcalculations at the enterprise level (Kalinowski and Karpiński 1984); and Derbin and Gandziarski 1985). As these changes will take place without good market signals, there is no guarantee, of course, that the new structure will be any more efficient than the one that was built in the past.

Poland's hard-currency indebtedness was $26.9 billion at the end of 1984 and, because of the need to convert unpaid interest into debt, it is not expected to be stabilized earlier than 1990–91 when it is likely to reach $33 or $34 billion (Majewski 1985). To service this debt, with the heavy dependence of the economy on imports from the West of not only modern technology but also of some essential raw materials and intermediate goods, exports to the West must expand quite considerably and this has to be accepted as the central point of development strategy. The economic system has to be adjusted to that strategy.

It seems that the minimum conditions for such an approach would involve, first of all, the introduction of a flexible price system based on transaction prices, the acceptance of profit as the success indicator throughout the economy, the allocation of producer goods by market relations between the suppliers and users, and a more liberalized labor market. All transactions between the FTOs and the producers or users of tradables should take place at transaction prices, and the price equalization system would have to be eliminated and replaced by tariffs and subsidies applied in some specific cases.

The elimination of price distortions on producer goods would make the calculation of profits and losses meaningful. It would help to separate the enterprises that are efficient, but do not show profits at the existing prices, from those whose expansion should be restricted or those that should be liquidated. The use of subsidies could be restricted. The financial strength of the efficient producers could be supported by bank credits available at the equilibrium rate of interest, while enterprises with some excess funds should be allowed to earn sufficiently high interest on their deposits. Similarly, exporters and importers should have the possibility of borrowing or accumulating foreign exchange in their bank accounts. The calculation of full costs on the basis of transaction prices in hard currency trade would make possible rational decisions concerning exports and imports (Zdyb 1985; and Józefiak 1985b).

On the basis of microdecisions within autonomous and profit maximizing enterprises—with the help of reasonably undistorted prices, positive real rates of interest, undistorted wages and a flexible rate of exchange—a more efficient structure of production and trade might evolve and, gradually, the old bureaucratic habits and mentality would be replaced by the business approach. This process would not be easy and would depend on a carefully conducted macroeconomic policy and a strategy of promoting exports and international industrial cooperation, as well as debt rescheduling. However, there does not seem to be any viable alternative to far-reaching economic reform as a necessary condition for the solution of Poland's balance-of-payments problems at the present time, without inflicting a prolonged stagnation on the economy. So far the economic reform in Poland has not evolved decisively in this direction and this has not been clearly stated in Plowiec's essay.

CHAPTER 15

Economic Reform and Foreign Trade in Poland: Comments on Chapter 13

David M. Kemme

Dr. Plowiec has presented a discussion of recent changes in foreign trade planning and management in Poland. More importantly, she has discussed these changes in historical perspective as well as in relation to contemporary changes in other areas of the economy. As such the essay can be divided into two distinct parts. The first is a history of foreign trade planning and management, highlighting three distinct periods: 1950–65—Strict methods of central planning and management; 1966–70—Partial reform of the foreign trade system; and 1971–81—Partial implementation of parametric methods. The second part discusses the current reform programs and their implementation —foreign trade being a significant part of the whole.

With respect to the historical discussion there appears to be an omission, namely, that relatively little attention was paid to the rationalization of *imports*. It appears that most economists and central planners in Poland were concerned with the rationalization of exports. Discussion of the optimization of trade tended to degenerate into a discussion of the efficiency of exports. Determination of imports was of secondary importance: central planners determined critically needed goods that were not produced domestically as part of the general economic plan. The Ministry of Foreign Trade (MFT) then provided further details to enterprises and FTOS. This omission may be especially important given the fact that near indiscriminate importing during the mid-1970s led to the severe economic problems of the late 1970s and 1980s. Montias (1982) describes the planning process of the late 1970s as one in which the politically more powerful ministries successfully secured resources and favorable plan targets often without the planning commission's participation. Alleged government corruption to avoid plan enforcement, the loss of the control function of the central bank, and the allure of Western technology and goods complicated the process. It was easier to import more from the West on credit than it was to make the difficult decisions necessary to retrench or reallocate resources.

With respect to exports it can be seen that from 1950 to 1981 there were many interesting changes. In nearly every subperiod there was a movement away from direct central planning toward an alternative that stressed rationalization and efficiency—ignoring arguments concerning the second best. In 1955–65 the calculation of various coefficients of export effectiveness eliminated the most inefficient transactions. I do not believe, however, that these calculations led to true optimization. In 1966–70 a more ambitious attempt to optimize involved the calculation of shadow profits. Over time, however, distortions were introduced, thereby decreasing shadow costs and increasing shadow profits. (Similar distortions were introduced with respect to revenues.) Throughout the period exchange rates were determined on the basis of the average cost, rather than marginal cost, of acquiring foreign exchange by export to the dollar and ruble trade regions. While the dichotomous exchange rate system discussed by Plowiec was marked as an important achievement, foreign prices and foreign competition still had little effect on the domestic economy. There were also novel experiments dealing with particular industries, pharmaceuticals, and shipbuilding in which foreign trade prices were used to calculate production costs, and profits were used as a source of funds for investment and bonuses. These experiments were deemed successful, but they also stand as isolated incidents.

The 1971 to 1981 period saw wider application of transaction prices in the earlier years (1971–72) as the domestic economic reforms that introduced the WOGS, or initiating units, were implemented. But still there was no linkage of export profits to the financial incentives of enterprise or FTO employees. Profits on exports were calculated with profits on domestic sales and, since profits on domestic sales could be increased much more easily, export production was again less important to any given enterprise. By 1975 the administrative structure giving WOGs and large enterprises more autonomy had collapsed and foreign trade decisionmaking had reverted to central planning. Thus by 1975 there were, as a practical matter, only a few minor differences from the system in operation during the 1950 to 1955 period. We may conclude that experiments concerning one sector, foreign trade, or selected industries, like pharmaceuticals or shipbuilding, have failed because the bulk of the economy continued to operate under a passive incentive system and central directives therefore inevitably returned.

The new reform period, which began with legislation passed in the winter of 1981 and continues to date, introduced major changes in the planning and management of the economy: plans are to take on more of a strategic-informative character and markets are to play a greater role in principle. It is important to note, however, that all of the premartial law proposals were not enacted by the Sejm later as proposed, and some of the bills enacted were not fully implemented. Some would argue that the most fundamental and meaningful elements have been omitted (e.g., the fact that the founding body of an enterprise rather than the workers' council of the enterprise is responsible for selecting the enterprise manager). Further, while central planning directives have been eliminated in principle, operational programs were introduced in several areas in which there were shortages of goods, or these were otherwise designated as priority areas. Foreign trade was one of the areas controlled by an operational program. Operational programs are now giving way to a system of government contracts that may be more promising, insofar as genuine liberalization is concerned.

There have been several additional changes in the area of foreign trade. The devisa zloty has been eliminated and a new exchange rate system has been introduced in which the zloty/dollar rate is based on a weighted market basket of convertible currencies and appears to be more flexible than in the past. I am not certain it is more meaningful though, since there was an immediate modification to what was to be a uniform exchange rate policy—the exchange rate for basic raw materials was initially set at a rate 40 percent below the general rate. The fact that there were two dollar exchange rates, and both foreign and domestic prices frequently changed, led central planners to abandon the use of transaction prices and generally made it impossible to evaluate the efficiency of foreign trade.

There were several important changes in institutional and organizational arrangements as well. The relationship between producers and FTOS is now more flexible—there are no obligatory relationships—and the MFT has granted more licenses to enterprises and associations to conduct trade. Both actions may weaken the monopoly position of FTOS, but to date most trade still takes place through these organizations due to cost advantages and availability of skilled personnel. There has also been the introduction of hard-currency retention accounts entitling exporters to some proportion of their hard-currency earnings. Unfortunately, the retention quota is based on the import intensity of production of the particular enterprise. If hard currency is of any value to the enterprise, this provides an incentive to increase imports. The stated goal, however, is to reduce hard-currency imports and increase exports. These actions indicate there is significant potential for meaningful change, but the current system of operation, on balance, appears to be little different from the mechanism of central directives of the past.

Before proceeding to Plowiec's conclusions let me add here that the essay tends to focus on issues relating primarily to Polish trade with the West. The developments of recent years that affect Polish-CMEA/Soviet relations should also be mentioned. There have been changes that in fact have further integrated Polish production facilities into the CMEA economy. For example, there have been numerous agreements between Polish enterprises and Soviet and other East European parties that allow for the sharing of idle or incomplete production facilities in Poland (Wolnicki 1985). In other cases equipment of major projects that were canceled has been sold to CMEA partners. The Soviet Union has also been instrumental in the selection of facilities to be completed and has then contracted for the output of these facilities. Wolnicki (1985) argues that the Polish economy today in comparison to the 1970s is more tightly bound to the Soviet Union by these bilateral production agreements and may have less room to maneuver in the future. In effect, the Soviet Union has succeeded in achieving a new type of economic integration with Poland that previously was resisted.

Now let me return to Plowiec's major conclusions and several questions that arise. First, central directives have been abolished, but these have been replaced by operational programs and governmental contracts. Will these programs atrophy or provide a mechanism for spontaneous regeneration of central planning? Nasilowski (1985) points out that the goal of integrating plan and market has yet to be described in a manner allowing its practical application. Nearly all of the new economic and financial criteria are subject to manipulation. Second, there has been a reform of retail prices both in terms of magnitude and price formation mechanisms. But will free market prices be replaced by negotiated (and then frozen) or officially fixed prices as soon as problems arise? Third, there is now greater self-reliance of enterprises, greater ability for them to determine wage structures and new relationships among enterprises. But when an enterprise faces financial difficulties the state inevitably grants financial assistance. The bargaining now is over the redistribution of financial resources with the goal of the enterprise being to increase the growth of income of its work force rather than to lower output targets or raise input allotments. Will increased efficiency and productivity result from this new process? Fourth, more meaningful exchange rates have been introduced, and they are more flexible. But if hard-currency imports are centrally allocated and there is little incentive to export, will the exchange rates serve anything but an accounting role? Finally, new relationships have been developed with CMEA countries, defined by production-sharing agreements. To what extent do these agreements represent a movement toward greater Soviet-Polish economic integration? Further, to what extent are these agreements a threat to the market orientation of the reform itself? Can the Polish economy move from central planning to a system integrating plan and market at the same time that there is movement toward greater integration with the CMEA and the Soviet Union? Does greater integration necessitate a larger degree of central planning, or can the Poles emulate the Hungarians—maintain domestic market mechanisms *and* trade and production agreements with the CMEA and the Soviet Union?

In summary, I must conclude that Poland has not passed the critical point of no return with respect to the reform. What have not yet been created are (1) autonomous enterprises that are free of excessive external influence, such as the rationing of the main producers' goods; (2) real financial constraints that effectively force enterprises to behave efficiently; (3) a reduction in the scale of enterprises in order to reduce monopoly power and therefore the need for state intervention; (4) a system of government contracting that is more competitive; and finally, a more flexible system of foreign trade and allocation of foreign exchange.

Notes

1. Economic Stabilization, Structural Adjustment, and Economic Reform

1. Holzman's seminal contributions on the macroeconomics of the Soviet Union and Eastern Europe include Holzman (1960a, and 1974a, chapter 5; and 1974b). Wiles (1968) also was a pioneer in analyzing the issue of external balance and the relationships between internal and external balance in centrally planned economies.

2. These ratios are calculated from data available from 1970 to 1981 in Vienna Institute for Comparative Economic Studies (1984) and for 1982 to 1984 in Vanous (1985). Consistent data were not available for Romania. Peak years for the investment ratio were 1974–75 for Bulgaria and Czechoslovakia, 1974–78 for Hungary, and 1972–78 for Poland. Because reliable data for most of these countries are not available for inventories, it is not possible to net them out from the accumulation fund in order to derive a figure for fixed investment. Some versions of the investment cycle would include inventories, however, and the accumulation fund may not be a bad measure of what the proponents of the investment cycle have in mind.

3. Estimated convertible currency trade balances would in general differ from the nonsocialist trade balances reported in table 1.1, but the general trends would be similar.

4. NMP produced minus NMP distributed actually equals a country's overall trade surplus plus losses to the national economy, a category for which data are not usually available. These data are based largely on United Nations Economic Commission for Europe (1985b), Vienna Institute (1984), and Vanous (1985).

5. To the extent that this increase in the growth rate of investment reflected a buildup in inventories of products normally exported to the convertible currency area, but in low demand because of the worldwide recession, it would not reflect the typical stage one adjustment behavior hypothesized earlier.

6. Of course, not all East European countries rely on such imports to the same extent. Czechoslovakia, for example, appears to follow a much more self-reliant industrial strategy. See Brada and Montias (1984), pp. 380–85.

2. Devaluation in Modified Planned Economies: A Preliminary Model for Hungary

European Department, International Monetary Fund. An earlier version of this paper was presented at the ninth U.S.-Hungarian Economics Roundtable, Berkeley, California, in June 1985. The author is grateful to Mark Allen, Peter Hole,

Anthony Lanyi, Paul Masson, Janos Somogyi, and Iqbal Zaidi for comments. Sole responsibility remains with the author for all interpretations and any errors or omissions. Views expressed herein do not necessarily reflect those of the institution with which the author is affiliated.

1. For a comparative study of exchange rate regimes in several planned economies, see Wolf (1985b). Various facets of the exchange rate system in the stylized CPE are explored in detail in Holzman (1974a, chapters 4, 10, and 15); and Wolf (1980, 1985b). Brabant (1985b) presents a comprehensive classification of and information on various exchange rates in the CMEA countries.

2. This combination of assumptions results in the prices of competitive nonruble tradables as well as of ruble tradables rising in proportion with the exchange rate, and the prices of flexibly priced nontradables also rising in proportion. Using the estimated weights from table 2.1, this would yield an elasticity of the overall domestic producers' price level with respect to an exchange rate change of 0.68.

3. Whether all domestic producer prices of goods within the competitive sector really move proportionately with their transaction prices is, of course, open to question. In a cross-section study of the Hungarian economy for the period 1981–83, Simon and Veress (1984) find no evidence of a systematic correlation between foreign trade and domestic prices. It is possible, of course, that the data available to the authors were simply too aggregative to pick up the correlations that did exist. As a greater number of enterprises become subject solely to the most liberal or "third" price rule mentioned in the text, it is possible that the correlation between domestic producer prices and transaction prices might increase for the competitive sector.

4. Exports to the ruble area amounted to about 18 percent of GDP in 1983. For purposes of calculating the weight of this composite good here, however, this higher percentage probably overstates the true weight of ruble exports in the economy. This is because while GDP measures only value added, exports are a gross concept. The same problem exists with respect to measuring the weight of nonruble exports. If the ratio of value added to gross value of output were higher for ruble exports than other goods, the 7 percent figure used in the text would, however, underestimate the weight of these goods in the economy.

5. Clearing accounts are maintained in transferable rubles (TRs), but each CMEA country attempts to avoid accumulating TR claims on the others because they cannot be automatically converted into claims on goods.

6. The increase in the relative profitability of the competitive tradable would be diminished somewhat in a model that explicitly incorporates intermediate goods. If, for simplicity, profitability is defined as the ratio of product price (P) to product cost (C), the percentage change in relative profitability for the competitive tradable would be equal to $(\hat{P}_T - \hat{P}_N) - (\hat{C}_T - \hat{C}_N)$, where a "$\hat{}$" denotes a percentage change in a variable. Because the material input coefficient for the nontradable will in general be less than that for the T good, we would expect $\hat{C}_T > \hat{C}_N$. This will make

reallocation from the N into the T good less attractive to producers than in our simpler model. In effect, the supply side relative price elasticity will be less than otherwise. As discussed in appendix 2.1, however, a lower substitution elasticity will also reduce the extent of price rise of the nontradable following devaluation from what it otherwise would be; therefore $(\hat{P}_T - \hat{P}_N)$ would be greater than in our model. The net supply side substitution effect with intermediates is likely to be less than in our model, but it is still likely to be positive. Wolf (in press) contains a model with an imported intermediate good.

7. A more detailed, but by no means comprehensive, discussion of the spillover effects of micro-disequilibrium on the consumption goods' market in planned economies may be found in Wolf (1985a) and the references therein. One would expect that the rather primitive substitution coefficient relating the N and T goods (see appendix 2.1) would be positively related to the underlying relative price elasticity of demand between these two goods.

8. Alternatively, the improvement in the competitive trade balance will be equal to the sum of (1) the reduced expenditure on the T good due to the higher price level, and (2) the increased excess supply of the T good induced by the change in relative prices.

9. The high degree of concentration of Hungarian industry, per se, should not cause the substitution effects to be negligible. For preliminary work, assuming a monopolistic market structure, see Wolf (1981). Also, the obstacles to rapid factor mobility among enterprises need not impede a reorganization of production *within* enterprises in response to changes in relative prices. For a summary of arguments on why elasticities may remain quite low in Hungary, see Wolf (1985b).

10. In terms of national prices, the ratio of the nontradable to tradable prices in 1975 was 0.74 for Hungary and an (unweighted) average of 0.92 for seven non-CMEA countries with roughly comparable per capita incomes (see Kravis et al. 1982, table 6.11). This difference, however, is probably due to a number of factors (see Marer 1985a).

11. A model of an MPE with a flexibly priced tradable and fixed price tradable-nontradable composite was first outlined in Wolf (1978). Aizenman (1981) examines the case of a market economy with a flexibly priced nontradable, and two flexibly priced tradables, one of which is subject to a quota.

12. See Kornai (1979) on the concept of forced substitution. For a brief analysis of this phenomenon in the familiar two-commodity general equilibrium framework, see Wolf (1985a).

3. Conditionality and Adjustment in Hungary and Yugoslavia

The research for this chapter was supported by a grant from the Institute of International Studies, University of California-Berkeley, and a grant from the Berkeley-Stanford Program on Soviet International Behavior. The chapter benefited from the helpful comments and suggestions of the editors of this volume.

1. While the major focus of this essay is on the role of the IMF, the World Bank has also started to play an increasingly important role. The Bank has instituted new forms of program lending, including structural adjustment loans, to assist countries in restructuring their economies in the medium term to deal with structural balance-of-payments problems. In theory, the IMF only lends short term to deal with short-term problems; and the Bank lends medium to long term to promote long-term development and structural change. In recent years, however, the distinction has become blurred as the IMF has had to roll over short-term loans and institute newer, medium-term instruments such as the extended fund facility (EFF); and the Bank has recognized that short-term crises in the balance of payments have medium- and long-term implications. The Bank's seal of approval is also important to private banks and increases the Bank's leverage in policy dialogue with recipient countries. However, while the distinctions and policy distance between the two institutions have thus narrowed in recent years, they still differ in their time horizon and basic approach.

2. The implicit model underlying the standard IMF adjustment program assumes that inflationary pressure is the result of excess demand. The simplest form of this model relates inflation to growth in the money supply that, in turn, is assumed to be the major factor behind excess demand. See Khan and Knight (1981) for a formal specification of an implicit IMF model.

3. There is continuing controversy on this point, as suggested in the work of Taylor (1981) and Robinson (1986).

4. For a complete discussion of differences in timing and enforcement of different types of IMF conditions, see Williamson (1982).

5. For a description of a typical CPE, see Brown and Neuberger (1968), and for a description of the shortage-economy model, see Kornai (1980a).

6. The basic features described here are those that seem to be the most important to achieving an understanding of how the economies functioned during the 1980–84 period. For a more detailed discussion of these economies both during this period and during earlier phases of the postwar period, see, for example, Tyson and Eichler (1980); and Hewett (1981).

7. In Hungary, profile restrictions specifying the composition of output continued to be applied to state enterprises through the end of 1984.

8. This perception is based on interviews carried out by the authors in Yugoslavia in 1981 and 1982 and in Hungary in 1983 and 1985.

9. For evidence on investment cycles in Hungary and Yugoslavia, see Bauer (1978); and Tyson (1983).

10. The value of medium- and long-term funds raised by Hungary in international capital markets is based on information contained in table 5.4.10, United Nations, Economic Commission for Europe, *Economic Survey of Europe in 1984–85* (1985.) The value of long-term capital inflow from commercial banks into Yugoslavia in 1984 is estimated from data contained in the National Bank of Yugoslavia (September 1984).

11. Available anecdotal evidence suggests that the IMF had to lobby hard to win

a commitment from the private banks for new medium- and long-term credits.

12. After hanging fire for several months, the loan was put together with strong pressure from the Bank of England to overcome objections by British banks.

13. In addition to such limits on domestic demand components, quantitative limits were set on foreign borrowing and foreign reserve changes in the Yugoslav-IMF agreements and presumably in the Hungarian agreements as well. Since the ultimate objective of these agreements was to improve the external economic situation, these kinds of quantitative limits were reflections of the desired or allowable pace of improvement expected by the IMF.

14. For an insightful discussion of enterprise responses to credit contraction in planned economies, see Wolf (1985a).

15. Tardos (1983) argues that especially during the squeeze on enterprise incomes that accompanied austerity in Hungary after 1980, inter-enterprise trade credit became a significant phenomenon there as well.

16. Khan and Knight's article (1981) contains a formal description of the major features of this model.

17. In the Yugoslav case the IMF negotiated a policy understanding on exchange rate movements during the period 1981–83 and, finally, adopted an explicit exchange rate target in 1984.

18. The IMF had at its disposal estimates of the overvaluation of the dinar from the computable general equilibrium (CGE) model developed by World Bank researchers. These estimates indicated that the dinar was overvalued by about 25 percent in 1980 despite a nominal devaluation of about 31 percent. By mid-1981 the inflation differential between Yugoslavia and its trading partners had more than offset the real effects of the devaluation. As a result of a devaluation in October 1982 under IMF pressure, the real effective exchange rate of the dinar fell by about 17 percent between the end of 1981 and the end of 1982, but this was not sufficient to eliminate the overvaluation of the exchange rate suggested by model simulations. In the case of Hungary the extent of overvaluation must have been uncertain in the minds of the IMF negotiators. There was a nominal devaluation against the dollar in 1981 and 1982, but the forint rate actually appreciated against the currencies of Hungary's major European trading partners during this period. In addition, the forint had appreciated against both the dollar and the European currencies in 1980, and there were no available model estimates of the extent of overvaluation stemming from this appreciation. Finally, given the soft budget constraints and the long history of restricting imports from Western markets to goods for which there were few domestic or CMEA substitutes, it must have been difficult for the IMF negotiators to understand the role of the exchange rate in Hungary's system let alone to estimate its equilibrium value.

19. Finally, it is at least possible, though nowhere documented, that the IMF was encouraged to adopt a more cautious role with the Hungarians so as not to stir up Soviet concern about or opposition to Hungarian membership in the IMF. If the IMF were perceived as forcing the Hungarians to adopt policies that they opposed for domestic or bloc reasons (and a large forint devaluation was arguably such a

policy), then Soviet concern about the effects of IMF membership on Hungarian autonomy was a likely result.

20. For empirical work on the links between devaluation and inflation in Yugoslavia, see Tyson (1977b); Tyson and Neuberger (1979); and Bajt (1985). Bajt argues that, although devaluation has an inflationary impact in Yugoslavia, the main reasons for increased inflation are the concentrated market structure that allows firms to increase their prices when price controls are relaxed and increases in personal incomes.

21. See table 3.2 for evidence on the activity of inflation and real money conditions in Yugoslavia during the period 1980–84.

22. See chapter 2 of this volume.

23. Evidence indicating a decline in export subsidy rates in light manufacturing, machinery, chemicals, metals, and food products is presented in Robinson (1986).

24. According to Kis, Robinson, and Tyson (1985), between 1981 and 1983 the ratio between the price received for dollar export sales and the price received for sales to domestic users fell in most of the major exporting sectors except machinery. This evidence suggests a noticeable deterioration in export incentives during this period, with some recovery in 1984 but not to 1981 levels.

25. A debit of about $1.2 billion was recorded in the errors and omissions category of the Yugoslav balance of payments with the convertible currency area in 1983. An average credit of about $650 million was recorded for this category in 1981–82. See International Monetary Fund, *International Financial Statistics*, various issues.

26. During 1981–83, both consumers and producers were confronted by a variety of new policies that restricted their ability to use foreign exchange holdings as they wished. For example, in 1982 limits were placed on the amount of foreign exchange that individuals could take out of the country; and enterprises were forced to hand over part of their foreign exchange earnings to the federal government to help service outstanding debt which it guaranteed.

27. Several enterprise managers interviewed in Hungary by Tyson in May 1985 indicated that interest rates had been unexpectedly increased sometime during 1980–84 on the outstanding portion of long-term loans contracted earlier at lower interest rates.

28. According to the National Bank of Yugoslavia estimates, interest rates behaved as follows during 1980–85:

	1980 August	1981 August	1982 June	1983 July	1984 July	1984 October	1985 January
Nominal long-term rates	12.0	12.0	18.0	38.0	48.0	57.0	62.0
Inflation in retail prices	30.4	46.0	30.0	39.0	50.7	55.6	62.0

This evidence suggests that Yugoslavia began to adhere to the real interest rate condition imposed by the 1984 IMF agreement by the last quarter of the year. Interest rates taken from the National Bank of Yugoslavia (June 1984 and June 1985).

29. Administrative control over the allocation of investment in Yugoslavia was weakened by inter-enterprise trade credit and other inter-enterprise forms of lending which made the final distribution of credit different from the one realized through administrative means. Also, the Yugoslav authorities did not have strong administrative controls over the distribution of enterprise retained income as the Hungarian authorities had. For these two reasons it seems likely that the Hungarian authorities had better control over the micro allocation of investment than did the Yugoslav authorities.

30. According to recent statistics reported by the United Nations, Hungary's imports from nonsocialist countries stagnated between 1981 and 1984 (United Nations, *Economic Bulletin for Europe*, 1985). The difference between the UN and Robinson results may be attributable to the fact that a portion of Hungary's convertible currency imports came from socialist countries.

31. The Yugoslav trade figures must be treated with caution and skepticism because of the anomalies introduced by the use of statistical exchange rates to convert trade flows denominated in convertible currencies other than the dollar into dollar values.

32. Of course, this pattern of export growth is attributable in part to the recovery in convertible currency export markets that occurred in 1983–84 after the sharp recession in 1981.

33. See, for example, the analysis of the effects of dinar overvaluation on export incentives and export growth in Robinson and Tyson (1985).

34. Under competitive pricing regulations, prices on domestic sales could be raised only if export prices increased and export profitability increased in convertible currency trade. Thus firms were encouraged to eliminate exports with below-average prices or profitability so they could more easily raise their domestic prices.

35. The stagnation in the dollar value of Hungary's convertible currency exports is partly the result of the appreciation of the dollar relative to the currencies of Hungary's major European trading partners. The dollar appreciation, along with the slower growth of European markets relative to the U.S. market, also, in part, explains why Hungary continued to lose market share in the developed countries (see Balassa 1988).

36. According to data reported by the United Nations Economic Commission for Europe, Hungarian exports to nonsocialist countries increased in real terms at an average annual rate of 6.5 percent between 1980 and 1984 (United Nations, *Economic Bulletin for Europe* 1985a). Estimates by Robinson show an average annual growth rate of 6.1 percent between 1981 and 1984. Most of the reported increase occurred in 1983 and 1984 after a stagnation in real exports between 1980 and 1982. Finally, a dramatic increase in energy and fuel exports in 1983 attributable to a large increase in reexports of Iranian and Libyan oil is partly responsible for the apparent growth in real exports (Wharton Econometric Forecasting Associates, 1984). If fuel and energy exports are excluded, exports to the convertible currency area grew at an average annual rate of about 5.5 percent between 1980 and 1984, according to the UN data.

37. Evidence from enterprise interviews conducted by Tyson in May 1985 supports

this interpretation. Enterprise managers reported that they had been under extreme pressure from state and party authorities to export even when it was unprofitable to do so and that their access to foreign exchange and investment credits was linked to their convertible currency export performance.

4. Industrial Policy in Eastern Europe

The findings reported here are in large part the result of my collaboration with J. Michael Montias on the industrial policies of the East European nations. Elements of the conceptual framework and much of the factual material, particularly that dealing with Poland, are the result of his research and are reported here with his kind permission and my deep appreciation. Any shortcomings and all conclusions are entirely my responsibility. The financial support of the National Council for Soviet and East European Research is gratefully acknowledged.

1. Indeed, much of the post-1968 period was characterized by the use of gross value of output, with all its attendant drawbacks, as the indicator of enterprise performance, as well as by a recentralization of financial and other controls over enterprise activity (Csaba 1983).

2. Vavroušek (1986) refers to some criteria, such as a desire for technological breakthroughs, economy-wide effects, and a consistency with the international division of labor. Csaba (1983, p. 80) mentions more specific, but nevertheless not very operational, criteria such as trends in the structure of production, the state of R&D, material-intensity of production, the size of production runs, and investment requirements.

3. Notice the contrast to the Czechoslovak case where development programs were only briefly administered in this way before being made subordinate to ministry departments.

4. A more extensive treatment of Hungarian industrial policy can be found in Brada (1984).

5. This analysis of Polish industrial policy is largely based on J. M. Montias's contributions to Brada and Montias (1984, 1985).

6. Clearly there are problems and disputes within CMEA over specialization. Such conflicts also exist within the European Community (EC), where industrial policy in sectors such as steel, computers, telecommunications, and aircraft has created tension. It is worth noting that in both static and dynamic terms the CMEA in fact appears to be at least as effective a regional integration scheme as the EC (Brada and Méndez 1985, 1988), despite the impressionistic claims to the contrary of many specialists such as those of Marrese and Vanous in this volume.

5. The Evolution of CMEA Institutions and Policies and the Need for Structural Adjustment

1 An English translation is available in *The Multilateral Economic Cooperation of Socialist States* (1977). For a commentary on this document, see Lavigne (1973).

2. The relevant statements are summarized in *Intensifikatsia proizvodstva v evropeiskikh*

stranakh SEV [CMEA]: *faktory ekonomicheskogo rosta* (1972).

3. See the reports on the thirty-fifth and thirty-sixth sessions of the CMEA in *Ekonomicheskaia Gazeta*, June 1981 and June 1982, respectively, as well as a lead article in *Pravda*, October 15, 1982, on "the orientation toward a deepening of socialist economic integration," which received extensive comment in Eastern Europe.

4. See, for instance, Köves (1983), who writes, "On the Soviet part, demands are formulated more and more definitely that those countries should transform their export structure in such a way that would . . . result in a pushing into the background of several sectors which have been developed dynamically up to now precisely according to Soviet demands" (pp. 131–32).

5. Mironov (1984), referring to an *ukaz* of May 22, 1983: "On the procedure of operations on the territory of the Soviet Union of joint organizations of the USSR and the other CMEA countries."

6. This was indeed realized, for example through several agreements concluded with Hungary in July 1983 for the implementation of Hungarian corn growing systems in the Ukraine and the establishment of a large poultry farm in Azerbaidjan. *Nepszabadsag*, July 30, 1983, as cited by *Radio Free Europe Background Report*, no. 195 (August 11, 1983).

7. By the end of 1983 some 198 multilateral agreements had been signed by CMEA members in relation to the target programs. This figure was already cited for late 1981–early 1982. (See Ultanbaev 1983, p. 21; and Golubev et al. 1983, p. 74.)

8. See the texts of these programs in *Ekonomicheskaia Gazeta*, no. 20, May 1984; no. 42, October 1984; no. 17, April 1984; no. 24, June 1985.

9. Ryzhkov (1984); Ryzhkov's statement merely indicated that an agreement would be needed if the Soviet Union was to supply more gas to Eastern Europe. Later the project was mentioned in a number of East European sources. All countries, including Romania, seem to be prepared to participate.

10. Pecsi (1983) puts the depreciation of the transferable ruble at 37 percent between 1974 and 1980 and the real interest rate at -1.8 percent.

11. The Hungarian prime minister, G. Lázár, was reported to be critical of the failure to implement this decision at the 1985 session of the CMEA (*Reuters*, June 26, 1985).

12. For Czechoslovak-Soviet relations see Lushnikov (1985, p. 93), who argues, "It would be rational to increase significantly the share of machinery and equipment in Soviet exports to Czechoslovakia."

6. CMEA Institutions and Policies versus Structural Adjustment

The author is a staff member of the Department of International Economic and Social Affairs of the Secretariat of the United Nations in New York. The views expressed here are his own and do not imply expression of any opinion whatsoever on the part of the UN secretariat.

1. The creation of such a union, chiefly among Czechoslovakia, the German Democratic Republic, Hungary, and Poland, was first advocated in Machowski (1973, pp. 18–19). Whereas Machowski saw this union as being then in statu nascendi, Brabant (1976) argued that it might be usefully explored, although political realities militated against its imminent emergence.

2. The full title reads: *The Comprehensive Program for the Further Extension and Improvement of Cooperation and the Development of Socialist Economic Integration by the CMEA Member Countries.*

3. Exceptions are a few of the more esoteric international economic organizations (IEOs) created in the late 1970s (e.g., Interlikhter in 1978).

4. I have examined the prehistory and achievements of the summit in greater detail in Brabant (1987).

5. Only some details of this agreement have been published as yet (*Rude Pravo*, July 10, 1984, pp. 1, 7). Others may be inferred from Strougal (1984, pp. 7–12).

6. For details, see Brabant (1987), pp. 133–39.

7. Brezhnev used the term *sovmestnaia firma*. This is a rather unusual designation, especially in view of the very carefully worded taxonomy of "international economic organizations (IEOs)" that has gradually evolved since the adoption of the integration program (see Brabant 1980, pp. 195–216). It is not clear from the context whether Brezhnev was advocating completely new organs or whether he had something more conservative in mind. In the Soviet Union, *firma* refers to an association of enterprises headed by a "leading enterprise" (see *Bol'shaia sovetskaia entsiklopediia*, vol. 27 [Moscow: Sovetskaia entsiklopediia, 1977], p. 471) and is therefore akin to the GDR's Kombinat. As will be conjectured below, the recommendation probably concerned new organs that would fit better into the traditional planning framework of the CPEs than the IEOs that proliferated in the early 1970s.

8. *Declaration of the main directions of further development and deepening of economic, scientific, and technological cooperation of the CMEA member countries* (henceforth Main Directions). The other published document, *Declaration of the CMEA member countries on the preservation of peace and international economic cooperation* (henceforth Preservation of Peace), is a major statement on international relations, especially between East and West, but will not be further discussed here because it does not directly add anything to the summit's implications for SEI. Both documents are available from many sources. I shall use Main Directions from *Ekonomicheskaia Gazeta*, 1984:26, pp. 4–5. The official communiqué of the summit (*Pravda*, June 15, 1984, p. 1) suggests that other documents were agreed upon. These may contain more concrete details of some of the statements in Main Directions.

9. This is the interpretation of L. Strougal (see Bratislava's *Pravda*, July 5, 1984, p. 3), one of the chief architects of the summit.

10. The full designation is "*concerted plan of multilateral integration measures*." None of it has ever been published in extenso.

11. Especially Cuba, Mongolia, and Vietnam.

12. For a comprehensive analysis of the target programs as they were formulated around 1980, see Brabant (1981, pp. 141ff.).

13. There is considerable misunderstanding about investment coordination and the joint financing of investment projects coming under the SEI umbrella. For an example, see Marer (1984, pp. 163–64).

14. Strougal affirmed (Bratislava's *Pravda*, July 5, 1984, p. 3), in connection with the summit, that monetary aspects deserve equal attention to plan coordination. On the other hand, a Romanian source (Silvestru 1984, pp. 17–18) sees the future of SEI chiefly in the context of national planning and plan coordination in areas where national and regional interests intersect. Marjai (1984 pp. 6ff.) makes it crystal clear that SEI will be advanced by whatever means and in whatever direction the interests of two or more members intersect.

15. The document's full title is *Basic Principles of the International Socialist Division of Labor*.

16. For all practical purposes the Soviet dollar price and world supply curves can be combined without any loss of generality, because the Soviet dollar price supply curve to Eastern Europe (e.g., S_{sw}^l in the diagram) asymptotically converges to the general dollar price supply curve (e.g., S_w^l in the diagram) over a rather narrow supply range (here indicated by AD in the case of S_{sw}^l); in turn, the general dollar price supply curve must coincide with the world supply curve to Eastern Europe.

17. I have discussed the realism of a 1975 "Moscow principle" that superseded the 1958 "Bucharest principles" in another context. For a few of the arguments, see Brabant 1984a, p. 138.

18. I do not believe that all CPEs are presently realistically aiming at full self-sufficiency in all agricultural products suitable to their climate. This is certainly the case for the more industrial crops, but applies to some degree also to foodstuffs.

19. I do not believe that all CPEs are presently realistically aiming at full self-sufficiency in all agricultural products suitable to their climate. This is certainly the case for the more industrial crops, but applies to some degree also to foodstuffs.

20. In fact, calls for scientific-technical cooperation can be traced all the way to the very beginning of the CMEA, especially the 2d council session in August 1949.

21. Lavigne's remarks regarding the GDR (Lavigne 1984, p. 32) are too facile. The commentary of an insider in the GDR's negotiations with the CMEA and its individual members (e.g., Seiffert 1983) will quickly dispel the view she propounds.

7. The Content and Controversy of Soviet Trade Relations with Eastern Europe, 1970–1984

Above all the authors gratefully acknowledge programming work, calculations, and editorial assistance from Charles Movit. Additional thanks go to Jason McDonald and Marcia Levenson for excellent research assistance. The authors also benefited from critical remarks by H. Steven Gardner, Ed Hewett, Thomas Wolf, Keith Crane, Josef Brada, Michael Murphy, and Perry Patterson as well as the attendees of the conference on the Soviet Union and Eastern Europe in the world economy.

1. The relationship between implicit Soviet trade subsidies and unconventional gains from trade and the derivation of the country ranking in terms of strategic, political, ideological, and economic support for the Soviet Union are discussed at length in Marrese and Vanous (1983a), pp. 68–86.

2. Having clarified the steps in the bargaining process and the interests of both the Soviet Union and its CMEA partners, we must also caution the reader that our use of the strong correlation between implicit trade subsidies and nonmarket benefits as evidence supporting our interpretation of Soviet-East European trade flows is valid only if all East European countries have equal bargaining power or if bargaining power and the size of nonmarket benefits are positively correlated.

3. Ed Hewett was instrumental in opening our eyes to the possibility that more credit should be given to the bargaining skills of East European leaders—who seek to convince the Soviets that political-economic stability in Eastern Europe is fragile —and the uncertainties Soviet leaders face regarding the actual links between their subsidies and political-economic stability. Perhaps, as Hewett suggests, the Soviets have overestimated the fragility of the East European political-economic system, and therefore overpaid for what they have been receiving. Poland may have played a major role in triggering a reassessment, which may have led the Soviets to reduce anticipated subsidies.

4. Our claim that the Soviets operate a cumbersome resource transfer system is supported by the presence of unanticipated subsidies. Unanticipated subsidies reflect the Soviets' inability to forecast wmps perfectly. Desai (1985) has criticized our earlier work by arguing that in our transfer-theoretic framework the Soviets must fix prices and quantities of trade simultaneously to achieve the desired level of transfer to a particular country. She implicitly believes, therefore, that we have ignored the possibility of unanticipated subsidization. In this paper it is especially clear that the observed level of subsidization depends on anticipations.

5. A detailed methodological appendix is available from the authors upon request.

6. The economic rationale for East European participation in CMEA is also extremely weak (see Marrese 1986), but the East European position is more complicated to present because of the presence of implicit subsidies.

8. Centrally Planned Economies in the IMF, the World Bank, and the GATT

The author thanks the following persons for valuable comments, without implying responsibility on their part for the facts and interpretations: Zdenek Drábek, Janos Nyerges, John Williamson, Thomas Wolf, an expert affiliated with the IMF who prefers to remain anonymous, and all the editors for useful suggestions concerning presentation.

1. Although the legally correct term is "contracting parties," I use "members" for brevity.

2. Although the decree ratifying Czechoslovakia's accession to the GATT was signed by Klement Gottwald, then prime minister of a communist government.

3. Based on the author's discussions in Moscow during the summer of 1986 with Soviet experts.

4. I owe this insight to John Williamson of the Institute for International Economics.

5. During the early 1980s a portion of the Fund's holdings of Chinese renminbi was designated and disbursed as a usable currency. This was made possible by China's strong balance-of-payments and reserve position at the time.

9. How to Create Markets in Eastern Europe: The Hungarian Case

1. The case of agriculture was to a certain extent different. The ancillary businesses of the members of cooperatives and of employees pay less for one hour's work than the state or cooperative sector does, but only the private activity offers opportunities for a significant increase of global income.

2. The differential nature of control becomes clearer when we add to the above the fact that the ministry of finance has issued 1,200 to 2,500 ordinances per year concerning companies. These ordinances are supplemented by those of other superior authorities, such as the Hungarian National Bank, branch ministries, and often local party organizations. These ordinances provide special allowances or aggravation under the circumstances of already differentiated control. Fifty percent of the ordinances are retrospective: for example, changing taxes on incomes generated in the past (Galik 1983).

3. Adam Angyal, manager of one of the largest industrial enterprises, the Hungarian Shipyards and Crane Factory, found it insulting that the main activity of company economists was not defined as setting down the foundations for the technical development of the shipyards but in bargaining with the authorities. Adam Angyal and others are right when they stress their efforts to shape and influence the technical aspects of production. Financial issues cannot cast doubt on this. Their allegations and critiques are limited only to stating that the method of financial regulation reviewed here does not give suitable criteria for satisfactory selection among alternative technical possibilities on the one hand, and that the success of the technical concept selected often has to be put into operation in bargaining with state administration on the other, meaning that often it is not the market that determines the success of a concept. Case study on the Hungarian Shipyards and Crane Factory (Angyal 1983).

4. Since 1980, after-tax profits used by the enterprise for investments or wage increases have been subject to a further tax.

5. The contradictory coexistence of the two standpoints is well described in two statements of finance minister I. Hetenyi: "Regarding subsidies related to production, the major question for me is whether it is normative or not. Namely, whether the state grants subsidy under defined targets and conditions and whether it is accessible for everyone, fulfilling conditions, because such a subsidy can be pro-

motive. Or it is such a subsidy which is sort of cried out to prolong in the majority of cases the lifetime of less efficient production" (Hetenyi 1981). "The stimulative character of control may be effective only if control is normative. That is, if the changes of income generation and rates and taxes of each similar economic unit are identical. It is not against the incentive effect if on a higher income there is imposed not a proportionate but higher burden (e.g., progressive taxation, provided its rate is rational, that is not hampering the quick development of more profitable firms). It emerged from normativity also that the regulation of companies with substantially different conditions, owing to objective reasons may be different as well" (Hetenyi 1982). That means: First, he takes a stand regarding uniform controls. In the second case, he deems it necessary not only to apply progressive taxation on incomes, but he also describes regulation as normative if it takes into account the difficulties of particular firms.

6. The decree regarding the NEM was intended to provide freedom for companies concerning investments only so far as the maintenance of the level of production is concerned. Capacity-increasing investment credits, granted by the bank, were to be determined by a decision whether such credits were in accordance with the plan and whether the returns were adequate. The ideological foundation of limited independence in the 1960s in Hungary is outlined by W. Brus (1966), who claimed, based on the economic views of O. Lange and M. Dobb, that "the market mechanism is not suitable . . . for forming major long-term trends of the economy, especially not for selecting major long-term and investment trends" (p. 165). From this he drew the conclusion that, in a reformed socialist economy, the center distributes funds for investments among the different branches by means of direct decisions, concretely determining capacity increase as a result of these investments (p. 170). He also points out that for the sake of "superiority" of the central plan, the central level controls the market mechanism, limiting the range established of direct decisions (p. 175).

10. The Politics of Creating Efficient Markets in Socialism

These comments were prepared while the author was a fellow at the Center for Advanced Studies in the Behavioral Sciences in Stanford, California. I am grateful for the financial support provided by the Exxon Educational Foundation during my stay there. The International Research and Exchange Board and the German Marshall Fund generously funded the field research I did in Hungary and France in 1981–82, upon which many of these comments are based.

12. Soviet Central Planning: Probing the Limits of the Traditional Model

I am grateful to Josef C. Brada, Thomas A. Wolf, Lincoln Gordon, Jerry Hough, and Gregory Grossman for their detailed comments on an earlier draft of this chapter. I also benefited greatly from discussion of the essay at the conference where the studies in this volume were presented.

1. An account of Gorbachev's reform program and its implications for the system appears in Hewett (1988).

2. This section draws on a somewhat lengthier discussion in Hewett (1984a).

3. I am not the first to use the term. See, for example, Brus (1979).

4. For more information on the 1965 reforms, see Schroeder (1968, 1971); Campbell (1968); Feiwel (1972); and Hewett (1988, chapter 5).

5. For more information on the industrial associations, see Gorlin (1976).

6. Since assuming the post of general secretary, Mikhail Gorbachev has indicated on numerous occasions his determination to pursue a broad set of reforms (see, for example, Gorbachev 1985a). Probably the strongest statement in that regard came at the Twenty-seventh Party Congress in February 1986 where Gorbachev (1986) actually called for a radical reform (radikalnaia reforma), words rich with symbolism because Soviet leaders traditionally have not used them. In fact, while Gorbachev does not talk often of radical reforms, and it is not yet clear precisely what he has in mind, it is clear that he intends to pursue major changes in the spirit of Andropov's brief period.

7. Hewett (1984b, chapter 2) discusses this. For an excellent and very detailed discussion, see Gustafson (1984).

8. See in particular Chernenko (1984b).

9. Even here there are some ambiguities, particularly for pensioners who may fear that reform-induced inflation will seriously erode their real income.

10. At least in the traditional system one can stand in line to acquire products, and in many cases it is possible to get away from work to do that. That is part of the egalitarian flavor of the traditional system. Under the reformed system flexible prices would considerably reduce lines and their egalitarian externalities; and discipline at the workplace would be tighter, so it would be more difficult in any event to get away and stand in lines.

11. RFE-RL (1983, p. 18). Although this essay at the time was unpublished, since then most views presented there have appeared in print in the USSR (Zaslavakaia 1985, 1986).

12. CIA 1983, p. 62.

13. Organization for Economic Cooperation and Development (OECD) Europe GNP growth rates in 1961–65 averaged 5.5 percent per annum; during 1980–81 there was, on average, no significant GNP growth (CIA 1983, p. 35).

14. It certainly has been the case in Hungary (see Hewett 1981).

15. Computed using production data from the report on fulfillment of the 1983 plan, *Ekonomicheskaia Gazeta*, no. 6 (February 1984), pp. 7–9.

16. " . . . now the situation at times is simply offensive: the starting materials are good, but the production is such that people prefer to overpay speculators for good tastefully manufactured commodities." Andropov (1983c, p. 4).

17. See particularly Gorbachev (1984, p. 12).

18. For a more detailed argument on this point with some help from a small econo-

metric model, see Hewett (1984c).

19. For a discussion of these and other partial reforms focused on the wage fund, see Aganbegian (1984).

13. Economic Reform and Foreign Trade in Poland

The author is grateful to Thomas A. Wolf for assistance in preparing the final text.

1. The years 1945–49 should be viewed as a period of reconstruction and of looking for new approaches. See Plowiec (1979).

2. For a discussion of the methodologies used in calculating these exchange rates, see Trzeciakowski (1978, chapter 10).

3. The concept of the submarginal exchange rate, which ensures the profitability of 75–85 percent of exports, derives from past Polish foreign trade experience. The curve of export profitability tends to rise sharply above this level because at this point most exports are only incidentally exported or are produced by artisans, cooperatives, and so forth that operate and set prices in conditions that are not typical of the economy as a whole. When the exchange rate is set at this submarginal level, it is sufficient to justify most exports and imports. At the same time all the incidental elements, internal and external, that influence the equilibrium level of the exchange rate are excluded. With the submarginal rate the central authorities are able to influence producers to diminish the costs of unprofitable exports, at least over the medium term. If the exchange rate were set at a lower rate, it would not be the main financial parameter, and the authorities would have to accommodate passively the unprofitable exports.

4. This is the law on principles of remuneration in the firms (*Dziennik Ustaw*, no. 5, 1984, section 25).

Bibliography

"A szovetkezeti mozgalom a reformfolyamatban" (The Cooperatives and the Reform Movement). *Valosag*, no. 3 (1984).

Adam, Jan. *Wage Control and Inflation in the Soviet Bloc Countries*. New York: Praeger, 1980.

Adamecz, P., and J. Komlos. *The Financing of Ventures with Great Risk*. Budapest: MTA Kozgazdasagtudomanyi Intezet, 1984.

Aganbegian, A. "Vazhnye pozitivnye sdvigi v ekonomicheskoi zhizni strany" (Important Positive Developments in the Life of the Country), *EKO* (June 1984), pp. 3–16.

Aizenman, Joshua. "Devaluation and Liberalization in the Presence of Tariff and Quota Restrictions," *Journal of International Economics*, vol. 11, no. 2 (June 1981), pp. 197–206.

Allen, Mark. "Adjustment in Planned Economies," *IMF Staff Papers*, vol. 29, pp. 398–421 (September 1982).

————. "Comment on the CMEA Financial System and Integration," in Paul Marer and John Michael Montias, eds. *East European Integration and East-West Trade*. Bloomington: Indiana University Press, 1980.

Altmann, Franz-Lothar. "Employment Policies in Czechoslovakia," in Jan Adam, ed. *Employment Policies in the Soviet Union and Eastern Europe*. New York: St. Martin's Press, 1982.

Alton, Thad. "East European GNPs: Origins of Product, Final Uses, Rates of Growth, and International Comparisons," in Joint Economic Committee, United States Congress, *East European Economies: Slow Growth in the 1980s, vol. 1*. Washington, D.C.: U.S. Government Printing Office, 1985.

Alton, Thad, Krzysztof Badach, Elizabeth Bass, and Gregor Lazarcik. *East European GNP by Origin and Domestic Final Uses of Gross Produce, 1965–1984*. Occasional Paper No. 89, New York: L. W. International Financial Research, 1985.

Andropov, Y. V. "Rech' General'nogo sekretaria Ts. K. KPSS Iu. V. Andropova na Plenume Ts. K. KPSS 22 Noiabria 1982 goda" (Speech of the General Secretary of the Central Committee of the CPSU at the November 12, 1982 Plenum of the Central Committee of the CPSU). *Pravda*, November 12, 1982a.

————. "Doklad General'nogo sekretaria Ts. K. KPSS Tovarishcha Iu. V. Andropova" (Speech of the General Secretary of the Central Committee of the CPSU, Comrade Iu. V. Andropov), *Ekonomicheskaia Gazeta*, no. 52 (December 1982b), pp. 3–5.

————. "Uchenie Karla Marksa i nekotorye voprosy sotsialisticheskogo stroitel'stva v SSSR" (The Teachings of Karl Marx, and Several Questions Concerning the Building of Socialism in the USSR), *Kommunist* (February 1983a), pp. 9–23.

———. "Vstrecha Iu. V. Andropova s Moskovskimi stankostroiteliami" (The Meeting of Iu. V. Andropov with the Moscow Machine Builders), *Ekonomicheskaia Gazeta*, no. 6 (February 1983b), pp. 3–4.

———. "Rech' General'nogo sekretaria Tsentralnogo Komitete KPSS na plenume Ts. K. KPSS 15 Iunia 1983 goda" (Speech of the General Secretary of the Central Committee of the CPSU on 15 June 1983), *Ekonomicheskaia Gazeta*, no. 25 (June 1983c), pp. 3–6.

———. "Tekst vystupleniia General'nogo sekretaria Ts. K. KPSS T-a Iu. V. Andropova" (The Text of the Presentation of the General Secretary of the Central Committee of the CPSU Comrade Iu. V. Andropov), *Ekonomicheskaia Gazeta*, no. 1 (January 1984), pp. 3–5.

Angyal, Adam. "Nagyvallalati szindroma" (The Large Enterprise Syndrome), *Kozgazdasagi szemle*, vol. 5, no. XXX (1983).

Assetto, Valerie J. *The Soviet Bloc in the IMF and the IBRD*. Boulder, Colo.: Westview Press, 1988.

Ayres, Robert L. *Banking on the Poor*. Cambridge, Mass.: MIT Press, 1983.

Backova, Viera. "K riadeniu z zabespecovaniu efektivnosti rozvojovych programov," *Politicka Eckonomie* vol. 34, no. 2 (1986), pp. 185–95.

Bajt, Alexander. *Kurskao osnovno, u datim uslovima i jedino sredstvo potsticanja izvoza*. Ljubljana: Ekonomski Institut Pravyne Fakultete, 1985.

Balassa, Andrea. "Central Development Programs in Hungary," *Acta Oeconomica* vol. 14, no. 1 (1975), pp. 91–108.

Balassa, Bela. "Adjustment Policies in Socialist and Private Market Economies," *Journal of Comparative Economics*, vol. 10, no. 2 (June 1986), pp. 138–59.

———. "The 'New Growth Path' in Hungary," in Josef C. Brada and Istvan Dobozi, eds. *The Hungarian Economy in the 1980s: Reforming the System and Adjusting to External Shocks*. Greenwich, Conn.: JAI Press (1988).

Baneth, Jean. "Foreword," in Paul Marer, ed. *Dollar GNPs of the USSR and Eastern Europe*. Baltimore: Johns Hopkins University Press for the World Bank, 1985.

Baryshnikov, N. and G. Galakhov. "Kapital'noe stroitel'stvo—reshaiushchii uchastok sotsialisticheskogo vosproizvodstva" (Capital Construction—a Decisive Element of Socialist Reproduction), *Planovoe khoziastvo* (March 1982), pp. 20–30.

Bauer, Tamas. "Investment Cycles in Planned Economics," *Acta Oeconomica*, vol. 21, no. 3 (March 1978), pp. 233–50.

———. "The Second Economic Reform and Ownership Relations. Some Considerations for the Further Development of NEM," *East European Economics*, vol. 22, nos. 3–4 (1984), pp. 33–87.

Belousov, R. S. "Nuzhna reshitel'naia perestroika" (A Decisive Restructuring is Needed), *EKO*, August 1983, p. 23.

Bentley, Raymond. *Technical Change in the German Democratic Republic*. Boulder, Colo., and London: Westview Press, 1984.

Berliner, Joseph S. "Planning and Management," in Abram Bergson and Herbert S. Levine, eds. *The Soviet Economy: Toward the Year 2000*. London: George Allen and Unwin, 1983.

Blaha, Jaroslav. "La mobilisation de la science et de la recherche tchecoslovaques au service de l'integration," *Le Courrier des Pays de l'Est*, no. 302 (January 1986), pp. 42–57.

Blaha, Jaroslav, and Anita Tirapolsky. "La Tchecoslovaquie dans les options industrielles du CAEM," *Le Courrier des Pays de l'Est*, no. 283, (April 1984), pp. 3–28.

Bobrowski, Cz. "Current Problems of the Polish Economic Reforms." Polish Ministry of Foreign Affairs, 1982.

Bogomolov, Oleg. *The World Socialist Economy*. Moscow: Nauka, 1986.

Bogomolov, O. T. *Strany sotsializma v mezhdunarodnom razdelenii* (The Socialist Countries in the International Division of Labor). Moscow: Nauka, 1980.

Bolz, Klaus, and Petra Pissulla. "GATT's Role in East-West Trade," *Intereconomics*, (March/April 1986).

Bornstein, Morris. "Economic Reform in Eastern Europe," in Joint Economic Committee, United States Congress, *East European Economics Post-Helsinki*. Washington, D.C.: U.S. Government Printing Office, 1977.

————. "The Administration of the Soviet Price System," *Soviet Studies*, vol. 30, no. 4 (January 1978), pp. 466–90.

Borokh, N. V., and V. S. Glagolev. *Strategicheskoe napravlenie sotrudnichestva* (Strategic Orientation of Cooperation). Moscow: Nauka, 1984.

Brabant, J. M. van. "Zur Rolle Mitteleuropas im Rahmen des Rats fur gegenseitige Wirtschaftshilfe," *Osteuropa Wirtschaft*, vol. 21, no. 1 (1976), pp. 1–20.

————. *Socialist Economic Integration—Aspects of Contemporary Economic Problems in Eastern Europe*. New York, N.Y.: Cambridge University Press, 1980.

————. "Target Programming—a New Instrument of Socialist Economic Integration?" *Jahrbuch der Wirtschaft Osteuropas-Yearbook of East-European Economics*, vol. 9, no. 1 (1981), pp. 141–84.

————. "The USSR and Socialist Economic Integration—A Comment," *Soviet Studies*, vol. 36, no. 1 (June 1984a), pp. 127–38.

————. "Socialist Economic Integration and the Global Economic Recession," *Osteuropa Wirtschaft*, vol. 29, no. 3 (1984b), pp. 192–212.

————. "The Relationship Between World and Socialist Trade Prices—Some Empirical Evidence," *Journal of Comparative Economics*, vol. 9, no. 3 (1985a), pp. 233–51.

————. "Exchange Rates in Eastern Europe: Types, Derivation, Application." Washington, D.C.: World Bank Staff Working Papers, no. 778, 1985b.

————. "The CMEA Summit and Socialist Economic Integration—a Perspective," *Jahrubuch der Wirtschaft Osteuropas-Yearbook of East European Economics*, vol. 12, no. 1 (1987), pp. 129–60.

Brada, Josef C. "Industrial Policy in Hungary: Lessons for America," *Cato Journal*, vol. 4, no. 2 (Fall 1984), pp. 485–505.

———. "Soviet Subsidization of Eastern Europe: The Primacy of Economics over Politics?" *Journal of Comparative Economics*, vol. 9, no. 4 (March 1985), pp. 80–92.

———. "Interpreting the Soviet Subsidization of Eastern Europe," in *International Organization*, (in press).

Brada, Josef C., and Jose A. Mendez. "Economic Integration Among Developed, Developing and Centrally Planned Economies," *Review of Economics and Statistics*, vol. 67, no. 4 (November 1985), pp. 549–56.

———. "An Estimate of the Dynamic Effects of Economic Integration," *Review of Economics and Statistics*, vol. 70, no. 1 (February 1988), pp. 163–68.

Brada, Josef C. and J. Michael Montias. "Industrial Policy in East Europe: A Three Country Comparison," *Journal of Comparative Economics*, vol.8, no. 4 (December 1984), pp.377–419.

———. "Industrial Policy in East Europe: A Comparison of Poland, Czechoslovakia, and Hungary," in Joint Economic Committee, United States Congress, *East European Economies: Slow Growth in the 1980s, vol. 1. Economic Performance and Policy*. Washington, D.C.: U.S. Government Printing Office, 1985.

Brandt, Willy. *North-South: A Programme for Survival*. (Report of the Independent Commission on International Development Issues.) Cambridge, Mass.: MIT Press, 1980.

Brezhnev, Leonid I. "Report of the CC to the 26th Congress and Current Tasks of the Party in the Field of Domestic and External Policy" (in Russian), in *Spravochnik partiinogo rabotnika*, vol. 22. Moscow: 1982.

Brown, Alan A., and Egon Neuberger. "Basic Features of a Centrally Planned Economy," in Alan Brown and Egon Neuberger, eds. *International Trade and Central Planning*. Berkeley: University of California Press, 1968.

Brus, Wlodzimierz. *A szocialista gazdasag mukodesenek altalanos problemai* (General Problems of the Operation of the Socialist Economy). Budapest: Kozgazdasagi es Jogi Konyvkiado, 1966.

Brus, Wlodzimierz. "The East European Reforms: What Happened to Them?" *Soviet Studies*, vol. 31, no. 2 (April 1979), pp. 257–67.

Burkett, John P. "Stabilization Measures in Yugoslavia: An Assessment of the Proposals of Yugoslavia's Commission for Problems of Economic Stabilization," in Joint Economic Committee, United States Congress, *East European Economies: Slow Growth in the 1980s, vol. 1*. Washington, D.C.: U.S. Government Printing Office, 1986.

Campbell, Robert. "Economic Reform in the USSR," *American Economic Review*, vol. 58, no. 2 (May 1968), pp. 547–58.

Central Intelligence Agency (CIA), *Handbook of Economic Statistics 1983*. Washington, D.C.: CIA, 1983.

Chandavarkar, Anand G. *The International Monetary Fund: Its Financial Organization and Activities*. Washington, D.C.: IMF, 1984.

Chernenko, Konstantin U. "Narod i partiia ediny. Vstrecha izbiratelei s general'nym sekretarem TsK KPSS K. U. Chernenko" (The People and the Party are United. A Meeting of the Voters with the General Secretary of the Communist Party of the Soviet Union, K. U. Chernenko). *Ekonomicheskaia Gazeta*, no. 11 (March 1984a), pp. 3–6.

————. "Vystuplenie tovarishcha K. U. Chernenko na vsesoiuznom ekonomicheskom soveshchanii po problemam agropromyshlennogo kompleksa" (The Speech of Comrade K. U. Chernenko at the All-Union Economic Conference on Problems of the Agro-Industrial Complex). *Kommunist*, no. 6 (April 1984b), pp. 19–20.

————. "Rech' tovarishcha K. U. Chernenko na plenume TsK KPSS 10 Apreia 1984 goda" (The Speech of Comrade K. U. Chernenko at the Plenum of the Central Committee of the Communist Party of the Soviet Union on April 10, 1984). *Ekonomicheskaia Gazeta*, no. 16 (April 1984c), pp. 3–4.

Clement, Hermann. "Planungszusammenarbeit und Entwicklung der RGW-Intrablockhandels in den 80er Jahren," in Heinrich Machowski, ed. *Harmonisierung der Wirtschaftspolitik in Osteuropa*. Berlin: Berlin Verlag Arno Spitz, 1985.

Colton, Timothy J. *The Dilemma of Reform in the Soviet Union*. New York: Council on Foreign Relations, 1984.

"Comecon Survey." *Economist*, April 20, 1985.

Consultative Economic Council. "Źródlapresji inflacyjnej," and "Handel Zagraniczny," *Życie Gospodarcze*, no. 14 (1984).

Csaba, Laszlo. *Economic Mechanism in the GDR and Czechoslovakia*. Budapest: Hungarian Scientific Council for World Economy, 1983.

————. "Comecon Perspectives for the 1980s," *Economies et Societes*, vol. 18, no. 2, serie G, no. 40 (February 1984a), pp. 5–44.

————. "Integration into the World Economy and the Cooperation in Planning," *Osteuropa Wirtschaft*, vol. 28, no. 2 (1984b), pp. 105–22.

————. "Joint Investments and Mutual Advantages in the CMEA—Retrospection and Prognosis," *Soviet Studies*, vol. 37, no. 2 (April 1985), pp. 227–47.

Dach, Z. "Polityka zatrudnienia w ramach reformy," *Gospodarka Planowa*, No. 11 (1984).

Derbin, K., and M. Gandziarski. "Propozycje kierunków specializacji eksportowej," *Handel Zagraniczny*, No. 2 (1985), pp. 3–6.

Desai, Padma. "Is the Soviet Union Subsidizing Eastern Europe?" *European Economic Review*, vol. 30, no. 1 (March 1985), pp. 107–16.

Dietz, Raimund. "Advantages/Disadvantages in USSR Trade with Eastern Europe—The Aspect of Prices," in Joint Economic Committee, United States Congress, *East European Economies: Slow Growth in the 1980s, vol. 2*. Washington, D.C.: U.S. Government Printing Office, 1986.

Dornbusch, Rudiger. "Devaluation, Money and Nontraded Goods," *American Economic Review*, vol. 63, no. 5 (December 1973), pp. 871–80.

————. *Open Economy Macroeconomics*. New York: Basic Books, 1980.

Driscoll, David D. *The International Monetary Fund: Its Evolution, Organization, and*

Activities. Washington, D.C.: IMF, 1984.

Dziennik Ustaw, various issues.

Edwards, Richard W. *International Monetary Cooperation*. Dobbs Ferry, New York: Transnational Publishers, 1985.

Ekonomicheskaia Gazeta, various issues.

Feiwel, George, ed. *The Soviet Quest for Economic Efficiency: Issues, Controversies, Reforms*. New York: Praeger, 1972.

Finanse, various issues.

Fomin, Boris. "Monetary and Financial Aspects of East-West Cooperation," in C. T. Saunders, ed. *Money and Finance in East and West*. Vienna: Springer-Verlag, 1978.

Foreign Trade Research Institute. *Polish Foreign Trade in 1966–1970 and Forecast for 1971–1975*. Warsaw: Foreign Trade Research Institute, 1972.

———. *East-West Economic Relations*. Warsaw: Foreign Trade Research Institute, 1973.

———. *Polish Foreign Trade in 1982*. Warsaw: Foreign Trade Research Institute, 1983.

Fox, Lesley. "Soviet Policy in the Development of Nuclear Power in Eastern Europe," in Joint Economic Committee, United States Congress, *Soviet Economy in the 1980s: Problems and Prospects, vol. 1*. Washington, D.C.: U.S. Government Printing Office, 1982.

Galik, Laszlo. "Interpretations Related to Normativity, and an Attempt to Outline the Operation of Normativity." Budapest: Research Institute of Finance, 1983.

GATT. "Memorandum to the Contracting Parties," September 10, 1986.

Gerschenkron, Alexander. *Economic Relations with the USSR*. New York: Committee on International Economic Policy, 1945.

Glinski, Bogdan. "Od limitu do normatywu," *Życie Gospodarcze*, no. 9 (1973).

Gold, Joseph. *Membership and Nonmembership in the International Monetary Fund*. Washington, D.C.: IMF, 1974.

Golubev, V. A., A. S. Shepeliuk, and A. S. Filipenko. *Vneshne-ekonomicheskie sviazi stran-chlenov SEV v usloviiakh sotsialisticheskoi integratsii* (The International Economic Relations of the CMEA-Member Countries in the Conditions of the Socialist Integration). Kiev: Naukova Dumka, 1983.

Gorbachev, Mikhail S. "Zakrepliat' dostignutoe, idti dal'she, povyshat' delovitost'. Vstrecha izbiratelei s M. S. Gorbachevym" (Reinforce What Has Been Achieved, Move Ahead, Increase a Businesslike Approach), *Sotsialisticheskaia Industriia* (March 1, 1984), pp. 1–2.

———. "Korennoi vopros ekonomisheskoi politiki partii" (The Urgent Question of the Party's Economic Policy), *Literaturnaia Gazeta* (June 12, 1985a), pp. 1–2.

———. "Doklad General'nogo sekretaria TsK KPSS tovarishcha Gorbacheva M. S." (Report of the General Secretary of the CC of the CPSU, Comrade M. S. Gorbachev), *Sotsialisticheskaia Industriia*, February 26, 1986.

Gorlin, Alice C. "Industrial Reorganization: The Associations," in Joint Economic

Committee, United States Congress, *Soviet Economy in a New Perspective*. Washington, D.C.: U.S. Government Printing Office, 1976.

Granick, David. *Enterprise Guidance in Eastern Europe*. Princeton: Princeton University Press, 1975.

Graziani, Giovanni. "La dependance energetique de l'Europe Orientale vis-à-vis de l'URSS: 1945–1981," *Revue d'etudes comparatives Est-Ouest*, vol. 14, no. 2 (June 1983), pp. 34–60.

Grinberg, L., M. Liubskii. "Tseny i valiutnye otnosheniia v sotrudnichestve stran SEV" (Prices and Value Relations in the Cooperation of the CMEA-Member Countries), *Voprosy Ekonomiki*, no. 6 (1985), pp. 99–107.

Grossman, Gregory. "The Party as Manager and Entrepreneur," in Gregory Guroff and Fred V. Carstensen, eds. *Entrepreneurship in Imperial Russia and the Soviet Union*. Princeton: Princeton University Press, 1983.

Gustafson, Thane. *Reform in Soviet Politics: Lessons of Recent Policies on Land and Water*. Cambridge: Cambridge University Press, 1981.

———. "Soviet Oil Policy and Energy Politics, 1970–85," mimeo, August 1984.

Hannigan, John B., and Carl H. McMillan. "Joint Investment in Resource Development: Sectoral Approaches to Socialist Integration," in Joint Economic Committee, United States Congress, *East European Economic Assessment: part 2, Regional Assessments*. Washington, D.C.: U.S. Government Printing Office, 1981.

———. *East European Responses to the Energy Crisis*. Ottawa: Carleton University, Institute of Soviet and East European Studies, East-West Commercial Relations Series, 1983.

Hetenyi, Istvan. "On Growth Planning and Financial Control," *Valosag*, no. 2 (1981).

———. "Targets and Means," *Nepszabadsag*, August 20, 1982.

Heti Vilaggazdasag, various issues.

Hewett, Ed A. "The Hungarian Economy: Lessons of the 1970s and Prospects for the 1980s," in Joint Economic Committee, United States Congress, *East European Economic Assessment, Part 1*. Washington, D.C.: U.S. Government Printing Office, 1981.

———. "Foreign Economic Relations," in Abram Bergson and Herbert S. Levine, eds. *The Soviet Economy: Toward the Year 2000*. London: George Allen and Unwin, 1983.

———. "Economic Reform in the Soviet Union and Eastern Europe," presented at the Conference on "Reform of the Chinese Political Order," Harwich Port, Mass., June 18–24, 1984a.

———. *Energy, Economics, and Foreign Policy in the Soviet Union*. Washington, D.C.: Brookings Institution, 1984b.

———. "Soviet Economic Performance in the 1980s: Constraints and Opportunities, presented at the Conference on the Soviet Economy: Performance, Prospects, and Impact," Washington, D.C., May 10–11, 1984c.

———. "Soviet Economic Relations with the CMEA Countries," in Philip Joseph, ed. *The Soviet Economy After Brezhnev*. Brussels: NATO, 1984d.

———. *Reforming the Soviet Economy: Equality vs. Efficiency*. Washington, D.C.: Brookings Institution, 1988.

Holzman, Franklyn D. "The Profit-Output Relationship of a Soviet Firm: Comment," *Canadian Journal of Economics and Political Science*, vol. 19, no. 4 (November 1953), pp. 523–31.

———. "Soviet Inflationary Pressures, 1928–1957: Causes and Cures," *Quarterly Journal of Economics*, vol. 74, no. 2 (May 1960a), pp 167–88.

———. "Some Financial Aspects of Soviet Foreign Trade," in Joint Economic Committee, United States Congress, *Comparisons of the United States and Soviet Economies, part 2*. Washington, D.C.: U.S. Government Printing Office, pp. 427–43, 1960b.

———. "Soviet Foreign Trade Pricing and the Question of Discrimination: A Customs Union Approach," *Review of Economics and Statistics*, vol. 44, no. 2 (May 1962), pp. 134–47.

———. "More on Soviet Bloc Trade Discrimination," *Soviet Studies*, vol. 17, no. 1 (July 1965), pp. 44–65.

———. *Foreign Trade Under Central Planning*. Cambridge, Mass.: Harvard University Press, 1974a.

———. "The Operation of Some Traditional Adjustment Mechanisms in the Foreign Trade of Centrally Planned Economies," in Alan A. Brown and Egon Neuberger, eds. *International Trade and Central Planning*. Berkeley: University of California Press, 1974b.

———. *International Trade Under Communism: Politics and Economics*. New York: Basic Books, 1976.

———. "Some Systemic Factors Contributing to the Convertible Currency Shortages of Centrally Planned Economies," *American Economic Review*, vol. 69, no. 2 (May 1979), pp. 76–80.

———. "Comecon: A Trade Destroying Customs Union?" *Journal of Comparative Economics*, vol. 9, no. 4 (December 1985), pp. 410–23.

———. "The Significance of Soviet Subsidies to Eastern Europe," *Comparative Economic Studies*, vol. 28, no. 1 (Spring 1986), pp. 54–65.

Hooke, A. W. *The International Monetary Fund: Its Evolution, Organization, and Activities*. Washington, D.C.: IMF, 1982.

Hough, Jerry F. *The Soviet Prefects*. Cambridge, Mass.: Harvard University Press, 1969.

Intensifikatsiia proizvodstva v evropeiskikh stranakh SEV: faktory ekonomicheskogo rosta (Intensification of Production in the European CMEA Countries: A Factor of Economic Growth). Moscow: Nauka, 1972.

International Herald Tribune, various issues.

International Institute for Economic Problems of the World Socialist System. *Problemy sovershenstvovaniia narodnokhoziaistvenykh struktur stran-chlenov SEV* (Problems of Improving the Macroeconomic Structures of the Member Countries of the CMEA). Moscow: MIEPMSS, 1984.

International Monetary Fund, *International Financial Statistics*, various issues.

Ivanov, Ivan D. *The Soviet Union in a Changing Global Economic Setting: The Prospects for Trade-Oriented Growth*, UNCTAD/ST/TSC/ 4, (April 1986).

Ivashov, P. "Agropromyshlennaia integratsia v deistvii" (The Agro-Industrial Integration Is Underway), *Ekonomicheskaia Gazeta*, no. 28 (July 1984).

Jackson, Marvin R. "Industrialization, Trade, and Mobilization in Romania's Drive for Economic Independence," in Joint Economic Committee, United States Congress, *East European Economies Post-Helsinki*. Washington, D.C.: U.S. Government Printing Office, 1977.

———. "Bulgaria's Economy in the 1970s: Adjusting Productivity to Structure," in Joint Economic Committee, United States Congress, *East European Economic Assessment: Part 1—Country Studies, 1980*. Washington, D.C.: U.S. Government Printing Office, 1981.

———. "Recent Economic Performance and Policy in Bulgaria," in Joint Economic Committee, United States Congress, *East European Economies: Slow Growth in the 1980s, Volume 3, Country Studies on Eastern Europe and Yugoslavia*. Washington, D.C.: United States Government Printing Office, 1986a.

———. "Romania's Debt Crisis: Its Causes and Cures," in Joint Economic Committee, United States Congress, *East European Economies: Slow Growth in the 1980s, Volume 3, Country Studies on Eastern Europe and Yugoslavia*. Washington, D.C.: U.S. Government Printing Office, 1986b.

Jeziorański, T. "Sukcesy, slabości, zagrożenia," *Życie gospodarcze*, no. 28 (1984).

Józefiak, C. "Ceny, reglamentacja, prace," *Życie gospardcze*, no. 5 (1985a).

———. "Struktura i funkcjonowanie przedsiebiorstw," *Życie gospodarcze*, no. 6 (1985b).

Kalinowski, W., and P. Karpiński. "Podstawowe zmiany w mechanizmach ekonomicznych reformy gospodarczej w 1984 roku," *Gospodarka Planowa*, no. 4 (1984), pp. 161–65.

Kemme, David M., and Keith Crane. "The Polish Economic Collapse: Contributing Factors and Economic Costs," *Journal of Comparative Economics*, vol. 8, no. 1 (March 1984), pp. 25–40.

Khan, Mohsin S., and Malcolm D. Knight. "Stabilization Programs in Developing Countries: A Formal Framework," *International Monetary Fund Staff Papers*, vol.28, no. 1 (March 1981), pp. 1–53.

Kirichenko, V. "O nekotorykh voprosakh dal'neishego sovershenstvovanie planirovaniia i upravleniia khoziastvom" (On Several Questions Concerning the Further Improvement of the Planning and Management of the Economy), *Planovoe khoziastvo* (September 1982), pp. 57–65.

Kis, Peter, Sherman Robinson, and Laura Tyson. "Computable General Equilibrium Models for Socialist Economies." Paper presented at the annual meetings of the American Economic Association, December 1985.

Kornai, Janos. "Resource-Constrained Versus Demand-Constrained Systems," *Econometrica*, vol. 47, no. 4 (August 1979), pp. 801–19.

———. *Economics of Shortage*, 2 vols. Amsterdam: North-Holland, 1980a.

————. "Hard and Soft Budget Constraint," *Acta Oeconomica*, vol. 25 (1980b), pp. 231–45.

————. "The Hungarian Reform Process: Visions, Hopes, and Reality," *Journal of Economic Literature*, vol. 24, no. 4 (December 1986), pp. 1687–1737.

Kornai, Janos, and A. Matits. "A koltsegvetesi Korlat yuhasagarol: vallalati adatok Alapjan," *Gazdasag*, vol. 16, no. 4 (1983).

Kostecki, M. M. *East-West Trade and the GATT System.* New York: St. Martin's Press, 1979.

Kotz, Laszlo. *Elgondolasok a hossutavu vagyonerdekeltseg alakulasarol* (Thoughts on Long-Term Interest in Property Rights). Budapest: Agrargazdasagi Kutato Intezet, 1984.

Köves, Andras. "Implicit Subsidies and Some Issues of Economic Relations Within the CMEA (Remarks on the Analyses Made by Michael Marrese and Jan Vanous)," *Acta Oeconomica*, vol. 31, nos. 1–2 (1983), pp. 125–36.

Kravis, Irving B., et al. *World Product and Income.* Baltimore: Johns Hopkins University Press, 1982.

Krueger, Anne O. "The Role of Home Goods and Money in Exchange Rate Adjustment," in Willy Sillekaerts, ed. *International Trade and Finance.* New York: International Arts and Sciences Press, 1974.

Krugman, Paul R. "Scale Economies, Product Differentiation, and the Pattern of Trade," *American Economic Review*, vol. 70, no. 5 (December 1980), pp. 950–59.

Kucera, Lubomir. "Spolupruce CSSR se socialistickymi zememi v oblash elektroenergetiky," *Planovane Hosporarstvi*, no. 12 (1984), pp. 52–58.

Kurenkov, Y. "Scientific and Technological Progress and Structural Changes in World Industrial Production," in, Zoltan Roman, ed. *Industrial Development and Industrial Policy.* Budapest: Akademiai Kiado, 1979.

Lampe, John R. *The Bulgarian Economy in the Twentieth Century.* New York: St. Martin's Press, 1986.

Lavigne, Marie. *Le Comecon (Le Programme du Comecon et l'integration socialiste).* Paris: Cujas, 1973.

————. "The International Monetary Fund and the Soviet Union," in F. Levcik, ed. *International Economy—Comparison and Interdependence.* Vienna: Springer-Verlag, 1978.

————. "The Soviet Union Inside Comecon," *Soviet Studies*, vol. 35, no. 2 (April 1983), pp. 135–53.

————. "The Evolution of CMEA Institutions and Policies and the Need for Structural Adjustment." Manuscript, 1984.

Ledworowski, D., R. Michalski, and Z. Piotrowski. "Kurs zlotego a koszty i ceny wewnetrzne," *Handel Zagraniczny*, no. 3 (1984), pp. 9–14.

Lewis, Jerry. "World Bank Courts Eastern Europe," *Wall Street Journal*, September 26, 1984.

Lushnikov, O. "Ekonomicheskie vzaimosviaizi SSSR i ChSSR" (The Economic Relations between the USSR and Czechoslovakia), *Voprosy Ekonomiki*, no. 6 (1985), pp. 91–98.

Machowski, Heinrich. "Die Funktion der DDR im RGW," *Deutschland Archiv*, vol. 6 (Special Issue, 1973).

———. "Die Produktionsspezialisierung im RGW am Beispiel der DDR," in Heinrich Machowski, ed. *Harmonisierung der Wirtschaftspolitik in Osteuropa*. Berlin: Berlin Verlag Arno Spitz, 1985.

Majewski, W. "Syndrom zadlużenia," *Nowosci*, June 7, 1985.

Maly, B. "Conditions for the Specialization of the Czechoslovak National Economic Complex," *Czechoslovak Economic Papers*, no. 22 (1984), pp. 38–41.

Marer, Paul. "Exchange Rates and Convertibility in Hungary's New Economic Mechanism," in Joint Economic Committee, United States Congress, *East European Economic Assessment, part 1*. Washington, D.C.: U.S. Government Printing Office, 1981.

———. "The Political Economy of Soviet Relations with Eastern Europe," in Sarah M. Terry, ed. *Soviet Policy in Eastern Europe*. New Haven, Conn., and London: Yale University Press, 1984.

———. *Dollar GNPs of the USSR and Eastern Europe*. Baltimore: Johns Hopkins University Press for the World Bank, 1985a.

———. "Alternative Estimates of the Dollar GNP and Growth Rates of the CMEA Countries," in Joint Economic Committee, United States Congress, *East European Economies: Slow Growth in the 1980s*, vol. 1. Washington, D.C.: U.S. Government Printing Office, 1985b.

———. "Economic Reform in Hungary" in Morris Bornstein, ed. *Comparative Economic Systems: Models and Cases*. Homewood, Ill.: Richard D. Irwin, 1985c.

———. *East-West Technology Transfer: A Study of Hungary, 1968–84*. Paris: OECD, 1986a.

———. "Growing Soviet International Economic Isolation and Severe Problems Ahead in the Foreign Trade Sector Prompt Top Soviet Economists to Advocate Membership in the IMF, World Bank, and the GATT," *PlanEcon Report*, vol. 2, no. 31, July 31, 1986b.

———. "Economic Reform in Hungary: From Central Planning to Regulated Market," in Joint Economic Committee, United States Congress, *East European Economies: Slow Growth in the 1980s*, vol. 3. Washington, D.C.: U.S. Government Printing Office, 1986c.

Marer, Paul, and W. Siwinski, eds. *Creditworthiness and Reform in Poland: Western and Polish Perspectives*. Bloomington: Indiana University Press, 1988.

Marjai, J. *A KGST csucsertekezlet es hazank*. Budapest, Hungary: Kossuth Konyvkiado, 1984.

Marrese, Michael. "The Evolution of Wage Regulation in Hungary." In P. W. Hare et al., eds. *Hungary: A Decade of Economic Reform*. London: Allen and Unwin, 1981.

———. "CMEA: Effective but Cumbersome Political Economy," *International Organi-*

zation, vol. 40, no. 2 (Spring 1986), pp. 287–327.

Marrese, Michael, and Jan Vanous. "Optimal Behavior in the Presence of Unconventional Gains from Trade." Discussion Paper No. 80–29. Department of Economics, University of British Columbia, Vancouver, August 1980.

———. "Soviet Subsidies to Eastern Economies," *Wall Street Journal*, January 15, 1982a.

———. "Soviet Policy Options in Trade Relations with Eastern Europe," in Joint Economic Committee, United States Congress, *Soviet Economy in the 1980s: Problems and Prospects*, part 1. Washington, D.C.: U.S. Government Printing Office, 1982b.

———. *Soviet Subsidization of Trade With Eastern Europe—A Soviet Perspective*. Berkeley: Institute of International Studies, University of California, 1983a.

———. "Unconventional Gains from Trade," *Journal of Comparative Economics*, vol. 7, no. 4 (December 1983b), pp. 382–99.

———. *Soviet-East European Trade Relations: Recent Patterns and Likely Future Developments*. Manuscript prepared for U.S. Department of State, Contract No. 1724–320182. Washington, D.C.: Wharton Econometric Forecasting Associates, October 1984.

Matejcek, P. "Setting Contractual Prices for Agricultural Products in Mutual Trade among CMEA-Member Countries," *Zahranicni Obchod*, no. 1 (1984), pp. 11–14. Translated in *J.P.R.S. East Europe Report*, no. 47/84 (April 1984).

Medvedev, P. A. *Upravlenie sotsialisticheskoi proizvodstva*. (The Management of Socialist Production). Moscow: Politizdat, 1983.

Mencinger, Joze. "A Quarterly Macroeconomic Model of the Yugoslav Economy." Unpublished doctoral dissertation, University of Pennsylvania, 1974.

Mendershausen, Horst. "Terms of Trade between the Soviet Union and Smaller Communist Countries," *Review of Economics and Statistics*, vol. 41, no. 2 (May 1959), pp. 106–18.

———. "The Terms of Soviet Satellite Trade," *Review of Economics and Statistics*, vol. 41, no. 2 (May 1960), pp. 152–63.

Michalski, R. "Problemy wdrażenia reformy w handlu zagranicznym w 1982," *Handel Zagraniczny*, no. 3 (1983).

Michalski, R., Z. Piotrowski, and J. Soldaczuk. "Rachunek wyrównawczy a system odpisow dewizowych i polityka kursowa," *Handel Zagraniczny*, nos. 7–8 (1983), pp. 6–9.

Mikul'skii, K., ed. *Problemy sbailansirovannosti sotsialisticheskoi ekonomiki* (Problems of Balancing in the Socialist Economy). Moscow: Ekonomika, 1984.

Mironov, N. V. "Pravovoi status sovmestnykh khoziaisvennykh organizatsii stranchlenov SEV na territorii SSSR" (The Legal Status of Joint Economic Organizations with CMEA-Member Countries on the Territory of the USSR), *Sovetskoe Gosudarstvo i Pravo*, no. 3 (1984), pp. 43–51.

Misiak, M. "Równowaga i efektywność," *Życie Gospodarcze*, no. 7, 1984.

Mittag, Gunter. "Ekonomicheskoe i nauko-technicheskoe sotrudnichestvo GDR a

SSSR," *Vosprosy Ekonomiki*, no. 5 (1985), pp. 134–40.

Monitor Polski, various issues.

Montias, J. Michael. "Poland—Roots of the Economic Crisis," *The ACES Bulletin*, vol. 24, no. 3 (Fall 1982), pp. 1–19.

Mroczkowski, Piotr. "History of Poland's Relations with the IMF and the World Bank," in Paul Marer and Wlodzimierz Siwinski, eds. *Creditworthiness and Reforms in Poland*. Bloomington: Indiana University Press, 1988.

(The) *Multilateral Economic Cooperation of Socialist States. A Collection of Documents*. Moscow: Progress Publishers, 1977.

(*Narkhoz* 19**), USSR Central Statistical Administration, *Narodnoe khoziastvo SSSR v 19**g: Statisticheskii ezhegodnik (Economy of the USSR in 19**: Statistical Yearbook)*. Moscow: Finansy i statistika, Annual. (The date in the reference corresponds to the year to which the yearbook applies; it is published the following year.)

Nasilowski, Mieczyslaw. "The Reform in a Straight Jacket," *Życie Gospodarcze*, no. 20, May 19, 1985.

National Bank of Yugoslavia, *Yugoslavia Economic Information Statement*, June 1984.

———. *Yugoslavia Economic Information Statement*, September 1984.

———. *Yugoslavia Economic Information Statement*, June 1985.

Nemeth, K. "Long-Term Foreign Economic Policy and Development of the Productive Structure in Hungary," *Acta Oeconomica*, vol. 19, nos. 3–4 (1977), pp. 237–53.

Neuberger, Egon. "Central Planning and Its Legacies: Implications for Foreign Trade," in Alan A. Brown and Egon Neuberger, eds. *International Trade and Central Planning*, Berkeley: University of California Press, 1968.

New York Times, various issues.

Nivollet, B. "On Devaluation in Centrally Planned Economies," mimeo, 1983.

Nyerges, Janos. "Hungary's Accession to GATT," *New Hungarian Quarterly*, vol. 17, no. 2 (1976), pp. 133–42.

Nyers, Reszo. "Tendencies of Tradition and Reform in CMEA Cooperation," *Acta Oeconomica*, vol. 30, no. 1 (1983), pp. 31–51; and *Soviet and Eastern European Foreign Trade*, vol. 20, no. 1 (1984), pp. 6–36.

Nyers, Rezso, and Marton Tardos. "What Economic Development Policy Should We Adopt?" *Acta Oeconomica*, vol. 22, nos. 1–2 (1979), pp. 11–31.

———. "The Necessity for Consolidation of the Economy and the Possibility for Development in Hungary," *Acta Oeconomica*, vol. 32, nos. 1–2 (1984), pp. 1–19.

Orr, Mark Z. "Eastern European Participation in the Tokyo Round of Multilateral Trade Negotiations," in Joint Economic Committee, United States Congress, *East European Economic Assessment, part 2*. Washington, D.C.: U.S. Government Printing Office, 1981.

Pecsi, Kalman. *The Future of Socialist Economic Integration*. Armonk: M. E. Sharpe, 1981.

———. "The Realization of the Principle of Mutual Interests in CMEA-Member Countries' Trade Between Themselves and the Influence of this Principle on the Prospects of Economic Growth in Eastern Europe During the Eighties." Paper prepared for a Conference of the Hungarian and American Economists, October 1983.

Pissulla, Petra. "Romania and Hungary and the IMF and Implications for Poland," in Paul Marer and Wlodzimierz Siwinski, eds. *Creditworthiness and Reform in Poland: Western and Polish Perspectives*. Bloomington: Indiana University Press, 1988.

Plowiec, Urszula. "Evolution of the Methods of Management in Polish Foreign Trade in 1944–1978," *Handel Zagraniczny*, no. 7 (1979).

———. *Handel zagraniczny. Polska reforma gospodarcza*. Warsaw: PWE, 1982.

Pokol, B. "Institutions Defending Interests of Social Strata in Forming Political Will," *Tarsadalomtudomanyi Kozlemenyek*, no. 1 (1985).

Poller, Rolan, and Istvan Tesner. "Socialist Economic Integration and the Investment Cooperation of the CMEA Countries," *Soviet and Eastern European Foreign Trade*, vol. 1, no. 1 (Spring 1984), pp. 6–26.

Portes, Richard, and David Winter. "Disequilibrium Estimates for Consumption Goods Markets in Centrally Planned Economies," *Review of Economic Studies*, vol. 47 (1980), pp. 137–59.

Poznański, Kazimierz. "Competition Between Eastern Europe and Developing Countries in the Western Market for Manufactured Goods," in Joint Economic Committee, United States Congress, *East European Economies: Slow Growth in the 1980s, vol. 2*, pp. 62–90. Washington, D.C.: U.S. Government Printing Office, 1986.

Pravda, various issues.

Radio Free Europe, *Background Reports*, various issues.

Robinson, Roger W., Jr. "East-West Trade and National Security," *Heritage Lectures*, no. 50 (February 11, 1986a).

———. "Financing the Soviet Union," *Wall Street Journal* (March 10, 1986b), p. 16.

Robinson, Sherman. "Hungary: Industry in the Macro Context." University of California, Department of Agricultural and Resource Economics, Working Paper, 1986.

Robinson, Sherman, and Laura Tyson. "Foreign Trade, Resource Allocation, and Structural Adjustment in Yugoslavia," *Journal of Comparative Economics*, vol. 9, no. 1 (March 1985), pp. 46–70.

Roman, Zoltan. "Industrial Policy in Hungary—Today and Tomorrow," *Acta Oeconomica*, vol. 21, nos. 3–4 (1978), pp. 1–27.

Root, Franklin R. *International Trade and Investment*. Cincinnati: South-Western Publishing, 1984.

Root, William A. "Trade Controls That Work," *Foreign Policy*, vol. 56, no. 3 (Fall 1984), pp. 61–80.

Rott, N. *A nepgazdasagi erdekkel egybevago vallati fejlesztesi tevekenyseg felttetelrendszere* (Conditions of Business Development in Harmony with the National Interest). Budapest: MTA Kozgazdasagi Intezet, 1984.

Rude Pravo, various issues.

Rumer, Boris. "Soviet Investment Policy: Unresolved Problems," *Problems of Communism*, vol. 31, no. 5 (September-October 1982), pp. 53–68.

Ruzmich, L. "Value Aspects in Developing the Process of International Socialist Integration," *Zahranicni Obchod*, no. 11, 1984. Translated in *Soviet and Eastern European Foreign Trade*, vol. 20, no. 4 (Winter 1984–85), pp. 7–31.

Ryzhkov, N. "Novyi etap sotrudnichestva bratskikh partii i gosudarstv" (A New Stage in the Cooperation between the Brother Parties and States). *Pravda* (July 30, 1984), p. 4.

Schroeder, Gertrude E. "Soviet Economic Reforms: A Study in Contradictions," *Soviet Studies*, vol. 20, no. 1 (July 1968), pp. 1–21.

———. "Soviet Economic Reform at an Impasse," *Problems of Communism*, vol. 19, no. 4 (July-August 1971), pp. 36–46.

———. "Soviet Economic Reform Decrees: More Steps on the Treadmill," in Joint Economic Committee, United States Congress, *Soviet Economy in the 1980s: Problems and Prospects*, part 1. Washington, D.C.: U.S. Government Printing Office, 1979.

Schweitzer, I. "Central Decisions—Enterprise Efforts," *Acta Oeconomica*, vol. 24, nos. 3–4 (1980), pp. 321–40.

Seiffert, W. *Kann der Ostblock überleben? Der Comecon und die Krise des sozialistischen Wirtschaftsystems*. Bergisch Gladbach: Gustav Lubbe Verlag, 1983.

Shiriaev, Iu., and O. D. Bakovetskii. *Sovershenstvovanie planovogo mekhanizma ekonomicheskogo sotrudnichestva stran-chlenov SEV* (Improving the Planning Mechanism of the Economic Cooperation of the CMEA-Member Countries). Moscow: Nauka, 1981.

Silvestru, I. "Dezvoltarea si perfectionarea colaborarii, in interesul reciproc, al cauzei socialismului si pacii," *Revista economica*, no. 25 (1984), pp. 17–18.

Simai, Mihaly. *International Technology Transfer and Economic Development in the Late 20th Century*. Budapest: Trends in World Economy, no. 48, 1983.

Simon, Andras and Maria Veress. "A kompetitiv arkepes es a tenyarak 1981–83-ban," mimeo, 1984.

Skolkova, Michaela. "Postaveni, uloha a perspektivy chemickeho prumislu v Ceskoslovenskych vnejsich ekonomickych vztazich," *Zahranicni Obchod*, vol. 39, no. 1 (1986), pp. 2–5.

Strougal, L. "Za dalsi rozvoj socialisticke ekonomicke integrace," *Nova Mysl*, vol. 38, nos. 7/8 (1984), pp. 3–12.

Szego, Andrea. "Ertek es a gazdasagi intezmenyrendszer" (Interest and the System of Economic Institutions). *Valosag*, no. 6, 1983.

———. "Vita a reform alternativakrol" (Debate on the Alternatives of the Reform). *Kritika*, no. 6, 1984.

Tardos, Marton. "The Role of Money: Economic Relations between the State and the Enterprises in Hungary," *Acta Oeconomica*, vol. 25, nos. 1–2 (1980), pp. 19–35.

———. Interview in *Ipargazdasag* (March 1983), pp. 52–53. Translated in *J.P.R.S. East Europe Report*, no. 2412, June 16, 1984.

Taylor, Lance. "IS/LM in the Tropics: Diagrammatics of the New Structuralist Macro Critique," in W. R. Cline and S. Weintraub, eds. *Economic Stabilization in Devel-*

oping Countries. Washington, D.C.: Brookings Institution, 1981.

———. *Structuralist Macroeconomics*. New York: Basic Books, 1983.

Terek, Juraj. "Prohlubovani mezinardni specializace a kooperace v resortu vseobecneho strojirenstvi," *Zahranicni Obchod*, vol. 38, no. 12 (1985), pp. 2–3.

Tiraspolsky, Anita, "Les choix energetiques a l'Est," *Le Courrier des pays de l'Est*, Special Issue "Panorame de l'Europe de l'Est," nos. 309–11 (August, September, October 1986), pp. 250–65.

Trzeciakowski, Witold. *Indirect Management in a Centrally Planned Economy*. Amsterdam: North-Holland, 1978.

Tsantis, Andreas C., and Roy Pepper. *Romania*. Washington, D.C.: The World Bank, 1979.

Tyson, Laura. "Liquidity Crises in the Yugoslav Economy: An Alternative to Bankruptcy," *Soviet Studies*, vol. 29, no. 2 (April 1977a), pp. 284–95.

———. "The Yugoslav Inflation: Some Competing Hypotheses," *Journal of Comparative Economics*, vol. 1, no. 2 (1977b), pp. 113–46.

———. *The Yugoslav Economic System and Its Performance in the 1970s*. Berkeley: Institute for International Studies, University of California, Berkeley, 1980.

———. "Investment Allocation: A Comparison of the Reform Experiences of Hungary and Yugoslavia," *Journal of Comparative Economics*, vol. 7, no. 2 (June 1983), pp. 288–303.

Tyson, Laura, and Egon Neuberger. "The Impact of External Economic Disturbances on Yugoslavia: Theoretical and Empirical Explanations," *Journal of Comparative Economics*, vol. 3, no. 4 (December 1979), pp. 346–74.

Tyson, Laura, and Gabriel Eichler. "Continuity and Change in the Yugoslav Economy in the 1970's and 1980's," in Joint Economic Committee, U.S. Congress, *East European Economic Assessment, part 1*, pp. 139–214. Washington, D.C.: U.S. Government Printing Office, 1980.

Ultanbaev, R. "Deistvennost dolgosrochnykh tselevykh" (The Significance of the Long-Term Target Programs), *Ekonomicheskaia Gazeta*, no. 36 (September 1983).

United Nations, Economic Commission for Europe. *Economic Bulletin for Europe*. New York: United Nations, 1985a.

———. *Economic Survey of Europe in 1984–1985*. New York: United Nations, 1985b.

United Nations. *World Economic Survey: 1985–1986*, supplement. New York: United Nations, 1986.

United States International Trade Commission. *49th Quarterly Report to the Congress and the Trade Policy Committee on Trade Between the United States and the Nonmarket Economy Countries During 1986*. Washington, D.C., March 1987.

(U.S. JEC) U.S. Congress, Joint Economic Committee. *East European Economic Assessment. Part 1. Country Studies. 1980*. Washington, D.C.: U.S. Government Printing Office, 1980.

———. *USSR: Measures of Economic Growth and Development, 1950–80*. Washington, D.C.: U.S. Government Printing Office, 1982.

———. *East-West Technology Transfer: A Congressional Dialogue with the Reagan Administration*. Washington, D.C.: U.S. Government Printing Office, 1984.

Vanous, Jan. "Diverging Trends in CMEA Economies in 1984." Washington, D.C.: PlanEcon Report, March 27, 1985.

Vavrousek, Josef. "Ekonomicka problematika vedeckotechnickeho rozvoje," *Politicka Ekonomie*, vol. 34, no. 8 (1986), pp. 847–57.

Vienna Institute for Comparative Economics. *Comecon Data 1983*. Vienna: 1984.

Wernik, A. "Zjawiska inflacyjne w latach siedemziesiatych," *Finanse*, no. 6 (1984), pp. 25–40.

Wharton Econometric Forecasting Associates. *Centrally Planned Economies: Current Analysis*, various issues.

Wiles, P. J. D. *Communist International Economics*. New York: Praeger, 1968.

Williamson, John H. *The Lending Policies of the International Monetary Fund*. Washington, D.C.: International Institute of Economics, 1982.

Wolf, Thomas A. "Exchange-Rate Adjustments in Small Market and Centrally Planned Economies," *Journal of Comparative Economics*, vol. 2, no. 3 (1978), pp. 226–45.

———. "On the Adjustment of Centrally Planned Economies to External Economic Disturbances," in Paul Marer and John Michael Montias, eds. *East European Integration and East-West Trade*. Bloomington: Indiana University Press, 1980.

———. "Foreign Trade Prices and Other Determinants of Hungarian Manufactures Exports to the West." Unpublished manuscript, 1981.

———. "Economic Stabilization in Planned Economies: Toward an Analytical Framework," *International Monetary Fund Staff Papers*, vol. 32, no. 1 (March 1985a), pp. 78–131.

———. "Exchange-Rate Systems and Adjustment in Planned Economies," *International Monetary Fund Staff Papers*, vol. 32, no. 2 (June 1985b), pp. 211–47.

———. "The Simultaneity of the Effects of Devaluation: Implications for Modified Planned Economies," *Acta Oeconomica*, in press.

Wolnicki, Miron. "Soviet Economic Crisis Management: The Case of Poland." Paper presented at the 26th Annual Meeting of the International Studies Association, Washington, D.C.: March 5–9, 1985.

Zaslavskaia, Tatiana. "Ekonomika skvoz' prizmu sotsiologii" (Economics through the Prism of Sociology), *EKO*, no. 7 (1985), pp. 3–22.

———. "Chelevecheskii faktor i sotsial'naia spravedlivost'" (The Human Factor and Social Justice), *Sovetskaia Kultura*, January 23, 1986.

Zdyb, Z. "Warunki efektywności systemu finansowego," *Finanse*, no. 3 (1985).

Życie Gospodarcze, various issues.

Index

economy, 53–56; in Poland, 358, 361; as a source of balance-of-payments problems, 54, 229; symptoms of, 6; in USSR, 325–327, 334–335
Exchange rate: IMF-Yugoslav agreement on, 389 n. 17; of planned economies, 386 n. 1; in Poland, 353–354, 373, 400 n. 3; tourist, 176. *See also* Devaluation, Dinar, Forint
Export incentives in Poland, 364–365, 380

Foreign trade organization (FTO): 341–342; in Poland, 357, 366–368
Forint, 389 n. 18
Fuels, East European imports of, 23–24, 168. *See also* Energy; Petroleum

General Agreement on Tariffs and Trade (GATT): conditions for membership, 227; East European membership in 28–29, 241–246; and MFN treatment, 235–248 passim; operation of, 234–236, 243; organization of, 227–228; origins, 225; reciprocity for Eastern Europe, 242, 245
German Democratic Republic (GDR): industrial policy in, 121–124; priority sectors of industry, 124; provision of nonmarket benefits to USSR, 193
Gerschenkron, Alexander, xii
Gierek, Edward, 126
Giscard d'Estaing, Valéry, 286
Gold, Josef, 227
Gorbachev, Mikhail, 306, 308, 311, 312, 315, 323, 337 n. 6, 399
Gosplan, 320, 326
Gossnab, 320
Gostev B., 166
Gottwald, Klement, 397 n. 2
Granada, 211
Greece, 195
Grossman, Gregory, 317

Hard currency retention in Poland, 356, 360, 361, 363–364, 381
Hard goods, 186
Harvard University, xii
Havasi, Ferenc, 281
Hewett, Ed A., 33, 396 n. 3
Holzman, Franklyn D., 3, 30, 216, 371, 385 n. 1, 386 n. 1; critique of Mendershausen,

xiv, 186; estimates of Soviet defense expenditures, xiii; government service, xii; at Harvard University, xii; military service, xi–xiii; theory of CMEA integration, xiv, 185
Holzman-Mendershausen debate, xiv, 186
Honecker, Erich, 123
Hough, Jerry, 317
House of Commons, 293
Hungarian Chamber of Commerce, 287
Hungarian Shipyards and Crane Factory, 397 n. 3
Hungarian Socialist Workers' Party, 125, 280, 289, 290, 291, 294, 295, 296, 298
Hungary: application for IMF membership, 240; borrowing from West, 82–83; concentration of industry, 387 n. 9; crisis in, 262; economic reforms in, 4, 60, 78–81, 267–270; evolution of economic mechanism, 260–263; exchange rate policy, 93–94, 102–103; exports to socialist countries, 125–126, 391 n. 36; GNP, 249–250; IMF stabilization program for, 252; industrial policy in, 125–126, 303; interest rate, 262, 390 n. 27; links between devaluation and inflation, 390 n. 20; macroeconomic policy, 81, 262; membership in the GATT, 244–245; price system, 42–45, 51–52; provision of nonmarket benefits to USSR, 193–194; redistribution of profits in, 266–268; reexports of Iranian and Libyan oil, 391 n. 36; trade with CMEA, 303–304; wages in, 269–270

Implicit Subsidies from USSR to Eastern Europe, xiv, 165–167. *See also* Soviet subsidies to Eastern Europe
Imports: as source of competitive pressure, 303; of Western machinery by Poland, 127
Industrial policy: in Bulgaria, 116–119; of CMEA countries 144–146, 152–153, 181–183; effect of CMEA on, 151; effect on production in Eastern Europe, 131–144, 152; in Hungary, 125–126, 303; material and energy intensiveness of, 152, 155; measurement of, 111–113; and pattern of employment in Eastern Europe, 131–144; pressure for in Eastern Europe, 21–23, 110, 159–161; similarity among East European countries, 134–141, 152. *See*

Editors and Contributors

Josef C. Brada is Professor of Economics at Arizona State University and formerly taught at Ohio State University and New York University. Aside from writing extensively on the Soviet and East European economies, particularly in the area of foreign trade, he is editor of the *Journal of Comparative Economics* and the journal *Soviet and East European Foreign Trade* and was formerly editor of *Comparative Economic Studies*.

Ed A. Hewett is Senior Fellow at the Brookings Institution. The author of *Reforming the Soviet Economy*, he has published widely on Soviet energy, Soviet and East European foreign trade, and the Hungarian economy. Formerly Associate Professor of Economics at the University of Texas at Austin, he is the editor of *Soviet Economy* and chairman of the National Council for Soviet and East European Research.

Thomas A. Wolf is Senior Economist, European Department, International Monetary Fund. He has written extensively on the micro- and macroeconomics of foreign trade in the Soviet Union and Eastern Europe and is author of the monograph *Foreign Trade in the Centrally Planned Economy*. He formerly was Associate Professor of Economics at Ohio State University.

Joseph S. Berliner is Professor of Economics (emeritus) at Brandeis University and Research Associate with the Russian Research Center at Harvard University. He is a leading scholar of the Soviet economy, having written extensively on enterprise management, economic reform, and technological progress in Soviet industry.

Jozef M. van Brabant is Chief of the Centrally Planned Economies Section, Department for International Economic and Social Affairs, the United Nations. He is the author of several books and numerous articles dealing with planned economies, with particular emphasis on the CMEA and Soviet–East European foreign trade relations.

Ellen Comisso is Professor of Politics at the University of California at San Diego. She has written extensively on the political systems and political economy of Eastern Europe, with particular emphasis on Hungary and Yugoslavia.

Zbigniew M. Fallenbuchl is Professor of Economics and Dean of the College of Social Sciences at the University of Windsor. He has written extensively, in several languages, on the Polish economy, including economic reform and foreign trade.

David M. Kemme is Assistant Professor of Economics at Wichita State University. He has published empirical studies regarding the Polish economy and has written on macroeconomic issues faced by planned economies generally. He formerly was on the faculty of the University of North Carolina at Greensboro.

Marie Lavigne is Professor of Economics and Director of the Center for International Economics of Socialist Countries at the University of Paris I (Pantheon Sorbonne). She has published widely in both French and English on the economies of Eastern Europe and the Soviet Union, particularly in the areas of foreign trade, CMEA integration, and economic reform.

Paul Marer is Professor of International Business at Indiana University. The author and editor of numerous books on Soviet and East European economics, including *Dollar GNPs of the USSR and Eastern Europe*, he has written extensively on East-West trade, intra-CMEA foreign trade, and the Hungarian economy.

Michael Marrese is Associate Professor of Economics at Northwestern University. He has published widely on the Hungarian economy and Soviet–East European foreign trade and is coauthor, with Jan Vañous, of *Soviet Subsidization of Trade with Eastern Europe*. He formerly taught at the University of British Columbia.

Urszula Plowiec is a Senior Research Fellow at the Foreign Trade Research Institute in Warsaw. She is one of the research pioneers in foreign trade reform in Poland, and in the early 1980s she was the head of a major commission that made proposals in this area. She is the author of numerous articles and books on Polish foreign trade, some translated into English.

Sherman Robinson is Professor of Economics at the University of California at Berkeley. Particularly well-known for his work in the field of computable general equilibrium models, he has written extensively on development planning models and international trade. He formerly taught at Princeton University and was a senior economist with the World Bank.

Márton Tardos is a head of section at the Institute of Economics of the Academy of Sciences in Budapest. The co-founder and general director of a private economics research institute in that city, he has published widely on the Hungarian economy, with a particular focus on the behavior of enterprises, the problems of economic reform, and foreign trade.

Laura D. Tyson is Professor of Economics at the University of California at Berkeley. A leading scholar of the Yugoslav economy, she has written extensively on the macroeconomic policy, foreign trade, and economic reforms of that country. Also the author of comparative studies, notably between Yugoslavia and Hungary, she formerly taught at Princeton University.

Jan Vañous is President and Research Director of PlanEcon, Inc., an economics consulting firm in Washington, D.C., devoted to analysis of the Soviet Union and Eastern Europe. A leading expert on Soviet and East European economic statistics and foreign trade, he formerly taught at the University of British Columbia.

Leyla Woods is an international economist, Office of Trade and Investment Analysis, U.S. Department of Commerce. Having spent time in Hungary as a graduate student of the University of California at Berkeley, she has published several articles on the Hungarian economy.

Library of Congress Cataloging-in-Publication Data
Economic adjustment and reform in Eastern Europe and Soviet Union :
essays in honor of Franklyn D. Holzman / edited by Josef C. Brada,
Ed A. Hewett, Thomas A. Wolf.
p.   cm.—(Duke Press policy studies)
Bibliography: p.
Includes index.
ISBN 0-8223-0852-5
1. Europe, Eastern—Economic policy. 2. Central planning—Europe,
Eastern. 3. Soviet Union—Economic policy. 4. Central planning—
Soviet Union. 5. Holzman, Franklyn D.   I. Holzman, Franklyn D.
II. Brada, Josef C., 1942–   III. Hewett, Edward A.   IV. Wolf,
Thomas A.   V. Series.
HC244.E235 1989
338.947—dc19   88-21130 CIP